Traveler's Language Guides: Russian

by
Holger von Rauch

Photos

Dr. J. Becker, Wahlscheid: 85; Bundesverband Selbsthilfe
Körperbehinderter, Krautheim: 79; Cycleurope, Bergisch-Gladbach:
61; E. Endress, Neuss: 183; Fordwerke AG: 56; Olga Grigoryeva,
Saarbrücken, and Holger von Rauch, Sulzbach/Saar: 42; HB-Verlag,
Achim Gaasterland: 17, 33, 49, 97, 147; Ifa, Stuttgart: 75, 119, 129;
Holger von Rauch, Sulzbach/Saar: 21, 141, 171; Wolpert
Fotodesign, Stuttgart: 11, 106–112, 154
Cover: Corbis, Corel-PhotoLibrary

All inquiries should be addressed to:
Barron's Educational Series, Inc.
250 Wireless Boulevard
Hauppauge, NY 11788
http://www.barronseduc.com

ISBN-13: 978-0-7641-3209-4
ISBN-10: 0-7641-3209-1
Library of Congress Control Number 2005921551

Printed in China
9 8 7 6 5 4 3 2 1

Cyrillic Letter	Transliteration (Journalistic Style)	Transliteration (Library of Congress)	English Symbol Used in Book
А, а	a	a	a
Б, б	b	b	b
В, в	v	v	v
Г, г	g	g	g
Д, д	d	d	d
Е, е	e (ye at beginning of a word)	e	ye
Ё, ё (Е, е)	e	e	yo
Ж, ж	zh	zh	zh
З, з	z	z	z
И, и	i	i	i
Й, й	y	i	y
К, к	k	k	k
Л, л	l	l	l
М, м	m	m	m

Pronunciation

Before the following vowels, consonants are "soft":
я; е; и; ё; ю and ь (soft position). In all other positions
they are "hard" (hard position).

When stressed, in the syllable preceding the stress, and in initial
position: **a** as in *amen*.
In other unstressed syllables, reduced to a sound between **a** and
o, like **i** in *it*.

b as in *bag*

v as in *vote*

g as in *gas*; before к and ч , like **ch** in *Bach, loch*;
in adjectival *gen sing* endings, like **v** in *vote*

In hard position: **d** as in *dot*; in soft position: palatalized, with
the tongue tip touching the hard palate.

After a vowel, after ь, after ъ, or in initial position, like **ye** in *yes*;
in unstressed position, reduced to a sound like **i** in *it*.

After a vowel, after ь, after ъ, or in initial position: **yo** as in *yo-yo*;
elsewhere, like **o** in *hello* (always stressed!)

zh as in *azure*

z as in *zoo*

ee as in *bee*; after ж, ш, and ц like ы (see ы, pages 8-9)

y as in *boy*

k as in *kayak*; not aspirated

l as in *lot*; velarized in hard position, with the back of the tongue
retracted toward the hard palate; in soft position, palatalized,
with the tongue against the hard palate.

m as in *mall*

Cyrillic Letter	Transliteration (Journalistic Style)	Transliteration (Library of Congress)	English Symbol Used in Book
Н, н	n	n	n
О, о	o	o	o
П, п	p	p	p
Р, р	r	r	r
С, с	s	s	s
Т, t	t	t	t
У, у	u	u	u
Ф, ф	f	f	f
Х, х	kh	kh	kh
Ц, ц	ts	ts	ts
Ч, ч	ch	ch	ch
Ш, ш	sh	sh	sh
Щ, щ	shch	shch	sh
ъ	omitted or "	"	
Ы, ы	y	y	y
Ь	omitted or '	'	'
Э, э	e	e	E
Ю, ю	yu	iu	yu
Я, я	ya	ia	ya

Pronunciation

In hard position: **n** as in *nose*; in soft position: palatalized, with the tongue against the hard palate.

o as in *hello* only when stressed; in syllable preceding stress and in initial position, like **a** in *amen*

p as in *papa*; not aspirated

r as in *rabbit*, but noticeably trilled as in Spanish *guitarra*

s as in *sun*

t as in *toe*: in hard position, not aspirated; in soft position, palatalized, with the tongue touching the hard palate

u as in *rule*

f as in *fun*

ch as in *Bach, loch*

ts as in *bats*

ch as in *cheap*

sh as in *show*

sh as in *sheep* or **st** as in *Christian*

"hard sign"; makes preceding consonant "hard"

resembles **y** in *hairy* or **ui** in *quick*

"soft sign"; indicates that the preceding consonant is "soft"

e as in *bet*

u as in *union*

ya as in *yahoo*; when unstressed, reduced to **i** as in *it*

To use this book, there is no need for you to learn the Cyrillic alphabet and the rules of Russian pronunciation: All the Russian words and phrases are also given here in a simplified approximation to get you started, with the stressed syllable indicated in capital letters. Please note the following special features:

- The stress of each word in Cyrillic letters is shown in this book with an accent mark [´]. Please use the stress indicated; otherwise, the word may be hard for Russians to understand.

- Consonants can be "hard" **ну** (NU) or "soft" **нет** (NYET). The soft **н** is like the **n** in *onion*. A consonant is hard unless it is followed by a soft vowel letter (**я, е, и, ё, ю**) or by the soft sign (**ь**).

- In final position or before a voiced consonant, **б, в, г, д, ж,** and **з** become their voiceless counterparts: **б→п, в→ф, г→к, д→т, ж→ш, з→с**. Examples: **юбка** *YUPka*, **нож** *NOSH*, **сад** *SAT*.

- The "journalistic style" of transliterating Cyrillic (see table, pages 6 and 8) is perhaps the most frequently used style by Russians in e-mail messages (see page 12). The Library of Congress system is used in American academic libraries.

Abbreviations Used in This Guide

a.	and
adv	adverb
adj	adjective
acc	accusative case
dat	dative case
f	feminine
gen	genitive
imperat	imperative
inf	infinitive
instr	instrumental case
ipf	imperfective
m	masculine
n	neuter
no.	noun
nom	nominative
o.	or
o.s.	oneself
pers pron	personal pronoun
pf	perfective
pl	plural
poss pron	possessive pronoun
prep	prepositional case
sing	singular
s.o.	someone
s.th.	something

Different Countries, Different Customs

Intercultural Tips

The Russian Language ...

...is the native language of at least 100 million people and is spoken—at least as a second language—by a total of more than 250 million people in various countries of Eastern Europe and Asia. Thus it is the most significant representative of the family of Slavic languages, which includes Czech and Bulgarian, among others. By the way, the Slavic languages are so similar that they generally are mutually intelligible, with a little effort.

In spite of the enormous land area of the Russian Federation (almost 1.8 times the size of the United States), there are no major differences between the dialects of the various regions, and anyone who knows Russian can easily be understood anywhere in the country (unlike foreign tourists who visit different regions of the United States!).

The Cyrillic Alphabet ...

...is often considered quite difficult, but many of the letters are identical or similar to those of the Roman, or Latin, alphabet, so there are relatively few that need to be learned from scratch. Learning the alphabet is worth the trouble if you travel to Russia, as street signs, information posted in public means of transportation, and other public notices normally use only Cyrillic. And once you have learned the alphabet, you will soon appreciate it, since it is an excellent means of representing the sounds of Russian. The popular cabbage soup, for example, has only two letters in Russian: щи, while some English methods of transcription use five: shchi. Although modern computers usually can produce Cyrillic fonts with no difficulty, it is still common practice to use the Latin alphabet in e-mail messages, and the most frequent systems of transliteration are based on those current in the English-speaking world.

Foreign Words ...

...are plentiful in Russian, and they often make it easier to communicate. In various periods of history, many Greek (пáфос [PAfas]—pathos), Latin (фóрмула [FORmula]—formula), French (пальтó [pal'TO]—coat), German (ландшáфт [lantSHAFT]—landscape), and English (фешенéбельный [fishyNYEbil'ny]—fashionable) words made their way into the Russian lexicon.

Russian Hospitality ...

... is legendary, and anyone who has ever visited the home of Russian friends (see page 14) knows what that means. In public, however, it is not considered good manners to show much emotion, so a friend's greeting when you meet on the street may seem strangely reserved. In Russia, good behavior means not attracting attention. Joy and displeasure are not expressed in a loud voice or through passionate gestures, and even the courteous smiles that are part of conversational good manners in America and Europe are less customary in Russia, and also not necessarily appropriate with strangers. (Service personnel in hotels that cater to many foreigners, for example, have to take special courses in smiling!) An adjustment period may be necessary before you can see a surly or seemingly indifferent face and recognize that it does not reflect an unfriendly attitude, but simply belongs to someone who is behaving with reserve, as the country's customs dictate.

The Interpersonal Distance ...

... that people maintain in social situations is much smaller than in English-speaking countries, despite this apparent reserve. If you have the feeling that someone is getting too close to you, he or she may not be expressing any particular intentions, but just maintaining a different culturally determined distance.
When standing in line, therefore, don't stay too far from the person in front of you; someone else may step in ahead of you to fill the gap, thinking that you are not in line. If there is a crowd (at subway entrances, for example), you definitely will encounter a little pushing and shoving, and even a bit of elbowing need not be interpreted right off the bat as an act of aggression, much less reciprocated.

When Greeting Someone ...

... it is not the general practice to shake hands as in the United States and Europe, and with women especially, it is best to let the other party take the initiative. If you know the other person well, or if you are in a private setting, hugs and kisses (even between men) are customary. Among young people, too, you will see the same range of greeting rituals as in other countries, all the way from a simple "Cool," to hugging and kissing.
Generally no detailed answer is expected when you are asked how you are, usually right after greetings are exchanged.

Patience ...

... unlike punctuality, for example, is one of the typical Russian virtues, and we seriously recommend that you practice it. People will not respond with understanding if you immediately start to complain angrily about a delay of an hour or so, an extended waiting period, or a postponed appointment.

Waiting Lines ..

... have become less common in Russia, but they are still part of daily life. If the line is orderly, simply take your place at the end, but if that is not the case, ask the crowd this question: "Кто последний?" [KTO paSLYEDni] ("Who's last in line?"). Then remember who is in front of you. When the next person comes up and asks the same question, answer by saying "Я" [YA] ("I am."). Certain categories of people (such as war veterans) are allowed to go to the head of the line. Sometimes a line is longer than it looks, because some people have asked others to hold their place in line for them.

When You're a Guest ...

... in the home of Russian friends, you can learn more about Russian life than anywhere else. It is a special privilege to be invited into the kitchen, because that is traditionally the center of real family life. But let's begin at the door of the apartment: Don't exchange greetings over the threshold; first enter the room, then greet your hosts, and then remove your coat and shoes (usually you'll be given a pair of slippers). Now it's time to present a little gift to your hosts, possibly a nice book that includes pictures of your home town, a typical souvenir, or a music CD or cassette. In addition, special delicacies, bottles of wine or other beverages, and flowers are always welcome.

The meal is usually abundant and may include several courses, which will not be visible at the outset, so make sure you don't eat too much right away! Russian etiquette requires that guests be urged to eat, so let your hosts have an opportunity to do so. And keep that in mind if you ever have Russian guests. If you really have had enough to eat, you may have to leave some food on your plate—contrary to custom—in order to convince your hosts that you are full.

Tea, Russian Style:

A strong brew (заварка [zaVARka]) is prepared in a small porcelain teapot. It is poured out into a teacup according to the drinker's taste and diluted with hot water (кипято́к [kipiTOK]) from the samovar or, in a pinch, from the hot-water kettle. Sweet jam (варе́нье [vaRYEn'ye]) is spooned into the cup (at least when at home and when a guest in someone's home).

With Business Contacts ...

... the rules that apply are similar to those in Western countries. Here, for example, shaking hands is customary. Don't dress too casually, and make sure you are well supplied with business cards. Once conversation begins, don't get to the point too quickly; chat a little first, possibly even discussing philosophical, historical, and literary topics.

Alcohol ...

... is consumed in Russia primarily in the form of во́дка [VOTka] ("vodka" is the diminutive form of the word вода́ [vaDA], or "water," so it means "little water"), and it has a firm place in social life. By refusing vodka altogether—at least, if you're a man—you're not exactly contributing to international understanding. It is advisable, however, to keep in mind the following special customs and their consequences:
1. Vodka is often drunk from glasses that hold far more than American shot glasses. Keep in mind that the alcohol content of classic Russian vodka is 40% (80 proof).
2. It is customary to empty the glass in one gulp every time.
3. It is an unwritten law that once opened, a Russian vodka bottle must be emptied. For this reason, many types of vodka are even sold in bottles that can't be closed again.
4. In addition to the commercially produced vodka from the large distilleries, there are low-quality fakes of these brands as well as home brews (самого́н [samaGON]) produced with varying degrees of expertise, and some of these can lead to health problems—so be cautious when buying vodka!

By the way, beer almost has the status of a non-alcoholic beverage in Russia, and occasionally quite elegant people are seen drinking from beer bottles out in public, on the street.

Crime and Corruption ...

...exist in Russia, just as in most other countries of the world, although they certainly do not permeate life to the extent that media reports frequently would have us believe. To ensure your personal safety, safeguard your belongings, and to prevent fraud, you should take the same precautions you would observe at other travel destinations.

By no means should you take the initiative of offering a bribe to any official! If someone feels inclined to help you out in return for a special consideration, that will be made clear to you. So if you ever find your patience at an end, just give some indication of that and be sure to ask what the usual procedure is. Small tokens, however, such as boxes of chocolates, with which you might seek to win over the strict lady in the reservation office, are definitely within the limits of good manners and are not considered corruption.

Religion ...

...has by no means died out, despite the seventy years of Soviet-mandated atheism. The largest religious denomination is the Russian Orthodox Church. If you visit a church, be sure not to show any bare skin; women are required to wear a headscarf (see 1st Corinthians 11:5). Observant visitors light candles. Normally there are no seats in the churches; the members of the congregation stand or kneel during the long liturgy. Orthodox Christians make the sign of the cross with the tips of their thumb, index finger, and ring finger (as a symbol of the Trinity), with the horizontal movement going from the right shoulder to the left, just the reverse of the Catholic custom. In addition to the Russian Orthodox Church and other Christian churches, the multinational country of Russia also has representatives of other religions, including Muslims, Jews, Buddhists, and others.

Travel Preparations

Reserving a Hotel Room by E-mail

Dear Sir or Madam,
I would like to reserve a single/double/two-bed room for the nights of June 24th and 25th. Please let me know whether you have any vacancies and what the total cost per night, including breakfast, would be.
Yours sincerely,

Uvazhaemye damy i gospoda,
Ya by khotel *m*/khotela *f* zakat' odnomestnyy nomer/dvukhmestnyy semeynyy nomer/dvukhmestnyy nomer na dve nochi s 24go po 25oe iyunya.
Pozhaluysta, soobshchite mne, yest' li u Vas svobodnyy nomer i skol'ko on stoit vklyuchaya zavtrak.
S uvazheniem,

Renting a Car by E-mail

Dear Sir or Madam,
I would like to rent a compact car/mid-sized car/luxury car/van from July 20th to 25th, from ... Airport. I will be departing from ... Airport, so I would like to return the car there. Please let me know what your rates are and what documents I will need.
Yours sincerely,

Uvazhaemye damy i gospoda,
Ya by khotel *m*/khotela *f* vzyat' naprokat malen'kiy avtomobil'/sredniy avtomobil'/limuzin/mikroavtobus s 20ogo po 25oe iyulya v aeroportu ... Ya vyletayu iz aeroporta ..., poetomu khotel *m*/khotela *f* by vernut' avtomobil' tam.
Pozhaluysta, soobshchite mne Vashi rastsenki i kakie dokumenty mne nado imet'.
S uvazheniem,

General Questions

I'm planning to spend my vacation in … (+ prep). Could you please give me information about accommodations in the area?
Я намереваюсь провести свой отпуск " … (+ prep). Не могли бы Вы мне предоставить информацию о том, где можно остановиться в регионе? [YA namiriVAyus' proviSTI SVOY OTpusk … ni-maGLI BY VY MNYE pridaSTAvit' infarMAtsyyu a-TOM, GDYE MOZHna astanaVItsa v-rigiOnye]

What kind of accommodations would you prefer?
Какой вид проживания Вы бы предпочли?
[kaKOY VIT prazhiVAniya VY BY pritpaCHLI]

a hotel
гостиницу [gaSTInitsu]

a tourist hostel
турбазу [turBAzu]

a pension (small hotel/boarding house)
пансион [pansiON]

bed and breakfast
комнату в частной квартире [KOMnatu f-CHASnay kvarTIrye]

a vacation apartment
квартиру [kvarTIru]

Questions About Accommodations

Hotel—Pension—Bed and Breakfast

I'm looking for a hotel, but nothing too expensive—something in the mid-price range.
Я ищу гостиницу, но не очень дорогую, скорее средней категории. [YA iSHU gaSTInitsu na ni-Ochin daraGUyu skaRYEye SRYEDni katiGOrii]

I'm looking for a hotel with a pool/a golf course/tennis courts.
Я ищу гостиницу с бассейном./с площадкой для игры в гольф./с теннисным кортом. [YA iSHU gaSTInitsu s-baSYEYnam/s-plaSHATkay dlya-iGRY v-GOL'F/s-TYEnisnym KORtam]

For how many people?
На сколько человек? [na-SKOL'ka chilaVYEK]

Are dogs allowed there?
А там разрешается ли иметь с собой собаку?
[a TAM razriSHAyitsa li iMYET'' s-saBOY saBAku]

Can you put an extra bed in the room?
Нельзя ли поставить ещё одну кровать в номере?
[nil'ZYA li pasTAvit yiSHO adNU kraVAT' v-NOmirye]

How much does it cost per week?
Сколько это стоит в неделю?
[SKOL'ka Eta STOit v-niDYElyu]

I'm looking for a vacation apartment or a summer cottage.
Я ищу квартиру на время отпуска или летний домик.
[YA iSHU kvarTIru na-VRYEmya OTpuska Ili LYETni DOmik]

Is there ...?
Есть ли ...? [YEST li]

a baby crib?
детская кровать [DYETskaya kraVAT']

a highchair?
высокий детский стульчик [vySOki DYETski STUL'chik]

a telephone?
телефон [tiliFON]

a washing machine?
стиральная машина [stiRAL'naya maSHYna]

Is electricity included in the price?
Аренда включает стоимость электроэнергии?
[aRYENda fklyuCHAyit STOimast' eliktraeNYERgii]

Are bed linens and towels provided?
Предоставляется ли постельное бельё и полотенца?
[pridastaVLYAyitsa li pasTYEL'naye biL'YO i palaTYENtsa]

Do I need to make a deposit?
Нужно ли оставить залог? [NUZHna li asTAvit' zaLOK]

When does the deposit/the rent have to be paid?
Когда надо заплатить залог?/за аренду?
[kagDA NAda zaplaTIT' zaLOK/za-aRYENdu]

Where and when can I pick up the keys?
Где и когда можно будет взять ключи?
[GDYE i kagDA MOZHna BUdit VZYAT' KLYUchi]

> Normally the rent has to be paid immediately upon occupancy
> ("при вселении" [pri-fsiLYEnii]).

General Information

Basic Phrases

Instead of using "да" [DA] ("yes"), people often answer with a word that was contained in the question:
"Вы сегодня приéхали?" [VY siVOdnya priYEkhali] ("Did you arrive today?")—"Сегодня." [siVOdnya] ("Today.")
"У Вас есть сáхар?" [u-VAS YEST SAkhar] ("Do you have any sugar?", literally: "Is there sugar with you?")—"Есть." [YEST] ("Yes, I do.", literally, "There is.")

Yes.
Да. [DA]

No.
Нет. [NYET]

Please.
Пожáлуйста. [paZHAlusta]

Thank you.
Спасибо! [spaSIba]

Thanks a lot!
Большóе спасибо! [bal'SHOye spaSIba]

Thanks. Same to you!
Спасибо, Вам тóже! [spaSIba VAM TOzhe]

You're welcome./Not at all!
Пожáлуйста! [paZHAlusta]/Нé за что! [NYE-za-shta]

Don't mention it!
Не стóит благодáрности! [ni-STOit blagaDARnasti]

Pardon me?/What did you say?
Извините, что Вы сказáли? [izviNItye SHTO VY skaZAli]

Of course.
Конéчно! [kaNYESHna]

Agreed!
Соглáсен! m [saGLAsin]/Соглáсна! f [saGLAsna]

Okay!
Хорошó! [kharaSHO]

All right!
Всё в поря́дке! [FSYO f-paRYATkye]

Excuse me!/Pardon me!
Извините! [izviNItye]

Just a second, please.
Минýтку, пожáлуйста. [miNUTku paZHAlusta]

That's enough!
Всё, хва́тит! [FSYO KHVAtit]

Help!
Помоги́те! [pamaGItye]

Who?
Кто? [KTO]

What?
Что? [SHTO]

Which?
Како́й? *m* [kaKOY]/**Кака́я?** *f* [kaKAya]
Како́е? *n* [kaKOye]/**Каки́е?** *pl* [kaKIye]

(To/For) Whom?
Кому́? [kaMU]

Whom?
Кого́? [kaVO]

Where?
Где? [GDYE]

Where is ...?/Where are ...?
Где ...? [GDYE]

Why?
Почему́? [pachiMU]

What ... for?/Why?
Заче́м? [zaCHEM]

How?
Как? [KAK]

How much?
Ско́лько *(+ gen sing)*? [SKOL'ka]

How many?
Ско́лько *(+ gen pl)*? [SKOL'ka]

How long?
Как до́лго? [KAK DOLga]

When?
Когда́? [kagDA]

(At) What time?/When?
В кото́ром часу́? [f-kaTOram chaSU]

I'd like ...
Я бы хоте́л *m*/**хоте́ла** *f* ... *(+ acc)* [YA BY khaTYEL/khaTYEla]

Is there ...?/Are there ...?
Есть ли ...? [YEST li]

0	ноль [NOL']
1	оди́н *m* [aDIN]/одна́ *f* [aDNA]/ одно́ *n* [aDNO]
2	два *m n* [DVA]/две *f* [DVYE]
3	три [TRI]
4	четы́ре [chiTYrye]
5	пять [PYAT']
6	шесть [SHEST']
7	семь [SYEM']
8	во́семь [VOsim']
9	де́вять [DYEvit']
10	де́сять [DYEsit']
11	оди́ннадцать [aDInatsat']
12	двена́дцать [dviNAtsat']
13	трина́дцать [triNAtsat']
14	четы́рнадцать [chiTYRnatsat']
15	пятна́дцать [pitNAtsat']
16	шестна́дцать [shistNAtsat']
17	семна́дцать [simNAtsat']
18	восемна́дцать [vasimNAtsat']
19	девятна́дцать [divitNAtsat']
20	два́дцать [DVAtsat']
21	два́дцать оди́н *m*/одна́ *f*/одно́ *n* [DVAtsat' aDIN/aDNA/aDNO]
22	два́дцать два *m n*/две *f* [DVAtsat' DVA/DVYE]
23	два́дцать три [DVAtsat' TRI]
24	два́дцать четы́ре [DVAtsat' chiTYrye]
25	два́дцать пять [DVAtsat' PYAT']
26	два́дцать шесть [DVAtsat' SHEST']
27	два́дцать семь [DVAtsat' SYEM']
28	два́дцать во́семь [DVAtsat' VOsim']
29	два́дцать де́вять [DVAtsat' DYEvit']
30	три́дцать [TRItsat']
31	три́дцать оди́н *m*/одна́ *f*/одно́ *n* [TRItsat' aDIN/aDNA/aDNO]
32	три́дцать два *m n*/две *f* [TRItsat' DVA/DVYE]
40	со́рок [SOrak]
50	пятьдеся́т [pidiSYAT]
60	шестьдеся́т [shyzdiSYAT]
70	се́мьдесят [SYEM'disit]
80	во́семьдесят [VOsim'disit]
90	девяно́сто [diviNOsta]
100	сто [STO]

101	сто оди́н *m*/одна́ *f*/одно́ *n* [STO aDIN/aDNA/aDNO]
200	две́сти [DVYEsti]
300	три́ста [TRIsta]
400	четы́реста [chiTYrista]
500	пятьсо́т [pit'SOT]
600	шестьсо́т [shyst'SOT]
3,000	три ты́сячи [TRI TYsichi]
4,000	четы́ре ты́сячи [chiTYrye TYsichi]
5,000	пять ты́сяч [PYAT' TYsich]
6,000	шесть ты́сяч [SHEST' TYsich]
1,000	ты́сяча [TYsicha]
2,000	две ты́сячи [DVYE TYsichi]
10,000	де́сять ты́сяч [DYEsit' TYsich]
100,000	сто ты́сяч [STO TYsich]
1,000,000	миллио́н [million]
first	пе́рвый *m* [PYERvy]/пе́рвая *f* [PYERvaya]/пе́рвое *n* [PYERvaye]
second	второ́й *m* [ftaROY]/втора́я *f* [ftaRAya]/второ́е *n* [ftaROye]
third	тре́тий *m* [TRYEti]/тре́тья *f* [TRYEtya]/тре́тье *n* [TRYEtye]
fourth	четвёртый *m* [chitVYORty]/ четвёртая *f* [chitVYORtaya] / четвёртое *n* [chitVYORtaye]
fifth	пя́тый [PYAty]
sixth	шесто́й [shySTOY]
seventh	седьмо́й [sid'MOY]
eighth	восьмо́й [vas'MOY]
ninth	девя́тый [diVYAty]
tenth	деся́тый [diSYAty]
1/2	полови́на [palaVIna]
1/3	треть *f* [TRYET']
1/4	че́тверть *f* [CHETvirt']
3/4	три че́тверти [TRI CHETvirti]
3.5 %	три це́лых и пять деся́тых проце́нта [TRI TSELykh i PYAT' diSYAtykh praTSYENta]
27º C	два́дцать семь гра́дусов [DVAtsat' SYEM' GRAdusaf]
–5º C	ми́нус пять (гра́дусов) [MInus PYAT' (GRAdusaf)]
the year 1999	ты́сяча девятьсо́т девяно́сто девя́тый год [TYsicha divit'SOT diviNOsta diVYAty GOT]
the year 2005	две ты́сячи пя́тый год [DVYE TYsichi PYAty GOT]
millimeter	миллиме́тр [miliMYETR]

25

centimeter	сантиме́тр [santiMYETR]
meter	метр [MYETR]
kilometer	киломе́тр [kilaMYETR]
square meter	квадра́тный метр [kvaDRATny MYETR]
liter	литр [LITR]
gram	грамм [GRAM]
half a kilo	полкило́ [palkiLO]
kilogram	килогра́мм [kiloGRAM]

Telling the Time

Time

What time is it?
Кото́рый час? [kaTOry CHAS]

It's ...
Сейча́с ... [siyCHAS]

(exactly) three o'clock.
(ро́вно) три часа́. [(ROVna) TRI chiSA]

about three o'clock.
о́коло трёх часо́в. [Okala TRYOKH chiSOF]

five after three.
пять мину́т четвёртого. [PYAT' miNUT chitVYORtava]

ten after three/three ten.
три часа́ де́сять мину́т. [TRI chiSA DYEsat' miNUT]

quarter after three/three fifteen.
че́тверть четвёртого. [CHETvirt' chitVYORtava]

three thirty.
полчетвёртого. [polchitVYORtava]

quarter to four.
без че́тверти четы́ре. [bis-CHETvirti chiTYrye]

five to four.
без пяти́ четы́ре. [bis-piTI chiTYrye]

noon./midnight.
по́лдень. [POLdin'] /по́лночь. [POLnach]

(At) What time?/When?
В кото́ром часу́? [f-kaTOram chiSU]/**Когда́?** [kagDA]

At one o'clock.
В час. [f-CHAS]

At two o'clock.
В два часа́. [v-DVA chiSA]

At about four o'clock.
Приме́рно в четы́ре часа́. [priMYERna f-chiTYrye chiSA]

In an hour.
Через час. [chirish-CHAS]

In two hours.
Через два часа́. [chiris-DVA chiSA]

Not before nine a.m.
Не ра́ньше девяти́ часо́в утра́. [ni-RAN'shy diviTI chiSOF uTRA]

After eight p.m.
По́сле восьми́ часо́в ве́чера. [POslye vas'MI chiSOF VYEchira]

Between three and four.
Ме́жду тремя́ и четырьмя́ часа́ми.
[MYEZHdu triMYA i chityr'MYA chiSAmi]

How long?
Как до́лго? [KAK DOLga]

For two hours.
Два часа́. [DVA chiSA]

From ten to eleven.
От десяти́ до оди́ннадцати часо́в. [ad-disiTI da-aDInatsati chiSOF]

Until five o'clock.
До пяти́ часо́в. [da-piTI chiSOF]

Since when?
С каки́х пор? [s-kaKIKH POR]

Since eight a.m.
С восьми́ часо́в утра́. [s-vas'MI chiSOF uTRA]

For half an hour (...).
Уже́ полчаса́ (как ...). [uZHE polchiSA (KAK)]

For a week (...).
Уже́ во́семь дней (как ...). [uZHE VOsim' DNYEY (KAK)]

about noon	о́коло полу́дня [Okala paLUdnya]
at lunchtime	вполдень [f-POLdin']
at night	но́чью [NOchyu]
during the day	днём [DNYOM]
earlier	ра́ньше [RAN'she]
early	ра́но [RAna]
every day	ка́ждый день [KAZHdy DYEN']
every day, daily	ежедне́вно [yizhyDNYEVna]
every hour, hourly	ежеча́сно [yizhyCHASna]
in a week	через неде́лю [chiris-niDYElyu]
in ten days	через де́сять дней [chiris-DYEsit' DNYEY]

in the afternoon	после обе́да [POslye aBYEda]
in the evening	ве́чером [VYEchiram]
in the morning	до обе́да [da-aBYEda]
in the morning	у́тром [Utram]
in two weeks	через две неде́ли [chiris-DVYE niDYEli]
last Monday	в про́шлый понеде́льник [f-PROshly paniDYEL'nik]
late	по́здно [POZna]
later	по́зже [POzhe]
next year	в сле́дующем году́ [f-SLYEduyushim gaDU]
now	сейча́с [siyCHAS], тепе́рь [tiPYER']
on Sunday	в воскресе́нье [v-vaskriSYEn'ye]
on the weekend	в конце́ неде́ли [f-kanTSE niDYEli]
once in awhile	вре́мя от вре́мени [VRYEmya at-VRYEmini]
recently	неда́вно [niDAVna]
sometimes	иногда́ [inagDA]
soon	ско́ро [SKOra]
ten minutes ago	де́сять мину́т наза́д [DYEsit' miNUT naZAT]
the day after tomorrow	послеза́втра [pasliZAFtra]
the day before yesterday ...	позавчера́ [pazafchiRA]
this morning/this evening ..	сего́дня у́тром [siVOdnya Utram]/ сего́дня ве́чером [siVOdnya VYEchiram]
this week	на э́той неде́ле [na-Etay niDYElye]
today	сего́дня [siVOdnya]
tomorrow	за́втра [ZAFtra]
tomorrow morning	за́втра у́тром [ZAFtra Utram]/
tomorrow evening	за́втра ве́чером [ZAFtra VYEchiram]
within a week	в тече́нии неде́ли [f-tiCHEnii niDYEli]
yesterday..............	вчера́ [fchiRA]

The Days of the Week

Monday...............	понеде́льник [paniDYEL'nik]
Tuesday...............	вто́рник [FTORnik]
Wednesday	среда́ [sriDA]
Thursday	четве́рг [chitVYERK]
Friday	пя́тница [PYATnitsa]
Saturday	суббо́та [suBOta]
Sunday	воскресе́нье [vaskriSYEn'ye]
on	в ... (+ acc) [f-...]

The Months

January	январь *m*	[yinVAR']
February	февраль *m*	[fiVRAL']
March	март	[MART]
April	апрель *m*	[aPRYEL']
May	май	[MAY]
June	июнь *m*	[iYUN']
July	июль *m*	[iYUL']
August	август	[AVgust]
September	сентябрь *m*	[sinTYABR']
October	октябрь *m*	[akTYABR']
November	ноябрь *m*	[naYABR']
December	декабрь *m*	[diKABR']
in ...	в ... *(+ prep)*	[f-...]

The Seasons

spring	весна	[viSNA]
in (the) spring	весной	[viSNOY]
summer	лето	[LYEta]
in (the) summer	летом	[LYEtam]
fall	осень *f*	[Osin']
in (the) fall	осенью	[Osin'yu]
winter	зима	[ziMA]
in (the) winter	зимой	[ziMOY]

Holidays

Legal holidays are marked with *.

New Year's Day (1/1–2)	Новый год *	[NOvy GOT]
Epiphany (1/19)	Крещение (Господне)	[kriSHEniye (gaSPODnye)]
Defenders of the Fatherland Day (2/23)	День *m* защитников Отечества	[DYEN' zaSHITnikaf aTYEchistva]
International Women's Day (3/8)	Международный женский день *	[mizhdunaRODny ZHENski DYEN']
Good Friday	Страстная пятница	[STRASnaya PYATnitsa]
Easter	Пасха (Христова)	[PASkha (khriSTOva)]
May Day, Spring and Labor Holiday (5/1–2)	Первое мая [PYERvaye MAya], Праздник весны и труда *	[PRAZnik viSNY i truDA]
Victory Day (5/9)	День *m* Победы *	[DYEN' paBYEdy]

29

Ascension Day	Вознесе́ние (Госпо́дне) [vazniSYEniye (gaSPOdnye)]
Pentecost	Тро́ица [TROitsa], День m Свято́й Тро́ицы [DYEN' sviTOY TROitsy]
Independence Day/ .... Declaration of Sovereignty of the Russian Federation (6/12)	День m приня́тия Деклара́ции о госуда́рственном суверените́те Росси́йской Федера́ции * [DYEN' priNYAtiya diklaRAtsyi a-gasuDARstvinam suviriniTYEtye raSIYskay fidiRAtsyi]
Assumption	Успе́ние [uSPYEniye]
Day of Accord and .... Conciliation (*formerly:* October Revolution Day, 11/7)	День m согла́сия и примире́ния * [DYEN' saGLAsiya i primiRYEniya] (Пра́здник Октя́брьской Револю́ции) [(PRAZnik akTYABR'skay rivaLYUtsyi)]
Constitution Day (12/12) ..	День m Конститу́ции * [DYEN' kanstiTUtsyi]
Christmas Eve	Соче́льник [saCHEL'nik]
New Year's Eve	Нового́дний ве́чер [navaGODny VYEchir]
Christmas (1/7)	Рождество́ Христо́во * [razhdiSTVO khriSTOva]

Can you tell me today's date, please?
Не могли́ бы Вы мне сказа́ть, како́е сего́дня число́?
[ni-maGLI BY VY MNYE skaZAT' kaKOye siVOdnya chiSLO]

Today is August 4th.
Сего́дня четвёртое а́вгуста. [siVOdnya chitVYORtaye AVgusta]

Until the Revolution, Russia used the Julian calendar (Old Style – ста́рый стиль [STAry STIL'], abbreviated SS or ст. ст.), while the rest of Europe followed the Gregorian calendar still in use today (New Style – но́вый стиль [NOvy STIL'], abbreviated NS or н. ст.). The difference in dates amounts to 13 days, as the old calendar lags behind the new one. The Russian Orthodox Church continues to use the Old Style calendar, so Christmas, for example, comes in January. Watch out with historical dates as well: The anniversary of the October Revolution (October 25, 1917 SS) now falls in November! Movable feasts (Easter, etc.) are observed on different dates than in Western Christendom.

What fantastic/terrible weather!
Кака́я прекра́сная/ужа́сная пого́да!
[kaKAya priKRASnaya/uZHASnaya paGOda]

It's very cold./hot./humid.
О́чень хо́лодно./жа́рко./ду́шно.
[Ochin' KHOladna/ZHARka/DUSHna]

It's foggy./windy.
Тума́нно. [tuMANna]/**Ве́трено.** [VYEtreno]

It's going to stay nice./bad.
Пого́да остаётся хоро́шей./плохо́й.
[paGOda astaYOtsa khaROshey/plaKHOY]

It's going to get warmer./colder.
Потепле́ет. [patiPLYEyit]/**Похолода́ет.** [pakhalaDAyit]

It's going to rain./snow.
Бу́дет дождь./снег. [BUdit DOSHT'/SNYEK]

The roads are slippery.
Доро́ги ско́льзкие. [daROgi SKOL'skiye]

You need snow chains.
Нужна́ цепь противоскольже́ния.
[nuzhNA TSEP' prativaskal'ZHEniya]

air	во́здух [VOZdukh]
calm	безве́трие [bizVYEtriye]
changeable	неусто́йчивый [niuSTOYchivy]
cloud	о́блако [Oblaka]
cloudburst	ли́вень m [LIvin']
cloudy, overcast	о́блачный [Oblachny]
cold	холо́дный [khaLODny]
fog	тума́н [tuMAN]
frost	моро́з [maROS]
glare ice	гололе́дица [galaLYEditsa]
gust of wind	поры́в ве́тра [paRYF VYEtra]
heat	жара́ [zhaRA]
high tide	прили́в [priLIF]
hot	жа́ркий [ZHARki]
humid	ду́шный [DUSHny]
ice	лёд [LYOT]
lightning	мо́лния [MOLniya]
low tide	отли́в [atLIF]
rain	дождь m [DOZHT']
rain shower	кратковре́менный дождь [kratkaVRYEminy DOZHT']
rainy	дождли́вый [dazhDLIvy]

31

snow	снег [SNYEK]
storm	бу́ря [BUrya]
sun	со́лнце [SONtse]
sunny	со́лнечный [SOLnichny]
temperature	температу́ра [timpiraTUra]
thunder	гром [GROM]
thunderstorm	гроза́ [graZA]
variable	переме́нчивый [piriMYENchivy]
warm	тёплый [TYOply]
weather forecast	прогно́з пого́ды [praGNOS paGOdy]
weather report	сво́дка пого́ды [SVOTka paGOdy]
wet	сыро́й [syROY]
wind	ве́тер [VYEtir]
wind speed	си́ла ве́тра [SIla VYEtra]

Colors

beige	бе́жевый [BYEzhivy]
black	чёрный [CHORny]
blue	си́ний [SIni]
brown	кори́чневый [kaRICHnivy]
colored	цветно́й [tsvitNOY]
gold(en)	золоти́стый [zalaTIsty]
gray	се́рый [SYEry]
green	зелёный [ziLYOny]
lilac	лило́вый [liLOvy]
multicolored	пёстрый [PYOstry]
orange	ора́нжевый [aRANzhyvy]
pink	ро́зовый [ROzavy]
plain	одноцве́тный [adnaTSVYETny]
purple, violet	фиоле́товый [fiaLYEtavy]
red	кра́сный [KRASny]
silver	серебри́стый [siriBRIsty]
sky blue	голубо́й [galuBOY]
turquoise	бирюзо́вый [biryuZOvy]
white	бе́лый [BYEly]
yellow	жёлтый [ZHOLty]
light blue/light green	све́тло-си́ний [SVYETla-SIni]
	све́тло-зелёный [SVYETla-ziLYOny]
dark blue/dark green	тёмно-си́ний [TYOMna-SIni]
	тёмно-зелёный [TYOMna-ziLYOny]

Blue (си́ний [SIni] and sky blue (голубо́й [galuBOY] are two completely different colors for Russians. Голубо́й [galuBOY] is also the colloquial word for homosexual (like English "gay").

"Здра́вствуйте!" [ZDRASTvuytye] ("Be healthy!") is a greeting that is suitable for every time of day and every occasion. The familiar form is "Здра́вствуй!" [ZDRASTvuy].

Saying Hello

Good morning!
До́брое у́тро! [DObraye Utra]

Hello!/Good afternoon!
До́брый день! [DObry DYEN']

Good evening!
До́брый ве́чер! [DObry VYEchir]

Hello!/Hi!
Приве́т! [priVYET]

What's your name? (respectful)
Как Вас зову́т? [KAK VAS zaVUT]

What's your name? (familiar)
Как тебя́ зову́т? [KAK tiBYA zaVUT]

My name is ...
Меня́ зову́т … [miNYA zaVUT …]

How are you?
Как Вы пожива́ете? [KAK VY pazhiVAyitye]

How are things?/How are you?
Как дела́? [KAG diLA]

Fine, thanks. And you?
Спаси́бо. А у Вас?/у тебя́? [spaSIba. a u-VAS/u-tiBYA]

A casual inquiry about someone's health does not require a detailed answer. Simply say "Хорошо́" [kharaSHO] ("fine"), "Норма́льно" [narMAL'na] ("fine"—literally: "normal"), "Ничего́" [nichiVO] ("not bad"—literally: "nothing"), if things are going well, and if they're not, say "Так себе" [TAK siBYE] ("so-so") or "Нева́жно" [niVAZHna] ("it doesn't matter"). It is bad manners to bluntly say "Пло́хо" [PLOkha] ("poorly"). It is even worse to say "Нехорошо́" [nikharaSHO] ("not well," "badly").

Russian names have three parts: the first name (и́мя) [Imya],
the patronymic (о́тчество) [Ochistva], and the family name
(фами́лия) [faMIliya]. The patronymic is formed from the
father's first name by attaching –ович [avich] or –евич [yivich]
for a man and –овна [avna] or –евна [yivna] for a woman (for
example, Ива́н Ива́нович [iVAN iVAnavich] or Зо́я Ива́новна
[ZOya iVAnavna]). The family name of a woman often has a
feminine ending. The politest form of address among Russians
is the first name and the patronymic. It generally is not used
with foreigners; they are addressed as господи́н/госпожа́
[gaspaDIN/gaspaZHA] plus the family name.

May I introduce you?
Познако́мьтесь! [paznaKOMtis']
This is ...
Э́то ... [Eta]
  Mrs./Ms. X.
  госпожа́ X. [gaspaZHA]
  Mr. X.
  господи́н X. [gaspaDIN]
  my husband.
  мой муж. [MOY MUSH]
  my wife.
  моя́ жена́. [maYA zhyNA]
  my son.
  мой сын. [MOY SYN]
  my daughter.
  моя́ дочь. [maYA DOCH]
  my boyfriend.
  мой друг. [MOY DRUK]
  my girlfriend.
  моя́ подру́га. [maYA paDRUga]
  my card.
  моя́ визи́тка. [maYA viZITka]

Saying Good-bye

Good-bye!
До свида́ния! [da-sviDAniya]

See you soon!
До ско́рой встре́чи! [da-SKOray FSTRYEchi]

See you tomorrow!
До за́втра! [da-ZAFtra]

Take care!
Счастли́во! [shchiSLIva]

Good night!
Споко́йной но́чи! [spaKOYnay NOchi]

Bye!
Пока́! [paKA]

Have a good trip!
Счастли́вого пути́! [shchiSLIvava puTI]

Polite Phrases

Requesting and Thanking

Please.
Пожа́луйста. [paZHAlusta]

Yes, please.
Да, пожа́луйста. [da paZHAlusta]

No, thank you!
Нет, спаси́бо! [NYET spaSIba]

May I?
Разреши́те? [razriSHYtye]

Sorry to bother you.
Прости́те за беспоко́йство. [praSTItye za-bispaKOYstva]

Excuse me, may I ask you something?
Извини́те, пожа́луйста, мо́жно Вас спроси́ть?
[izviNItye paZHAlusta MOZHna VAS spraSIT']

Could you help me, please?
Не могли́ бы Вы мне помо́чь? [ni-maGLI BY VY MNYE paMOCH]

Can I ask you a favor?
Могу́ ли я Вас попроси́ть об одолже́нии?
[maGU li YA VAS papraSIT' ab-adalZHEnii]

Would you mind just ...
Бу́дьте добры́, ... (+ imperat) [BUT'tye daBRY]

Thanks/Thanks a million, you've been a great help.
Большо́е/Огро́мное спаси́бо, Вы мне о́чень помогли́.
[bal'SHOye/aGROMnaye spaSIba VY MNYE Ochin' pamaGLI]

That was very nice of you.
Э́то бы́ло о́чень ми́ло с Ва́шей стороны́.
[Eta BYla Ochin' MIla s-VAshy staraNY]

Could you please tell me ...
Не могли́ бы Вы мне сказа́ть, ...
[ni-maGLI BY VY MNYE skaZAT']

36

Could you recommend ..., please?
Не могли́ бы Вы мне порекомендова́ть, … *(+ acc)*
[ni-maGLI BY VY MNYE parikamindaVAT']

Thank you!
Спаси́бо! [spaSIba]

Yes, thank you!
Спаси́бо, с удово́льствием! [spaSIba s-udaVOL'stviyim]

That's really nice of you, thank you!
О́чень любе́зно, спаси́бо! [Ochin' lyuBYEZna spaSIba]

You're welcome!/My pleasure!
Пожа́луйста! [paZHAlusta]/Не́ за что. [NYE-za-shta]

In questions, Russians do not use the word "please." Instead, requests phrased as questions often employ the negative form (with не [ni-], "not"). You can also introduce a polite question with "Извини́те, пожа́луйста, ..." [izviNItye paZHAlusta] or "Прости́те, ..." [praSTItye] ("Excuse me, ...").

Apologies

I'm sorry!
Извини́те! [izviNItye]

Excuse me!
Прости́те! [praSTItye]

I'm very sorry.
О́чень сожале́ю! [Ochin' sazhaLYEyu]

No problem!/Don't worry about it!
Ничего́ стра́шного! [nichiVO STRASHnava]
Не беспоко́йтесь! [ni-bispaKOYtis']

I'm afraid that's impossible.
К сожале́нию, э́то невозмо́жно.
[k-sazhaLYEniyu Eta nivazMOZHna]

Congratulations/Wishes

Congratulations!
Серде́чно поздравля́ю! [sirDYECHna pazdraVLYAyu]

Happy birthday!/name day!
Поздравля́ю с днём рожде́ния!/с имени́нами!
[pazdraVLYAyu z-DNYOM raZHDYEniya/s-imiNInami]

Happy holiday!
С пра́здником! [s-PRAZnikam]

Happy New Year!
С Но́вым го́дом! [s-NOvym GOdam]

37

Good luck!
Уда́чи! [uDAchi]/**Больши́х успе́хов!** [bal'SHIKH uSPYEkhaf]

Get well soon!
Поправля́йтесь!/Поправля́йся! [papravLYAYtis'/papravLYAYsa]

The custom of crossing one's fingers is unknown in Russia. Instead, people say "Ни пу́ха ни пера́!" [ni-PUkha ni-piRA] ("good luck") and respond with "К чёрту!" [k-CHORtu] ("to hell with it!").

Opinions and Feelings

Agreement and Conversational Responses

Good.
Хорошо́. [kharaSHO]

Right.
Пра́вильно. [PRAvil'na]

Agreed!
Согла́сен! *m* [saGLAsin]/**Согла́сна!** *f* [saGLASna]

It's a deal!
Договори́лись! [dagavaRIlis']

That's all right!
Всё в поря́дке! [FSYO f-paRYATkye]

Okay!
Ла́дно! [LADna]

Exactly!
То́чно! [TOCHna]

Really?
Пра́вда? [PRAVda]

How interesting!
Интере́сно! [intiRYESna]

How nice!
Как здо́рово! [KAK ZDOrava]

I understand.
Понима́ю. [paniMAyu]

I agree entirely.
Я с Ва́ми соверше́нно согла́сен. *m*/согла́сна. *f*
[YA s-VAmi savirSHENna saGLAsin/saGLASna]

That's right.
Э́то пра́вда. [Eta PRAVda]

Gladly./I'd love to.
С удовóльствием. [s-udaVOL'stviyim]

Refusal

I don't have time.
У меня нет врéмени. [u-miNYA NYET VRYEmini]

I don't want to.
Мне не хóчется. [MNYE ni-KHOchitsa]

I can't agree to that.
Я с э́тим не соглáсен *m.*/не соглáсна *f.*
[YA s-Etim ni-saGLAsin/ni-saGLASna]

That's out of the question!
Об э́том не мóжет быть и рéчи! [ab-Etam ni-MOzhit BYT' i RYEchi]

Certainly not!/No way!
Ни в кóем слýчае! [ni f-KOyim SLUchaye]

I don't like this at all.
Э́то мне вообщé не нрáвится. [Eta MNYE vaapSHE ni-NRAvitsa]

Preferences

I (don't) like it.
Э́то мне (не) нрáвится. [Eta MNYE (ni-)NRAvitsa]

I'd rather ...
Я предпочитáю ... (+ *acc*) [YA pritpachiTAyu]

I'd really like ...
Бóльше всегó мне хотéлось бы ...
[BOL'shy fsiVO MNYE khaTYElas' BY]

I'd like to find out more about it.
Об э́том хотéлось бы бóльше узнáть.
[ab-Etam khaTYElas' BY BOL'shy uZNAT']

Expressing Ignorance

I don't know.
Не знáю. [ni-ZNAyu]

I have no idea.
Поня́тия не имéю. [paNYAtiya ni-iMYEyu]

Indecision

It makes no difference to me.
Мне всё равнó. [MNYE FSYO ravNO]

I don't know yet.
Ещё не знáю. [yiSHO ni-ZNAyu]

Maybe.
Мóжет быть. [MOzhit BYT']

Probably.
Вероя́тно. [viraYATna]

Delight—Enthusiasm

Great!
Великоле́пно! [vilikaLYEPna]

Wonderful!
Прекра́сно! [priKRASna]

Fine!/Good!
Здо́рово! [ZDOrava]

Fantastic!
Кла́ссно! [KLASna]

Contentment

I'm completely satisfied.
Я соверше́нно дово́лен. *m*/дово́льна. *f*
[YA savirSHENna daVOlin/daVOL'na]

I can't complain.
Я не могу́ пожа́ловаться. [YA ni-maGU paZHAlavatsa]

Everything worked out perfectly.
Всё получи́лось отли́чно. [FSYO paluCHIlas' atLICHna]

Boredom

How boring!/What a bore!
Как ску́чно! [KAK SKUSHna]

Totally boring!
Тоска́ зелёная! [taSKA ziLYOnaya]

Astonishment—Surprise

Really?
Пра́вда? [PRAVda]

Amazing!
Как удиви́тельно! [KAK udiVItil'na]

Incredible!
Невероя́тно! [niviraYATna]

Relief

It's lucky that ...!
К сча́стью, ...! [k-SHAST'yu]

Thank God!
Сла́ва Бо́гу! [SLAva BOgu]

Finally!/At last!
Наконе́ц-то! [nakaNYETS-ta]

Composure

Don't panic/get excited!
То́лько без па́ники. [TOL'ka bis-PAniki]

Don't worry about a thing.
Не пережива́йте. [ni-pirizhyVAYtye]

Annoyance

How annoying!
Вот э́то доса́дно! [VOT Eta daSADna]

Damn!
Чёрт побери́! [CHORT pabiRI]

That's enough!
Хва́тит! [KHVAtit]

I'm sick of it.
Мне надое́ло. [MNYE nadaYEla]

That's outrageous!
Кака́я на́глость! [kaKAya NAglast']

It's a disgrace!
Э́то безобра́зие! [Eta bizaBRAziye]

That can't be true!
Э́того быть про́сто не мо́жет! [Etava BYT' PROsta ni-MOzhit]

Rebuking

What do you think you're doing!
Что Вы взду́мали! [SHTO VY VZDUmali]

Don't you dare come near me!
Не приближа́йтесь ко мне́! [ni-pribliZHAYtis' ka-MNYE]

That's completely out of the question.
Об э́том не мо́жет быть и ре́чи.
[ab-Etam ni-MOzhit BYT' i RYEchi]

Regret—Disappointment

Oh no!
Бо́же! [BOzhy]

I'm sorry.
Сожале́ю. [sazhaLYEyu]

I'm really sorry for ...
Я и́скренне сожале́ю за ... (+ acc). [YA ISkrinye sazhaLYEyu za-]

What a shame!
Жаль! [ZHAL']

The number 3—The thumb isn't used until you reach 5.

1, 2, ...—When counting off, bend your fingers inward, starting with the little finger.

Flicking your neck with a finger is a reference to "drinking alcohol" (and usually a good deal!).

"Taxi!"—Move your hand up and down, as if to signal "slow down, please."

Spitting three times over your left shoulder is a way to ward off bad luck.

"Honestly, with all my heart."

How nice!
Как краси́во! [KAK kraSIva]

That's wonderful!
Э́то чуде́сно! [Eta chuDYESna]

That's really nice of you!
Это о́чень ми́ло с Ва́шей/с твое́й стороны́!
[Eta Ochin' MIla s-VAshy/s-tvaYEY staraNY]

It's nice to be with you.
С Ва́ми/С тобо́й о́чень прия́тно. [s-VAmi/s-taBOY Ochin' priYATna]

The lunch/dinner was really excellent!
Обе́д/Ужин был бесподо́бен! [aBYET/Uzhin BYL bispaDObin]

You're such a good cook!
Вы так вку́сно гото́вите! [VY TAK FKUSna gaTOvitye]

It's really gorgeous here!
Здесь так ска́зочно! [ZDYES' TAK SKAzachna]

That looks great!
Э́то вы́глядит хорошо́! [Eta VYglyadit kharaSHO]

The dress looks good on you.
Пла́тье сиди́т на Вас/на тебе́ хорошо́.
[PLAt'ye siDIT na-VAS/na-tiBYE kharaSHO]

cosy, comfy (place)	ую́тный [uYUTny]
delicious	вку́сный [FKUSny]
excellent	отли́чный [atLICHny]
friendly	дружелю́бный [druzhyLYUBny]
impressive	впечатля́ющий [fpichatLYAyushi]
lovely	краси́вый [kraSIvy]
pleasant	прия́тный [priYATny]
polite	любе́зный [lyuBYEZny]
pretty	хоро́шенький [khaROshyn'ki]
wonderful	чуде́сный [chuDYESny]

Personal Information

How old are you?
Ско́лько Вам/тебе́ лет? [SKOL'ka VAM/tiBYE LYET]

I'm thirty-nine.
Мне три́дцать де́вять. [MNYE TRItsat' DYEvit']

What do you do for a living?
Чем Вы занима́етесь?/ты занима́ешься?
[CHEM VY zaniMAyitis'/TY zaniMAyishsa]

I'm a(n) ...
Я ... [YA ...]

I work for ...
Я рабо́таю у ... (+ gen); в; на ... (+ prep). [YA raBOtayu u-...; f-...; na-...]

I'm retired.
Я пенсионе́р/ка. [YA pinsiaNYER/ka]

I'm still in school.
Я ещё учу́сь в шко́ле. [YA yiSHO uCHUS' f-SHKOlye]

I'm a college student.
Я студе́нт/ка. [YA stuDYENT/ka]

Where are you from?
Отку́да Вы?/ты? [atKUda VY/TY]

I'm from ...
Я из ... (+ gen) [YA IS ...]

Have you been in ... long?
Вы/Ты уже́ до́лго в ... (+ prep)? [VY/TY uZHE DOLga f-...]

I've been here since ...
Я здесь уже́ ... [YA ZDYES' uZHE ...]

How long are you staying here?
Ско́лько вре́мени Вы пробу́дете/ты пробу́дешь здесь?
[SKOL'ka VRYEmini VY praBUditye/TY praBUdish ZDYES']

Is this your first time here?
Вы/Ты здесь впервы́е? [VY/TY ZDYES' fpirVYye]

Do you like it here?
Вам нра́вится? [VAM NRAvitsa]

Are you married?
Вы жена́ты? m [VY zhyNAty]/Вы за́мужем? f [VY ZAmuzhym]

Do you have any children?
У Вас есть де́ти? [u-VAS YEST DYEti]

Yes, but they're all grown up.
Есть, но они́ уже́ взро́слые. [YEST NO aNI uZHE VZROslyye]

How old are your children?
Ско́лько Ва́шим де́тям лет? [SKOL'ka VAshym DYEtyam LYET]

My daughter is eight (years old) and my son is five (years old).
До́чери — во́семь, а сы́ну — пять. [DOchiri VOsim' A SYnu PYAT']

44

Do you have a hobby?
У Вас/У тебя́ есть хо́бби? [u-VAS/u-tiBYA YEST KHObi]

I spend a lot of time with my children.
Я провожу́ мно́го вре́мени со свои́ми детьми́.
[YA pravaZHU MNOgo VRYEmini sa-svaImi dit'MI]

I like to read.
Я люблю́ чита́ть. [YA lyuBLYU chiTAT']

I surf a lot on the Internet.
Я мно́го гуля́ю по Интерне́ту. [YA MNOga gulYAyu pa-intirNYEtu]

I enjoy working in the garden/yard.
Я охо́тно рабо́таю в саду́. [YA aKHOTna raBOtayu f-saDU]

I do a little painting.
Я немно́го рису́ю. [YA niMNOgo riSUyu]

I collect antiques./stamps.
Я коллекциони́рую антиква́рные ве́щи./почто́вые ма́рки.
[YA kaliktsyaNIruyu antiKVARnyye VYEshi/pachTOvyye MARki]

What are you interested in?
Чем Вы в це́лом интересу́етесь? [CHEM VY f-TSElam intiriSUyitis']

I'm interested in ...
Я интересу́юсь ... (+ instr). [YA intiriSUyus']

I'm a member of ...
Я член ... (+ gen). [YA CHLYEN]

... is one of my favorite pastimes.
... одна́ из са́мых мои́х люби́мых заня́тии.
... [aDNA is-SAmykh maIKH lyuBImykh zaNYAtii]

cooking	вари́ть/свари́ть [VArit'/SVArit']
doing handicrafts	мастери́ть/смастери́ть [mastiRIT'/smastiRIT']
drawing	рисова́ть/нарисова́ть [risaVAT'/narisaVAT']
learning languages	занима́ться/заня́ться языка́ми [zaniMAtsa/zaNYAtsa yizyKAmi]
listening to music	слу́шать/послу́шать му́зыку [SLUshat'/paSLUshat' MUzyku]
making music	занима́ться/заня́ться му́зыкой [zaniMAtsa/zaNYAtsa MUzykoi]
painting	рисова́ть/нарисова́ть кра́сками [risaVAT'/narisaVAT KRASkami]
reading	чита́ть/прочита́ть [chiTAT'/prachiTAT']

relaxing	расслабля́ться/рассла́биться
	[rasslaBLYAtsa/rasSLAbitsa]
traveling	путеше́ствовать/попутеше́ствовать
	[putiSHESTvavat'/paputiSHESTvavat']

Fitness ➤ also Active Vacations

How do you keep in shape?
Как Вы подде́рживаете свою́ фо́рму?
[KAK VY padDYERzhyvayitye svaYU FORmu]

I jog./swim./ride a bike.
Я занима́юсь пробе́жкой./занима́юсь пла́ванием./ката́юсь на велосипе́де. [YA zaniMAyus' praBYEZHkay/zaniMAyus' PLAvaniyim/kaTAyus' na-vilasiPYEdye]

I play tennis/volleyball once a week.
Раз в неде́лю игра́ю в те́ннис./в волейбо́л.
[RAS v-niDYELyu iGRAyu f-TEnis/v-valiBOL]

I go to a fitness center regularly.
Я регуля́рно хожу́ в фитнес-це́нтр.
[YA riguLYARna khaZHU f-fitnis-TSENTR]

What kind of sports do you do?
Каки́м спо́ртом Вы занима́етесь?
[kaKIM SPORtam VY zaniMAyitis']

I play ...
Я игра́ю в ... (+ acc). [YA iGRAyu ...]

I like ...
Я люблю́ ... (+ inf). [YA lyuBLYU ...]

Can I play too?
Мо́жно мне с ва́ми игра́ть? [MOZHna MNYE s-VAmi iGRAT']

Making a Date

Do you have any plans for tomorrow evening?
У Вас/У тебя́ есть каки́е-то пла́ны на за́втра ве́чером?
[u-VAS/u-tiBYA YEST kaKIye-ta PLAny na-ZAFtra VYEchiram]

Shall we go there together?
Пошли́ вме́сте? [paSHLI VMYEStye]

Could we go somewhere together this evening?
Мо́жет, сего́дня ве́чером куда́-нибудь пойдём вме́сте?
[MOzhit siVOdnya VYEchiram kuDA-nibut' payDYOM VMYEStye]

May I take you out for dinner tomorrow evening?
Мо́жно Вас/тебя́ пригласи́ть на у́жин за́втра?
[MOZHna VAS/tiBYA priglaSIT' na-Uzhyn ZAFtra]

When should we meet?
Когда встретимся? [kagDA FSTRYEtimsa]

Let's meet at nine o'clock in front of .../in ...
Давайте/Давай встретимся в девять часов перед ...
*(+ instr)./*в ... *(+ prep)*.
[daVAYtye/daVAY FSTRYEtimsa v-DYEvit' chiSOF pirit- .../f- ...]

I'll pick you up.
Я заеду за Вами./за тобой. [YA zaYEdu za-VAmi/za-taBOY]

Can I see you again?
Я могу с Вами/с тобой снова встретиться?
[YA maGU s-VAmi/s-taBOY SNOva FSTRYEtitsa]

That was really a nice evening!
Это был приятный вечер! [Eta BYL priYATny VYEchir]

You have beautiful eyes.
У тебя красивые глаза. [u-tiBYA kraSIvye glaZA]

I like the way you laugh.
Мне нравится, как ты смеёшься.
[MNYE NRAvitsa KAK TY smiYOSHsa]

I like you.
Ты мне нравишься. [TY MNYE NRAvishsa]

I think you're great!
Ты такой классный! *m* [TY taKOY KLASny]
Ты такая классная! *f* [TY taKAya KLASnaya]

I love you!
Я тебя люблю! [YA tiBYA lyuBLYU]

Do you have a steady boyfriend?/a steady girlfriend?
У тебя есть бойфрэнд?/гёрлфрэнд?
[u-tiBYA YEST boyFRENT/gyorlFRENT]

Do you live with someone?
Ты с кем-то живёшь? [TY s-KYEM-ta zhyVYOSH]

Are you married?
Ты женат? *m*/замужем? *f* [TY zhyNAT/ZAmuzhym]
  I'm divorced.
  Я разведён. *m*/разведена. *f* [YA razviDYON/razvidiNA]
  We're separated.
  Мы живём отдельно. [MY zhyVYOM adDYEL'na]

Do you want to come back to my place?
Пойдёшь со мной ко мне? [payDYOSH sa-MNOY ka-MNYE]

No, slow down a moment!
Нет, это слишком быстро для меня.
[NYET Eta SLISHkam BYstra dlia-miNYA]

Please go now!
Пожа́луйста, уходи́! [paZHAlusta ukhaDI]

Please leave me alone!
Оста́вьте меня́ в поко́е!! [aSTAF'tye miNYA f-paKOye]

Stop that right now!
Переста́ньте сейча́с же! [piriSTAN'tye siyCHAZH-zhy]

Communication Problems

Pardon me?/What did you say?
Извини́те, как Вы сказа́ли? [izviNItye KAK VY skaZAli]

I can't understand you.
Я Вас/тебя́ не понима́ю. [YA VAS/tiBYA ni-paniMAyu]

Could you please repeat that?
Повтори́те/Повтори́, пожа́луйста. [paftaRItye/paftaRI paZHAlusta]

Could you please speak a little bit slower?
Говори́те/Говори́ поме́дленнее, пожа́луйста.
[gavaRItye/gavaRI paMYEDliniye paZHAlusta]

I understand.
Я понима́ю. [YA paniMAyu]

I understood.
Я по́нял. *m*/поняла́. *f* [YA POnyil/POnila]

Do you speak ...
Вы говори́те .../Ты говори́шь ...
[VY gavaRItye/TY gavaRISH]

  German?
  по-неме́цки? [pa-niMYETski]
  English?
  по-англи́йски? [pa-anGLIski]
  French?
  по-францу́зски? [pa-franTSUski]

I only speak a little ...
Я говорю́ то́лько немно́го ... [YA gavaRYU TOL'ka niMNOga ...]'

Could you please write it down for me?
Не могли́ бы Вы мне э́то написа́ть?
[ni-maGLI BY VY MNYE Eta napiSAT']

Take Note!

If you are walking around in a Russian city, it is best to exercise a little caution. Possible stumbling blocks such as rough spots, holes, and protruding pieces of metal, as well as slippery patches of ice in winter, will occupy part of your attention, but make sure you still devote some of it to the other road users, because drivers always have the right of way, even at pedestrian crossings. And if some driver flashes his lights, it's probably not because he's giving you an opportunity to cross the street, but because he wants you to stay out of the way!

Asking for Directions

Useful Words

left	налéво	[naLYEva]
right	напрáво	[naPRAva]
straight ahead	прямо	[PRYAma]
in front of	перед ... (+ instr)	[pirit-]
behind	за ... (+ instr)	[za-]
next to	рядом с ... (+ instr)	[RYAdam s-]
across from	напрóтив ... (+ gen)	[naPROtif]
here	здесь	[ZDYES']
there	там	[TAM]
near	блúзко adv	[BLISka]
far	далекó adv	[daliKO]
to	в ... (+ acc) [f-...]; на ... (+ acc) [na- ...]	
traffic light	светофóр	[svitaFOR]
street	ýлица	[Ulitsa]
road	дорóга	[daROga]
street corner	ýгол	[Ugal]
intersection	перекрёсток	[piriKRYOstak]
curve	поворóт	[pavaROT]

Directions

Excuse me please, how do you get to ...? (on foot)
Извинúте, как пройтú до ... (+ gen)? [izviNItye KAK prayTI da- ...]

Excuse me please, how do you get to ...? (by car)
Извинúте, как проéхать до ... (+ gen)?
[izviNItye KAK praYEkhat' da- ...]

Keep going straight ahead until you get to ...
Всё врéмя прямо до ... (+ gen). [FSYO VRYEmya PRYAma da- ...]

Then turn left/right at the traffic light.
Потом у светофора повернуть налево./направо.
[paTOM u-svitaFOra pavirNUT' naLYEva/naPRAva]

Follow the signs.
Следите за указателями. [sliDItye za-ukaZAtilyami]

Is it far from here?
Это далеко отсюда? [Eta daliKO otSYUda]

It's really close.
Это совсем рядом. [Eta saFSYEM RYAdam]

Excuse me, is this the road to ...?
Это дорога в ... *(+ acc)*?/на ... *(+ acc)*? [Eta daROga f- .../na- ...]

Excuse me, where is ..., please?
Скажите, пожалуйста, где ...? [skaZHYtye paZHAlusta GDYE]

I'm sorry, I don't know.
К сожалению, не знаю. [k-sazhaLYEniyu ni-ZNAyu]

I'm not from here.
Я не отсюда. [YA ni-atSYUda]

Go straight ahead/turn left/turn right.
Идите прямо./налево./направо. [iDItye PRYAma/naLYEva/naPRAva]

At the first/At the second intersection, turn left./turn right.
На первом/На втором перекрёстке налево./направо.
[na-PYERvam/na-ftaROM piriKRYOSTkye naLYEva/naPRAva]

Go across ...
Перейдите ... [piriDItye ...]
  the bridge.
  мост. [MOST]
  the square.
  площадь. [PLOshchat']
  the street.
  улицу. [Ulitsu]

The best thing would be to take the number ... bus.
Лучше всего сесть на автобус номер ...
[LUchy fsiVO SYEST' na-aFTObus NOmir ...]

At the Border

Passport Check

Your passport, please.
Ваш паспорт, пожалуйста! [VASH PASpart paZHAlusta]

Do you have a visa?
У Вас есть виза? [u-VAS YEST VIza]

Can I get a visa here?
Можно получить визу здесь? [MOZHna paluCHIT' VIzu ZDYES']

Customs

Do you have anything to declare?
У Вас есть това́ры, кото́рые на́до записа́ть в деклара́цию?
[u-VAS YEST taVAry kaTOryye NAda zapiSAT' v-diklaRAtsyyu]

Please pull over to the right/the left.
Вста́ньте спра́ва!/сле́ва! [FSTAN'tye SPRAva/SLYEva]

Open the trunk/this suitcase.
Откро́йте бага́жник!/э́тот чемода́н!
[atKROYtye baGAZHnik/Etat chimaDAN]

Do I have to pay duty on this?
На́до плати́ть по́шлину за э́то? [NAda plaTIT' POSHlinu za-Eta]

Personal Data

birthplace	ме́сто рожде́ния [MESto rozhDEniya]
date of birth	да́та рожде́ния [DAta raZHDYEniya]
first name	и́мя *n* [Imya]
last name	фами́лия [faMIliya]
maiden name	де́вичья фами́лия [DYEvichya faMIliya], бы́вшая фами́лия [BYFshaya faMIliya]
marital status	семе́йное положе́ние [siMYEYnaye palaZHEniye]
married	жена́тый *m*/за́мужем *f* [zhyNAty/ZAmuzhem]
single	холосто́й *m*/не за́мужем *f* [khalaSTOY/ni-ZAmuzhym]
widowed	вдове́ц *m*/вдова́ *f* [vdaVYETS/vdaVA]
nationality	гражда́нство [graZHDANstva]
patronymic	о́тчество [Ochistva]
personal data	ли́чные све́дения [LICHnyye SVYEdiniya]
place of residence	местожи́тельство [mistaZHYtil'stva]

At the Border

American	америка́нец *m*/америка́нка *f* [amiriKAnits/amiriKANka]
arrival	въезд [VYEZT]
border	грани́ца [graNItsa]
border crossing	пограни́чный контро́льно-пропускно́й пункт [pagraNICHny kanTROL'na-prapuskNOY PUNKT]
customs	тамо́жня [taMOZHnya]
customs duties	тамо́женные по́шлины *f pl* [taMOzhinyye POSHliny]
departure	вы́езд [VYyezt]

52

driver's license	водительские права [vaDItil'skiye praVA]
duty	пошлина [POSHlina]
duty-free	беспошлинный [bisPOSHliny]
green insurance card	зелёная страховая карта [zilYOnaya strakhaVAya KARta]
ID card, identification	удостоверение личности [udastaveRYEniye LICHnasti]
license plate	номерной знак [nomirNOY ZNAK]
passport	заграничный паспорт [zagraNICHny PASpart]
passport check	паспортный контроль [PASpartny kanTROL']
subject to duty	облагаемый пошлиной [ablaGAyimy POSHlinay]
valid	действительный [dyistVItil'ny]
visa	виза [VIza]

Cars and Motorcycles

If you plan to drive a vehicle into CIS countries, you need to get plenty of information beforehand. Consult embassies/consulates, automobile clubs, and other organizations to find out about border crossing points, regulations, insurance, gas stations, and the like.

Signs and Information

Остановка запрещена	No Stopping
стройка	Road Construction
Плохая дорога	Bad Road
Опасно	Danger
Скользко	Slippery Road
Крутой спуск	Steep Hill
объезд	Detour
Внимание: дети	Caution: Children
Въезд запрещён	No Entry
Высокое напряжение	High Voltage
больница	Hospital
грузовик	Truck
Внимание, Осторожно	Caution
Аварийная служба	Road Assistance
Выезд (с автомагистрали)	Exit Ramp
Не загораживать выезд	Keep Exit Clear
Парковка запрещена	No Parking
Опасный поворот	Dangerous Curve
Объездная дорога	Bypass

The State Inspectorate for Road Traffic Safety, GIBDD [ge-i-be-de-de] (Госуда́рственная Инспе́кция Безопа́сности Доро́жного Движе́ния [gasuDARstvinaya inSPYEKtsyya bizaPASnasti daROZHnava dviZHEniya]), which still is commonly known by the name of the previous organization, ГАИ [gai], ensures the observance of traffic regulations and oversees the technical inspection of vehicles. If you have any contact with its representatives, it is advisable to behave with restraint.

Roadways, Regulations ...

country road	шоссе́ [shaSSE]
entrance	въезд [VYEZT]
entrance ramp	въезд/съезд [VYEZT/SYEZT]
exit ramp	вы́езд [VYyezt]
fine	штраф [SHTRAF]
freeway, interstate	автомагистра́ль f [aftamagiSTRAL']
freeway toll	пла́та за прое́зд [PLAta za-praYEZT]
gas station	автозапра́вочная ста́нция [aftazaPRAvachnaya STANtsyya]
highway, expressway	скоростна́я доро́га [skarasNAya daROga]
hitchhike	е́хать/прое́хать автосто́пом [YEkhat/praYEkhat' aftaSTOpam]
legal alcohol limit	допусти́мое содержа́ние алкого́ля в крови́ [dapuSTImaye sadirZHAniye alkaGOLya f-kraVI]

There is a general ban on driving while drinking (0.0%).

main road	гла́вная доро́га [GLAVnaya daROga]
radar speed check, speed trap	рада́рный контро́ль ско́рости [raDARny kanTROL' SKOrasti]
rest area, service area	(авто)стоя́нка [(afta)staYANka]
road sign	доро́жный указа́тель [daROZHny ukaZAtil']
secondary road	второстепе́нная доро́га [ftarastiPYEnaya daROga]
toll	доро́жная по́шлина [daROZHnaya POSHlina]
traffic jam	зато́р [zaTOR]

54

At the Gas Station ➤ also At the Garage

Where's the nearest gas station, please?

Где ближа́йшая автозапра́вочная ста́нция?
[GDYE bliZHAYshaya aftazaPRAvachnaya STANtsyya]

I'd like ... liters of ...

Мне ну́жно … ли́тров …*(+ gen)* [MNYE NUZHna ... LItraf ...]

"A-95" gas

бензи́на "А-девяно́сто пять" [binZIna a-diviNOsta PYAT']

> A distinction is made not between regular and premium, but according to octane numbers: А-72, А-76, АИ-80, АИ-92, АИ-93, АИ-95, АИ-98 (often only А is used, rather than АИ). The higher the octane number, the higher is the quality of the fuel. In some places an additional type, "Су́пер-люкс" [supir-LYUKS], is sold; it allegedly is the highest quality. For Western-made automobiles, А(И)-95 or higher is recommended.

Diesel.

ди́зельного то́плива. [DIzil'nava TOpliva]

... rubles' worth, please.

Запра́вьте, пожа́луйста, на ... рубле́й.
[zaPRAF'tye paZHAlusta na-... ruBLYEY]

Fill it up, please.

По́лный бак, пожа́луйста. [POLny BAK paZHAlusta]

Please check the oil.

Прове́рьте, пожа́луйста у́ровень ма́сла.
[praVYER'tye paZHAlusta Uravin' MAsla]

I need a road map of this area.

Мне нужна́ ка́рта автомоби́льных доро́г э́той о́бласти.
[MNYE nuzhNA KARta aftamaBIL'nykh daROK Etay Oblasti]

Parking

> Looking for a parking place in Moscow is not exactly fun. If possible, you'll do better to head for a Park-and-Ride lot (стоя́нка-перехва́тчик [staYANka-piriKHVAchik]).

Excuse me please, is there a place to park around here?

Извини́те, здесь есть побли́зости парко́вка?
[izviNItye ZDYES' YEST paBLIzasti parKOFka]

55

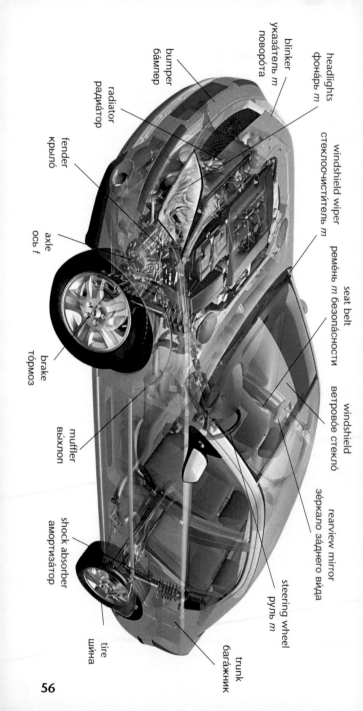

headlights
фонарь *m*

blinker
указатель *m*
поворота

bumper
бампер

radiator
радиатор

fender
крыло

axle
ось *f*

brake
тормоз

muffler
выхлоп

shock absorber
амортизатор

tire
шина

windshield wiper
стеклоочиститель *m*

seat belt
ремень *m* безопасности

windshield
ветровое стекло

rearview mirror
зеркало заднего вида

steering wheel
руль *m*

trunk
багажник

56

Can I park here?
Мо́жно здесь оста́вить маши́ну?
[MOZHna ZDYES' aSTAvit' maSHYnu]

Is there a place to park with an attendant?
Здесь есть охраня́емая парко́вка?
[ZDYES' YEST akhraNYAyimaya parKOFka]

Is there an attendant on duty?
Парко́вка охраня́ется? [parKOFka akhraNYAyitsa]

How much is it per hour to park?
Ско́лько сто́ит парко́вка в час?
[SKOL'ka STOit parKOFka f-CHAS]

Is the parking garage/lot open all night?
Парко́вка круглосу́точная? [parKOFka kruglaSUtachnaya]

A Breakdown

My car's broken down.
Я потерпе́л *m*/потерпе́ла *f* ава́рию.
[YA patirPYEL/patirPYEla aVAriyu]

I have a flat tire.
У меня́ спусти́ла ши́на. [u-miNYA spuSTIla SHYna]

Is there a garage near here?
Здесь есть побли́зости автомастерска́я?
[ZDYES' YEST paBLIzasti aftamastirSKAya]

Could you call the emergency road service, please?
Не могли́ бы Вы вы́звать авари́йную слу́жбу?
[ni-maGLI BY VY VYzvat' avaRIYnuyu SLUZHbu]

Would you please send me a mechanic?
Не могли́ бы Вы присла́ть мне автомеха́ника?
[ni-maGLI BY VY priSLAT' MNYE aftamiKHAnika]

My car has to be towed.
Мою́ маши́ну на́до отбукси́ровать.
[maYU maSHYnu NAda adbukSIravat']

Could you lend me some gas?
Вы не могли́ бы вы́ручить меня́ бензи́ном?
[VY ni-maGLI BY VYruchit' miNYA binZInam]

Could you help me change the tire, please?
Вы не могли́ бы помо́чь мне поменя́ть колесо́?
[VY ni-maGLI BY paMOCH MNYE pamiNYAT' kaliSO]

Could you give me a lift to the nearest car repair shop?
Вы не мо́жете подвезти́ меня́ до ближа́йшей
автомастерско́й? [VY ni-MOzhytye padviSTI miNYA da-bliZHAYshy
aftamastirSKOY]

breakdown	ава́рия [aVAriya]
emergency flashers	авари́йная светова́я сигнализа́ция [avaRIYnaya svitaVAya signaliZAtsyya]
first-aid kit	апте́чка [apTYECHka]
gas canister	кани́стра для бензи́на [kaNIstra dli-binZIna]
jack	автомоби́льный домкра́т [aftamaBIL'ny damKRAT]
jumper cables	пусковы́е про́воды *m pl* [puskaVYye PROvady]
parking garage	(многоэта́жный) па́ркинг [mnagaeTAZHny PARkink]
road assistance	авари́йная слу́жба [avaRIYnaya SLUZHba]
spare tire	запасно́е колесо́ [zapasNOye kaliSO]
tools	инструме́нты *m pl* [instruMYENty]
to tow (away)	букси́ровать/отбукси́ровать [bukSIravat'/adbukSIravat']
towing service	слу́жба техни́ческой по́мощи [SLUZHba tekhNIchiskay POmashi]
tow rope	буксиро́вочный трос [buksiROvachny TROS]
tow truck	буксиро́вочный автомоби́ль [buksiROvachny aftamaBIL']
warning triangle	предупреди́тельный треуго́льник [pridupriDItil'ny triuGOL'nik] знак авари́йной остано́вки [ZNAK avaRIYnay astaNOFki]

At the Garage

The engine won't start.
Дви́гатель не заво́дится. [DVIgatil' ni-zaVOditsa]

There's something wrong with the engine.
С дви́гателем что-то не в поря́дке.
[s-DVIgatilim SHTO-ta ni-f-paRYATkye]

... is/are faulty.
... испо́рчен. *m*/испо́рчена. *f*/испо́рчено. *n*/испо́рчены. *pl*
[...isPORchin/isPORchina/isPORchino/isPORchiny]

It's losing oil.
Течёт ма́сло. [tiCHOT MAsla]

When will the car be ready?/the motorcycle be ready?
Когда́ маши́на бу́дет гото́ва?/мотоци́кл бу́дет гото́в?
[kagDA maSHYna BUdit gaTOva/mataTSYKL BUdit gaTOF]

(Roughly) how much will it cost?
Ско́лько э́то бу́дет (приме́рно) сто́ить?
[SKOL'ka Eta BUdit (priMYERna) STOit']

(traffic) accident	доро́жно-тра́нспортное происше́ствие [daROZHna-TRANspartnoye praiSHESTviye], ДТП [de-te-PE]
air filter	возду́шный фи́льтр [vazDUSHny FILTR']
alarm system	противоуго́нная сигнализа́ция [prativauGOnaya signaliZAtsyya]
antifreeze	антифри́з [antiFRIS]
automatic transmission	автомати́ческая переда́ча [aftamaTIchiskaya piriDAcha]
blinker	указа́тель *m* поворо́та [ukaZAtil' pavaROta]
brake	то́рмоз [TORmas]
brake fluid	тормозна́я жи́дкость [tarmaZNAya ZHYTkast']
brake lights	стоп-сигна́л [stop-sigNAL]
bright lights	да́льний свет [DAL'ni SVYET]
bumper	ба́мпер [BAMpir]
car repair shop, garage	мастерска́я [mastirSKAya]
clutch	сцепле́ние [stsyPLYEniye]
coolant	охлажда́ющая вода́ [akhlaZHDAyushaya vaDA]
damage	поврежде́ние [pavriZHDYEniye]
defect, flaw	неиспра́вность *f* [niiSPRAVnast']
dimmed lights	бли́жний свет [BLIZHny SVYET]
electronic immobilizer	электро́нная противоуго́нная блокиро́вка [elikTROnaya prativauGOnaya blakiROFka]
emergency blinkers	авари́йная светова́я сигнализа́ция [avaRIInaya svitaVAya signaliZAtsyya]
gas pedal	педа́ль *f* акселера́тора [piDAL' aksiliRAtara]
gas pump	бензонасо́с [binzanaSOS]
gear	ско́рость *f* [SKOrast']
first gear	пе́рвая ско́рость [PYERvaya SKOrast']
neutral	холосто́й ход [khalaSTOY KHOD]
reverse	за́дний ход [ZADni KHOD]
generator	генера́тор [giniRAtar]
headlight	фона́рь *m* [faNAR']
hood	капо́т дви́гателя [kaPOT DVIgatilya]
horn	кла́ксон [KLAKsan]
ignition	зажига́ние [zazhyGAniye]
motor, engine	дви́гатель *m* [DVIgatil']
muffler	вы́хлоп [VYkhlap]
oil	ма́сло [MAsla]
oil change	сме́на ма́сла [SMEna MAsla]

parking brake	ручно́й то́рмоз [ruchNOY TORmas]
parking lights	габари́тные фа́ры *m pl* [gabaRITnyye FAry]
radiator	радиа́тор [radiAtar]
rearview mirror	зе́ркало за́днего ви́да [ZYERkala ZADniva VIda]
seat belt	реме́нь *m* безопа́сности [riMYEN' bizaPASnasti]
short-circuit	коро́ткое замыка́ние [kaROTkaye zamyKAniye]
snow tire	зи́мняя ши́на [ZIMnyaya SHYna]
spark plug	свеча́ зажига́ния [sviCHA zazhyGAniya]
speedometer	спидо́метр [spiDOmitr]
starter	ста́ртер [STARtir]
taillight	за́дний фона́рь [ZADni faNAR']
tank	бак [BAK]
tire	ши́на [SHIna]
transmission	переда́ча [piriDAcha]
trunk	бага́жник [baGAZHnik]
wheel	колесо́ [kaliSO]
windshield	ветрово́е стекло́ [vitraVOye stiKLO]
windshield wiper	стеклоочисти́тель *m* [stiklaachiSTItil']

Accident

There's been an accident.
Произошло́ доро́жно-тра́нспортное происше́ствие.
[praizaSHLO daROZHna-TRANSpartnoye praiSHESTviye]

Quick! Please call ...
Пожа́луйста, вы́зовите сро́чно ...
[paZHAlusta VYzavitye SROCHna ...]

an ambulance!
ско́рую по́мощь. [SKOruyu POmash]

the police!
мили́цию. [miLItsyyu]

the fire department!
пожа́рную кома́нду. [paZHARnuyu kaMANdu]

Do you have a first-aid kit?
У Вас есть перевя́зочный материа́л?
[u-VAS YEST piriVYAzachny matiriAL]

You ...
Вы ... [VY ...]

didn't yield the right of way.
нару́шили пра́во преиму́щественного прое́зда.
[naRUshili PRAva priiMUshistvinava praYEZda]

didn't signal your turn.
не пода́ли знак поворо́та. [ni-paDAli ZNAK pavaROta]

You ...
Вы ...[VY ...]

were driving too fast.
сли́шком бы́стро е́хали. [SLISHkam BYStra YEkhali]

ran a red light.
прое́хали при кра́сном све́те. [praYEkhali pri-KRASnam SVYEtye]

Give me your name and address.
Скажи́те мне Ва́шу фами́лию и Ваш а́дрес.
[skaZHYtye MNYE VAshu faMIliyu i VASH Adris]

Thanks for your help.
Большо́е спаси́бо за Ва́шу по́мощь.
[bal'SHOye spaSIba za-VAshu POmash]

Car, Motorcycle, and Bike Rental

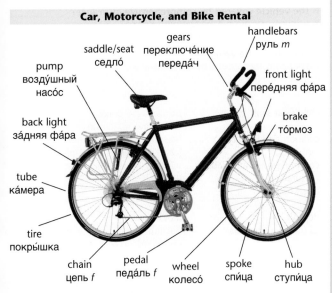

gears
переключе́ние
переда́ч

handlebars
руль *m*

saddle/seat
седло́

pump
возду́шный
насо́с

front light
пере́дняя фа́ра

back light
за́дняя фа́ра

brake
то́рмоз

tube
ка́мера

tire
покры́шка

chain
цепь *f*

pedal
педа́ль *f*

wheel
колесо́

spoke
спи́ца

hub
ступи́ца

I'd like to rent ... for two days/for a week.
Хочу́ взять напрока́т ... *(+ acc)* на два дня./на неде́лю.
[khaCHU VZYAT' napraKAT ... na-DVA DNYA/na-niDYElyu]

a(n) (all-terrain) vehicle/car
автомоби́ль (высо́кой проходи́мости)
[aftamaBIL' vySOkay prakhaDImasti]

a motorcycle
мотоци́кл [mataTSYKL]

a scooter
моторо́ллер [mataROlir]

a moped
мопе́д [maPYET]

61

a moped
мопéд [maPYET]

a bike
велосипéд [vilasiPYET]

How much does it cost per day/per week?
Скóлько э́то стóит в день?/в недéлю?
[SKOL'ka Eta STOit v-DYEN'/v-niDYElyu]

Does that include unlimited mileage?
В стóимость включáется неограни́ченный проéзд?
[f-STOimast' fklyuCHAyitsa niagraNIchiny praYEST]

How much does it cost per kilometer?
Скóлько стóит оди́н киломéтр? [SKOL'ka STOit aDIN kilaMYETR]

Is the vehicle covered by comprehensive insurance?
У маши́ны пóлное страховáние кáско?
[u-maSHYny POLnaye strakhaVAniye KASka]

Can I turn in the vehicle in ...?
Возмóжно ли бýдет сдать маши́ну в … *(+ prep)*?
[vazMOZHna li BUdit ZDAT' maSHYnu f- …]

child's car seat	дéтское сидéнье [DYETskaye siDYEn'ye]
collision and liability insurance	части́чное страховáние кáско [chasTICHnaye strakhaVAniye KASka]
comprehensive and liability insurance	пóлное страховáние кáско [POLnaye strakhaVAniye KASka]
crash helmet	защи́тный шлем [zaSHITny SHLYEM]
deposit	залóг [zaLOK]
to (make a) deposit	оставля́ть/остáвить в залóг [astaVLYAT'/aSTAvit' v-zaLOG]
driver's license	води́тельские правá [vaDItil'skiye praVA]
green insurance card	зелёная страховáя кáрта [ziLYOnaya strakhaVAya KARta]
ignition key	ключ зажигáния [KLYUCH zazhyGAniya]
kidney belt	пóяс-протéктор [POyis-praTYEKtar]
papers	докумéнты *m pl* [dakuMYENty]
sunroof	люк [LYUK]
weekend rate	тари́ф выходнóго дня [taRIF vykhadNOva DNYA]

Making a Flight Reservation

Moscow has five airports: When you are planning to fly via Moscow, find out whether you will have to change airports, and allow enough time for making the transfer.

Could you tell me when the next plane leaves for ...?

Не могли́ бы Вы мне сказа́ть, когда́ бу́дет сле́дующий самолёт в ... (+ acc)? [ni-maGLI BY VY MNYE skaZAT' kagDA BUdit SLYEduyushi samaLYOT f- ...]

Are there still seats available?

Есть ещё биле́ты? [YEST yiSHO biLYEty]

I'd like a one-way ticket to ...

Мне ну́жен биле́т в ... (+ acc) в одну́ сто́рону.
[MNYE NUzhin biLYET f- ... v-adNU STOranu]

I'd like a round-trip ticket to ...

Хочу́ заказа́ть биле́т на самолёт в ... (+ acc) туда́ и обра́тно.
[khaCHU zakaZAT' biLYET na-samaLYOT f- ... tuDA i aBRATna]

How much is an economy class/business class/first-class ticket?

Ско́лько сто́ит биле́т в экономи́ческий класс?/в би́знес-класс?/в пе́рвый класс? [SKOL'ka STOit biLYET v-ekanaMIchiski KLAS/v-BIZnis KLAS/f-PYERvy KLAS]

Smoking or non-smoking?

Куря́щий и́ли некуря́щий? [kurYAshi Ili nikurYAshi]

I'd like ...

Мне, пожа́луйста, ... [MNYE paZHAlusta]

a window seat.

ме́сто у окна́. [MYESta u-akNA]

an aisle seat.

ме́сто у прохо́да. [MYESta u-praKHOda]

I'd like to cancel/change this reservation.

Я хочу́ аннули́ровать/поменя́ть э́тот биле́т.
[YA khaCHU anuLIravat'/pamiNYAT' Etat biLYET]

At the Airport

Where's the ... check-in counter, please?
Где прохо́дит регистра́ция биле́тов авиакомпа́нии ...?
[GDYE praKHOdit rigiSTRAtsyya biLYEtaf aviakamPAnii ...]

Could I see your ticket, please.
Ваш биле́т, пожа́луйста. [VASH biLYET paZHAlusta]

Can I take this as carry-on baggage?
Мо́жно взять э́то как ручно́й бага́ж?
[MOZHna VZYAT' Eta KAK ruchNOY baGASH]

On Board

Could you bring me a glass of water, please?
Не могли́ бы Вы мне принести́ стака́н воды́?
[ni-maGLI BY VY MNYE priniSTI staKAN vaDY]

Could I have a (another) pillow/blanket, please?
Не могли́ бы Вы мне принести́ (ещё) одну́ поду́шку?/одно́
покрыва́ло? [ni-maGLI BY VY priniSTI (yiSHO) adNU
paDUSHku/adNO pakryVAla]

Would you mind switching places with me?
Вы не возража́ете, е́сли мы поменя́емся места́ми?
[VY ni-vazraZHAyitye YEsli MY pamiNYAyimsa miSTAmi]

Arrival ➤ also Lost-and-Found Office

My baggage is missing.
Мой бага́ж потеря́лся. [MOY baGASH patirYALsa]

My suitcase has been damaged.
Повреди́лся мой чемода́н. [pavriDILsa MOY chimaDAN]

Where does the bus to ... leave from?
Отку́да отхо́дит авто́бус в сто́рону ... (+ gen)?
[atKUda atKHOdit aFTObus f-STOranu ...]

➤ also Train

airline	авиакомпа́ния [aviakamPAniya]
airport	аэропо́рт [aeraPORT]
airport shuttle/bus	авто́бус-экспре́сс [aFTObus-ekSPRYES]
airport tax	аэропорто́вый сбор [aeraPORTny ZBOR]
arrival	прибы́тие [priBYtiye]
arrival time	вре́мя прибы́тия [VRYEmya priBYtiya]
baggage	бага́ж [baGASH]
baggage cart	теле́жка [tiLYESHka]

baggage check-in	оформле́ние и сда́ча багажа́ [afarmLYEniye i ZDAcha baGAzha]
baggage claim	вы́дача багажа́ [VYdacha baGAzha]
boarding pass	поса́дочный тало́н [paSAdachny taLON]
cancel	аннули́ровать *ipf a. pf* [anuLIravat']
to change (a flight reservation)	меня́ть/поменя́ть [miNYAT'/pamiNYAT']
to check in	регистри́роваться/ зарегистри́роваться [rigisTRIravatsa/zarigisTRIravatsa]
connection	переса́дка [piriSATka]
delay	опозда́ние [apaZDAniye]
domestic flight	вну́тренний полёт [VNUtrini paLYOT]
duty-free shop	магази́н беспо́шлинной торго́вли [magaZIN bisPOSHlinay tarGOvli]
emergency chute	эвакуацио́нный трап [evakuatsyOny TRAP], го́рка [GORka]
emergency exit	запа́сный вы́ход [zaPASny VYkhat]
emergency landing	вы́нужденная поса́дка [VYnuzhdinaya paSATka]
excess baggage	переве́с [piriVYES]
flight	полёт [paLYOT]
flight attendant	стю́ард/стюарде́сса [STYUart/styuarDYEsa]
gate	вы́ход на поса́дку [VYkhat na-paSATku]
international flight	междунаро́дный полёт [mizhdunaRODny paLYOT]
landing	приземле́ние [prizimLYEniye]
life jacket	спаса́тельный жиле́т [spaSAtil'ny zhiLYET]
passenger	пассажи́р/ка [pasaZHYR/ka]
pilot	пило́т [piLOT]
security check	контро́ль *m* безопа́сности [kanTROL' bizaPASnasti]
stopover/layover	промежу́точная поса́дка [pramiZHUtachnaya paSATka]
takeoff	вы́лет [VYlit]
terminal	термина́л [tirmiNAL]

Buying Tickets

Arrange for your tickets as far in advance as possible, since most trains require reservations.

Two tickets to ..., please.
Два билéта до ... *(+ gen)*, пожáлуйста.
[DVA biLYEta da- ... paZHAlusta]

A ticket to ..., please.
Пожáлуйста, одйн билéт до ... *(+ gen)*
[paZHAlusta aDIN biLYET da- ...]

one-way
в однý стóрону [v-adNU STOranu]
round-trip
тудá и обрáтно [tuDA i aBRATna]
on August 4th
на четвёртое áвгуста [na-chitVYORtaye AVgusta]
for the No. ... train
на пóезд № ... [na-POyist NOmir ...]

The upper/lower berth, please.
Вéрхнюю/Нйжнюю пóлку, пожáлуйста.
[VYERKHnyuyu/NIZHnyuyu POLku paZHAlusta]

Is there a reduced fare for children/for students?
Есть ли льгóты для детéй?/для студéнтов?
[YEST L'GOty dli-diTYEY/dli-stuDYENtaf]

Because of the long distances, trips usually take so long that you have to spend the night on the train. Thus most trains are equipped with sleeper and couchette cars. The following categories are offered:
—СВ [es-VE]: luxury-class sleeping car
—купéйный вагóн [kuPYEYny vaGON]: compartment car, usually with four-person compartments (четырёхмéстное купé [chityryokhMYESnaye kuPE]), sometimes with two-person compartments (двухмéстное купé [dvukhMYESnaye kuPE])
—плацкáртный вагóн [platsKARTny vaGON]: couchette car, not divided into compartments
—óбщий вагóн [OPshi vaGON]: simple car, without real sleeping accommodations

66

What time will I have a connection to the train to ...?
Во ско́лько часо́в у меня́ бу́дет переса́дка на по́езд в ...
(+ acc)? [va-SKOL'ka chiSOF u-miNYA BUdit piriSATka na-POyist f- ...]

How often do I have to change trains?
Ско́лько переса́док? [SKOL'ka piriSAdak]

At the Train Station

Can I check my suitcase/bicycle as baggage?
Могу́ ли я сдать свой чемода́н/велосипе́д в бага́ж по́езда?
[maGU li YA ZDAT' SVOY chimaDAN/vilasiPYET v-baGASH POyizda]

Excuse me, which platform does the train to ... leave from?
Извини́те, с како́го пути́ отправля́ется по́езд в ... *(+ acc)*?
[izviNItye s-kaKOva puTI atpravLYAyitsa POyist f- ...]

Train No. ... from ... is running ten minutes late.
По́езд но́мер ... из ... *(+ gen)* прибыва́ет с опозда́нием на
де́сять мину́т.
[POyist NOmir is-... pribyVAyit s-apaZDAniyim na-DYEsit' miNUT]

On the Train

Smoking is prohibited in every car of the train. People smoke
in the connecting areas between cars.

Excuse me, is this seat free?
Извини́те, э́то ме́сто свобо́дно? [izviNItye Eta MYESta svaBODna]

May I open/close the window?
Мо́жно откры́ть/закры́ть окно́? [MOZHna atKRYT'/zaKRYT' akNO]

Excuse me, I think that's my seat.
Извини́те, ка́жется, э́то моё ме́сто.
[izviNItye KAzhytsa Eta maYO MYESta]

Here is my seat reservation.
Вот мой биле́т. [VOT MOY biLYET]

Signs and Information

Расписа́ние поездо́в	Timetable
отправле́ние/прибы́тие	departures/arrivals
Спра́вочная	Information
носи́льщики	porters
Ж	women's restroom
М	men's restroom
за́нято/свобо́дно	occupied/vacant
Ко́мната ма́тери и ребёнка	mother-and-child room
Биле́тная ка́сса	ticket window
Железнодоро́жное аге́нтство	seat reservation and
по брони́рованию и прода́жам	ticket sales center
биле́тов	

Куре́ние запрещено́	No Smoking
Стоя́нка такси́	Taxi Stand
Метро́/При́городные поезда́	subway/commuter trains
Ка́мера хране́ния	baggage lockers, baggage check-room
теле́жки	baggage carts
Зал ожида́ния	Waiting Room
Мили́ция	Train Police

Sometimes intercity buses offer an economical alternative to train travel. For information, reservations, and departure platforms, go to the автовокза́л [aftavagZAL] (bus station).

➢ also Plane

accompanying person	сопровожда́ющее лицо́ [sapravazhDAyushiye liTSO]
additional charge	допла́та [daPLAta]
arrival	прибы́тие [priBYtiye]
baggage	бага́ж [baGASH]
baggage check-in counter	бага́жное отделе́ние [baGAZHnaye addiLYEniye], бага́жная ка́сса [baGAZHnaya KAsa]
baggage deposit	ка́мера хране́ния [KAmira khraNYEniya]
car number	но́мер ваго́на [NOmir vaGOna]
child's ticket	де́тский биле́т [DYETski biLYET]
compartment	купе́ [kuPYE]
conductor	конду́ктор [kanDUKtar]
corridor	прохо́д [praKHOT]
departure	отправле́ние [atpraVLYEniye]
dining car	ваго́н-рестора́н [vaGON-ristaRAN]
fare	сто́имость f прое́зда [STOimast' praYEZda]
to get off	выходи́ть/вы́йти [vykhaDIT'/VYti]
to get on	сади́ться/сесть [saDItsa/SYEST']
head conductor	нача́льник/нача́льница поезда́ [naCHAL'nik/naCHAL'nitsa POyizda]
locker	ка́мера хране́ния [KAmira khraNYEniya]
main railroad station	гла́вный вокза́л [GLAVny vagZAL]
reduction	льго́ты f pl [L'GOty]
reservation	брони́рование [braNIravaniye]
round-trip ticket	биле́т в о́ба конца́ [biLYET v-Oba kanTSA]
seat reservation	плацка́рта [platsKARta]
severely handicapped person	инвали́д [invaLIT]

smoking compartment	купе́ для куря́щих [kuPYE dli-kuRYAshikh]
snack cart	передвижно́й буфе́т [piridvizhNOY buFYET]
to stamp one's ticket	компости́ровать/прокомпости́ровать [kampaSTIravat'/prakampaSTIravat']
stop, stay	остано́вка [astaNOFka]
ticket	(проездно́й) биле́т [(prayizNOY) biLYET]
ticket counter	биле́тная ка́сса [biLYETnaya KAsa]
ticket inspection	контро́ль m биле́тов [kanTROL' biLYEtaf]
timetable	расписа́ние [raspiSAniye]
track	путь m [PUT']
train	по́езд [POyist]
train conductor	проводни́к/проводни́ца [pravadNIK/pravadNItsa]

The проводни́к [pravadNIK] or проводни́ца [pravadNItsa] checks tickets, shows people their seats, hands out bed linens, and pours hot tea.

train station	вокза́л [vagZAL]
window seat	ме́сто у окна́ [MYESta u-akNA]

Ship

Information

When does the next ship/ferry for ... leave?
Когда́ отхо́дит сле́дующий кора́бль/паро́м в ... *(+ acc)*?
[kagDA atKHOdit SLYEduyushi kaRABL'/paROM f- ...]

How long does the crossing take?
Как до́лго дли́тся рейс? [KAK DOLga DLItsa REYS]

When do we land at ...?
Когда́ мы прибу́дем в ... *(+ acc)*? [kagDA MY priBUdim f- ...]

How long do we stop in ...?
Как до́лго мы бу́дем стоя́ть в ... *(+ prep)*?
[KAK DOLga MY BUdim staYAT' f- ...]

I'd like ..., please.
Пожа́луйста, ... [paZHAlusta ...]

  a ticket to ...
  оди́н биле́т до ... *(+ gen)*. [aDIN biLYET da- ...]
  first class
  в пе́рвом кла́ссе [f-PYERvam KLAsye]

tourist class
в тури́стическом кла́ссе [f-turiSTIchiskam KLAsye]

a single cabin
одноме́стную каю́ту [adnaMYESnuyu kaYUtu]

a double cabin
двухме́стную каю́ту [dvukhMYESnuyu kaYUtu]

a ticket for the (round-trip) tour at three o'clock
оди́н биле́т на экску́рсию в пятна́дцать часо́в.
[aDIN biLYET na-ekSKURsiyu f-pitNAtsat' chiSOF]

On Board

Where's the dining room/the restaurant/the lounge, please?
Где столо́вая?/рестора́н?/каю́т-компа́ния?
[GDYE staLOvaya/ristaRAN/kaYUT-kamPAniya]

I don't feel well.
Я чу́вствую себя́ нехорошо́. [YA CHUSTvuyu siBYA nikharaSHO]

Please call the ship's doctor.
Позови́те корабе́льного врача́, пожа́луйста.
[pazaVItye karaBYEL'nava vraCHA paZHAlusta]

Could you give me something for seasickness, please?
Не могли́ бы Вы мне дать сре́дство от морско́й боле́зни?
[ni-maGLI BY VY MNYE DAT' SRYETstva at-marSKOY baLYEZni]

cabin	каю́та [kaYUta]
captain	капита́н [kapiTAN]
coast	морско́й бе́рег [marSKOY BYErik]
cruise	круи́з [kruIS]
deck	па́луба [PAluba]
excursion	экску́рсия на бе́рег [ekSKURsiya na-BYErik]
ferry	паро́м [paROM]
hovercraft	гли́ссер [GLIsir], су́дно на возду́шной поду́шке [SUDna na-vazDUSHnay paDUSHkye]
hydrofoil	су́дно на подво́дных кры́льях [SUDna na-padVODnykh KRYL'yikh]
to land at	прича́ливать/прича́лить в … (+ prep) [priCHAlivat'/priCHAlit' f- …]
life jacket	спаса́тельный жиле́т [spaSAtil'ny zhiLYET]
life preserver	спаса́тельный круг [spaSAtil'ny KRUK]
lifeboat	спаса́тельная ло́дка [spaSAtil'naya LOTka]
mainland	су́ша [SUsha]
port, harbor	порт [PORT]
reservation	бро́ня [BROnya]
rough sea	волне́ние (мо́ря) [valNYEniye (MOrya)]

seasickness	морская болезнь
	[marSKAya baLYEZN']
steamship	пароход [paraKHOT]
ticket	(проездной) билет
	[(prayizNOY) biLYET]
tour (round trip)	экскурсия [ekSKURsiya]
wharf	набережная [NAbirizhnaya]

Local Public Transportation

Excuse me, where's the nearest ...
Скажите, пожалуйста, где ближайшая …
[skaZHYtye paZHAlusta GDYE bliZHAYshaya ...]

bus stop?
остановка автобуса? [astaNOFka aFTObusa]

trolleybus stop?
остановка троллейбуса? [astaNOFka traLYEYbusa]

collective taxi stop?
остановка маршрутного такси?
[astaNOFka marshRUTnava taKSI]

streetcar stop?
остановка трамвая? [astaNOFka tramVAya]

subway station?
станция метро? [STANtsyya miTRO]

Which line goes to ...?
Какой номер идёт в … *(+ acc)*?/до … *(+ gen)*?
[kaKOY NOmir iDYOT f- ...]

When does the first/last (subway) train go to ...?
Когда идёт первый/последний поезд метро в … *(+ acc)*?
[kagDA iDYOT PYERvy/paSLYEDny POyist miTRO f- ...]

Does this bus go to ...?
Этот автобус идёт до … *(+ gen)*? [Etat aFTObus iDYOT da- ...]

How many stops is it to ...?
Сколько остановок до … *(+ gen)*? [SKOL'ka astaNOvak da- ...]

Where do I have to get off/change?
Где мне выходить?/пересесть?
[GDYE MNYE vykhaDIT'/piriSYEST']

Could you please tell me when I have to get off?
Не могли бы Вы мне сообщить, когда мне нужно будет
выходить? [ni-maGLI BY VY MNYE saapSHIT' kagDA MNYE NUZHna
BUdit vykhaDIT']

A ticket, please.
Один билет, пожалуйста. [aDIN biLYET paZHAlusta]

Normally you can buy tickets (билéты [biLYEty]) for the bus, trolleybus, and streetcar from the conductor, from the driver, or at many kiosks. If you have a single-use ticket, have it stamped once you have boarded, by inserting it in the special machine that will stamp the date and time on it. A flat rate is charged for the entire city, but if you transfer, you need another ticket.

Tickets (билéты [biLYEty]) or tokens (жетóны [zhyTOny]) for the subway are available at the station entrances. The tickets are read by a special device at the turnstile. After inserting the ticket, remember to remove it from the device again before going through! There are also various machine-readable commuter passes. Instead of билéт [biLYET], you will often hear the old term талóн [taLON] as well.

bus	автóбус [aFTObus]
bus station	автовокзáл [aftavagZAL]
cable car	зубчáтая желéзная дорóга [zupCHAtaya zhyLYEZnaya daROga]
city bus	городскóй автóбус [garatSKOY aFTObus]
commuter train	пригородный пóезд [PRIgaradny POyist], электричка [elikTRICHka]
conductor	кондуктор [kanDUKtar]
day pass	однодневный билéт [adnaDNYEVny biLYET]
departure	отправлéние [atpraVLYEniye]
direction	направлéние [napraVLYEniye]
end of the line	конéчная стáнция [kaNYECHnaya STANtsyya]
fare	стóимость f проéзда [STOimast' praYEZda]
to get on	садиться/сесть [saDItsa/SYEST']
intercity bus	междугорóдный автóбус [mizhdugaRODny aFTObus]
local train	пригородный пóезд [PRIgaradny POyist], электричка [elikTRICHka]
machine that stamps/ punches tickets	компóстер [kamPOstir]
monthly pass	мéсячный билéт [MYEsichny biLYET], абонемéнт [abaniMYENT]
pass for ... rides	билéт на- ... поéздок [biLYET na- ... paYEZdak]
schedule	расписáние [raspiSAniye]

to stamp one's ticket	компости́ровать/прокомпости́ровать [kampaSTIravat'/prakampaSTIravat']
start of the line	коне́чная остано́вка [kaNYECHnaya astaNOFka]
stop	остано́вка [astaNOFka]
streetcar	трамва́й [tramVAY]
subway	метро́ [miTRO]
ticket	(проездно́й) биле́т [(prayizNOY) biLYET]
ticket-taker	контролёр [kantraLYOR]
trolleybus	тролле́йбус [traLYEYbus]
weekly pass	однонеде́льный биле́т [adnaniDYEL'ny biLYET], абонеме́нт [abaniMYENT]

Taxi

Behind the wheel of vehicles with a taxi sign, you will usually find a trained driver who knows his way around town. But you can also try to stop any passing car by signaling with your hand and agreeing on a price for the ride. However, especially in large cities, you run the risk of getting picked up by criminals. In such places it is best to telephone for a taxi. Be especially careful with private taxis that wait in front of train stations, hotels, and international airports in particular. Always negotiate the fare in advance, and make sure that it is clear which currency you intend to use! In some cases, drivers suddenly try to collect the agreed-on fare in dollars or euros instead of rubles.

Excuse me, where is the nearest taxi stand?
Не могли́ бы Вы мне сказа́ть, где здесь побли́зости стоя́нка такси́?
[ni-maGLI BY VY MNYE skaZAT' GDYE ZDYES' paBLIzasti staYANka taKSI]

Could you please call me a taxi?
Не могли́ бы Вы мне вы́звать такси́?
[ni-maGLI BY VY MNYE VYzvat' taKSI]

Hello? Please send a taxi to the address ... right away/at ... o'clock (tomorrow).
Алло́! Мне, пожа́луйста, такси́ по а́дресу ... пря́мо сейча́с./на (за́втра,) ... часо́в. [aLO MNYE paZHAlusta taKSI pa-Adrisu ... PRYAma siyCHAS/na- (ZAFtra) ... chiSOF]

Where would you like to go?
Куда́ Вы е́дете? [kuDA VY YEditye]

73

To the train station, please.
До вокза́ла, пожа́луйста. [da-vagZAla paZHAlusta]

To the ... Hotel, please.
До гости́ницы ..., пожа́луйста. [da-gaSTInitsy ... paZHAlusta]

To ... Street, please.
До у́лицы ..., пожа́луйста. [da-Ulitsy ... paZHAlusta]

To ..., please.
До ... *(+ gen)*, пожа́луйста. [da-... paZHAlusta]

How much will it cost per kilometer?
Ско́лько сто́ит прое́зд за киломе́тр?
[SKOL'ka STOit praYEST za-kilaMYETR]

How much will it cost to ...?
Ско́лько сто́ит до ... *(+ gen)*? [SKOL'ka STOit da-...]

That's too much!
Это сли́шком мно́го! [Eta SLISHkam MNOga]

Could you stop here, please?
Останови́тесь здесь, пожа́луйста. [astanaVItyes' ZDYES'
paZHAlusta]

Could you please give me a receipt?
Вы мне мо́жете вы́писать квита́нцию?
[VY MNYE MOzhytye VYpisat' kviTANtsyyu]

That's for you.
Это Вам. [Eta VAM]

to buckle up	пристёгиваться/пристегну́ться [priSTYOgivatsa/pristiGNUtsa]
flat rate	о́бщая цена́ [OPshaya tsyNA]
house number	но́мер до́ма [NOmir DOma]
kilometer rate	тари́ф за киломе́тр [taRIF za-kilaMYETR]
receipt	квита́нция [kviTANtsyya]
seat belt	реме́нь *m* безопа́сности [riMYEN' bizaPASnasti]
to stop	остана́вливаться/останови́ться [astaNAvlivatsa/astanaVItsa]
taxi driver	води́тель/ница такси́ [vaDItil'/nitsa taKSI]
taxi stand	стоя́нка такси́ [staYANka taKSI]
tip	чаевы́е [chayiVYye]

The Russians' love of children, which travelers are certain to encounter, has as yet found little expression in child-friendly facilities and offerings of the sort found in Western countries.

Useful Questions

Could you please tell me whether there's a playground here?
Здесь есть де́тская площа́дка?
[ZDYES' YEST' DYETskaya plaSHATka]

Do you have child-care personnel here?
Здесь есть персона́л по ухо́ду за детьми́?
[ZDYES' YEST' pirsaNAL pa-uKHOdu za-dit'MI]

From what age up?
Со ско́льки лет? [sa-SKOL'ka LYET]

Do you know anyone who could babysit for us?
Вы зна́ете кого́-нибудь, кто мог бы посиде́ть с на́шим ребёнком?
[VY ZNAyitye kaVO-nibut' KTO MOK BY pasiDYET' s-NAshym riBYONkam]

Are there activities for children?
Предлага́ются ли мероприя́тия для дете́й?
[pridlaGAyutsa li mirapriYAtiya dlia-diTYEY]

Is there a reduced rate for children?
Есть ли ски́дка для дете́й? [YEST li SKITka dlia-diTYEY]

Could you please tell me where I can get diapers?
Не могли́ бы Вы мне сказа́ть, где мо́жно купи́ть пелёнки?
[ni-maGLI BY VY MNYE skaZAT' GDYE MOZHna kuPIT' piLYONki]

On the Road

We're traveling with a young child. Could we have seats right at the front?
Мы путеше́ствуем с ребёнком. Не могли́ бы мы сесть впереди́?
[MY putiSHESTvuyim s-riBYONkam. ni-maGLI BY MY SYEST' f-piriDI]

Do you have a child's seat belt?
У Вас есть де́тский реме́нь безопа́сности?
[u-VAS YEST DYETski riMYEN' bizaPASnasti]

Do you possibly have any crayons and paper?/a coloring book?
У Вас не найдётся карандаше́й и бума́ги?/кни́жки-раскра́ски?
[u-VAS ni-nayDYOtsa karandaSHEY i buMAgi/KNIshki-rasKRAski]

Do you rent children's car seats?
Вы даёте напрока́т де́тские автомоби́льные сиде́нья?
[VY daYOtye napraKAT DYETskiye aftamaBIL'nyye siDYEn'ya]

Do you have a highchair?
У Вас есть детский стульчик? [u-VAS YEST DYETski STUL'chik]

Do you serve children's portions?
Предлагаете детские порции? [pridlaGAyitye DYETskiye PORtsyi]

Could you warm up this baby bottle please?
Не могли бы Вы подогреть бутылочку?
[ni-maGLI BY VY padaGRYET' buTYlachku]

Is there a diaper changing room here?
Здесь есть комната для пеленания грудных детей?
[ZDYES' YEST KOMnata dlia-piliNAniya grudNYKH diTYEY]

Could you please tell me where I can breast-feed my baby?
Не могли бы Вы мне сказать, где я могу покормить
ребёнка грудью? [ni-maGLI BY VY MNYE skaZAT' GDYE YA maGU
pakarMIT' riBYONka GRUd'yu]

amusement park	парк с аттракционами [PARK s-atraktsyOnami]
baby bottle	бутылочка [buTYlachka]
baby food	детское питание [DYETskaye piTAniye]
baby monitor	бебифон [bibiFON], радионяня [radioNYAnya]
babysitter	бэбиситтер [bebiSItir]
bottle warmer	подогреватель *m* бутылочек [padagriVAtil' buTYlachik]
cap	шапочка [SHApachka]
changing table	столик для пеленания [STOlik dlia-piliNAniya]
child's car seat	детское сиденье [DYETskaye siDYEn'ye]
child-care service	уход за детьми [uKHOT za-dit'MI]
children's clothing	детская одежда [DYETskaya aDYEZHda]
children's pool	детский бассейн [DYETski baSYEYN]
coloring book	книжка-раскраска [KNISHka-rasKRASka]
crib	детская кровать [DYETskaya kraVAT']
diapers	пелёнки *f pl* [piLYONki]
feeding bottle	бутылочка с соской [buTYlachka s-SOskay]
inner tube	плавательный круг [PLAvatil'ny KRUK]
nanny	няня [NYAnya]
(baby bottle) nipple	соска [SOska]
pacifier	пустышка [puSTYshka]
playground	детская площадка [DYETskaya plaSHATka]

playmate	друг/подруга [DRUK/paDRUga]
reduced rate for children	скидка для детей [SKITka dlia-diTYEY]
sandbox	песочница [piSOCHnitsa]
sandcastle	крепость *f* из песка [KRYEpast' is-piSKA]
sunscreen	защита от солнца [zaSHIta at-SONtsa]
toys	игрушки *f pl* [iGRUSHki]
wading pool	детский бассейн [DYETski baSYEYN]
water wings	надувные крылышки для плавания [naduvNYye KRYlyshki dlia-PLAvaniya]

Health

Could you please tell me whether there's a pediatrician here?
Вы не скажете мне, есть ли здесь детский врач?
[VY ni-skaZHYtye MNYE YEST li ZDYES' DYETski VRACH]

My child has ...
У моего ребёнка … [u-mayiVO riBYONka ...]

He is allergic to ...
У него аллергия от … *(+ gen)* [u-niVO alirGIya at- ...]

He has thrown up.
У него рвота. [u-niVO RVOta]

He has diarrhea.
У него понос. [u-niVO paNOS]

He has been bitten.
Кто-то его укусил. [KTO-ta yiVO ukuSIL]

allergy	аллергия [alirGIya]
chickenpox	ветряная оспа [VYEtrinaya Ospa]
childhood disease	детская болезнь [DYETskaya baLYEZN']
children's hospital	детская больница [DYETsaka bal'NItsa]
cold	простуда [praSTUda]
fever	температура [timpiraTUra]
German measles	краснуха [krasNUkha]
head cold	насморк [NAsmark]
insect bite	укус насекомого [uKUS nasiKOmava]
measles	корь *f* [KOR']
mumps	свинка [SVINka]
oral electrolyte maintenance solution	раствор электролитов [rastVOR eliktraLItaf]
rash	сыпь *f* [SYP']
scarlet fever	скарлатина [skarlaTIna]
vaccination record	справка о прививках [SPRAFka a-priVIFkakh]
whooping cough	коклюш [kakLYUSH]

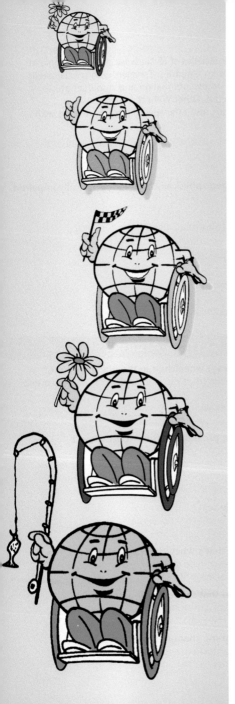

Travelers with Disabilities

There are far fewer facilities of all kinds for disabled people in Russia than in Western countries. Travelers with special needs will find extensive access information and resources at *www.access-able.com*. Other Websites, such as *www.frommers.com*, also offer special tips for travelers with disabilities.

I'm ...
Я ... [YA ...]

physically challenged./physically disabled./physically impaired.
инвали́д. [invaLIT]

mobility-impaired.
передвига́юсь с трудо́м. [piridviGAyus' s-truDOM]

I have ...
У меня́ ... [u-miNYA]

a visual disability.
наруше́ние зре́ния. [naruSHEniye ZRYEniya]

multiple sclerosis.
рассе́янный склеро́з. [raSEYany skliROS]

Getting Around

Can I take my (folding) wheelchair in the plane with me?
Могу́ ли я взять в самолёт свою́ (складну́ю) инвали́дную коля́ску?
[maGU li YA VZYAT' f-samaLYOT svaYU (skladNUuyu) invaLIDnuyu kaLYAsku]

Will a wheelchair be provided at the airport when I depart/arrive?
Бу́дет ли предоста́влена инвали́дная коля́ска в порту́ отправле́ния?/назначе́ния? [BUdit li pridaSTAvlina invaLIDnaya kaLYAska f-parTU atpraVLYEniya/naznaCHEniya]

Could I have an aisle seat?
Могу́ ли я получи́ть ме́сто у прохо́да?
[maGU li YA paluCHIT' MYESta u-praKHOda]

Is there a restroom that's wheelchair-accessible?
Есть ли туале́т, приспосо́бленный для инвали́дов?
[YEST li tuaLYET prispaSObliny dlia-invaLIdaf]

Is there a washroom that's wheelchair-accessible?
Есть ли умыва́льная для инвали́дов?
[YEST li umyVAL'naya dlia-invaLIdaf]

Could someone help me change flights/trains?
Мог бы кто-нибудь помо́чь мне при переса́дке?
[MOK BY KTO-nibut' paMOCH MNYE pri-piriSATkye]

Are the doors of the train at ground level?
Нахо́дится ли вход в тра́нспорт на у́ровне земли́?
[naKHOditsa li FKHOT f-TRANSpart na-Uravnye zimLI]

Do the platforms have ramps for wheelchair users?
Обору́дованы ли платфо́рмы накло́нными въе́здами для инвали́дных коля́сок? [abaRUdavany li platFORmy naKLOnymi VYEZdami dlia-invaLIDnykh kaLYAsak]

Do you have cars with hand controls for the physically challenged?
Есть ли у Вас инвали́дные автомоби́ли с ручны́м нажа́тием га́за?
[YEST li u-VAS invaLIDnyye aftamaBIli s-ruchNYM naZHAtiyim GAza]

Do you rent RVs suitable for wheelchair users?
Вы даёте напрока́т ке́мперы, приспосо́бленные для инвали́дов?
[VY daYOtye napraKAT KYEMpery prispaSOblinyye dlia-invaLIdaf]

Is it possible to rent hand-operated bikes here?
Мо́жно здесь взять напрока́т инвали́дные велосипе́ды?
[MOZHna ZDYES' VZYAT' napraKAT invaLIDnyye vilasiPYEdy]

Accommodations

Could you please send me information about which hotels/campgrounds in ... have special facilities for the disabled?
Не могли́ бы Вы мне посла́ть информа́цию о том, каки́е гости́ницы/ке́мпинги в ... (+ prep) располага́ют специа́льным обору́дованием для инвали́дов? [ni-maGLI BY VY MNYE paSLAT' infarMAtsyyu a-TOM kaKIye gaSTInitsy/KYEMpingi f- ... raspalaGAyut spitsyAL'nym abaRUdavaniyim dlia-invaLIdaf]

What kind of floor does the room have?
Како́е в но́мере половое́ покры́тие?
[kaKOye f-NOmirye palaVOye paKRYtiye]

Museums, Sights, Theater ...

Is an elevator for mobility-impaired people available at the exhibition?
На вы́ставке предусмо́трен лифт для инвали́дов?
[na-VYstafkye priduSMOtrin LIFT dlia-invaLIdaf]

Are there special (city) sightseeing tours for the deaf?
Прово́дятся ли специа́льные экску́рсии (по го́роду) для глухи́х?
[praVOdyitsa li spitsyAL'nyye ekSKURsii (pa-GOradu) dlia-gluKHIKH]

Can the induction loop system for the hard of hearing be turned on?

Можно включить систему индукционной связи для слабослышащих? [MOZHna fklyuCHIT' siSTYEmy induktsiOnay SVYAzi dlia-slabaSLYshashikh]

Are there museum tours/theater performances for deaf-mutes?/for the blind?

Проводятся ли музейные экскурсии/театральные представления для глухонемых?/слепых?
[praVOdyitsa li muZYEYnyye ekSKURsii/tiaTRAL'nyye pritstaVLYEniya dlia glukhaniMYKH/sliPYKH]

accessible	доступный [daSTUPny]
accompanying person	сопровождающее лицо [sapravaZHDAyushiye liTSO]
association for the disabled	общество инвалидов [OPshistva invaLIdaf]
at ground level	на уровне земли [na-Uravnye zimLI]
automatic door	автоматическая дверь [aftamaTIchiskaya DVYER']
automatic door opener . . .	устройство для автоматического открывания дверей [uSTROYstva dli-aftamaTIchiskava atkryVAniya dvirYEY]
barrier-free	свободный от заграждений [svaBODny at-zagraZHDYEni]
blind	слепой [sliPOY]
boarding assistance	приспособление для инвалидов при посадке [prispasaBLYEniye dlia-invaLIdaf pri-paSATke]
Braille	шрифт Брайля [SHRIFT BRAilya]
cabin for wheelchair users *(ship)*	каюта, приспособленная для инвалидных колясок [kaYUta prispaSOblinaya dlia-invaLIDnykh kaLYAsak]
cane	трость f для слепых [TROST' dlia-sliPYKH]
crutch	костыль m [kaSTYL']
deaf	глухой [gluKHOY]
deaf-mute	глухонемой [glukhaniMOY]
disabled identification card .	удостоверение инвалидности [udastaviRYEniye invaLIDnasti]
door width	ширина дверного проёма [shyriNA dvirNOva praYOma]
epilepsy	эпилепсия [epiLYEPsiya]
grip, handle	поручни m pl [POruchni]

hand throttle *(car)*	ручно́е нажа́тие га́за [ruchNOye naZHAtiye GAza]
hand-operated bike	велосипе́д с ручны́м при́водом [vilasiPYET s-ruchNYM PRIvadam], рукоба́йк [rukaBAYK]
handrail	пери́ла *n pl* [piRIla]
hard of hearing	слабослы́шащий [slabaSLYshashi]
headphones	нау́шники [naUSHniki]
hearing aid	слухово́й аппара́т [slukhaVOY apaRAT]
height	высота́ [vysaTA]
incline	подъём [padYOM]
induction loop system	индукцио́нная петля́ [induktsyOnaya pitLYA]
mentally handicapped	душевнобольно́й [dushevnabal'NOY]
mobility impaired person	с трудо́м передвига́ющийся [s-truDOM piridviGAyushisa]
mute	немо́й [niMOY]
paralyzed	парализо́ванный [paraliZOvany]
parking for the disabled	автостоя́нка для инвали́дов [aftastaYANka dlia-invaLIdaf]
person in need of care	нужда́ющийся в ухо́де [nuZHDAyushi v-uKHOdye]
physical disability	физи́ческий недоста́ток [fiZIchiski nidaSTAtak]
platform lift	подъёмный лифт [padYOMny LIFT]
provision of service for the disabled	обслу́живание инвали́дов [apSLUzhyvaniye invaLIdaf]
ramp	накло́нный въезд [naKLOny VYEST]
ramp (for wheelchairs)	накло́нный въезд (для инвали́дных коля́сок) [naKLOny VYEST dlia-invaLIDnykh kaLYAsak]
sanitary facilities	санита́рно-гигиени́ческие устро́йства [saniTARna-gigiyiNIchiskiye uSTROYstva]
seeing eye dog	соба́ка-поводы́рь [saBAka-pavaDYR']
services for the disabled	слу́жба социа́льной по́мощи [SLUZHba satsyAL'nay POmashi]
severely disabled person	инвали́д вы́сшей гру́ппы [invaLIT VYshey GRUpy]
shower seat	инвали́дное сиде́нье для душевы́х каби́н [invaLIDnaye siDYEn'ye dlia-dushiVYKH kaBIN]
sign language	же́стов язы́к [ZHEstaf yiZYK]
social services	социа́льное обеспече́ние [satsyAL'naye abispiCHEniye], собе́с [saBYES]
step	ступе́нь *f* [stuPYEN']

stepless access	вход без ступе́ней [FKHOT bis-stuPYEnyi]
suitable for the disabled ...	приспосо́бленный для инвали́дов [prispaSObliny dlia-invaLIdaf]
text telephone	текстофо́н [tekstaFON]
threshold	поро́г двери́ [paROK dviRI]
transportation service	тра́нспортные услу́ги [TRANSpartnyye uSLUgi]
visually impaired	слабови́дящий [slabaVIDyishi]
wheelchair	инвали́дная коля́ска [invaLIDnaya kaLYAska]
electric wheelchair	электри́ческая инвали́дная коля́ска [elikTRIchiskaya invaLIDnaya kaLYAska]
folding wheelchair	складна́я инвали́дная коля́ска [skladNAya invaLIDnaya kaLYAska]
on-board wheelchair	бортова́я инвали́дная коля́ска [bartaVAya invaLIDnaya kaLYAska]
wheelchair accessible	приспосо́бленный для инвали́дных коля́сок [prispaSObliny dlia-invaLIDnykh kaLYAsak]
wheelchair-accessible car .. (train)	ваго́н, приспосо́бленный для инвали́дных коля́сок [vaGON prispaSObliny dlia-invaLIDnykh kaLYAsak]
wheelchair-accessible .... restroom	туале́т, приспосо́бленный для инвали́дов [tuaLYET prispaSObliny dlia-invaLIdaf]
wheelchair user	передвига́ющийся в инвали́дной коля́ске [piridviGAyushisa v-invaLIDnay kaLYAskye]
width	ширина́ [shyriNA]
width of the corridor	ширина́ коридо́ра [shyriNA kariDOra]

Accommodations

Information

Sometimes the category and the price of a hotel are completely unrelated. Many hotels charge foreigners higher rates, while others refuse to accept any foreign guests at all.

Could you recommend ..., please?
Не могли́ бы Вы мне порекомендова́ть ...?
[ni-maGLI BY VY MNYE parikamindaVAT' ...]

a good hotel
хоро́шую гости́ницу [khaROshuyu gaSTInitsu]

an inexpensive hotel
дешёвую гости́ницу [diSHOvuyu gaSTInitsu]

a bed-and-breakfast/boarding house
ча́стный пансио́н [CHASny pansiON]

Is it centrally located/near the beach?
Э́то бли́зко от це́нтра?/от пля́жа?
[Eta BLISka at-TSENtra/at-PLYAzha]

Is it quiet?
Там ти́хо? [TAM TIkha]

Is there ... here?
А здесь есть ...? [A ZDYES' YEST ...]

a campground
ке́мпинг [KYEMpink]

a youth hostel
хо́стел [KHOstil]

a student dorm
студе́нческое общежи́тие [stuDYENchiskaye apshiZHYtiye]

There are only a few youth hostels that are members of the International Youth Hostel Federation. In some towns, student dorms offer simple, inexpensive accommodations when classes are not in session.

Hotel—Pension—Bed-and-Breakfast

At the Reception Desk

I have a room reservation. My last name is ...
Я заказа́л m/заказа́ла f у Вас но́мер. Моя́ фами́лия …
[YA zakaZAL/zakaZAla u-VAS NOmir. maYA faMIliya ...]

Do you have a vacancy ...
У Вас есть свобо́дный но́мер …
[u-VAS YEST svaBODny NOmir ...]

for one night?
на одну́ ночь? [na-adNU NOCH]

for two nights?
на две но́чи? [na-DVYE NOchi]

for a week?
на неде́лю? [na-niDYElyu]

No, I'm afraid not.
Нет, к сожале́нию. [NYET k-sazhaLYEniyu]

Yes, what kind of room would you like?
Есть. Како́й но́мер Вы жела́ете?
[YEST. kaKOY NOmir VY zhyLAyitye]

I'd like ...
Я бы хоте́л m/хоте́ла f … [YA BY khaTYEL/khaTYEla ...]

a single room
одноме́стный но́мер [adnaMYESny NOmir]

a double room
двухме́стный но́мер [dvukhMYESny NOmir]

a quiet room
ти́хий но́мер [TIkhi NOmir]

with a shower
с ду́шем [z-DUshym]

with a bath
с ва́нной [s-VAnay]

with a balcony
с балко́ном [s-balKOnam]

with a terrace
с терра́сой [s-tiRAsay]

on the courtyard
с окно́м во двор [s-akNOM va-DVOR]

with a view of the sea/of the lake
с ви́дом на мо́ре/на о́зеро [s-VIdam na-MOrye/na-Ozira]

Unlike Western Europeans, Russians count floors the same way as Americans. The ground floor is counted as the first floor, and so forth.

Can I see the room?

Мо́жно посмотре́ть но́мер? [MOZHna pasmaTRYET' NOmir]

Could I see another room, please?

А мо́жно посмотре́ть друго́й но́мер?
[A MOZHna pasmaTRYET' druGOY NOmir]

I'll take this room.

Я беру́ э́тот но́мер. [YA biRU Etat NOmir]

Could you please put a third bed/a child's bed in the room?

Не могли́ бы Вы поста́вить в но́мер тре́тью крова́ть?/
де́тскую крова́ть? [ni-maGLI BY VY paSTAvit' v-NOmir TRYEt'yu
kraVAT'/DYETSkayu kraVAT']

How much is the room with ...

Ско́лько сто́ит но́мер ... [SKOL'ka STOit NOmir ...]

breakfast?

с за́втраком? [z-ZAFtrakam]

breakfast and dinner?

с за́втраком и у́жином. [z-ZAFtrakam i Uzhinam]

all meals?

с по́лным пансио́ном? [s-POLnym pansiOnam]

Please fill out the registration form.

Запо́лните, пожа́луйста, регистрацио́нный лист.
[zapalNItye paZHAlusta rigistratsyOny LIST]

May I see your passport/your identification, please?

Ваш па́спорт/Ва́ше удостовере́ние ли́чности, пожа́луйста.
[VASH PASpart/VAshy udastaviRYEniye LICHnasti paZHAlusta]

Please have my bags brought up to my room.

Прошу́ принести́ мой бага́ж в но́мер.
[praSHU priniSTI MOY baGASH v-NOmir]

Where can I park the car?

Где мо́жно поста́вить маши́ну?
[GDYE MOZHna paSTAvit' maSHYnu]

In our garage.

В на́шем гараже́. [v-NAshym garaZHE]

In our parking lot (with an attendant on duty).

На на́шей (охраня́емой) стоя́нке.
[na-NAshey akhraNYAyimay staYANkye]

Asking for Service ≻ also Breakfast

What time is breakfast?
Когда́ начина́ется за́втрак? [kagDA nachiNAyitsa ZAFtrak]

When is lunch/dinner served?
Когда́ подаётся обе́д?/у́жин? [kagDA padaYOtsa aBYET/Uzhin]

Where is the restaurant?
Где столо́вая? [GDYE staLOvaya]

Where is breakfast served?
Где подаётся за́втрак? [GDYE padaYOtsa ZAFtrak]

Please give me a wake-up call tomorrow morning at ... o'clock.
Разбуди́те меня́ за́втра у́тром в ... часо́в, пожа́луйста.
[razbuDItye miNYA ZAFtra Utram f- ... chiSOF paZHAlusta]

Would you please bring me ...
Принеси́те мне, пожа́луйста, ... [priniSItye MNYE paZHAlusta ...]

  a towel/a piece of soap.
  полоте́нце./кусо́к мы́ла. [palaTYENtse/kuSOK MYla]

  a (another) blanket.
  (ещё) одно́ одея́ло. [(yiSHO) adNO adiYAla]

How does ... work?
Как рабо́тает ...? [KAK raBOtayit]

Room number 24, please!
Но́мер два́дцать четы́ре, пожа́луйста!
[NOmir DVAtsit' chiTYrye paZHAlusta]

Is there any mail for me?
На моё и́мя есть корреспонде́нция?
[na-maYO Imya YEST karispanDYENtsyya]

Where can I ...
Где здесь мо́жно ... [GDYE ZDYES' MOZHna ...]

  get something to drink?
  попи́ть? [paPIT']

  rent a car?
  взять напрока́т маши́ну? [VZYAT' napraKAT maSHYnu]

  make a phone call?
  позвони́ть по телефо́ну? [pazvaNIT' pa-tiliFOnu]

Can I leave my valuables in your safe?
Мо́жно отда́ть Вам це́нные ве́щи на хране́ние в сейф?
[MOZHna adDAT' VAM TSEnyye VYEshi na-khraNYEniye f-SEYF]

Can I leave my baggage here?
Мо́жно здесь оста́вить бага́ж?
[MOZHna ZDYES' aSTAvit' baGASH]

Complaints

The room hasn't been cleaned today.
Сегóдня мой нóмер не прúбран.
[siVOdnya MOY NOmir ni-PRIbran]

The air conditioning doesn't work.
Кондиционéр не рабóтает. [kanditsyaNYER ni-raBOtayit]

The water faucet leaks.
Кран течёт. [KRAN tiCHOT]

There's no (hot) water.
Нет (горячей) водьí. [NYET (garYAchi) vaDY]

The toilet/The sink is plugged up.
Туалéт засорён./Рáковина засоренá.
[tuaLYET zasaRYON/RAkavina zasariNA]

I'd like to have a different room.
Я бы хотéл m/хотéла f поменять нóмер.
[YA BY khaTYEL/khaTYEla pamiNYAT' NOmir]

Departure

I'm leaving this evening/tomorrow at ... o'clock.
Я уéду сегóдня вéчером/зáвтра в ... часóв.
[YA uYEdu siVOdnya VYEchiram/ZAFtra f- ... chiSOF]

When do I have to check out?
До котóрого чáса нáдо освободúть нóмер?
[da-kaTOrava CHAsa NAda asvabaDIT' NOmir]

Could you prepare the bill, please?
Приготóвьте счёт, пожáлуйста. [prigaTOF'tye SHOT paZHAlusta]

Do you take credit cards?
Вы принимáете кредúтные кáрточки?
[VY priniMAyitye kriDITnyye KARtachki]

Could you please call a taxi for me?
Закажúте для меня таксú, пожáлуйста.
[zakaZHYtye dli-miNYA taKSI paZHAlusta]

Thank you very much for everything. Goodbye!
Большóе спасúбо за всё! До свидáния!
[bal'SHOye spaSIba za-FSYO. da-sviDAniya]

adapter	переходнúк	[pirikhodNIK]
air conditioning	кондиционéр	[kanditsyaNYER]
armchair	крéсло	[KRYEsla]
ashtray	пéпельница	[PYEpil'nitsa]
balcony	балкóн	[balKON]
bath towel	купáльное полотéнце	
		[kuPAL'naye palaTYENtse]
bathroom	вáнная	[VANnaya]

bathtub	ва́нна [VANna]
bed	крова́ть f [kraVAT']
bed linen	посте́льное бельё [paSTYEL'naye biL'YO]
bedside table	ночно́й сто́лик [nachNOY STOlik]
bellboy	швейца́р [shviyTSAR], портье́ [parT'YE]
bidet	биде́ [biDE]
blanket	одея́ло [adiYAla]
breakfast	за́втрак [ZAFtrak]
breakfast buffet	шве́дский стол [SHVYETski STOL]
breakfast room	буфе́т [buFYET], рестора́н [ristaRAN]
chair	стул [STUL]
chambermaid	го́рничная [GORnichnaya]
change of linen	сме́на белья́ [SMYEna biL'YO]
to clean	убира́ть/убра́ть [ubiRAT'/uBRAT']
closet	шкаф [SHKAF]
coat hangers	пле́чики m pl [PLYEchiki]
cockroach	тарака́н [taraKAN]
dining room	столо́вая [staLOvaya]
dinner	у́жин [Uzhin]
door code	дверно́й код [dvirNOY KOT]
elevator	лифт [LIFT]
to extend (the stay)	продлева́ть/продли́ть (пребыва́ние) [pradliVAT'/praDLIT' (pribyVAniye)]
fan	вентиля́тор [vintiLYAtar]
floor supervisor	дежу́рная [diZHURnaya]
floor, story	эта́ж [eTASH]
full board	по́лный пансио́н [POLny pansiON]
garage	гара́ж [gaRASH]
glass	стака́н [staKAN]
half-board, breakfast and dinner	непо́лный пансио́н [niPOLny pansiON], за́втрак и у́жин [ZAFtrak i Uzhin]
handheld shower	душ с ручны́м смеси́телем [DUSH s-ruchNYM smiSItilyim]
heating	отопле́ние [ataPLYEniye]
high season	разга́р сезо́на [razGAR siZOna]
key	ключ [KLYUCH]
lamp	ла́мпа [LAMpa]
light(ing)	освеще́ние [asviSHEniye]
light switch	выключа́тель m [vyklyuCHAtil']
lightbulb	(электри́ческая) ла́мпочка [(elikTRIchiskaya) LAMpochka]
lounge	ко́мната о́тдыха [KOMnata ODdykha]
lunch	обе́д [aBYET]
mattress	матра́с [maTRAS]
mini-bar	бар в но́мере [BAR v-NOmirye]
mirror	зе́ркало [ZYERkala]

ACCOMMODATIONS

91

motel	мотель *m* [maTYEL']
mug	кружка [KRUSHka]
notepad	блокнот [blakNOT]
off season	послесезонный период [paslisiZOny piRIat]
parking lot	стоянка [staYANka]
patio, terrace	терраса [tiRAsa]
pension, boarding house	пансион [pansiON]
phone in the room	телефон в номере [tiliFON v-NOmirye]
pillow	подушка [paDUSHka]
place setting (for breakfast)	набор (для завтрака) [naBOR (dli-ZAFtraka)]
place to sleep	ночлег [nachLYEK]
plug	штепсель *m* [shTEPsil], вилка [VILka]
preseason	время до начала сезона [VRYEmya da-naCHAla siZOna]
price list	прейскурант цен [priyskuRANT TSEN]
(e.g., for the mini-bar)	
radio	радио [RAdia]
reading lamp	ночник [nachNIK]
reception (desk)	администрация [adminiSTRAtsyya]
reception area	фойе [faYE]
registration	регистрация [rigiSTRAtsyya]
to repair	чинить/починить [chiNIT'/pachiNIT']
reservation	бронирование [braNIravaniye]
room	комната [KOMnata]
safe	сейф [SEYF]
shoe polish	набор для чистки обуви [naBOR dli-CHISTki Obuwi]
shower	душ [DUSH]
shower curtain/door	занавеска для душа [zanaVYESka dlia-DUsha]/ дверь *f* от душевой кабинки [DVYER' ad-dushyVOY kaBINki]
showerhead	головка смесителя [gaLOFka smiSItilya]
shuttle bus	автобус-шаттл [aFTObus-shatl]
sink	раковина [RAkavina]
socket	розетка [raZETka]
stationery	почтовая бумага [pachTOvaya buMAga]
swimming pool	бассейн [baSYEYN]
table	стол [STOL]
television lounge	телевизионная комната [tiliviziOnaya KOMnata]
television, TV	телевизор [tiliVIzar]

toilet	туалéт [tuaLYET]
toilet paper	туалéтная бумáга [tuaLYETnaya buMAga]
towel	полотéнце [palaTYENtse]
tumbler	стакáн [staKAN]
wastepaper basket	корзúна для мýсора [karZIna dlia-MUsara]
water	водá [vaDA]
cold water	холóдная водá [khaLODnaya vaDA]
hot water	горячая водá [garYAchaya vaDA]
water faucet	кран [KRAN]
window	окнó [akNO]
wool blanket	шерстянóе одеяло [shyrstyiNOye adiYAla]

Vacation Cottages and Apartments

Is electricity/water included in the rental price?
Арéнда включáет стóимость электроэнéргии и воды?
[aRYENda fklyuCHAyit STOimast' eliktraeNYERgii i vaDY]

Are pets allowed?
Разрешáется имéть с собóй домáшние живóтные?
[razriSHAyitsa iMYET' s-saBOY daMASHnyye zhiVOTnyye]

Where is the garbage container?
Где нахóдится контéйнер для мýсора?
[GDYE naKHOditsa kanTYEYnir dlia-MUsara]

Do we have to clean the place ourselves before we leave?
Нам нýжно самúм убрáть перед отъéздом?
[NAM NUZHna saMIM uBRAT' pirid-at'YEZdam]

additional costs	дополнúтельные расхóды m pl [dapalNItil'niye rasKHOdy]
apartment	квартúра [kvarTIra]
bedroom	спáльня [SPAL'nya]
bunk bed	двухъярусная кровáть [dvukhYArusnaya kraVAT']
cabin	дáча [DAcha]
central heating	центрáльное отоплéние [tsynTRAL'naye ataPLYEniye]
coffee maker	кофевáрка [kafiVARka]
cottage	дáча [DAcha]
day of arrival	день m прибытия [DYEN' priBYtiya]
dish towel	кýхонное полотéнце [KUkhanaye palaTYENtse]
dishes	посýда [paSUda]
dishwasher	посудомóечная машúна [pasudaMOyichnaya maSHYna]

electricity	электри́чество [elikTRIchistva]
farm	крестья́нская уса́дьба [kriST'YANskaya uSAD'ba], ху́тор [KHUtar]
final clean-up	убо́рка перед отъе́здом [uBORka pirid-at'YEZdam]
garbage	му́сор [MUsar]
kitchen	ку́хня [KUKHnya]
living room	жила́я ко́мната [zhyLAya KOMnata]
microwave oven	микроволно́вая печь [mikravalNOvaya PYECH]
owner	хозя́ин (до́ма) [khaZYAin (DOma)]
pets	дома́шние живо́тные n pl [daMASHnyye zhiVOTnyye]
refrigerator	холоди́льник [khalaDIL'nik]
rent	аре́нда [aRYENda]
to rent	сдава́ть/сдать внаём [zdaVAT'/ZDAT' vnaYOM]
returning the keys	переда́ча ключе́й [piriDAcha klyuCHEY]
sleeper sofa	дива́н(-крова́ть) [diVAN(-kraVAT')]
stove	плита́ [pliTA]
electric stove	электри́ческая плита́ [elikTRIchiskaya pliTA]
gas stove	га́зовая плита́ [GAzavaya pliTA]
studio	сту́дио [STUdia]
toaster	то́стер [TOstir]
tourist camp	туристи́ческая ба́за [turiSTIchiskaya BAza], турба́за [turBAza]
voltage	(электри́ческое) напряже́ние [(elikTRIchiskaye) napriZHEniye]
washing machine	стира́льная маши́на [stiRAL'naya maSHYna]
water usage	потребле́ние воды́ [patriBLYEniye vaDY]

Camping

Could you please tell me whether there's a campground near here?

Вы не ска́жете, есть ли побли́зости ке́мпинг?
[VY ni-SKAzhytye YEST li paBLIzasti KYEMping]

Do you have space for another RV?/another tent?

Есть ли у Вас ещё ме́сто для карава́на?/для пала́тки?
[YEST li u-VAS yiSHO MYESta dlia-karaVAna/dlia-paLATki]

How much does it cost per day and per person?
Сколько стоит один день проживания на одного человека?
[SKOL'ka STOit aDIN DYEN' prazhyVAniya na-adnaVO chilaVYEka]

What's the charge ...
Сколько надо платить ... [SKOL'ka NAda plaTIT' ...]

  for the car?
  за машину? [za-maSHYnu]

  for the trailer?
  за караван? [za-karaVAN]

  for the RV?
  за кемпер? [za-KYEMpir]

  for the tent?
  за палатку? [za-paLATku]

Do you rent trailers?
Вы даёте напрокат караваны? [VY daYOtye napraKAT karaVAny]

We'll be staying for ... days./weeks.
Мы здесь пробудем ... дней./недели.
[MY ZDYES' praBUdim ... DNYEY/niDYEli]

Where are ...
Где ... [GDYE ...]

  the toilets?
  туалеты? [tuaLYEty]

  the washrooms?
  умывальные? [umyVAL'nyye]

  the showers?
  душевые? [dushiVYye]

Are there electrical hookups here?
Здесь подведено электричество?
[ZDYES' padvidiNO elikTRIchistva]

Where can I exchange gas canisters?
Где можно менять газовые баллоны?
[GDYE MOZHna miNYAT' GAzavyye baLOny]

Is the campground guarded at night?
Кемпинг охраняется ночью? [KYEMpink akhraNYAyitsa NOch'yu]

to camp	жить *ipf* в палатке [ZHYT' f-paLATkye]
campground	кемпинг [KYEMping]
camping	кемпинг [KYEMping]
camping guide	путеводитель *m* по кемпингам [putivaDItil' pa-KYEMpingam]
camping permit	пропуск [PROpusk]
clothes dryer	сушилка для белья [suSHYLka dlia-biL'YA]
drinking water	питьевая вода [pityiVAya vaDA]

electrical hookup	подвод электричества [padVOT elikTRIchistva]
electrical outlet	розе́тка [raZYETka]
electricity	электри́чество [elikTRIchistva]
gas camping stove	га́зовая пли́тка [GAzavaya PLITka]
gas canister/cartridge	га́зовый балло́н [GAzavy baLON]
hammer	молото́к [malaTOK]
kerosene lantern	кероси́новая ла́мпа [kiraSInavaya LAMpa]
plug	штéпсель *m* [SHTYEPsil'], ви́лка [VILka]
propane gas	пропа́н [praPAN]
reservation	предвари́тельная зая́вка [pridvaRItil'naya zaYAFka]
RV, camper	ке́мпер [KYEMpir]
sink	мо́йка для посу́ды [MOYka dlia-paSUdy]
stove	пли́тка [PLITka]
tent	пала́тка [paLATka]
tent peg	ко́лышек [KOlyshyk]
tent pole	пала́точная сто́йка [paLAtachnaya STOYka]
tether line	пала́точная верёвка [paLAtachnaya viRYOFka]
trailer	карава́н [karaVAN]
washroom	умыва́льная [umyVAL'naya]
water	вода́ [vaDA]
water canister	кани́стра для воды́ [kaNIstra dli-vaDY]

Eating and Drinking

Types of places to eat in Russia:

Рестора́н [ristaRAN]: restaurant (don't just order drinks!)

Столо́вая [staLOvaya]: simple café, like a canteen or cafeteria

Тракти́р [trakTIR] (tavern, pub), **Кафе́-рестора́н** [kaFYE-ristaRAN] (café-restaurant): these often sell typical Russian dishes from a self-service buffet (шве́дский стол [SHVYETski STOL]) at fixed prices

Кафе́ [kaFYE] (café), **Кафе́-бар** [kaFYE-BAR] (café-bar)

Кафете́рий [kafiTYEri] (cafeteria), **Кафе́-моро́женое** [kaFYE-maROzhinaye] (ice-cream shop), **Конди́терская** [kanDItirskaya] (pastry shop), **Ча́йная** [CHAYnaya] (tea room): these terms represent a great variety of establishments—from stand-up cafés to actual restaurants

Буфе́т [buFYET] (buffet), **Бистро́** [biSTRO] (bistro), **Бутербро́дная** [butirBRODnaya] (sandwich shop), **Заку́сочная** [zaKUsachnaya] (snack bar), **Соси́сочная** [saSIsachnaya] (sausage shop), and others: these establishments are like snack bars, often without seats

Пивна́я [pivNAya]: very simple place serving beer

Is there ... here?

Где здесь … ? [GDYE ZDYES' ...]

a good restaurant

хоро́ший рестора́н [khaROshi ristaRAN]

an inexpensive restaurant

недорого́й рестора́н [nidaraGOY ristaRAN]

Where can I get a good/a cheap meal near here?

Где здесь мо́жно побли́зости хорошо́/недо́рого поку́шать?
[GDYE ZDYES' MOZHna paBLIzasti kharaSHO/niDOraga paKUshat']

At the Restaurant

For dinner in high-class restaurants, you need to wear evening clothes. Do not take overcoats and other outerwear with you into the dining room. Typically, loud live music for dancing is played later in the evening.

I'd like to reserve a table for four for this evening.
Я бы хоте́л *m*/хоте́ла *f* зарезерви́ровать стол на четырёх
челове́к на сего́дняшний ве́чер.
[YA BY khaTYEL/khaTYEla zarizirVIravat' STOL na-chityRYOKH chilaVYEK
na-siVOdnishni VYEchir]

Is this table free?
Э́тот стол свобо́ден? [Etat STOL svaBOdin]

A table for two/for three, please.
Стол на двои́х/на трои́х, пожа́луйста.
[STOL na-dvaIKH/na-traIKH paZHAlusta]

Where is the restroom, please?
Где туале́т? [GDYE tuaLYET]

Do you mind if I smoke?
Мо́жно кури́ть? [MOZHna kuRIT']

> A more elegant way of asking where the restrooms are: "Где
> мо́жно помы́ть ру́ки?" [GDYE MOZHna paMYT' RUki] (Where
> can I wash my hands?). Smoking is prohibited in many places,
> but some establishments offer special smoking areas.

Ordering

Excuse me, could I have ...
Официа́нт, ... [afitsyANT ...]

   the menu, please.
   меню́, пожа́луйста! [miNYU paZHAlusta]

   the list of beverages, please.
   ка́рту напи́тков, пожа́луйста! [KARtu naPITkaf paZHAlusta]

What can you recommend?
Что Вы мне посове́туете? [SHTO VY MNYE pasaVYEtuyitye]

Do you have vegetarian dishes?/low-fat meals?
У Вас есть вегетариа́нские блю́да?/диети́ческие блю́да?
[u-VAS YEST vigitariANskiye BLYUda/diyiTIchiskiye BLYUda]

Do you serve children's portions?
Предлага́ете де́тские по́рции? [pridlaGAyitye DYETskiye PORtsii]

Are you ready to order?
Вы уже́ вы́брали? [VY uZHE VYbrali]

I'll have ...
Я возьму́ ... [YA vaz'MU]

I'll have the ... as an appetizer/as an entrée/for dessert.
На заку́ску/На пе́рвое/На второ́е/На десе́рт возьму́ ...
[na-zaKUSku/na-PYERvaye/na-ftaROye/na-diSYERT vaz'MU ...]

No appetizer for me, thank you.
Мне не надо закуски, спасибо. [MNYE ni-NAda zaKUSki spaSIba]

I'm afraid we're out of the ...
К сожалению, не осталось ... *(+ gen)*.
[k-sazhaLYEniyu ni-aSTAlas' ...]

That dish has to be ordered in advance.
Это блюдо надо было заранее заказать.
[Eta BLYUda NAda zaRAniye zakaZAT']

Could I have ... instead of ...?
Вместо ... *(+ gen)* можно получить ... *(+ acc)*?
[VMYESta ... MOZHna paluCHIT' ...]

I'm allergic to ... Could you make this dish without ...?
Я не выношу ... *(+ acc)*. Вы могли бы приготовить это
блюдо без ... *(+ gen)*?
[YA ni-vynaSHU ... VY maGLI BY prigaTOvit' Eta BLYUda bis-...]

How would you like your steak?
Как Вам приготовить мясо? [KAK VAM prigaTOvit' MYAsa]
  well-done
  хорошо прожаренное [kharaSHO praZHArinaye]
  medium rare
  полупрожаренное [palupraZHArinaye]
  rare
  слегка поджаренное [slikhKA padZHArinaye]

What would you like to drink?
Что Вы будете пить? [SHTO VY BUditye PIT']

A glass of ..., please.
Стакан ... *(+ gen)*, пожалуйста. [staKAN ...paZHAlusta]

A bottle of/Half a bottle of ..., please.
Бутылку/Полбутылки ... *(+ gen)*, пожалуйста.
[buTYLku/palbuTYLki ... paZHAlusta]

With ice, please.
Со льдом, пожалуйста. [sa-L'DOM paZHAlusta]

Enjoy your meal!
Приятного аппетита! [priYATnava apiTIta]

Would you like anything else?
Хотите ещё чего-нибудь? [khaTItye yiSHO chiVO-nibut']

Bring us ..., please.
Принесите нам ..., пожалуйста. [priniSItye NAM ... paZHAlusta]

Could you please bring us some more bread?/water?/wine?
Вы не принесёте ещё хлеба?/воды?/вина?
[VY ni-priniSYOtye yiSHO KHLYEba/vaDY/viNA]

Complaints

We need (another) ...
Здесь не хвата́ет ... *(+ gen)* [ZDYES' ni-khvaTAyit ...]

Have you forgotten ...?
Вы забы́ли мой *m*/мою́ *f*/моё *n*/мои́ *pl* ...?
[VY zaBYli MOY/maYU/maYO/maI ...]

That's not what I ordered.
Я э́того не зака́зывал. *m*/не зака́зывала. *f*
[YA Etava ni-zaKAzyval/ni-zaKAzyvala]

The soup is cold./too salty.
Суп холо́дный./пересо́ленный. [SUP khaLODny/piriSOliny]

The meat is tough./too fatty.
Мя́со жёсткое./сли́шком жи́рное.
[MYasa ZHOSTkaye/SLISHkam ZHYRnaye]

The fish is not fresh.
Ры́ба несве́жая. [RYba ni-SVYEzhaya]

Would you take this back, please.
Возьми́те э́то обра́тно, пожа́луйста.
[vaz'MItye Eta aBRATna paZHAlusta]

Send the manager over, please.
Позови́те ме́неджера, пожа́луйста.
[pazaVItye MYEnedzhyra paZHAlusta]

The Bill

Could we have the check, please?
Счёт, пожа́луйста! [SHOT paZHAlusta]

Could we have that on one check, please?
О́бщий счёт, пожа́луйста. [OPshi SHOT paZHAlusta]

Give us separate checks, please.
Посчита́йте нам, пожа́луйста, отде́льно.
[pashiTAYtye NAM paZHAlusta adDYEL'na]

> Sometimes you'll see these words on the menu:
> "Обслу́живание не включено́ в счёт. Мы рассчи́тываем
> на Ва́ше усмотре́ние." [apSLUzhivaniye ni-fklyuchiNO f-SHOT.
> MY raSHItyvayim na-VAshy usmaTRYEniye]. "A service charge is
> not included. We leave that to your discretion."

Is service included?
Обслу́живание включено́? [apSLUzhivaniye fklyuchiNO]

There seems to be a mistake on the check.
Мне ка́жется, счёт неве́рен. [MNYE KAzhitsa SHOT niVYErin]

101

I didn't have that.
Я э́того не получи́л. *m*/не получи́ла. *f*
[YA Etava ni-paluCHIL/ni-paluCHIla]

I had ...
У меня́ был *m*/была́ *f*/бы́ло *n*/бы́ли *pl* ...
[u-miNYA BYL/byLA/BYlo/BYli]

Did you enjoy your meal?
Вам бы́ло вку́сно? [VAM BYla FKUSna]

The food was excellent.
Еда́ была́ отли́чная. [yiDA byLA atLICHnaya]

That's for you.
Э́то Вам. [Eta VAM]

Keep the change.
Сда́чи не на́до. [ZDAchi ni-NAda]

Vodka is often drunk with meals. In a group, the vodka is
drunk by everyone at the same time, with people raising their
glasses to each other and giving a toast (тост [TOST]).
Customarily the glass is emptied in one gulp, "до дна́" [da-
DNA] ("to the bottom"), and a little tidbit (заку́ска [zaKUSka])
is eaten immediately thereafter.

At the Table

What are you going to drink?
Что Вы бу́дете/ты бу́дешь пить? [SHTO VY BUditye/TY BUdish PIT']

I'm going to have ...
Я бу́ду ... *(+ acc)* [YA BUdu ...]

No vodka for me, please.
Мне во́дку не на́до. [MNYE VOTku ni-NAda]

May I fill your glass?
Мо́жно Вам/тебе́ нали́ть? [MOZHna VAM/tiBYE naLIT']

To your health!
За Ва́ше/За твоё здоро́вье! [za-VAshy/za-tvaYO zdaROv'ye]

To being together!
За встре́чу! [za-FSTRYEchu]

To friendship!
За дру́жбу! [za-DRUZHbu]

Would you please pass me the ...
Пода́йте, пожа́луйста, ... *(+ acc)*. [paDAYtye paZHAlusta ...]

Would you like some more ...?
Бу́дете/Бу́дешь ещё ... *(+ acc).* [BUditye/BUdish yiSHO ...]

No thank you, I've had plenty.
Спаси́бо, я сыт. *m*/сыта́. *f* [spaSIba YA SYT/syTA]

This is on me.
За э́то я бу́ду плати́ть. [za-Eta YA BUdu plaTIT']

When you express your thanks for something to eat or drink,
you'll hear this response: "На здоро́вье!" [na-zdaROv'ye].

➢ also Groceries

appetizer	заку́ска [zaKUska]
artificial sweetener	сахари́н [sakhaRIN]
ashtray	пе́пельница [PYEpil'nitsa]
bland diet	диети́ческое пита́ние [diyiTIchiskaye piTAniye]
bone	кость *f* [KOST']
bowl	ми́ска [MIska]
breakfast	за́втрак [ZAFtrak]
carafe	графи́н [graFIN]
children's meal	де́тское блю́до [DYETskaye BLYUda]
cook	по́вар/повари́ха [POvar/pavaRIkha]
corkscrew	што́пор [SHTOpar]
course	блю́до [BLYUda]
cup	ча́шка [CHASHka]
daily special	блю́до дня [BLYUda DNYA]
dessert	десе́рт [diSYERT]
diabetic	диабе́тик [diaBYEtik]
dinner	у́жин [Uzhin]
dish	блю́до [BLYUda]
dressing	со́ус [SOus]
drink	напи́ток [naPItak]
dry (wine)	сухо́е [suKHOye]
entrée	второ́е (блю́до) [ftaROye (BLYUda)]
fishbone	ры́бья кость [RYb'ya KOST']
fork	ви́лка [VILka]
glass	стака́н [staKAN]
shot glass	рю́мочка [RYUmachka]
water glass	стака́н [staKAN]
wine glass	бока́л [baKAL], фуже́р [fuZHER]
grill	гриль *m* [GRIL']
hard	твёрдый [TVYORdy]
homemade	дома́шний [daMASHni]
hot	горя́чий [gaRYAchi]

(to be) hungry	(быть) го́лоден *m*/голодна́ *f*/ го́лодны *pl* [(BYT') GOladin/galaDNA/galaDNY]
ketchup	ке́тчуп [KYEchup]
knife	нож [NOSH]
lunch	обе́д [aBYET]
mayonnaise	майоне́з [mayaNYES]
menu	меню́ *n* [miNYU]
mustard	горчи́ца [garCHItsa]
napkin	салфе́тка [salFYETka]
non-alcoholic	безалкого́льный [bizalkaGOL'ny]
oil	ма́сло [MAsla]
on tap	наливно́е [nalivNOye]
order	зака́з [zaKAS]
pan-fried food	жарко́е на сковороде́ [ZHARkaye na-skavaraDYE]
pepper	пе́рец [PYErits]
pepper shaker	пе́речница [PYErichnitsa]
place setting	прибо́р [priBOR]
plate	таре́лка [taRYELka]
portion	по́рция [PORtsyya]
salad bar	сала́т-буфе́т [saLAT-buFYET]
salt	соль *f* [SOL']
salt shaker	соло́нка [saLONka]
saucer	блю́дце [BLYUtsy]
to season	приправля́ть/припра́вить [pripraVLYAT'/priPRAvit']
seasoning	пря́ность *f* [PRYAnast'], спе́ция [SPYEtsyya]
service person	официа́нт [afitsyANT]
set meal	ко́мплексное блю́до [KOMpliksnaya BLYUda]
silverware	прибо́р [priBOR]
slice	ло́мтик [LOMtik]
soup	суп [SUP], пе́рвое (блю́до) [PYERvaye (BLYUda)]
soup bowl	глубо́кая таре́лка [gluBOkaya taRYELka]
specialty of the house	фи́рменное блю́до [FIRminaye BLYUda]
spoon	ло́жка [LOSHka]
teaspoon	ча́йная ло́жка [CHAYnaya LOSHka]
spot	пятно́ [pyitNO]
straw	соло́минка [saLOMnika]
sugar	са́хар [SAkhar]
sweet (wine)	сла́дкое [SLATkaye]
tablecloth	ска́терть *f* [SKAtirt']
tip	чаевы́е [chayiVYye]

toothpick	зубочи́стка [zubaCHISTka]
vegetarian	вегетариа́нский [vigitariANski]
vinegar	у́ксус [UKsus]
waiter/waitress	официа́нт/ка [afitsyANT/ka]
water	вода́ [vaDA]

Preparation

au gratin	запечённый [zapiCHOny]
baked	печёный [piCHOny]
boiled	варёный [vaRYOny], отварно́й [atvarNOY]
braised	тушёный [tuSHOny]
done	гото́вый [gaTOvy]
grilled	на гри́ле [na-GRIlye]
juicy	со́чный [SOCHny]
lean	по́стный [POSny]
pan-fried	на сковороде́ [na-skavaraDYE]
raw	сыро́й [syROY]
roasted	жа́реный [ZHAriny]
spit-roasted	на ве́ртеле [na-VYERtilye]
sautéed	жа́реный [ZHAriny]
smoked	копчёный [kapCHOny]
sour	ки́слый [KIsly]
spicy	о́стрый [Ostry]
steamed	па́реный [PAriny]
stewed	тушёный [tuSHOny]
stuffed	начинённый [nachiNYOny]
sweet	сла́дкий [SLATki]
tender	не́жный [NYEZHny]
tough	жёсткий [ZHOSTki]
well-done	прожа́ренный [praZHAriny]

EATING AND DRINKING

boiled
варёный

cooked/simmered
приготóвленный

steamed
па́реный

in a bain-marie/
double boiler
в водяно́й ба́не

sautéed
жа́реный

deep-fried
во фритю́ре

grilled
на гри́ле

105

ginger имби́рь

garlic
чесно́к

onion
лук

dill
укро́п

bay leaf
лавро́вый лист

rosemary
розмари́н

marjoram/oregano
майора́н/орега́н

cilantro/coriander
ки́нза

parsley
петру́шка

basil
базили́к

nutmeg мускáтный орéх

chili peppers
чи́ли

red (hot) pepper
о́стрый пéрец

chives
лук-рéзанец

sage
шалфéй

chervil
купы́рь *m*

thyme
тимья́н

savory
чáбер

lovage
сюбисто́к

109

I'd like ...

Я бы хотел *m*/хотéла *f* ...

I'd like ...
Я бы хотéл m/хотéла f ...

Меню / Menu

(especially typical dishes are marked with *)

The typical sequence of courses is appetizer – soup – entrée – dessert – tea or coffee. Pancakes (блины [bliNY]) can also be ordered as a main dish.

Холодные закуски	Cold Appetizers
Ассорти [asarTI] *sing a. pl*	assortment *(of appetizers/cold cuts)*
Бутерброд [butirBROT]	open-face sandwich
Ветчина (с гарниром) [vichiNA (s-garNIram)]	ham (with garnish)
Икра (красная/чёрная) * [iKRA (KRASnaya/CHORnaya)]	caviar (red/black)
Колбаса [kalbaSA]	sausage
твердокопчёная [tvyordakapCHOnaya], сырокопчёная [syrakapCHOnaya]	hard sausage
летнего копчения [LYETniva kapCHEniya]	summer sausage
Крабы [KRAby] *m pl*	crabs
Окорок московский * [Okarak maSKOFski]	Moscow ham
Паштет (из дичи/из печени) [pashTYET (iz-DIchi/is-PYEchini)]	paté (of wild game/liver)
Рыба [RYba]	fish
горячего копчения [gaRYAchiva kapCHEniya]	cooked
холодного копчения [khaLODnava kapCHEniya]	smoked
под маринадом [pad-mariNAdam]	marinated
Горбуша [garBUsha]	humpbacked salmon
Кёта [KYEta]	Siberian salmon
Лосось [laSOS'] *m*	salmon
Палтус [PALtus]	halibut
Севрюга [siVRYUga]	sturgeon
Сельдь f [SYEL'T], Селёдка [siLYOTka]	herring
Сёмга [SYOMga]	salmon
Салат здоровье [saLAT zdaROv'ye], Витаминный салат [vitaMIny saLAT], овощной салат [avashNOY saLAT]	mixed vegetable salad
Салат из помидоров с огурцами (с яйцом) [saLAT is-pamiDOraf s-agurTSAmi (s-yiyTSOM)]	tomato and cucumber salad (with egg)

113

Салáт Оливьé/Столи́чный *	Russian salad with
[saLAT aliV'YE/staLICHny]	chicken/with meat
Яйцó [yiyTSO]	egg
под майонéзом [pad-mayaNYEzam] ..	(hard-boiled) with mayonnaise
фарширóванное [farshiROvanaye] ...	stuffed

Пéрвые блю́да	Soups
Бульóн [buL'YON]	bouillon/consommé
(говя́жий/кури́ный)	(beef/chicken consommé)
[gaVYAzhi/kuRIny]	
с яйцóм [s-yiyTSOM]	with an egg
с пирожкáми [s-piraSHKAmi]	with pirozhki
	(small Russian pastries)
Борщ (украи́нский) *	borshch (Ukrainian)
[BORSH (ukraINski)]	*(beet and cabbage soup)*
Грибнáя соля́нка *	mushroom solyanka
[gribNAya saLYANka]	
Грибнóй суп [gribNOY SUP]	mushroom soup
Молóчный суп [maLOCHny SUP]	milk soup
Рассóльник * [raSOL'nik]	rassolnik *(soup with chicken, rice, pickled cucumbers)*
Ры́бный суп [RYBny SUP]	fish soup
Соля́нка * [saLYANka]	solyanka *(soup with vegetables, pickled cucumbers, olives, meat or fish)*
Суп с фрикадéльками	soup with meatballs
[SUP s-frikaDYEL'kami]	
Ухá * [uKHA]	fish soup
Щи f pl * [SHI]	cabbage soup
свéжие [SVYEzhyye]	made with fresh cabbage
ки́слые [KIslyye]	made with sauerkraut
пóстные [POSnyye]	without meat

Ры́бные блю́да	Fish
Ры́ба [RYba]	fish
Кáмбала [KAMbala]	plaice
Карп [KARP]	carp
Лещ [LYESH]	bream
(Морскóй) óкунь [(marSKOY) Okun'] ..	(sea) bass
Пáлтус [PALtus]	halibut
Сазáн [saZAN]	wild carp
Сом [SOM]	catfish
Судáк [suDAK]	pike-perch
Трескá [triSKA]	cod
Ýгорь m [Ugar']	eel

Форе́ль f [faRYEL']	trout
Щу́ка [SHUka]	pike
по-по́льски [pa-POL'ski]	with egg sauce

Мясны́е блю́да	Meat
Мя́со [MYAsa]	meat
Бара́нина [baRAnina]	mutton
Говя́дина [gaVYAdina]	beef
Кро́лик [KROlik]	rabbit
Свини́на [sviNIna]	pork
Теля́тина [tiLYAtina]	veal
натура́льная [natuRAL'naya]	roast
ру́бленная [RUblinaya]	chopped
мо́лотая [MOlataya]	finely ground
Биф-стро́ганофф [bif-STROganaf]	beef stroganoff
Бифште́кс [bifSHTYEKS]	steak
Гуля́ш [guLYASH]	goulash
Котле́ты f pl [katLYEty]	meatballs; chops; cutlets
Котле́ты f pl по-ки́евски * [katLYEti pa-Klyifski]	pan-fried chicken croquettes
Отбивны́е [adbivNYye]	cutlets; chops
Пельме́ни (сиби́рские) * [pil'MYEni (siBIRskiye)]	meat-filled dumplings (Siberian)
Ромште́кс [ramSHTYEKS]	rump steak
Шашлы́к [shaSHLYK]	shashlik, shish kebab
Шни́цель [SHNItsyl']	schnitzel

Гарни́ры и припра́вы	Garnishes and Accompaniments
Карто́фель m [karTOfil']	potatoes
карто́фель m фри [karTOfil' FRI]	french fries
Лапша́ [lapSHA]	noodles
Овощно́е ассорти́ [avashNOye asarTI]	assorted vegetables
Рис [RIS]	rice
Майоне́з [mayaNYES]	mayonnaise
Смета́на * [smiTAna]	sour cream
Грибы́ m pl (све́жие/сушёные) [griBY (SVYEzhyye/suSHOnyye)]	mushrooms (fresh/dried)
запечённые [zapiCHOnyye]	baked
жа́реные [ZHArinyye]	fried

Диети́ческие блю́да	Vegetarian Dishes
Ка́ша * [KAsha] (гре́чневая/ма́нная/овся́ная/ри́совая) [GRYECHnivaya/MAnaya/afSYAnaya/RIsavaya]	groats (buckwheat/semolina/oat/rice)
на молоке́ [na-malaKYE]	with milk

Моло́чный суп [maLOCHny SUP]	milk soup
Омле́т [amLYET]	omelet
Сы́рники *m pl* * [SYRniki]	cheese fritters
(со смета́ной) [sa-smiTAnay]	with sour cream
Творо́жная запека́нка *	baked cottage cheese
[tvaROZHnaya zapiKANka]	pudding
Яи́чница (болту́нья/глазу́нья)	cooked eggs
[yaICHnitsa (balTUn'ya/glaZUn'ya)]	(scrambled/fried)

Вы́печка/Мучны́е изде́лия	Baked Goods
Блины́ *m pl* * [bliNY]	pancakes
с варе́ньем [s-vaRYEn'yem]	with jam
с икро́й * [s-iKROY]	with caviar
с мёдом [s-MYOdam]	with honey
со смета́ной [sa-smiTAnay]	with sour cream
с творо́гом [s-TVOragam]	with cottage cheese
Бу́лочки *f pl* (сла́дкие)	(sweet) buns/rolls
[BUlachki (SLATkiye)]	
с изю́мом [s-yZYUmam]	with raisins
с варе́ньем [s-vaRYEn'yim]	filled with jam
Пиро́г/Пирожки́ *m pl* * [piROK/pirashKI] .	cake/pastries
из дрожжево́го те́ста	made with yeast dough
[iz-drazhyVOva TYESta]	
из слоёного те́ста [is-slaYOnava TYESta]	made with puff pastry
с зелёным лу́ком [z-ziLYOnym LUkam]	with leeks
с капу́стой [s-kaPUstay]	with cabbage
с мя́сом [s-MYAsam]	with meat
с ри́сом [s-RIsam]	with rice
с яйцо́м [s-yiyTSOM]	with eggs
с варе́ньем [s-vaRYEn'yim]	with jam
с лимо́ном [s-liMOnam]	with lemon
с творого́м [s-tvaraGOM]	with cottage cheese
Расстега́й * [rastiGAY]	small open pie with filling

Десе́рты	Desserts
Моро́женое [maROzhinaye]	ice cream
(сли́вочное/шокола́дное)	(ice cream/chocolate
[SLIvachnaye/shakaLADnaye]	ice cream)
с варе́ньем [s-vaRYEn'yim]	with jam
с сиро́пом [s-siROpam]	with syrup
с фру́ктами [s-FRUKtami]	with fruits
с шокола́дом [sh-shakaLADam]	with chocolate sauce

Ice cream is very popular at all times of year, whatever the outside temperature.

Напи́тки — Beverages

Чай (с лимо́ном) [CHAY (s-liMOnam)]	tea (with lemon)
Ко́фе *m* (по-туре́цки/эспре́ссо) [KOfye (pa-tuRYETSki/esPRYEso)]	coffee (Turkish/espresso)
с молоко́м [s-malaKOM]	with milk
со сли́вками [sa-SLIFkami]	with cream
Компо́т * [kamPOT]	compote, served hot or cold
из сухофру́ктов/из све́жих фру́ктов [is-sukhaFRUKtaf/is-SVYEzhykh FRUKtaf]	made with dried/fresh fruits
Кисе́ль *m* [kiSYEL']	sweet, thickened fruit drink (hot or cold)
Квас * [KVAS]	kvass *(fermented beverage made from stale bread, with low alcohol content)*
Сок/Напи́ток [SOK/naPItak]	juice/diluted juice
виногра́дный [vinaGRADny]	grape juice
вишнёвый [vishNYOvy]	cherry juice
сли́вовый [SLIvavy]	plum juice
тома́тный [taMATny]	tomato juice
фрукто́вый [frukTOvy]	fruit juice
я́блочный [YAblachny]	apple juice
Лимона́д [limaNAT]	carbonated beverage
Минера́льная вода́ [miniRAL'naya vaDA]	mineral water

Алкого́льные напи́тки	Alcoholic Beverages
Пи́во [PIva]	beer
оте́чественное [aTYEchistvinaye]	domestic
и́мпортное [IMpartnaye]	imported
Вино́ бе́лое/кра́сное [viNO BYElaye/KRASnaye]	white wine/red wine
(полу)сухо́е [(palu)suKHOye]	(semi-)dry
сла́дкое [SLATkaye]	sweet
креплёное [kriPLYOnaye]	fortified
армя́нское [arMYANskaye]	Armenian
грузи́нское [gruZINskaye]	Georgian
молда́вское [malDAFskaye]	Moldavian
Шампа́нское [shamPANskaye]	champagne, sparkling wine
брют [BRYUT]	brut
(полу)сухо́е [(palu)suKHOye]	(semi-)dry
(полу)сла́дкое [(palu)SLATkaye]	(semi-)sweet
сове́тское [saVYETskaye]	Soviet
кры́мское [KRYMskaye]	Crimean
Насто́йка [naSTOYka], Нали́вка [naLIFka], Ликёр [liKYOR]	liqueur, cordial
Конья́к [kaN'YAK], Бре́нди [BRYENdi]	cognac, brandy

EATING AND DRINKING

армя́нский [arMYANski] . . . . Armenian
грузи́нский [gruZINski] . . . . Georgian
дагеста́нский [dagiSTANski] . . . . Dagestani
францу́зский [franTSUski] . . . . French
Во́дка [VOTka] . . . . vodka
оте́чественная [aTYEchistvinaya] . . . . domestic
и́мпортная [IMpartnaya] . . . . imported

Alcoholic beverages are served by the gram (50 grams, 100 grams, etc.).

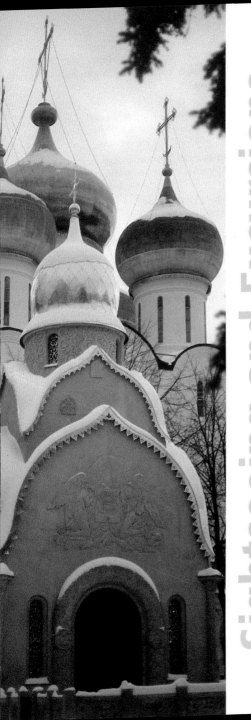

At the Tourist Information Office

I'd like a map of ..., please.
Мне ну́жен план го́рода ... *(+ gen)*. [MNYE NUzhin PLAN GOrada ...]

Do you have a calendar of events for this week?
У Вас есть програ́мма мероприя́тий на э́ту неде́лю?
[u-VAS YEST praGRAma mirapriYAtiy na-Etu niDYElyu]

Are there sightseeing tours of the town/city?
Прово́дятся ли авто́бусные экску́рсии по го́роду?
[praVOdyitsa li aFTObusnyye ekSKURsii pa-GOradu]

How much does the tour cost, please?
А ско́лько сто́ит экску́рсия? [a SKOL'ka STOit ekSKURsiya]

Places of Interest—Museums

Opening Hours, Guided Tours, Admission

Could you please tell me what places of interest there are here?
Не ска́жете, каки́е здесь есть достопримеча́тельности?
[ni-SKAzhytye kaKlye ZDYES' YEST dastaprimiCHAtil'nasti]

You've really got to see/visit ...
Вам обяза́тельно на́до осмотре́ть/посети́ть ... *(+ acc)*.
[VAM abyaZAtil'na NAda asmaTRYET'/pasiTIT' ...]

When is the museum open?
Когда́ музе́й откры́т? [kagDA muZYEY atKRYT]

When does the next guided tour start?
Когда́ начнётся сле́дующая экску́рсия?
[kagDA nachNYOTsa SLYEduyushaya ekSKURsiya]

Are there tours in English, too?
Прово́дятся ли экску́рсии на англи́йском языке́?
[praVOdyitsa li ekSKURsii na-anGLIYskam yizyKYE]

Are we allowed to take photographs here?
Мо́жно фотографи́ровать? [MOZHna fatagraFIravat']

Two tickets, please.
Два биле́та, пожа́луйста! [DVA biLYEta paZHAlusta]

Two adults and one child.
Два взро́слых и оди́н де́тский. [DVA VZROslykh i aDIN DYETski]

Are there discounts for ...
Есть ли ски́дки для ... [YEST li SKITki dlia-...]
  children?
  дете́й? [diTYEY]
  students?
  студе́нтов? [stuDYENtaf]

senior citizens?
пенсионе́ров? [pinsiaNYEraf]

groups?
групп? [GRUP]

Is there an exhibition catalog?
Есть ли катало́г экспона́тов вы́ставки?
[YEST li kataLOK ekspaNAtaf VYstafki]

Is this/that ...?
Э́то ...? [Eta ...]

When was this building built?/restored?
Когда́ э́то зда́ние бы́ло постро́ено?/реставри́ровано?
[kagDA Eta ZDAniye BYla paSTROyino/ristaVRIravana]

Who painted this picture?
Кто нарисова́л э́ту карти́ну? [KTO narisaVAL Etu karTInu]

Do you have a poster/a postcard/a slide of this picture?
У Вас есть репроду́кция э́той карти́ны на плака́те?/на
откры́тке?/на диапозити́ве? [u-VAS YEST ripraDUKtsyya Etai
karTIny na-plaKAtye/na-atKRYTkye/na-diapaziTIvye]

General

art	иску́сство [isKUstva]
birthplace	родно́й го́род [radNOY GOrat]
center of town, downtown	центр го́рода [TSENTR GOrada]
changing of the guard	сме́на карау́ла [SMYEna karaUla]
district, part of town	райо́н [rayON],
	часть f го́рода [CHAST' GOrada]
finds	нахо́дки f pl [naKHOTki]
guide	гид [GIT], экскурсово́д [ekskursaVOT]
(guided) tour	экску́рсия (с экскурсово́дом)
	[ekSKURsiya (s-ekskursaVOdam)]
historical preservation	охра́на па́мятников
	[aKHRAna PAMyitnikaf]
history	исто́рия [iSTOriya]
house	дом [DOM]
king/queen	коро́ль/короле́ва [kaROL'/karaLYEva]
lane	переу́лок [piriUlak]
market	ры́нок [RYnak]
museum	музе́й [muZYEY]
museum of ethnography	этнографи́ческий музе́й
	[etnagraFIchiski muZYEY]
opening hours	часы́ m pl рабо́ты [chiSY raBOty]
park	парк [PARK]
pedestrian zone	пешехо́дная зо́на
	[pishyKHOTnaya ZOna]

121

to reconstruct	реконструи́ровать *ipf a. pf* [rikanstruIravat']
religion	рели́гия [riLIgiya]
remains	оста́тки *f pl* [aSTATki]
to restore	реставри́ровать *ipf a. pf* [ristaVRIravat']
sights	достопримеча́тельности *f pl* [dastaprimiCHAtil'nasti]
sightseeing tour of the town	экску́рсия по го́роду [ekSKURsiya pa-GOradu]
street	у́лица [Ulitsa]
suburb	при́город [PRIgarat]
symbol	си́мвол [SIMval]
tour	осмо́тр [aSMOTR]
tourist information office	бюро́ по тури́зму [byuRO pa-tuRIZmu]
work	тво́рчество [TVORchistva]

Architecture

abbey	абба́тство [aBATstva]
altar	алта́рь *m* [alTAR']
arcade	арка́да [arKAda]
arch	а́рка [ARka], свод [SVOT]
archeology	археоло́гия [arkhiaLOgiya]
architect	архите́ктор [arkhiTYEKtar]
architecture	архитекту́ра [arkhitikTUra]
armory	оруже́йная пала́та [aruZHEYnaya paLAta]
baptismal font	купе́ль *f* [kuPYEL']
basilica	бази́лика [baSIlika]
bell tower	звонница [ZVOnitsa]
bridge	мост [MOST]
building	зда́ние [ZDAniye]
capital	капите́ль *f* [kaPItil']
carpet	ковёр [kaVYOR]
castle	за́мок [ZAmak]
cathedral	собо́р [saBOR]
ceiling	потоло́к [pataLOK]
cellar	подва́л [paDVAL]
cemetery	кла́дбище [KLADbishe]
chapel	часо́вня [chiSOVnya]
chimes	кура́нты *m pl* [kuRANty]
church	це́рковь *f* [TSERkaf']
church with a tented roof	шатро́вая це́рковь [shaTROvaya TSERkaf']
citadel	цитаде́ль *f* [tsytaDYEL']
city wall	городска́я стена́ [garatSKAya stiNA]
cloister	кры́тая галере́я [KRYtaya galiRYEya]

column, pillar	коло́нна [kaLOna], столб [staLO]
covered market	кры́тый ры́нок [KRYty RYnak]
crypt	кри́пта [KRIPta]
dome	ку́пол [KUpal]
edifice	сооруже́ние [saaruZHEniye]
excavations	раско́пки *f pl* [raSKOPki]
façade	фаса́д [faSAT]
fortress	кре́пость *f* [KRYEpast']
fountain	фонта́н [fanTAN]
gable	фронто́н [fronTON]
gates	воро́та *n pl* [varaTA]
grave, tomb	моги́ла [maGIla]
inner courtyard	вну́тренний двор [VNUtriny DVOR]
inscription	на́дпись *f* [NATpis']
mausoleum	мавзоле́й [mavzaLYEY]
memorial	мемориа́л [mimariAL]
monastery/convent	монасты́рь *m* [manaSTYR']
monument	па́мятник [PAmitnik]
mosque	мече́ть *f* [miCHET']
nave	неф [NYEF]
obelisk	обели́ск [abiLISK]
onion-shaped dome	лу́ковица [LUkavitsa]
opera	о́пера [Opira]
palace	дворе́ц [dvaRYETS], пала́ты *f pl* [paLAty]
place of pilgrimage	ме́сто пало́мничества [MYESta paLOMnichistva]
portal	порта́л [parTAL]
pulpit	ка́федра [KAfidra]
to rebuild	восстана́вливать/восстанови́ть [vastaNAvlivat'/vastanaVIT']
ring wall	кольцево́й вал [kal'tsyVOY VAL]
roof	кры́ша [KRYsha]
ruins	разва́лины *f pl* [raZVAliny], руи́ны *f pl* [rulny]
sacristy	ри́зница [RIZnitsa]
square	пло́щадь *f* [PLOshat']
steeple	колоко́льня [kalaKOL'nya]
stronghold	кре́пость *f* [KRYEpast']
summer palace	ле́тний дворе́ц [LYETni dvaRYETS]
synagogue	синаго́га [sinaGOga]
temple	храм [KHRAM]
the old town, historical district	ста́рая часть го́рода [STAraya CHAST' GOrada]
theater	теа́тр [tiATR]
tombstone	надгро́бный па́мятник [nadGROBny PAmitnik]
tower	ба́шня [BASHnya]

treasury	сокро́вищница [saKROvishnitsa]
triumphal arch	триумфа́льные воро́та *n pl* [triumFAL'nyye varaTA]
university	университе́т [univirsiTYET]
vault	свод [SVOT]
wall	стена́ [stiNA]
window	окно́ [akNO]
wing	крыло́ [kryLO]
winter palace	зи́мний дворе́ц [ZIMni dvaRYETS]
wood construction	деревя́нная констру́кция [diriVYAnaya kanSTRUKtsyya]

Visual Arts

arts and crafts	прикладно́е иску́сство [prikladNOye isKUstva]
bronze	бро́нза [BRONza]
canvas	холст [KHOLST]
ceramics	кера́мика [kiRAmika]
Christ	Христо́с [khriSTOS]
copperplate engraving	гравю́ра на ме́ди [graVYUra na-MYEdi]
copy	ко́пия [KOpiya]
cross	крест [KRYEST]
crucifix	распя́тие [rasPYAtiye]
drawing	рису́нок [riSUnak]
drawing(s), graphic art	гра́фика [GRAfika]
easel painting	станко́вая жи́вопись [stanKOvaya ZHYvapis']
etching, engraving	гравю́ра [graVYUra]
exhibit	экспона́т [ekspaNAT]
exhibition	вы́ставка [VYstafka]
gallery	галере́я [galiRYEya]
glass painting	жи́вопись *f* по стеклу́ [ZHYvapis' pa-stiKLU]
Gobelin (tapestry)	гобеле́н [gabiLYEN]
god/goddess	бог/боги́ня [BOK/baGInya]
gold work, goldsmith's art	ювели́рное иску́сство [yuviLIRnaye isKUstva]
icon	ико́на [iKOna]
iconostasis	иконоста́с [ikanaSTAS]
Last Judgment	стра́шный суд [STRASHny SUT]
lithography	литогра́фия [litaGRAfiya]
model	моде́ль *f* [maDYEL']
mosaic	моза́ика [maZAika]
nude	акт [AKT], обнажённая нату́ра [abnaZHOnaya naTUra]
original	по́длинник [PODlinik]
painter	жи́вописец [ZHYvapisits]
painting *(picture or portrait)*	карти́на [karTIna]

painting *(type of art)*	жи́вопись *f* [ZHYvapis']
paradise	рай [RAY]
photography	фотогра́фия [fataGRAfiya]
picture	о́браз [Obras]
plastic art	пла́стика [PLAstika]
porcelain	фарфо́р [farFOR]
portrait	портре́т [parTRYET]
poster	плака́т [plaKAT]
pottery	гонча́рное иску́сство [ganCHARnaye isKUstva]
prophet	проро́к [praROK]
revival	воскресе́ние [vaskriSYEniye]
royal gates *(of the iconostasis)*	ца́рские врата́ *n pl* [TSARskiye vraTA]
sculptor	ску́льптор [SKUL'Ptar]
sculpture	скульпту́ра [skul'pTUra]
silk-screen print(ing)	трафаре́тная печа́ть [trafaRYETnaya piCHAT']
statue	ста́туя [STAtuya]
still life	натюрмо́рт [natyurMORT]
terracotta	терракóта [tiraKOta]
Testament (Old/New)	заве́т (ве́тхий/но́вый) [zaVYET (VYETkhi/NOvy)]
torso	торс [TORS]
Trinity	тро́ица [TROitsa]
vase	ва́за [VAza]
Virgin Mary, Madonna	богома́терь [bagaMAtir'], богоро́дица [bagaROditsa]
watercolor	акваре́ль *f* [akvaRYEL']
woodcarving	резьба́ [riz'BA]
xylography	ксилогра́фия [ksilaGRAfiya]

Styles and Periods

ancient	дре́вний [DRYEVni]
applied arts	прикладно́е иску́сство [prikladNOye isKUstva]
Art Nouveau	стиль *m* моде́рн [STIL' maDYERN]
atheism	атеи́зм [atiIZM]
avant-garde	аванга́рд [avanGART]
Baroque	баро́кко [baROka]
boyar/boyar's wife	боя́рин/боя́рыня [baYArin/baYArynya]
Bronze Age	бро́нзовый век [BRONzavy VYEK]
Byzantine	византи́йский [vizanTIski]
century	столе́тие [staLYEtiye], век [VYEK]
Chinese	кита́йский [kiTAYski]
Christianity	христиа́нство [khristiANstva]
civil war	гражда́нская война́ [grazhDANskaya vayNA]
classicism	классици́зм [klasiTSYZM]

125

constructivism	конструктиви́зм [kanstruktiVIZM]
cubism	куби́зм [kuBIZM]
Decembrist Uprising	восста́ние декабри́стов [vaSTAniye dikaBRIstaf]
dynasty	дина́стия [diNAstiya]
Enlightenment	просвеще́ние [prasviSHEniye]
expressionism	экспрессиони́зм [eksprisiaNIZM]
February Revolution	февра́льская револю́ция [fiVRAL'skaya rivaLYUtsyya]
Freemason	масо́н [maSON]
Greek	гре́ческий [GRYEchiski]
Greeks	гре́ки [GRYEki]
heathen, pagan	язы́ческий [yiZYchiski]
heyday, prime	вре́мя расцве́та [VRYEmya rasTSVYEta]
high culture	высо́кая культу́ра [vySOkaya kul'TUra]
impressionism	импрессиони́зм [imprisiaNIZM]
Islam	исла́м [isLAM]
Jew/Jewess	евре́й/ка [yiVRYEY/ka]
Kievan Rus	(Ки́евская) Русь [KIyifskaya RUS']
Kremlin	кремль m [KRYEML']
mannerism	маньери́зм [man'yiRIZM]
metropolitan (relig.)	митрополи́т [mitrapaLIT]
Middle Ages	средневеко́вье [sridniviKOv'ye]
minaret	минаре́т [minaRYET]
modern	совреме́нный [savriMYEny]
Mongol(ian)	монго́льский [manGOL'ski]
October Revolution	октя́брьская револю́ция [akTYABR'skaya rivaLYUtsyya]
Old Believer	старове́рческий [staraVYERchiski]
Old Church Slavonic	старославя́нский [staraslaVYANski]
Old Russian	старору́сский [staraRUSki]
Oriental	восто́чный [vaSTOCHny]
Orthodox	правосла́вный [pravaSLAVny]
patriarch	патриа́рх [patriARKH]
period, epoch	эпо́ха [ePOkha]
Phoenicians	финики́яне pl [finiKIyanye]
pilgrimage	пало́мничество [paLOMnichistva]
prehistoric	доистори́ческий [daistaRIchiski]
prince/princess	князь/княги́ня [KNYAS'/knyaGInya]
realism (socialist)	реали́зм (социалисти́ческий) [riaLIZM (satsyaliSTIchiski)]
Renaissance	возрожде́ние [vazraZHDYEniye], ренесса́нс [riniSANS]
rococo	рококо́ [rakaKO]
Romanesque style	рома́нский стиль [raMANski STIL']
romanticism	рома́нтика [raMANtika]
Russian	росси́йский [raSIYski]

to Russify	русифици́ровать *ipf a. pf* [rusifiTSYravat']
school	шко́ла [SHKOla]
secular	све́тский [SVYETski]
serfdom	крепостно́е пра́во [kripasNOye PRAva]
Slavic	славя́нский [slaVYANski]
East/West/South	восто́чно-/за́падно-/ю́жно- [vaSTOCHna-/ZApadna-/YUZHna-]
Slavs	славя́не [slaVYAnye]
Soviet era	сове́тское вре́мя [saVYETskaye VRYEmya]
Stone Age	ка́менный век [KAminy VYEK]
style	стиль *m* [STIL']
suprematism	супремати́зм [suprimaTIZM]
surrealism	сюрреали́зм [syuriaLIZM]
symbolism	символи́зм [simvaLIZM]
Tatars	тата́ры [taTAry]
the Golden Ring	Золото́е кольцо́ [zalaTOye kal'TSO]
tsar/tsaritsa	царь/цари́ца [TSAR'/tsaRItsa]
tsarist era	ца́рское вре́мя [TSARskaye VRYEmya]
Turks	ту́рки [TURki]
Varangians	варя́ги [vaRYAgi]
Vikings	ви́кинги [VIkingi]
war	война́ [vayNA]
Western European	западноевропе́йский [zapadnayivraPYEYski]

Excursions

Where are we leaving from?
Отку́да мы отправля́емся? [atKUda MY atpraVLAYyimsa]

When should we meet?
Когда́ встре́тимся? [kagDA FSTRYEtimsa]

Will we pass by ...?
Прое́дем ми́мо ... *(+ gen)*? [praYEdim MImа ...]

Are we going to see ..., too?
Посети́м та́кже ...? [pasiTIM TAGzhy ...]

When are we going back?
Когда́ мы уе́дем обра́тно [kagDA MY uYEdim aBRATna]

amusement park	парк культу́ры и о́тдыха [PARK kulTUry i ODdykha]
botanical gardens	ботани́ческий сад [bataNIchiski SAT]
canyon, gorge	уще́лье [uSHEl'ye]
caravanserai	карава́н-сара́й [karavan-saRAY]
cave	пеще́ра [piSHEra]

day trip	однодне́вная экску́рсия [adnaDNYEVnaya ekSKURsiya]
dripstone cave	сталакти́товая пеще́ра [stalakTItavaya piSHEra]
excursion, trip	экску́рсия [ekSKURsiya]
fishing village	рыба́цкий посёлок [ryBATSki paSYOlak]
forest fire	лесно́й пожа́р [lisNOY paZHAR]
forest, woods	лес [LYES]
grotto	грот [GROT]
lake	о́зеро [Ozira]
landscape	пейза́ж [piyZASH]
lava	ла́ва [LAva]
lighthouse	мая́к [maYAK]
lookout point	смотрова́я площа́дка [smatraVAya plaSHATka]
market	ры́нок [RYnak]
mountain	гора́ [gaRA]
mountain pass	го́рный перехо́д [GORny piriKHOT]
mountains	го́ры *f pl* [GOry]
museum of local history and culture	краеве́дческий музе́й [krayiVYETchiski muZYEY]
museum village	музе́й-дере́вня [muZYEY-diRYEVnya]
national park; nature reserve	запове́дник [zapaVYEDnik]
observatory	обсервато́рия [apsirvaTOriya]
open-air museum	музе́й под откры́тым не́бом [muZYEY pad-atKRYtym NYEbam]
place of pilgrimage	ме́сто пало́мничества [MYESta paLOMnichistva]
river	река́ [riKA]
rock	скала́ [skaLA]
spring	исто́чник [iSTOCHnik]
summit, peak	верши́на [virSHYna]
surroundings	окре́стность *f* [aKRYESnast']
swamp	боло́то [baLOta]
tour	экску́рсия [ekSKURsiya]
tour around the island	экску́рсия по о́строву [ekSKURsiya pa-Ostravu]
valley	доли́на [daLIna]
volcano	вулка́н [vulKAN]
waste ground	пу́стошь *f* [PUstash']
waterfall	водопа́д [vadaPAT]
wildlife park	охо́тничий парк [aKHOTnichi PARK]
zoo	зоопа́рк [zaaPARK]

Active Vacations

Swimming

Excuse me please, is there a (an) ... here?
Извините, пожалуйста, здесь есть …
[izviNItye paZHAlusta ZDYES' YEST …]

swimming pool
бассейн? [baSYEYN]

outdoor pool
открытый бассейн? [atKRYty baSYEYN]

indoor pool
крытый бассейн? [KRYty baSYEYN]

One ticket, please.
Один билет, пожалуйста! [aDIN biLYET paZHAlusta]

Can you tell me where the ... are?
Вы не скажете мне, где … [VY ni-SKAzhytye MNYE GDYE …]

showers
душевые? [dushyVYye]

changing rooms
гардеробные кабины? [gardiROBnyye kaBIny]

Только для умеющих плавать!	For swimmers only!
Прыгать в воду запрещается!	No diving allowed!
Купание запрещено!	No swimming allowed!
Опасное течение!	Dangerous current!

Is the beach ...
Пляж … [PLYASH …]

sandy?
песчаный? [pisCHAny]

rocky/stony?
каменистый? [kamiNIsty]

Are there sea urchins/jellyfish/Is there algae here?
Здесь есть морские ежи?/медузы?/водоросли?
[ZDYES' YEST marSKIye yiZHY/miDUzy/VOdarasli]

Is there a strong current?
Течение сильное? [tiCHEniye SIL'naye]

Can you tell me whether it's dangerous for children?
Для детей опасно? [dlia-diTYEY aPASna]

When is low tide/high tide?
Когда бывает отлив?/прилив? [kagDA byVAyit atLIF/priLIF]

I'd like to rent ...
Я хочу взять напрокат … *(+ acc)* [YA khaCHU VZYAT' napraKAT …]

a deck chair.
шезлонг. [shyzLONK]

a beach umbrella.
зонт от со́лнца. [ZONT at-SONtsa]
a boat.
ло́дку. [LOTku]
a pair of water skis.
во́дные лы́жи. [VODnyye LYzhy]

How much is it per hour?/per day?
Ско́лько э́то сто́ит в час?/в день?
[SKOL'ka Eta STOit f-CHAS/v-DYEN']

air mattress	надувно́й матра́с [NAduvnoy maTRAS]
beach volleyball	бич-волейбо́л [BICH-valiyBOL]
children's pool	де́тский бассе́йн [DYETski baSYEYN]
jet ski	ску́тер [SKUtir]
lifeguard	плове́ц-спаси́тель [plaVYETS-spaSItil']
nudist beach	пляж нуди́стов [PLYASH nuDIstaf]
paddle boat	во́дный велосипе́д [VODny vilasiPYET]
sunbathing area	луг для лежа́ния [LUK dlia-liZHAniya]
superintendent, head lifeguard	смотри́тель *m* [smaTRItil']
to swim	пла́вать *ipf* [PLAvat'], плыть/поплы́ть [PLYT'/paPLYT']
swim fins	ла́сты *m pl* [LAsty]
swimmer	пло́ве́ц/пловчи́ха [plaVYETS/plafCHIkha]
wading pool	де́тский бассе́йн [DYETski baSYEYN]
to go water skiing	ката́ться на во́дных лы́жах [kaTAtsa na-VODnykh LYzhakh]
water skis	во́дные лы́жи *f pl* [VODnyye LYzhy]
water wings	надувны́е крылы́шки для пла́вания [naduvNYye KRYlyshki dlia-PLAvaniya]
windbreak	защи́та от ве́тра [zaSHIta at-VYEtra]

Other Activities and Sports

What athletic facilities are available here?
Каки́е здесь есть возмо́жности занима́ться спо́ртом?
[kaKIye ZDYES' YEST vazMOzhnasti zaniMAtsa SPORtam]

Is there ... here?
Здесь есть ... [ZDYES' YEST ...]

a golf course
площа́дка для игры́ в гольф [plaSHATka dlia-iGRY v-GOL'F]
a tennis court
те́ннисный корт [TYEnisny KORT]

Could you please tell me where I can go fishing/hiking here?
Не ска́жете мне, где здесь мо́жно лови́ть ры́бу?/ходи́ть
в похо́д?
[ni-SKAzhytye MNYE GDYE ZDYES' MOZHna laVIT' RYbu/khaDIT'
f-paKHOT]

Where can I rent ...?
Где мо́жно взять напрока́т ...?
[GDYE MOZHna VZYAT' napraKAT ...]

I'd like to take a course for beginners/an advanced course.
Я бы хоте́л m/хоте́ла f взять уро́ки ... (+ gen) для начина́ющих./
для продви́нутых. [YA BY khaTYEL/khaTYEla VZYAT' uROki ... dlia-
nachiNAyushikh/dlia-praDVInutykh]

Water Sports

boat trip *(on a houseboat)*	во́дная экску́рсия (в ба́рже для жилья́) [VODnaya ekSKURsiya (v-BARzhy dli-zhyL'YA)]
boating license	права́ на управле́ние ло́дкой [praVA na-upraVLYEniye LOTkay]
canoe	кано́э [kaNOe]
canyoning	ка́нионинг [KAnianink]
houseboat	ба́ржа для жилья́ [BARzha dlia-zhyL'YA]
oars	вёсла *n pl* [VYOSla]
to paddle	ката́ться на байда́рке [kaTAtsa na-bayDARkye]
paddle boat	байда́рка [bayDARka]
pickup service	обра́тный подъём [aBRATny padYOM]
power boat	мото́рная ло́дка [maTORnaya LOTka]
rafting	ра́фтинг [RAFtink], сплав по реке́ [SPLAF pa-riKYE]
regatta	рега́та [riGAta]
to row	грести́/погрести́ [griSTI/pagriSTI]
row boat	гребна́я ло́дка [gribNAya LOTka]
rubber boat	надувна́я ло́дка [naduvNAya LOTka]
to sail	пла́вать *ipf* под па́русом [PLAvat' pat-PArusam]
sailboat	па́русная ло́дка [PArusnaya LOTka]
sailing trip	экску́рсия на па́русной ло́дке [ekSKURsiya na-PArusnay LOTkye]
to surf	ката́ться *ipf* на доске́ [kaTAtsa na-daSKYE]
surfboard	се́рфинг [SYERfink]
wind direction	направле́ние ве́тра [napraVLYEniye VYEtra]
windsurfing	виндсе́рфинг [vintSYERfink]

Diving

to dive	нырять/нырнуть [nyRYAT'/nyrNUT']
dive mask	водолазная маска [vadaLAZnaya MAska]
diving equipment	водолазное снаряжение [vadaLAZnaye snaryiaZHEniye]
harpoon	гарпун [garPUN]
oxygen tank	кислородный баллон [kislaRODny baLON]
scuba diving	погружение под воду с водолазным снаряжением [pagruZHEniye pad-VOdu s-vadaLAZnym snaryiaZHEniyim]
snorkel	шноркель m [SHNORkil']
to go snorkeling	плавать ipf со шноркелем [PLAvat' sa-SHNORkilim]
wet suit	водолазный костюм [vadaLAZny kaSTYUM]

Fishing

deep-sea fishing	рыболовство на открытом море [rybaLOFstva na-atKRYtam MOrye]
to go fishing	удить/поудить [uDIT'/pauDIT']
fishing license	лицензия на ловлю рыб [liTSENziya na-LOVlyu RYP]
fishing rod	удочка [Udachka]
harbor master's office	портовое управление [partaVOye upraVLYEniye]
off season	запретное время для ловли рыб [zaPRYETnaya VRYEmya dlia-LOVli RYP]

Ball Games

ball	мяч [MYACH]
basketball	баскетбол [baskidBOL]
goal (score)	гол [GOL]
(posts)	ворота n pl [vaROta]
goalie, goalkeeper	вратарь m [VRAtar']
halftime	тайм [TAYM]
handball	гандбол [gandBOL]
net	сетка [SYETka]
rugby	регби [RYEGbi]
soccer ball	футбол [fudBOL]
soccer field	футбольное поле [fudBOL'naye POlye]
soccer game	футбольный матч [fudBOL'ny MACH]
team	команда [kaMANda]
volleyball	волейбол [valyiBOL]

Tennis and Badminton

badminton	бадминтон [badminTON]
doubles	парная игра [PARnaya iGRA]
racquet	ракетка [raKYETka]
shuttlecock	бадминтон [badminTON]
singles	одиночная игра [adiNOCHnaya iGRA]
squash	сквош [SKVOSH]
table tennis, ping-pong	настольный теннис [naSTOL'ny TYEnis]
tennis	теннис [TYEnis]
tennis racquet	теннисная ракетка [TYEnisnaya raKYETka]

Physical Fitness and Weight Training

aerobics	аэробика [aeRObika]
bodybuilding	бодибилдинг [badiBILdink]
fitness center, health club, gym	фитнес-центр [fitnis-TSENTR]
fitness training	тренировка (по физической подготовке) [triniROFka (pa-fiZIchiskay padgaTOFkye)]
gymnastics	гимнастика [gimNAstika]
jazz aerobics	ритмическая гимнастика [ritMIchiskaya gimNAstika]
jogging	пробежка [praBYESHka]
to go jogging	бегать *ipf* [BYEgat']
spinal column physiotherapy	лечебная гимнастика (для позвоночника) [liCHEBnaya gimNAstika (dlia-pazvaNOCHnika)]
stretching	растяжка [raSTYASHka]

Wellness

The embodiment of well-being is the Russian steam bath (русская баня [RUskaya BAnya]). In terms of the setup, it resembles a sauna, but the heat is not quite so high. Instead, water is continually ladled onto heated rocks to keep the humidity level up. Here's how the Russians do it: flail yourself with a leafy bunch of birch twigs to stimulate your circulation, and then conclude the procedure by jumping into the snow or plunging into a cold river or lake, or at least by taking a cold shower.

Jacuzzi	джакузи *n* [dzhaKUzi]
massage	массаж [maSASH]
pool	бассейн [baSYEYN]
sauna	сауна [SAuna] финская баня [FINskaya BAnya]

solarium	соля́рий [saLYAri]
steam bath	парна́я ба́ня [parNAya BAnya], ру́сская ба́ня [RUskaya BAnya]

Biking

The bicycle is almost unknown as an urban means of transportation. Instead, it is considered a piece of equipment for sports and recreation and, consequently, you will look in vain for bike paths and you should not count on any consideration and understanding on the part of car drivers.

bicycle, bike	велосипе́д [vilasiPYET]
bike helmet	велосипе́дный шлем [vilasiPYEDny SHLYEM]
bike path	велосипе́дная доро́жка [vilasiPYEDnaya daROSHka]
bike trip	пое́здка на велосипе́де [paYESTka na-vilasiPYEdye]
cycling	велоспо́рт [vilaSPORT]
mountain bike	го́рный велосипе́д [GORny vilasaPYET]
pump	насо́с [naSOS]
racing bike	го́ночный велосипе́д [GOnachny vilasiPYET]
to ride a bike	ката́ться на велосипе́де [kaTAtsa na-vilasiPYEdye]
scooter	самока́т [samaKAT]
tire repair kit	принадле́жности для ремо́нта ка́меры [pronadLYEZHnasti dlia-riMONta KAmiry]
trekking bike	тре́ккинговый велосипе́д [TRYEkingavy vilasiPYET], гибри́дный велосипе́д [giBRIDny vilasiPYET]
(inner) tube	ка́мера [KAmira]

Hiking and Mountain Climbing

I'd like to go hiking in the mountains.
Хочу́ соверши́ть похо́д в го́ры.
[khaCHU savirSHYT' paKHOT v-GOry]

Can you show me an interesting route on the map?
Вы мо́жете показа́ть мне интере́сный маршру́т по ка́рте?
[VY MOzhytye pakaZAT' MNYE intiRYESny marshRUT pa-KARtye]

day trip	однодне́вный похо́д [adnaDNYEVny paKHOT]
free climbing	ла́зание по скала́м [LAzaniye pa-skaLAM]

hike	поход [paKHOT]
to go hiking	ходить *ipf* в поход [khaDIT' f-paKHOT], идти/пойти в поход [iTI/payTI f-paKHOT]
hiking map	туристская карта [tuRISTskaya KARta]
hiking path	туристская тропа [tuRISTskaya traPA]
mountain climbing, mountaineering	альпинизм [al'piNIZM]
route	маршрут [marshRUT]
safety rope	страховочный канат [straKHOvachny kaNAT]
shelter	туристский приют [tuRISTski priYUT]
trail	дистанционная туристская тропа [distantsyOnaya tuRISTskaya traPA]
trekking	треккинг [TRYEkink]

Horseback Riding

horse	лошадь *f* [LOshat']
to go horseback riding	ездить *ipf* верхом [YEZdit' virKHOM]
polo	поло [POlo]
ride	выезд верхом [VYyist virKHOM]
riding lesson	урок верховой езды [uROK virkhaVOY yizDY]
riding, equestrian sport	конный спорт [KOnny SPORT]
saddle	седло [siDLO]
stable	конюшня [kaNYUSHnya]

Golf

golf	гольф [GOL'F]
golf ball	мяч [MYACH]
golf club *(implement)*	клюшка для гольфа [KLYUshka dlia-GOL'fa]
golf club *(organization)*	гольф-клуб [gol'f-KLUP]
golf course	поле для игры в гольф [POlye dlia-iGRY v-GOL'F]
hole	лунка [LUNka]

Flying

ascent	подъём [padYOM]
gliding	планеризм [planiRIZM]
hang gliding	дельтапланеризм [dil'taplaniRIZM]
hot-air balloon	воздушный баллон [vazDUSHny baLON]
parachuting	парашютизм [parashuTIZM]
paragliding	парапланеризм [paraplaniRIZM]
parasailing	парасейлинг [paraSYEYlink]

A one-day ski pass, please.
Билéт на одúн день, пожáлуйста. [biLYET na-aDIN DYEN' paZHAlusta]

When is the last trip up the mountain/down the mountain?
Во скóлько послéдний подъём?/спуск?
[va-SKOL'ka paSLYEDni padYOM/SPUSK]

bunny lift	дéтский подъёмник [DYETski padYOMnik]
cable railway	фуникулёр [funikuLYOR], подъёмник [padYOMnik], канáтная дорóга [kaNATnaya daROga]
chairlift	крéсельная канáтная дорóга [KRYEsil'naya kaNATnaya daROga], сидéния [siDYEniya]
cross-country skis	гóночные лы́жи f pl [GOnachnyye LYzhy]
curling	кёрлинг [KYORlink]
day pass	билéт нá день [biLYET NA-din']
downhill skis	гóрные лы́жи f pl [GORnyye LYzhy]
ice hockey	хоккéй на льду [khaKYEY na-L'DU]
ice skates	конькú m pl [kan'KI]
ice skating	бег на конькáх [BYEK na-kan'KAKH]
ice-skating rink	катóк [kaTOK]
middle station	срéдняя стáнция [SREDniya STANtsyya]
powder snow	ры́хлый снег [RYKHly SNYEK]
ski binding	лы́жное креплéние [LYZHnaye kriPLYEniye]
ski goggles	лы́жные очкú m pl [LYZHnyye achKI]
ski instructor	инстрýктор по катáнию на лы́жах [inSTRUKtar pa-kaTAniyu na-LYzhakh]
ski poles	лы́жные пáлки f pl [LYZHnyye PALki]
skiing lessons	урóки m pl катáния на лы́жах [uROki kaTAniya na-LYzhakh]
to go skiing	катáться на лы́жах [kaTAtsa na-LYzhakh]
skis	лы́жи f pl [LYzhy]
sled, toboggan	сáни f pl [SAni]
to go sledding	катáться ipf на санях [kaTAtsa na-saNYAKH]
snowboard	сноубóрд [snauBORT]
station at the bottom of the ski lift	нúжняя стáнция [NIZHnaya STANtsyya]
summit station	вéрхняя стáнция [VYERKHniya STANtsyya]

touring skis	туристские лыжи f pl
	[tuRISTskiye LYzhy]
tow lift, T-bar	бугельный подъёмник
	[BUgil'ny padYOMnik]
track	лыжня [lyzhNYA]
weekly pass	билет на неделю [biLYET na-niDYElyu]

Other Sports

bowling	боулинг [BOulink]
to go bowling	играть/сыграть в кегли
	[iGRAT'/syGRAT' f-KYEgli]
bungee jumping	банджи-джампинг [BANdzhy-
	DZHAMpink], тарзанка [tarZANka]
inline skates, rollerblades	йнлайн скейт [INlayn SKEYT],
	ролики m pl [ROliki]
miniature golf	мини-гольф [MIni-gol'f]
roller skates	роликовые коньки m pl
	[ROlikavyye kan'KI]
to go roller-skating	кататься на роликах
	[kaTAtsa na-ROlikakh]
skateboard	скейтбóрд [skiytBORT]
to go skateboarding	кататься на скейтборде
	[kaTAtsa na-skiytBORdye]
track and field events	лёгкая атлетика [LYOKHkaya atLYEtika]

Sporting Events

Could you please tell me what sporting events there are here?
Вы не скажете мне, какие здесь спортивные мероприятия
проводятся? [VY ni-SKAzhytye MNYE kaKIye ZDYES' sparTIVnyye
mirapriYAtiya praVOdyitsa]

I'd like to watch the soccer game.
Я бы хотел m/хотела f посмотреть футбол.
[YA BY khaTYEL/khaTYEla pasmaTRYET' fudBOL]

When/Where is it?
Когда/Где это будет? [kagDA/GDYE Eta BUdit]

How much does it cost to get in?
Сколько стоит вход? [SKOL'ka STOit FKHOT]

What's the score?
Какой идёт счёт? [kaKOY iDYOT SHOT]

Two to one.
Два-один. [DVA-aDIN]

A tie, one to one.
Один-один. [aDIN-aDIN]

Foul!
Нарушение! [naruSHEniye]

138

Nice shot!
Хоро́ший уда́р. [khaROshi uDAR]

Goal!
Гол! [GOL]

athlete	спортсме́н/ка [spartsMYEN/ka]
athletic field	спорти́вная площа́дка [sparTIVnaya plaSHATka]
bicycle race	велого́нка [vilaGONka]
championship	чемпиона́т [chimpiaNAT]
contest, match	соревнова́ние [sarivnaVAniye]
defeat, loss	пораже́ние [paraZHEniye]
free kick	свобо́дный уда́р [svaBODny uDAR]
game	игра́ [iGRA]
kickoff	нача́льный уда́р [naCHAL'ny uDAR]
to lose	прои́грывать/проигра́ть [praIgryvat'/praiGRAT']
offside	офса́йд [afSAYT]
pass	переда́ча [piriDAcha]
penalty	11-метро́вый уда́р [aDInatsat'-miTROvy uDAR], пена́льти n [piNAL'ti]
penalty box	штрафна́я пло́щадь [shtrafNAya PLOshat']
penalty kick	штрафно́й уда́р [shtrafNOY uDAR]
program	програ́мма [praGRAma]
race	го́нка [GONka]
referee, umpire	ре́фери [rifiRI]
stadium	стадио́н [stadiON]
ticket (of admission)	(входно́й) биле́т [(fkhadNOY) biLYET]
ticket stand	ка́сса [KAsa]
tie	ничья́ [niCHYA]
to win	выи́грывать/вы́играть [vyIgryvat'/VYigrat']
victory, win	побе́да [paBYEda]

Creative Vacations

I'd like to attend ...
Я бы хоте́л m/хоте́ла f приня́ть уча́стие в ... *(+ prep)*.
[YA BY khaTYEL/khaTYEla priNYAT' uCHAstiye f- ...]

a pottery course.
ку́рсах по гонча́рству [KURsakh pa-ganCHARstvu]

a Russian course.
ку́рсах ру́сского языка́ [KURsakh RUskava yizyKA]

for beginners.
для начина́ющих [dlia-nachiNAyushikh]

for advanced learners.
для продви́нутых [dlia-praDVInutykh]

139

How many hours per day does it meet?
Ско́лько часо́в в день предполага́ется?
[SKOL'ka chiSOF v-DYEN' pritpalaGAyitsa]

Is the number of participants limited?
Коли́чество уча́стников ограни́чено?
[kaLIchistva uCHASnikaf agraNIchino]

Do you need any previous knowledge?
Тре́буются ли предвари́тельные зна́ния?
[TRYEbuyutsa li pridvaRItil'nyye ZNAniya]

When is the registration deadline?
Како́й срок пода́чи зая́вки? [kaKOY SROK paDAchi zaYAFki]

Are the costs of materials included?
Включа́ется ли в сто́имость расхо́д на материа́лы?
[fklyuCHAyitsa li f-STOimast' rasKHOT na-matiriAly]

What should I bring along?
Что принести́ с собо́й? [SHTO priniSTI s-saBOY]

belly dancing	та́нец живота́ [TAnits zhyvaTA]
cooking	кулина́рное мастерство́ [kuliNARnaye mastirSTVO]
course	курс [KURS], (usually pl): ку́рсы [KURsy]
dance theater	танцева́льный теа́тр [tantsyVAL'ny tiATR]
drama workshop	актёрская мастерска́я [akTYORskaya mastirSKAya]
drumming	игра́ на бараба́не [iGRA na-baraBAnye]
language courses	языковы́е ку́рсы m pl [yazykaVYE KURsy]
life drawing, nude drawing	рисова́ние обнажённых нату́р [risaVAniye abnaZHOnykh naTUR]
oil painting	жи́вопись f ма́слом [ZHYvapis' MAslam]
painting	жи́вопись f [ZHYvapis']
photography	фотографи́рование [fatagraFIravaniye]
silk painting	жи́вопись f на шёлке [ZHYvapis' na-SHOLkye]
theater ensemble	театра́льная тру́ппа [tiaTRAL'naya TRUpa]
watercolor painting	акваре́льная жи́вопись [akvaRYEL'naya ZHYvapis']
wood carving	резьба́ по де́реву [riz'BA pa-DYErivu]
working with gold	златокузне́чество [zlatakuZNYEchistva]
workshop	мастерска́я [mastirSKAya]
yoga	йо́га [YOga]

Entertainment

Theater – Concert – Movies

Theater, opera, and concert tickets can be purchased from ticket offices (театра́льная ка́сса [tiaTRAL'naya KAsa]) in town or at the various performance halls and theaters. In addition, hotels often have tickets for good seats available at higher prices—sometimes even if the performance actually is already sold out.

Could you please tell me what's playing at the theater tonight?
Вы не ска́жете мне, что идёт сего́дня ве́чером в теа́тре?
[VY ni-SKAzhytye MNYE SHTO iDYOT siVOdnya VYEchiram f-tiAtrye]

What's on at the movies tomorrow night?
Что за́втра ве́чером идёт в кино́?
[SHTO ZAFtra VYEchiram iDYOT f-kiNO]

Can you recommend a good play?
Вы не посове́туете мне хоро́ший спекта́кль?
[VY ni-pasaVYEtuyitye MNYE khaROshi spikTAKL']

When does the performance start?
Когда́ начина́ется представле́ние?
[kagDA nachiNAyitsa pritstaVLYEniye]

Where can I get tickets?
Где мо́жно взять биле́ты? [GDYE MOZHna VZYAT' biLYEty]

Two tickets for tonight, please.
Два биле́та на сего́дняшний ве́чер, пожа́луйста.
[DVA biLYEta na-siVOdnyishni VYEchir paZHAlusta]

Two ...-ruble seats, please.
Два ме́ста за ... рубле́й, пожа́луйста.
[DVA MYESta za- ... ruBLYEY paZHAlusta]

Can I have a program, please?
Мо́жно взять програ́ммку?
[MOZHna VZYAT' praGRAMku]

advance ticket sales	предвари́тельная прода́жа [pridvaRItil'naya praDAzha]
coat check	гардеро́б [gardiROP]
festival	фестива́ль *m* [fistiVAL']
intermission	антра́кт [anTRAKT], переры́в [piriRYF]
performance	представле́ние [pritstaVLYEniye]
program (booklet)	програ́ммка [praGRAMka]
ticket (of admission)	(входно́й) биле́т [(fkhadNOY) biLYET]
ticket office	ка́сса [KAsa]

Theater

act	акт [AKT]
actor/actress	актёр/актри́са [akTYOR/akTRIsa]
ballet	бале́т [baLYET]
box	ло́жа [LOzha]
cabaret	теа́тр ма́лых форм [tiATR MAlykh FORM]
cabaret artiste	арти́ст-сати́рик [arTIST-satiRIK]
(dress) circle *(seating)*	я́рус [YArus]
comedy	коме́дия [kaMYEdiya]
dancer	танцо́вщик/танцо́вщица [tanTSOFshik/tanTSOFshitsa]
drama	пье́са [P'YEsa]
folk play	наро́дная пье́са [naRODnaya P'YEsa]
intermission	антра́кт [anTRAKT]
music hall, variety theater	варьете́ [var'yiTE]
musical	мю́зикл [MYUzikl]
open-air theater	ле́тний теа́тр [LYETni tiATR]
opera	о́пера [Opira]
operetta	опере́тта [apiRYEta]
orchestra *(seating)*	парте́р [parTYER]
performance	представле́ние [pritstaVLYEniye]
piece	пье́са [P'YEsa]
play	спекта́кль *m* [spikTAKL']
premiere	премье́ра [priM'YEra]
production	инсцениро́вка [instsyniROFka]
repertoire	репертуа́р [ripirtuAR]
revue theater	теа́тр миниатю́р [tiATR miniaTYUR]
theater	теа́тр [tiATR]
tragedy	траге́дия [traGYEdiya]

Concert

blues	блюз [BLYUZ]
choir	хор [KHOR]
classical music	класси́ческая му́зыка [klaSIchiskaya MUzyka]
composer	компози́тор [kampaZItar]
concert	конце́рт [kanTSERT]
chamber concert	ка́мерный конце́рт [KAmirny kanTSERT]
church concert	конце́рт церко́вной му́зыки [kanTSERT tsirKHOVnay MUzyki]
symphony concert	симфони́ческий конце́рт [simfaNIchiski kanTSERT]
conductor	дирижёр [diriZHOR]
folk	фолькло́р [fol'kLOR]
folk music	наро́дная му́зыка [naRODnaya MUzyka]
jazz	джаз [DZHES]

orchestra	оркéстр [arKYESTR]
pop	поп [POP]
rap	рэп [REP]
reggae	рéгги [RYEgi]
rock	рок [ROK]
singer	певéц/певи́ца [piVYETS/piVItsa]
soloist	соли́ст/ка [saLIST/ka]
soul	сóул [SOul]
techno	тéхно [TYEKHna]

Movies

directed by	режиссýра [rizhySUra]
film, movie	фильм [FIL'M]
action film	боеви́к [bayiVIK]
black-and-white film	чёрно-бéлый фильм [CHORna-BYEly FIL'M]
cartoon, animated film	мультфи́льм [mul'tFIL'M]
classic	клáссика [KLAsika]
comedy	комéдия [kaMYEdiya]
documentary film	документáльный фильм [dakuminTAL'ny FIL'M]
drama	мелодрáма [milaDRAma]
science fiction film	наýчная фантáстика [naUCHnaya fanTAStika]
short film	короткометрáжка [karatkamiTRASHka]
thriller	три́ллер [TRIlir]
Western	вéстерн [VYEStirn]
main role	глáвная роль [GLAVnaya ROL']
movie actor/actress	киноактёр/киноактри́са [kinaakTYOR/kinaakTRIsa]
movie theater	кинó [kiNO]
theater showing lesser-known or classic films	репертуáрное кинó [ripirtuARnaye kiNO]
original version	первоначáльный текст [pirvanaCHAL'ny TYEKST]
special effects	спецэффéкты *m pl* [spyetseFYEKty]
subtitles	субти́тры *m pl* [supTItry]

Nightlife

What is there to do here in the evenings?
Чем мóжно здесь заня́ться вéчером?
[CHEM MOZHna ZDYES' zaNYAtsa VYEchiram]

Is there a nice bar around?
Есть здесь уютное кафе? [YEST ZDYES' uYUTnaye kaFYE]

Where can you go dancing here?
Где можно здесь потанцевать?
[GDYE MOZHna ZDYES' patantsyVAT']

May I have this (another) dance?
(Ещё) потанцуем? [(yiSHO) patanTSUyim]

band	группа [GRUpa]
bar	бар [BAR]
casino	казино [kaziNO]
to dance	танцевать/потанцевать [tantsyVAT'/patantsyVAT']
dance band	танцевальный оркестр [tantsyVAL'ny arKYESTR]
disco, club	дискотека [diskaTYEka]
folklore	фольклор [fal'kLOR]
folklore evening	фольклорный вечер [fal'kLORny VYEchir]
formal attire	вечернее платье [viCHERniye PLAt'ye]
gambling	азартная игра [aZARTnaya iGRA]
to go out (somewhere)	выходить/выйти (куда-нибудь) [vykhaDIT'/VYti (kuDA-nibut')]
live music	живая музыка [zhyVAya MUzyka]
nightclub	ночной клуб [nachNOY KLUP]
party	вечеринка [vichiRINka]
show	ревю *n* [reVYU], шоу *n* [SHOu]
tavern, pub	кафе [kaFYE], пивная [pivNAya], бар [BAR]

Festivals and Events

Could you please tell me when the ... festival takes place?
Вы не скажете мне, когда проходит фестиваль ... (+ *gen*)?
[VY ni-SKAzhytye MNYE kagDA praKHOdit fistiVAL' ...]

from ... to ...
с ... (+ *gen*) по ... (+ *acc*) [s- ... pa- ...]
every year in August
ежегодно в августе [yizhyGODna v-AVgustye]
every other year
каждые два года [KAZHdyye DVA GOda]

Can anyone take part?
Каждый может участвовать? [KAZHdy MOzhyt uCHAStvavat']

brass band	духово́й орке́стр [dukhaVOY arKYESTR]
carnival	карнава́л [karnaVAL]
circus	цирк [TSYRK]
fair	я́рмарка [YARmarka]
festival	фестива́ль *m* [fistiVAL']
fireworks	фейерве́рк [fiyirVYERK]
flea market	барахо́лка [baraKHOLka]
folk festival	наро́дные гуля́ния [naRODnyye guLYAniya]
Olympic games	олимпиа́да [alimpiAda]
parade	ше́ствие [SHESTviye]
procession	проце́ссия [praTSEsiya]

Shopping

Questions

In many places you will look in vain for specialty stores. However, many small shops and even kiosks have quite a varied selection of goods. Thus practically everything available in the West can be obtained somewhere. If you need something special, it may be the case that you have to look for it long and hard. If at all possible, try to bring with you from home all the personal hygiene products, health-related items, and gadgets you will need.

I'm looking for ...
Я ищу́ ... *(+ acc).* [YA iSHU]

I'd like ...
Я бы хоте́л *m*/хоте́ла *f* ... *(+ acc).* [YA BY khaTYEL/khaTYEla]

May I help you?
Я могу́ Вам помо́чь? [YA maGU VAM paMOCH]

Are you being helped?
Вас уже́ обслу́живают? [VAS uZHE apSLUzhyvayut]

Thank you, I'm just looking around.
Спаси́бо, я то́лько смотрю́. [spaSIba YA TOL'ka smaTRYU]

Do you have ...?
У Вас есть ...? [u-VAS YEST ...]

Can I get you anything else?
Что-нибудь ещё? [SHTO-nibut' yiSHO]

Making Purchases

In some stores, you have to pay at a separate cashier's counter (ка́сса [KAsa]). First, in the department where the item you want is displayed, ask what the price is, and then go to the cashier. After you tell the clerk the price and the department and pay for the item, you will be given a receipt. Go back to the department, present the receipt, and you will receive your purchase.

How much is it?
Ско́лько э́то сто́ит? [SKOL'ka Eta STOit]

That's expensive!
Но э́то же до́рого! [NO Eta zhe DOraga]

Is this on sale?
Вы даёте ски́дку? [VY daYOtye SKITku]

Fine, I'll take it.
Хорошо, я беру́. [kharaSHO YA biRU]

Do you take credit cards?
Вы принима́ете креди́тные ка́рточки?
[VY priniMAyitye kriDITnyye KARtachki]

Stores and Shops

Excuse me, where can I find ...?
Извини́те, где мо́жно найти́ ... *(+ acc)*?
[izviNItye GDYE MOZHna nayTI ...]

вре́мя рабо́ты – opening hours
откры́то .... **open**
закры́то, не рабо́тает .... **closed**
пра́здничные выходны́е до ... .. **on vacation until ...**

The terms given below in quotation marks can be seen on signs displayed outside stores or on directory signboards in larger department stores.

antiques shop	антиква́рный магази́н [antiKVARny magaZIN]
art dealer	магази́н худо́жественных изде́лий [magaZIN khuDOzhistvinykh izDYEli], «Иску́сство» [isKUstva]
bakery	бу́лочная [BUlachnaya], «Хлеб» [KHLYEP]
bookstore	кни́жный магази́н [KNIZHny magaZIN], «Кни́ги» [KNIgi]
boutique	сало́н мо́дных това́ров [salon MODnykh taVAraf]
butcher shop	мясна́я ла́вка [misNAya LAFka], «Мя́со» [MYAsa]
candy store	конди́терская [kanDItirskaya]
catering service	доста́вка проду́ктов на́ дом [daSTAFka praDUKtaf NA-dam]
dairy store	моло́чная [maLOCHnaya]
delicatessen	гастроно́м [gastraNOM]
department store	универма́г [univirMAK]
drugstore	галантере́я [galantiRYEya]

Pharmacies sell toiletries as well as pharmaceutical products.

dry cleaner's	химчи́стка [khimCHISTka]
electrical appliance store ..	магази́н электротова́ров [magaZIN eliktrataVAraf]
flea market	барахо́лка [baraKHOLka]
florist's	цвето́чный магази́н [tsviTOCHny magaZIN]
fruit and vegetable store ..	овощно́й магази́н [avashNOY magaZIN], «О́вощи и фру́кты» m pl [Ovashi i FRUKty]
grocery store	продово́льственный магази́н [pradaVOL'stviny magaZIN], «Проду́кты» m pl [praDUKty]
hairdresser's/barber's	парикма́херская [parikMAkhirskaya]
hardware store	магази́н строи́тельных това́ров [magaZIN straItil'nykh taVAraf]
health food store	магази́н диети́ческих проду́ктов [magaZIN diyiTIchiskikh praDUKtaf]
jeweler's	ювели́рный магази́н [yuviLIRny magaZIN]
laundromat	пра́чечная на самообслу́живание [PRAchichnaya na-samaapSLUzhyvaniye]
laundry	пра́чечная [PRAchichnaya]
leather goods store	магази́н кожгалантере́йных изде́лий [magaZIN kazhgalantiRYEYnykh izDYEli]
liquor store	виново́дочный магази́н [vinaVOdachny magaZIN]
market	ры́нок [RYnak]
music store	но́тный магази́н [NOTny magaZIN]; магази́н музыка́льных инструме́нтов [magaZIN muzyKAL'nykh instruMYENtaf]
newspaper stand	газе́тный кио́ск [gaZYETny kiOSK]
optician's	о́птика [OPtika]
pastry shop	конди́терская [kanDItirskaya]
perfume store	парфюме́рия [parfyuMYEriya]
pharmacy	апте́ка [apTYEka]
photo store	магази́н фототова́ров [magaZIN fatataVAraf]
sausage store	магази́н колба́сных изде́лий [magaZIN kalBASnykh izDYEli]
seafood store	ры́бный магази́н [RYBny magaZIN], «Ры́ба» [RYba]
second-hand store	комиссио́нный магази́н [kamisiOny magaZIN]
shoe store	обувно́й магази́н [abuvNOY magaZIN], «О́бувь» f [Obuf']

shoemaker's	сапо́жник [saPOZHnik], «Ремо́нт о́буви» [riMONT Obuvi]
souvenir shop	сувени́рный магази́н [suviNIRny magaZIN]
sporting goods store	магази́н спортова́ров [magaZIN sparttaVAraf]
stationery store	магази́н канцтова́ров [magaZIN kantstaVAraf]
supermarket	суперма́ркет [supirMARkit]
tailor/dressmaker	портно́й/портни́ха [partNOY/partNIkha], «Ателье́» [atiL'YE]
thrift store	утильсырьё [util'syR'YO]
tobacco store	таба́чный магази́н [taBACHny magaZIN]
toy store	магази́н игру́шек [magaZIN iGRUshyk], «Де́тский мир» [DYETski MIR]
travel agency	тураге́нтство [turaGYENTstva]
watchmaker's	часова́я мастерска́я [chasaVAya mastirSKAya]
wine merchant's	ви́нный магази́н [VIny magaZIN]

Books, Magazines, and Stationery

I'd like ...
Я бы хоте́л *m*/хоте́ла *f* ... *(+ acc)* [YA BY khaTYEL/khaTYEla ...]

an American newspaper.
америка́нскую газе́ту. [amiriKANskuyu gaZYEtu]

an English-language newspaper.
газе́ту на англи́йском языке́. [gaZYEtu na-anGLIskam yizyKYE]

a magazine.
журна́л. [zhurNAL]

a travel guide.
путеводи́тель *m*. [putivaDItil']

a hiking map of this area.
маршру́тную тури́стскую ка́рту э́того райо́на.
[marshRUTnuyu tuRISTskuyu KARtu Etava raYOna]

Books, Magazines, and Newspapers

book	кни́га [KNIga]
city map	план(-схе́ма) го́рода [PLAN(-SKHYEma) GOrada]
comic book	ко́микс *m* [KOmiks]
cookbook	пова́ренная кни́га [paVArinaya KNIga]
dictionary	слова́рь *m* [slaVAR']
illustrated magazine	иллюстри́рованный журна́л [ilyuSTRIravany zhurNAL]
magazine	журна́л [zhurNAL]

map	(географи́ческая) ка́рта [(giagraFIchiskaya) KARta]
mystery/detective novel	детекти́в [ditikTIF]
newspaper	газе́та [gaZYEta]
(daily) newspaper	(ежедне́вная) газе́та [(yizhyDNYEVnaya) gaZYEta]
novel	рома́н [raMAN]
road map	ка́рта автомоби́льных доро́г [KARta aftamaBIL'nykh daROK]
travel guide	путеводи́тель *m* [putivaDItil']
women's magazine	же́нский журна́л [ZHENski zhurNAL]

Stationery

ballpoint pen	(ша́риковая) ру́чка [SHArikavaya RUCHka]
block	блокно́т [blakNOT]
color pencil	цветно́й каранда́ш [TzvetNOY karanDASH]
coloring book	кни́жка-раскра́ска [KNIzhka-rasKRASka]
envelope	конве́рт [kanVYERT]
notebook	записна́я кни́жка [zapisNAya KNIzhka]
notepaper	почто́вая бума́га [pachTOvaya buMAga]
paper	бума́га [buMAga]
pencil	каранда́ш [karanDASH]
postcard	откры́тка [atKRYTka]
stationery	канцтова́ры *m pl* [kantstaVAry]

CDs and Cassettes

➤ also Electrical Goods and Concert

Do you have any CDs/cassettes by ...?
У Вас есть компакт-ди́ски/кассе́ты ... *(+ gen)*?
[u-VAS YEST kampak-DISki/kaSYEty ...]

I'd like a CD with ... music.
Я бы хоте́л *m*/хоте́ла *f* компакт-ди́ск с ... му́зыкой.
[YA BY khaTYEL/khaTYEla kampak-DISK s- ... MUzykay]

Could I listen to a little of this, please?
Мо́жно послу́шать? [MOZHna paSLUshat']

cassette	кассе́та [kaSYEta]
CD (compact disc)	компакт-ди́ск [kampak-DISK]
CD player (portable)	CD-пле́йер [si-di-PLYEyir]
DVD	DVD (дивиди́) [diviDI]
headphones	нау́шники [naUSHniki]

| speaker | громкоговори́тель *m* [gramkagavaRItil'] |
| Walkman | плéйер [PLYEyir] |

Toiletries

after-shave lotion	лосьóн для бритья́ [laS'YON dlia-briT'YA]
band-aid	плáстырь *m* [PLAstyr']
brush	щётка [SHOTka]
chapstick	гигиени́ческая помáда [gigiyiNIchiskaya paMAda]
comb	расчёска [rasCHOSka]
condom	презервати́в [prizirvaTIF]
contouring pencil	кóнтурный каранда́ш [KONturny karanDASH]
cotton balls	вáта [VAta]
cotton swabs	вáтные пáлочки *f pl* [VATnyye PAlachki]
cream	(космети́ческий) крем [(kasmiTIchiski) KRYEM]
dental floss	нить *f* для чи́стки зу́бов [NIT' dlia-CHISTki ZUbof]
deodorant	дезодорáнт [dizadaRANT]
detergent powder	стирáльный порошóк [stiRAL'ny paraSHOK]
dishcloth	кýхонное полотéнце [KUkhanaye palaTYENtse]
dishwashing brush	щётка для мытья́ посу́ды [SHOTka dlia-myT'YA paSUdy]
dishwashing liquid	срéдство для мытья́ посу́ды [SRYETstva dlia-myT'YA paSUdy]
elastic hair band	рези́нка для волóс [riZINka dlia-vaLOS]
hair gel	гель *m* для волóс [GYEL' dlia-vaLOS]
hairpins	закóлки *f pl* для волóс [zaKOLki dlia-vaLOS]
hairspray	лак для волóс [LAK dlia-vaLOS]
hand cream	крем для рýк [KRYEM dlia-RUK]
lipstick	губнáя помáда [gubNAya paMAda]
mascara	тушь *f* для ресни́ц [TUSH dlia-risNITS]
mirror	зéркало [ZYERkala]
moisturizing cream	увлажня́ющий крем [uvlazhNYAyushi KRYEM]
nail polish	лак для ногтéй [LAK dlia-nakTYEY]
nail polish remover	жи́дкость *f* для сня́тия лáка [ZHYTkast' dlia-SNYAtiya LAka]
nail scissors	нóжницы *f pl* для ногтéй [NOZHnitsy dlia-nakTYEY]

I'd like ...

154

night cream	ночной крем [nachNOY KRYEM]
panty liners	гигиени́ческие прокла́дки *f pl* [gigiyiNIchiskiye praKLATki]
paper tissues	бума́жные носовы́е платки́ *m pl* [buMAZHnyye nasaVYye platKI]
perfume	духи́ *m pl* [duKHI]
powder	пу́дра [PUdra]
razor, shaver	бри́твенный аппара́т [BRITviny apaRAT]
razor blades	ле́звия *n pl* [LYEZviya]
sanitary napkins	гигиени́ческие прокла́дки *f pl* [gigiyiNIchiskiye praKLATki]
shampoo	шампу́нь *m* [shamPUN']
shaving brush	помазо́к [pamaZOK]
shaving cream	пе́на для бритья́ [PYEna dlia-briT'YA]
shower gel	гель *m* для ду́ша [GYEL' dlia-DUsha]
soap	мы́ло [MYla]
sun cream	крем от со́лнца [KRYEM at-SONtsa]
sun protection factor	солнцезащи́тный фа́ктор [sontsyzaSHITny FAKtar]
suntan lotion	молочко́ от со́лнца [malachKO at-SONtsa]
suntan oil	ма́сло от со́лнца [MAsla at-SONtsa]
tampons	тампо́ны *m pl* [tamPOny]
mini/normal/super/ super plus	ми́ни/норма́льные/су́пер/ су́пер-плюс [MIni/narMAL'nyye/SUpir/SUpir-PLYUS]
tea-tree oil	ма́сло ча́йного де́рева [MASla CHAYnava DYEriva]
toilet paper	туале́тная бума́га [tuaLYETnaya buMAga]
toiletries	галантере́я [galantiRYEya]
toothbrush	зубна́я щётка [zubNAya SHOTka]
toothpaste	зубна́я па́ста [zubNAya PASta]
toothpicks	зубочи́стки *f pl* [zubaCHISTki]
tweezers	пинце́т [pinTSET]

Electrical Goods

> ➤ also Photo Supplies and CDs and Cassettes

adapter	ада́птер [aDAPtir]
alarm clock	буди́льник [buDIL'nik]
battery	батаре́йка [bataRYEYka]
battery charger	заря́дное устро́йство [zaRYADnaye uSTROYstva]
cable	ка́бель *m* [KAbil']
extension cord	удлини́тель *m* [udliNItil']

hairdryer	. . . .	фен [FYEN]
light bulb	. . . .	электри́ческая ла́мпочка [elikTRIchiskaya LAMpachka]
notebook	. . . .	тетра́дь [tyeTRAT']
organizer	. . . .	электро́нный секрета́рь [elikTROny sikriTAR'], орга́на́йзер [argaNAYzir]
plug	. . . .	штéпсель m [SHTYEPsil'], ви́лка [VILka]
pocket calculator	. . . .	(микро)калькуля́тор [(mikra)kal'kuLYAtar]
storage battery	. . . .	аккумуля́тор [akumuLYAtar]

Photo Supplies

> also Filming and Photographing

Film for slides is generally hard to find.

I'd like ...
Я бы хоте́л m/хоте́ла f ... (+ acc) [YA BY khaTYEL/khaTYEla ...]
  a roll of film for this camera.
  плёнку для э́того фотоаппара́та.
  [PLYONku dlia-Etava fataapaRAta]
  a roll of color film.
  цветну́ю плёнку. [tsvitNUyu PLYONku]
  a roll of film for slides.
  диафи́льм. [diaFIL'M]
  a roll of film with 36/24/12 exposures.
  плёнку на три́дцать шесть/на два́дцать четы́ре/на двена́дцать ка́дров. [PLYONku na-TRItsat' SHEST'/na-DVAtsat' chiTYrye/na-dviNAtsat' KAdraf]

The ... doesn't work.
... не рабо́тает. [... ni-raBOtayit]

This is broken. Can you repair/fix it?
Вот э́то слома́лось. Вы мо́жете э́то починить?
[VOT Eta slaMAlas'. VY MOzhytye Eta pachNIT']

black-and-white film	. . . . .	чёрно-бе́лая плёнка [CHORna-BYElaya PLYONka]
camcorder	. . . .	видеока́мера с магнитофо́ном [vidiaKAmira s-magnitaFOnam]
(writable) CD	. . . .	(запи́сываемый) компакт-ди́ск [(zaPIsyvayemy) kampak-DISK]
digital camera	. . . .	цифрово́й фотоаппара́т [tsyfraVOY fataapaRAT]

digital video camera	цифровáя видеокáмера [tsyfraVAya vidiaKAmira]
DVD	DVD (дивиди́) [diviDI]
film speed	светочувстви́тельность *f* [svitachufSTVItil'nast]
flash	вспы́шка [FSPYSHka]
instant camera	поларóид [palaROit]
lens	ли́нза [LINza]
light meter	экспонóметр [ekspaNOmitr]
objective	объекти́в [abyikTIF]
self-timer, delayed action shutter release	автоспýск [aftaSPUSK]
shutter	спуск [SPUSK]
storage battery	аккумуля́тор [akumuLYAtar]
storage card	кáрта пáмяти [KARta PAMyiti]
telephoto lens	телеобъекти́в [tiliabyikTIF]
tripod	штати́в [SHTAtif]
underwater camera	фотоаппарáт для подвóдных съёмок [fataapaRAT dlia-padVODnykh SYOmak]
video camera	видеокáмера [vidiaKAmira]
video cassette	видеокассéта [vidiakaSYEta]
video film	ви́део [VIdia], видеофи́льм [vidiaFIL'M]
video recorder	видеомагнитофóн [vidiamagnitaFON]

Hairdresser/Barber

Shampoo and blow-dry, please.
Мне, пожáлуйста, помы́ть и посуши́ть гóлову.
[MNYE paZHAlusta paMYT' i pasuSHYT' GOlavu]

Wash-and-cut/Dry-cut, please.
Меня́ подстриги́те с мытьём/без мытья́, пожáлуйста.
[miNYA patstriGItye s-myT'YOM/biz-myTYA paZHAlusta]

I'd like ...
Я бы хотéл *m*/хотéла *f* ... (+ acc) [YA BY khaTYEL/khaTYEla ...]

Just trim the ends.
Мне тóлько кóнчики волóс подстри́чь.
[MNYE TOL'ka KONchiki vaLOS patSTRICH]

Not too short/Really short/A bit shorter, please.
Не óчень кóротко/Óчень кóротко/Покорóче, пожáлуйста.
[ni-Ochin' KOratka/Ochin' KOratka/pakaROchi paZHAlusta]

I'd like a shave, please.
Побрéйте меня́, пожáлуйста. [paBRYEYtye miNYA paZHAlusta]

157

Would you please trim my mustache/beard?
Подстриги́те, пожа́луйста, усы́./бо́роду.
[patstriGItye paZHAlusta uSY/BOradu]

Thank you very much. Everything's fine.
Спаси́бо большо́е. Всё о́чень хорошо́.
[spaSIba bal'SHOye. FSYO Ochin' kharaSHO]

bangs	чёлка [CHOLka]
beard	борода́ [baraDA]
blond	белоку́рый [bilaKUry]
to blow dry	суши́ть/вы́сушить фе́ном [suSHYT'/VYsushyt' FYEnam]
to comb	причёсывать/причеса́ть [priCHOsyvat'/prichiSAT']
curlers, rollers	бигуди́ f pl [biguDI]
curls	ку́дри f pl [KUdri]
dandruff	пе́рхоть f [PYERkhat']
to dye	кра́сить/покра́сить [KRAsit'/paKRAsit']
hair	во́лосы m pl [VOlasy]
dry hair	сухи́е во́лосы m pl [suKHIye VOlasy]
oily hair	жи́рные во́лосы m pl [ZHYRnyye VOlasy]
hairpiece	накла́дка [naKLATka]
hairstyle, hairdo	причёска [priCHOska]
highlights	мели́рование [miLIravaniye]
layered cut	ступе́нчатая причёска [stuPYENchataya priCHOska]
mustache	усы́ m pl [uSY]
part	пробо́р [praBOR]
perm(anent)	химзави́вка [khimzaVIFka]
to put in a rinse	подкра́шивать/подкра́сить [patKRAshyvat'/patKRAsit']
to set	укла́дывать/уложи́ть [uKLAdyvat'/ulaZHYT']
shampoo	шампу́нь m [shamPUN']
to style (hair)	де́лать/сде́лать причёску [DYElat'/ZDYElat' priCHOsku]
wig	пари́к [paRIK]

Household Goods

aluminum foil	(алюми́ниевая) фольга́ [(alyuMIniyivaya) fal'GA]
bottle opener	открыва́лка [atkryVALka]
can opener	консервооткрыва́тель m [kansirvaatkryVAtil']
candles	све́чи f pl [SVYEchi]

158

charcoal	у́голь *m* для гри́ля [Ugal' dlia-GRIlya]
clothes line	бельева́я верёвка [bilyiVAya viRYOFka]
clothespins	прище́пки *f pl* [priSHEPki]
cooler bag	су́мка-холоди́льник [SUMka-khalaDIL'nik]
corkscrew	што́пор [SHTOpar]
denatured alcohol	денатури́рованный спирт [dinatuRIravany SPIRT]
disposable cup	одноразовый стака́н [adnaRAzavy staKAN]
fork	ви́лка [VILka]
freezer pack	аккумуля́тор хо́лода [akumuLYAtar KHOlada]
garbage bag	му́сорный мешо́к [MUsarny miSHOK]
glass	стака́н [staKAN]
household goods	хозтова́ры *m pl* [khastaVAry]
immersion heater	кипяти́льник [kipiyTIL'nik]
kerosene	кероси́н [kiraSIN]
knife	нож [NOSH]
needle	игла́ [igLA]
paper napkins	бума́жные салфе́тки *f pl* [buMAZHnyye salFYETki]
plastic bag	мешо́к [miSHOK], паке́т [paKYET]
plastic wrap	прозра́чная фольга́ [praZRACHnaya fal'GA]
pocket knife	перочи́нный но́жик [piraCHIny NOzhik]
safety pin	(безопа́сная) була́вка [(bizaPASnaya) buLAFka]
scissors	но́жницы *f pl* [NOZHnitsy]
spoon	ло́жка [LOSHka]
string	верёвка [viRYOFka]
thermos flask/bottle	те́рмос [TYERmas]
wire	про́волока [PROvalaka]

Groceries

What can I do for you?
Что Вам уго́дно? [SHTO VAM uGODna],
Что Вы жела́ете? [SHTO VY zhyLAyitye]

I'd like ..., please.
Да́йте мне ..., пожа́луйста. [DAYtye MNYE ... paZHAlusta]

  a kilo of ...
  килогра́мм ... *(+ gen)* [kiloGRAM ...]

  a piece of ...
  кусо́к ... *(+ gen)* [kuSOK ...]

a package of ...
па́чку ... *(+ gen)* [PACHku ...]

a jar of ...
ба́нку ... *(+ gen)* [BANku ...]

a can of ...
ба́нку ... *(+ gen)* [BANku ...]

a bottle of ...
буты́лку ... *(+ gen)* [buTYLku ...]

a bag.
мешо́к. [miSHOK]

Could you slice it, please?
Пожа́луйста, поре́жьте на ло́мтики.
[paZHAlusta paRYESHtye na-LOMtiki]

Is it all right if it's a little more?
Мо́жет быть Вам побо́льше? [MOzhyt BYT' VAM paBOL'shy]

Will there be anything else?
Что-нибудь ещё? [SHTO-nibut' yiSHO]

Could I try some of that, please?
Мо́жно попро́бовать? [MOZHna paPRObavat']

No, thanks. That'll be all.
Спаси́бо, э́то всё. [spaSIba Eta FSYO]

Fruits and Nuts

almonds	минда́ль *m* [minDAL']
apples	я́блоки *n pl* [YАblaki]
apricots	абрико́сы *m pl* [abriKOsy]
bananas	бана́ны *m pl* [baNAny]
bird cherries	черему́хи *f pl* [chiriMUkhi]
blackberries	ежеви́ки *f pl* [yizhyVIki]
blueberries	голуби́ки *f pl* [galuBIki]
cherries	чере́шни *f pl* [chiRYESHni]
coconut	коко́с [kaKOS]
cranberries	клю́квы *f pl* [KLYUKvy]
currants	сморо́дины *f pl* [smaROdiny]
figs	инжи́ры *m pl* [inZHYry]
fruit	фру́кты *m pl* [FRUKty]
grapefruit	гре́йпфрут [GRYEYPfrut]
grapes	виногра́д [vinaGRAT]
lemons	лимо́ны *m pl* [liMOny]
melon *(honeydew/cantaloupe)*	ды́ня [DYnya]
(watermelon)	арбу́з [arBUS]
nuts	оре́хи *m pl* [aRYEkhi]
oranges	апельси́ны *m pl* [apil'SIny]
peaches	пе́рсики *m pl* [PYERsiki]
pears	гру́ши *f pl* [GRUshy]

pineapple	ананас [anaNAS]
plums	сливы f pl [SLIvy]
strawberries	земляники f pl [[zimlyiNIki]
tangerines	мандарины m pl [mandaRIny]
whortleberries	черники f pl [chirniKI]

Vegetables

artichokes	артишоки m pl [artiSHOki]
asparagus	спаржа [SPARzha]
avocado	авокадо [avaKAda]
beans	фасоль m [faSOL']
green beans	стручковый фасоль [STRUCHkavy faSOL']
white beans	бобы m pl [baBY]
cabbage	капуста [kaPUsta]
carrots	морковь f [marKOF']
cauliflower	цветная капуста [tsvitNAya kaPUsta]
celery	сельдерей [sil'diRYEY]
chickpeas, garbanzos	нут [NUT]
chicory	цикорий [tsyKOri]
corn	кукуруза [kukuRUza]
cucumber	огурец [aguRYETS]
dill	укроп [uKROP]
eggplants	баклажаны m pl [baklaZHAny]
fennel	фенхель m [FYENkhil']
garlic	чеснок [chiSNOK]
green onions	зелёный лук [ziLYOny LUK]
head of lettuce	кочанный салат [koCHAny saLAT]
leek	лук-порей [luk-paRYEY]
lentils	чечевица [chichiVItsa]
lettuce	салат [saLAT]
mushrooms	грибы m pl [griBY]
olives	маслины f pl [maSLIny]
onions	лук (репчатый) [LUK (ripCHAty)]
parsley	петрушка [piTRUSHka]
peas	горох [gaROKH]
pepper	перец [PYErits]
potatoes	картофель m [karTOfil']
pumpkin, squash	тыква [TYKva]
radishes	редиска [riDISka]
ramson	черемша [chirimSHA]
red beets	свёкла n pl [SVYOkla]
spinach	шпинат [shpiNAT]
tomatoes	помидоры m pl [pamiDOry]
turnip	репа [RYEpa]
vegetables	овощи m pl [Ovashi]

Bakery Products and Confectionery

baked goods	печéнье [piCHEn'ye]
bar of chocolate	шокола́дка [shakaLATka]
bread	хлеб [KHLYEP]
black bread	чёрный хлеб [CHORny KHLYEP]
rye bread	ржано́й хлеб [rzhaNOY KHLYEP]
white bread	бéлый хлеб [BYEly KHLYEP]
(fancy) cake, pastry	пиро́жное [piROZHnaye]
candy bar	шокола́дная пли́тка [shakaLADnaya PLITka]
candy, bon bons	конфéты m pl [kanFYEty]
chewing gum	жва́чка [ZHVACHka]
chocolate	шокола́д [shakaLAT]
cookies	(бискви́тное) печéнье [(biSKVITnaye) piCHEn'ye]
honey	мёд [MYOT]
ice cream	моро́женое [maROzhinaya]
jam	варéнье [vaRYEn'ye], джем [DZHEM]
muesli	мю́сли n sing u. pl [MYUsli]
pie, cake	пиро́г [piROK]; кекс [KYEKS]
roll, bun	бу́лочка [BUlachka]
rolled oats	овся́ные хло́пья [afSYAnyye KHLOp'ya]
sandwich	бутербро́д [butirBROT]
sweets	сла́дости f pl [SLAdasti]

Eggs and Dairy Products

butter	ма́сло [MAsla]
buttermilk	па́хта [PAKHta]
cheese	сыр [SYR]
hard cheese	твёрдый сыр [TVYORdy SYR]
soft cheese	мя́гкий сыр [MYAKHki SYR]
cottage cheese	творо́г [tvaROK]
cream	сли́вки f pl [SLIFki]
eggs	я́йца n pl [YAYtsa]
kefir (kind of yogurt)	кефи́р [kiFIR]
milk	молоко́ [malaKO]
low-fat milk	обезжи́ренное молоко́ [abiZHYrinnaye malaKO]
sour cream	смета́на [smiTAna]
yogurt	йо́гурт [YOgurt]

Meat and Sausages

bacon	шпик [SHPIK], са́ло [SAla]
beef	говя́дина [gaVYAdina]
chicken	ку́рица [KUritsa]
chop, cutlet	отбивна́я котлéта [adbivNAya katLYEta]

cold cuts	ассортú *n sing u. pl* [asarTI]
finely ground pork sausage	сарде́лька [sarDYEL'ka]
frankfurters, hot dogs	сосúски *f pl* [saSIski]
ground meat	(мясно́й) фарш [misNOY FARSH]
ham	ветчина́ [vichiNA], о́корок [Okarak]
boiled ham	варёный о́корок [vaRYOny Okarak]
cured ham	сырокопчёная ветчина́ [syrakapCHOnaya vichiNA]
jerky	вя́леное мя́со [VYAlinaye MYAsa]
lamb	бара́нина [baRAnina]
liver paté	печёночный паште́т [piCHOnachny paSHTYET]
meat	мя́со [MYAsa]
mutton	бара́нина [baRAnina]
pork	свинúна [sviNIna]
rabbit	кро́лик [KROlik]
salami	саля́ми *f pl* [saLYAmi]
sausage	колбаса́ [kalbaSA]
stew, goulash	гуля́ш [guLYASH]
veal	теля́тина [tiLYAtina]

Fish and Seafood

caviar (red/black)	икра́ (кра́сная/чёрная) [iKRA (KRASnaya/CHORnaya)]
crabs	кра́бы *m pl* [KRAby]
crayfish	рак [RAK]
eel	у́горь *m* [Ugar']
fish	ры́ба [RYba]
herring	сельдь *f* [SYEL'T'], селёдка [siLYOTka]
lobster	ома́р [aMAR]
mackerel	ску́мбрия [SKUMbriya]
mussels	раку́шки *f pl* [raKUSHki]
oysters	у́стрицы *f pl* [Ustritsy]
perch	о́кунь *m* [Okun']
pike	щу́ка [SHUka]
salmon	лосо́сь *m* [laSOS']
shrimp	креве́тки *f pl* [kriVYETki]
smoked cod	копчёная треска́ [kapCHOnaya triSKA]
sole	морско́й язы́к [marSKOY yiZYK]
sturgeon	осётр [aSYOTR]
trout	форе́ль *f* [faRYEL']
tuna	туне́ц [tuNYETS]
Venus mussels	мúдии *f pl* [MIdii]

Miscellaneous

bouillon cube	бульо́нный ку́бик [buLYOny KUbik]
butter	ма́сло [MAsla]

cereal grains	крупá [kruPA]
chestnuts	каштáны *m pl* [kashTAny]
flour	мукá [muKA]
margarine	маргарúн [margaRIN]
mayonnaise	майонéз [mayaNYES]
mustard	горчúца [garCHItsa]
noodles	лапшá [lapSHA]
olive oil	олúвковое мáсло [aLIFkavaye MAsla]
rice	рис [RIS]
salt	соль *f* [SOL']
sugar	сáхар [SAkhar]
vegetable oil	растúтельное мáсло [raSTItil'naye MAsla]
vinegar	ýксус [UKsus]

Beverages

apple juice	яблочный сок [YAblachny SOK]
beer	пúво [PIva]
non-alcoholic beer	безалкогóльное пúво [bisalkaGOL'naye PIva]
champagne	шампáнское [shamPANskaye]
coffee	кóфе *m* [KOfye]
decaffeinated coffee	декофéйновый кóфе [dikafiInavy KOfye], кóфе *m* без кофéина [KOfye bis-kafiIna]
mineral water	минерáльная водá [miniRAL'naya vaDA]
carbonated	газирóванная [gaziROvanaya]
non-carbonated	не газирóванная [ni-gaziROvanaya]
orange juice	апельсúновый сок [apil'SInavy SOK]
soda pop	лимонáд [limaNAT]
tea	чай [CHAY]
black tea	чай [CHAY]
chamomile tea	ромáшковый чай [raMASHkavy CHAY]
fruit tea	фруктóвый чай [frukTOvy CHAY]
green tea	зелёный чай [ziLYOny CHAY]
peppermint tea	мя́тный чай [MYATny CHAY]
rose hip tea	чай из шипóвника [CHAY ish-shyPOVnika]
tea bags	чай в пакéтиках [CHAY f-paKYETikakh]
wine	винó [viNO]
red wine	крáсное винó [KRASnaye viNO]
rosé, blush	рóзовое винó [ROzavaye viNO]
white wine	бéлое винó [BYElaye viNO]

Fashion

> ➢ also Colors

Clothing

Can you show me ..., please?
Вы не покáжете мне ...? [VY ni-paKAzhytye MNYE ...]

Can I try it on?
Мóжно примéрить? [MOZHna priMYErit']

What size do you take?
Какóй у Вас размéр? [kaKOY u-VAS razMYER]

It's too ...
Это слúшком ... для меня. [Eta SLISHkam ... dlia-miNYA]

tight./big, baggy.
тéсно. [TYESna]/широкó. [shiraKO]

short./long.
кóротко. [KOratka]/длúнно. [DLIna]

small./large.
мáло. [MAla]/великó. [viliKO]

It's a good fit. I'll take it.
Это сидúт хорошó. Я это возьмý.
[Eta siDIT kharaSHO. YA Eta vaZ'MU]

It's not quite what I'm looking for.
Это не то, что я хочý. [Eta ni-TO SHTO YA khaCHU]

bathing cap	купáльная шáпочка [kuPAL'naya SHApachka]
bathing suit	купáльник [kuPAL'nik]
bathing trunks	плáвки f pl [PLAFki]
beachrobe	купáльный халáт [kuPAL'ny khaLAT]
bikini	бикúни n [biKIni]
blazer	блéйзер [BLYEYzir]
blouse	блýзка [BLUSka]
bodysuit	бóди m [BOdi]
bow tie	бáбочка [BAbachka]
bra	бюстгáльтер [byuzdGAL'tir]
cap	шáпка [SHAPka]
cardigan	вязаная кóфта [VYAzanaya KOFta]
clothing	одéжда [aDYEZHda]
(over) coat	пальтó [pal'TO]
cotton	хлóпок [KHLOpak]
dress	плáтье [PLAt'ye]
gloves	перчáтки f pl [pirCHATki]
hat	шляпа [SHLYApa]
sunhat	шляпа от сóлнца [SHLYApa at-SONtsa]
jacket	кýртка [KURTka]

jeans	джи́нсы *m pl* [DZHYNsy]
leggings	ле́ггинсы *m pl* [LYEginsy]
linen	лён [LYON]
muffler	шарф [SHARF]
panties	тру́сики *m pl* [TRUsiki]
pants	брю́ки *f pl* [BRYUki]
pantyhose	колго́тки *f pl* [kalGOTki]
parka	штормо́вка [shtarMOFka]
raincoat	непромока́емый плащ [nipramaKAyimy PLASH]
scarf	шарф [SHARF]
shirt	руба́шка [ruBASHka]
shorts	шо́рты *m pl* [SHORty]
silk	шёлк [SHOLK]
skipants	лы́жные брю́ки *f pl* [LYZHnyye BRYUki]
skirt	ю́бка [YUPka]
sleeve	рука́в [ruKAF]
socks	носки́ *m pl* [naSKI]
stockings	чулки́ *m pl* [chulKI]
suit *(man's)*	костю́м [kaSTYUM]
suit *(woman's)*	костю́м [kaSYTUM]
sweater, pullover	сви́тер [SVItir], пуло́вер [puLOvir]
sweatpants	спорти́вные брю́ки [sparTIVnyye BRYUki]
sweatsuit	спорти́вный костю́м [sparTIVny kaSTYUM]
tie	га́лстук [GALstuk]
T-shirt	футбо́лка [fudBOLka]
umbrella	зо́нт(ик) [ZONT(ik)]
underpants	трусы́ *m pl* [TRUsy]
undershirt	ни́жняя соро́чка [NIZHniya saROCHka]
underwear	ни́жнее бельё [NIZHniye biL'YO]
vest, waistcoat	жиле́т [zhiLYET]
wool	шерсть *f* [SHERST']

Cleaning

I'd like to have these things cleaned/laundered, please.
Хочу́ сдать э́ти ве́щи в чи́стку./в сти́рку.
[khaCHU ZDAT' Eti VYEshi f-CHISTku/f-STIRku]

When will they be ready?
Когда́ бу́дут гото́вы? [kagDA BUdut gaTOvy]

laundry	сти́рка [STIRka]
to dry clean	отдава́ть/отда́ть в химчи́стку [addaVAT'/adDAT' f-khimCHISTku]
to iron	гла́дить/вы́гладить [GLAdit'/VYgladit']

Optician

Would you please fix these glasses for me?
Не могли́ бы Вы почини́ть э́ти очки́?
[ni-maGLI BY VY pachiNIT' Eti achKI]

I'm near-sighted./far-sighted.
У меня́ близору́кость./дальнозо́ркость.
[u-miNYA blizaRUkast'/dal'naZORkast']

What's your eye prescription?
Како́й у Вас дио́птрий? [kaKOY u-VAS diOPtri]

... in the right eye, ... in the left eye
пра́вый глаз ..., ле́вый глаз ... [PRAvy GLAS ..., LYEvy GLAS ...]

When can I pick up my glasses?
Когда́ мо́жно бу́дет забра́ть очки́?
[kagDA MOZHna BUdit zaBRAT' achKI]

I'd like ...
Я бы хоте́л m/хоте́ла f ... (+ acc) [YA BY khaTYEL/khaTYEla ...]

  some storage solution
  жи́дкость для хране́ния [ZHYTkast' dlia-khraNYEniya]

  some cleaning solution
  жи́дкость для очи́стки [ZHYTkast'dlia-aCHISTki]

  for hard/soft contact lenses.
  для твёрдых/для мя́гких конта́ктных линз.
  [dlia-TVYORdykh/dlia-MYAKHkikh kanTAKTnykh LINS]

  some sunglasses.
  солнцезащи́тные очки́. [sontsyzaSHITnyye achKI]

  binoculars.
  бино́кль. [biNOKL']

Shoes and Leather Goods

I'd like a pair of ...
Мне, пожа́луйста, па́ру ... [MNYE paZHAlusta PAru ...]

I take a size ...
Мой разме́р ... [MOY razMYER ...]

They're too tight./too big.
Они́ сли́шком те́сные./сли́шком больши́е.
[aNI SLISHkam TYESnyye/SLISHkam bal'SHYye]

backpack	рюкза́к	[ryukZAK]
bag	су́мка	[SUMka]
belt	по́яс	[POyis]
boots	сапоги́ m pl	[sapaGI]
flip-flops	рези́новые та́почки f pl	[riZInavyye TApachki]
fur coat	шу́ба	[SHUba]

heel	каблу́к [kaBLUK]
leather coat	ко́жаное пальто́ [KOzhanaye pal'TO]
leather jacket	ко́жаная ку́ртка [KOzhanaya KURTka]
leather pants	ко́жаные брю́ки *f pl*
	[KOzhanyye BRYUki]
purse	(да́мская) су́мочка
	[(DAMskaya) SUmachka]
rubber boots	рези́новые сапоги́ *m pl*
	[riZInavyye sapaGI]
sandals	санда́лии *f pl* [sanDAlii]
shoe	о́бувь *f* [Obuf']
shoe brush	сапо́жная щётка
	[saPOZHnaya SHOTka]
shoe polish	крем для о́буви [KRYEM dlia-Obuvi]
shoelaces	шнурки́ *m pl* (для о́буви)
	[SHNURki (dlia-Obuvi)]
shoulder bag	су́мка через плечо́
	[SUMka chiris-pliCHO]
ski boots	лы́жные боти́нки *m pl*
	[LYZHnyye baTINki]
sneakers	гимнасти́ческие ту́фли *f pl*
	[gimnaSTIchiskiye TUfli]
sole	подмётка [padMYOTka]
suitcase	чемода́н [chimaDAN]
travel bag	доро́жная су́мка [daROZHnaya SUMka]

Souvenirs

I'd like ...
Я бы хоте́л *m*/хоте́ла *f* ... *(+ acc)* [YA BY khaTYEL/khaTYEla ...]

a nice souvenir.
краси́вый сувени́р. [kraSIvy suviNIR]

something typical of this area.
что-нибудь характе́рное для э́тих мест.
[SHTO-nibut' kharakTYERnaye dlia-Etikh MYEST]

How much do you want to spend?
На каку́ю су́мму Вы рассчи́тываете?
[na-kaKUyu SUmu VY raSHCHItyvayitye]

I'd like something that's not too expensive.
Хочу́ что-нибудь не сли́шком дорого́е.
[khaCHU SHTO-nibut' ni-SLISHkam daraGOye]

That's really pretty.
Вот э́то краси́во. [VOT Eta kraSIva]

Thanks, but I didn't find the right thing.
Спаси́бо, но я ничего́ подходя́щего не нашёл. *m*/не нашла́. *f*
[spaSIba NO YA nichiVO patkhaDYAshivo ni-naSHOL/ni-naSHLA]

amber	янта́рь *m* [yinTAR']
artificial	иску́сственный [isKUstviny], синтети́ческий [sintiTIchiski]
ceramics	кера́мика [kiRAmika]
crystal	хруста́ль *m* [khruSTAL']
decoration, ornamentation	украше́ние [ukraSHEniye]
embroidery	вы́шивка [VYshyfka]
genuine	настоя́щий [nastaYAshi]
gift	пода́рок [paDArak]
Gzhel porcelain	гжель *f* [GZHEL']
handmade	ручна́я рабо́та [ruchNAya raBOta]
lapis lazuli	лазури́т [lazuRIT]
malachite	малахи́т [malaKHIT]
matryoshka	матрёшка [maTRYOSHka]
mother of pearl	перламу́тр [pirlaMUTR]
music box	музыка́льная шкату́лка [muzyKAL'naya shkaTULka]
national costume	национа́льный костю́м [natsyaNAL'ny kaSTYUM]
porcelain	фарфо́р [farFOR]
pottery	гонча́рные изде́лия [ganCHARnyye izDYEliya]
regional product	ме́стное изде́лие [MYESnaye izDYEliye]
rock crystal	го́рный хруста́ль [GORny khruSTAL']
samovar	самова́р [samaVAR]
tacky	безвку́сный [bizFKUSny]
traditional folk art store	магази́н наро́дных изде́лий [magaZIN naRODnykh izDYEli]
turquoise	бирюза́ [biryuZA]
wood carving	резьба́ [riz'BA]

Tobacco

A pack/A carton of...
Па́чку/Блок ... *(+ gen)* [PACHku/BLOK ...]
filter-tipped/without filter, please.
с фи́льтром/без фи́льтра, пожа́луйста!
[s-FIL'tram/bis-FIL'tra paZHAlusta]

Ten cigars/cigarillos, please.
Де́сять сига́р/сига́рок, пожа́луйста.
[DYEsit' siGAR/siGArak paZHAlusta]

A pack/A tin of cigarette/pipe tobacco, please.
Одну́ па́чку/Одну́ ба́нку сигаре́тного/тру́бочного табака́,
пожа́луйста. [adNU PACHku/adNU BANku
sigaRYETnava/TRUbachnava tabaKA paZHAlusta]

Some Russian smokers are fond of папиросы [papiROsy]: Half of each cigarette consists of strong black tobacco, while the other half is a long cardboard tube that serves as a mouthpiece. The best-known brand is "Беломорканал" [bilamarkaNAL].

ashtray	пепельница [PYEpil'nitsa]
cigar	сигара [siGAra]
cigarette	сигарета [sigaRYEta]
cigarillo	сигарка [siGARka]
lighter	зажигалка [zazhyGALka]
matches	спички f pl [SPICHki]
pipe	трубка [TRUPka]

Jewelry

bracelet	браслет [braSLYET]
brooch	брошка [BROSHka]
costume jewelry	бижутерия [bizhuTYEriya]
diamond	алмаз [alMAS]
earrings	серьги f pl [SYER'gi]
emerald	изумруд [izumRUT]
gold	золото [ZOlata]
gold-plated	позолоченный [pazaLOchiny]
jewelry	драгоценности [dragoTSYEnosti]
necklace	цепочка [tsyPOCHka]
pearl	жемчуг [ZHEMchuk]
pearl necklace	бусы f pl [BUsy]
pendant	кулон [kuLON]
ring	кольцо [kal'TSO]
silver	серебро [siriBRO]
silver-plated	посеребрённый [pasiriBRYOny]
tiepin	булавка для галстука [buLAFka dlia-GALstuka]
travel alarm	дорожный будильник [daROZHny buDIL'nik]
wristwatch	наручные часы m pl [naRUCHnyye chiSY]
ladies'/men's	дамские/мужские [DAMskiye/mushSKIye]
mechanical	механические [mikhaNIchiskiye]
waterproof	водонепроницаемые [vadanipraniTSAyimyye]

АПТЕКА

Health

At the Pharmacy

Can you give me something for ..., please?
Не могли бы Вы мне дать средство от ... *(+ gen)*?
[ni-maGLI BY VY MNYE DAT' SRYETstva at- ...]

aspirin . . . . аспирин [aspiRIN]

band-aid . . . . пластырь *m* [PLAstyr']

burn ointment . . . . мазь *f* от ожогов [MAS' at-aZHOgaf]

cardiac stimulant . . . . сердечно-сосудистое средство
[sirDYECHna-saSUdistaye SRYETstva]

condom . . . . презерватив [prizirvaTIF]

cotton balls, cotton-wool . . вата [VAta]

cough syrup . . . . микстура от кашля
[mikSTUra at-KASHlya]

disinfectant . . . . дезинфицирующее средство
[dizinfiTSYruyushiye SRYETstva]

drops . . . . капли *f pl* [KApli]

ear drops . . . . капли *f pl* в уши [KApli v-Ushy]

elastic bandage . . . . эластичный бинт [elaSTICHny BINT]

eye drops . . . . глазные капли *f pl* [glazNYye KApli]

gauze bandage . . . . (марлевый) бинт [(MARlivy) BINT]

headache tablets . . . . таблетки *f pl* от головной боли
[taBLYETki ad-galaVNOY BOli]

insect repellent . . . . средство от укусов
[SRYETstva at-uKUsaf]

insulin . . . . инсулин [insuLIN]

iodine (tincture of) . . . . . . настойка йода [naSTOYka YOda]

laxative . . . . слабительное средство
[slaBItil'naye SRYETstva]

medicine . . . . лекарство [liKARstva]

ointment . . . . мазь *f* [MAS']

painkillers . . . . болеутоляющие таблетки *f pl*
[baleutoLYAyushiye taBLYETki]

pill, tablet . . . . таблетка [taBLYETka]

powder . . . . пудра [PUdra]

prescription . . . . рецепт [riTSEPT]

remedy . . . . средство [SRYETstva]

sleeping pills . . . . снотворное (в таблетках)
[snaTVORnaye (f-taBLYETkakh)]

sunburn ointment . . . . . . мазь *f* от солнечных ожогов
[MAS' at-SOLnichnykh aZHOgaf]

suppository . . . . свечка [SVYECHka]

thermometer . . . . градусник [GRAdusnik]

throat lozenges . . . . таблетки *f pl* от боли в горле
[taBLYETki ad-BOli v-GORlye]

tincture of chamomile	насто́йка рома́шки
	[naSTOYka raMASHki]
tranquilizer, sedative	успока́ивающее сре́дство
	[uspaKAivayushiye SRYETstva]
vitamin pills	витами́н в табле́тках
	[vitamin f-taBLYETkakh]

Package Circular

соста́в	**Composition**
спо́собы примене́ния	Directions
противопоказа́ния	**Contraindications**
побо́чные де́йствия	Side effects
взаимоде́йствия	Drug interations
дозиро́вка	**Dosage:**
оди́н раз/не́сколько раз в	Take … once/several times a day
день принима́ть …	
одну́ табле́тку	1 pill
два́дцать ка́пель	20 drops
одну́ ме́рную кру́жку	1 dosage cup
до еды́, перед едо́й	Before meals
по́сле еды́	After meals
на пусто́й желу́док	On an empty stomach
запи́ть водо́й не разжёвывая	Take with water and swallow whole
раствори́ть в воде́	Dissolve in water
раста́ять во рту	Let dissolve in your mouth
нару́жный	External use
нанести́ то́нким сло́ем на	Apply thin layer to skin and rub in
ко́жу и втира́ть	
грудны́е де́ти	Infants
де́ти (до … лет)	Children (up to age of …)
взро́слые	Adults
Держа́ть в недосту́пном для	Keep away from children!
дете́й ме́сте!	

At the Doctor's

Could you recommend a/an …?

Вы не могли́ бы мне порекомендова́ть … *(+ acc)*?
[VY ni-maGLI BY MNYE parikamindaVAT' …]

doctor
врача́ [vraCHA]

optometrist
окули́ста [akuLIsta]

gynecologist
гинеко́лога [giniKOlaga]

173

ear, nose, and throat specialist
ло́ра [LOra], оториноларинго́лога [atarinalarinGOlaga]
dermatologist
дермато́лога [dirmaTOlaga]
pediatrician
де́тского врача́ [DYETskava vraCHA]
urologist
уро́лога [uROlaga]
dentist
зубно́го врача́ [zubNOva vraCHA]

Where's his/her office?
Где он/она́ принима́ет? [GDYE ON/ONA priniMAyit]

Medical Complaints

What's the trouble?
На что Вы жа́луетесь? [na-SHTO ZHAluyitis'],
Что беспоко́ит? [SHTO bispaKOit]

I'm running a temperature.
У меня́ жар. [u-miNYA ZHAR]

I often feel nauseous.
Ме́ня ча́сто тошни́т. [miNYA CHASta tashNIT]

I often feel dizzy.
У меня́ ча́сто кру́жится голова́.
[u-miNYA CHASta KRUzhytsa galaVA]

I have a bad cold.
Я си́льно простуди́лся. m/простуди́лась. f
[YA SIL'na prastuDILsa/prastuDIlas']

I have a headache./a sore throat.
У меня́ боли́т голова́./го́рло. [u-miNYA baLIT galaVA/GORla]

I have a cough.
У меня́ ка́шель. [u-miNYA KAshil']

I've been stung (or bitten) by a/an ...
Меня́ укуси́л m/укуси́ла f ... [miNYA ukuSIL/ukuSIla ...]

I have an upset stomach.
У меня́ разболе́лся желу́док. [u-miNYA razbaLYELsa zhyLUdak]

I have diarrhea./constipation.
У меня́ поно́с/запо́р. [u-miNYA paNOS/zaPOR]

The food here doesn't agree with me.
Я не переношу́ здесь еду́. [YA ni-pirinaSHU ZDYES' yiDU]

I've hurt myself.
Я пора́нился. m/пора́нилась. f [YA paRAnilsa/paRAnilas']

I fell down.
Я упа́л. m/упа́ла. f [YA uPAL/uPAla]

Can you give/prescribe me something for ...?
Не могли́ бы Вы мне дать/прописа́ть что-нибудь от … *(+ gen)*? [ni-maGLI BY VY MNYE DAT'/prapiSAT' SHTO-nibut' at- ...]

I usually take ...
Обы́чно я принима́ю … *(+ acc)*. [aBYCHna YA priniMAyu ...]

I have high/low blood pressure.
У меня́ повы́шенное/пони́женное давле́ние. [u-miNYA paVYshynaye/paNIzhynaye daVLYEniye]

I'm a diabetic.
Я диабе́тик [YA diaBYEtik]

I'm pregnant.
Я бере́менна. [YA biRYEmina]

I had ... recently.
Неда́вно у меня́ был *m*/была́ *f*/бы́ло *n*/бы́ли *pl* … *(+ nom)*. [niDAVna u-miNYA BYL/byLA/BYla/BYly ...]

What can I do for you?
Чем я могу́ помо́чь? [CHEM YA maGU paMOCH]

Where does it hurt?
Где у Вас боли́т? [GDYE u-VAS baLIT]

I have pain here.
Здесь у меня́ боли́т. [ZDYES' u-miNYA baLIT]

Please get undressed/roll up your sleeve.
Пожа́луйста, разде́ньтесь./приподними́те рука́в. [paZHAlusta rasDYEN'tis'/pripadniMItye ruKAF]

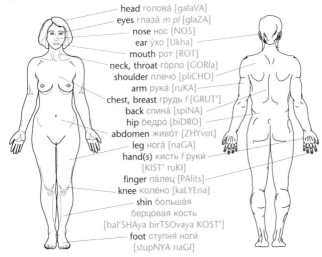

head голова́ [galaVA]
eyes глаза́ *m pl* [glaZA]
nose нос [NOS]
ear у́хо [Ukha]
mouth рот [ROT]
neck, throat го́рло [GORla]
shoulder плечо́ [pliCHO]
arm рука́ [ruKA]
chest, breast грудь *f* [GRUT']
back спина́ [spiNA]
hip бедро́ [biDRO]
abdomen живо́т [ZHYvot]
leg нога́ [naGA]
hand(s) кисть *f* руки́ [KIST' ruKI]
finger па́лец [PAlits]
knee коле́но [kaLYEna]
shin больша́я берцо́вая кость [bal'SHAya birTSOvaya KOST']
foot ступня́ ноги́ [stupNYA naGI]

Take a deep breath. Hold your breath.
Сде́лайте глубо́кий вдох. Придержи́те дыха́ние.
[ZDYElaytye gluBOki VDOKH. pridirZHYtye dyKHAniye]

We need to take a blood/urine sample.
На́до сде́лать ана́лиз кро́ви./мочи́.
[NAda ZDYElat' aNAlis KROvi/maCHI]

We need to have you X-rayed.
На́до сде́лать Вам рентге́н. [NAda ZDYElat' VAM rindGYEN]

You need an operation.
Вам на́до сде́лать опера́цию. [VAM NAda ZDYElat' apiRAtsyyu]

You need to spend a few days in bed.
Вы должны́ соблюда́ть не́сколько дней посте́льный режи́м.
[VY dalzhNY sablyuDAT' NYEskal'ka DNYEY paSTYEL'ny riZHYM]

It's nothing serious.
Ничего́ серьёзного. [nichiVO sirYOZnava]

I've been vaccinated against ...
Я приви́т *m*/приви́та *f* про́тив ... *(+ gen)*.
[YA priVIT/priVIta PROtif- ...]

At the Hospital

How long will I have to stay here?
Как до́лго я здесь пробу́ду? [KAK DOLga YA ZDYES' praBUdu]

I'd like ..., please.
Да́йте мне ..., пожа́луйста. [DAYtye MNYE ... paZHAlusta]

a glass of water
стака́н воды́ [staKAN vaDY]

a painkiller
болеутоля́ющую табле́тку [baleutoLYAyushuyu taBLYETku]

a sleeping pill
снотво́рную [snaTVORnuyu]

a hot-water bottle
гре́лку [GRYELku]

Illnesses and Complaints

abscess	абсце́сс [apsTSES]
AIDS	СПИД [SPID]
allergic to ...	аллерги́я от ... *(+ gen)* [alirGIya at- ...]
apoplectic attack	(апоплекси́ческий) уда́р [apaplikSIchiski uDAR]
appendicitis	аппендици́т [apindiTSYT]
asthma	а́стма [ASTma]
backache	боль *f* в спине́ [BOL' f-spiNYE]
bleeding	кровотече́ние [kravatiCHEniye]
blood poisoning	зараже́ние кро́ви [zaraZHEniye KROvi]
bone fracture	перело́м ко́сти [piriLOM KOsti]

176

broken	слóманный [SLOmany]
bronchitis	бронхи́т [branKHIT]
bruise	уши́б [uSHYP]
burn	ожóг [aZHOK]
cancer	рак [RAK]
cardiac infarction	инфáркт миокáрда [inFARKT miaKARda]
chest pain	ангúна [anGIna]
cholera	холéра [khaLYEra]
circulatory disorder	нарушéние кровообращéния [naruSHEniye kravaabraSHEniya]
cold	простýда [praSTUda]
colic	кóлики f pl [KOliki]
concussion	сотрясéние мóзга [satriSYEniye MOZga]
constipation	запóр [zaPOR]
contagious	зарáзный [zaRAZny]
cramp	сýдорога [SUdaraga]
cut	рéзаная рáна [RYEzanaya RAna]
diabetes	диабéт [diaBYET]
diarrhea	понóс [paNOS]
difficulty breathing	удýшье [uDUshye]
diphtheria	дифтери́я [diftiRIya]
dizziness	головокружéние [galavakruZHEniye]
faint	óбморок [OBmarak]
fever	температýра [timpiraTUra]
flu	грипп [GRIP]
food poisoning	пищевóе отравлéние [pishiVOye atraVLYEniye]
gas	гáзы m pl [GAzy]
hay fever	аллерги́ческий рини́т [alirGIchiski riNIT]
head cold	нáсморк [NASmark]
headache	головнáя боль [galavNAya BOL']
heart attack	сердéчный при́ступ [sirDYECHny PRIstup]
heart defect	порóк сéрдца [paROK SYERtsa]
heart trouble	сердéчные недýги m pl [sirDYECHnyye niDUgi]
heartburn	изжóга [iZHOga]
hemorrhoids	геморрóй [gimaROY]
hepatitis	гепати́т [gipaTIT]
hernia	паховáя гры́жа [pakhaVAya GRYzha]
high blood pressure	высóкое кровянóе давлéние [vySOkaye kraviNOye daVLYEniye]
hoarse	хри́плый [KHRIply]
illness	болéзнь f [baLYEZN']
impaired balance	нарушéние координáции движéний [naruSHEniye kaardiNAtsyi dviZHEni]

impaired vision	наруше́ния зре́ния [naruSHEniye ZRYEniya]
indigestion	расстро́йство пищеваре́ния [raSTROYstva pishivaRYEniya]
infection	инфе́кция [inFYEKtsyya]
inflammation	воспале́ние [vaspaLYEniye]
injury	ране́ние [raNYEniye]
insomnia	бессо́нница [biSOnitsa]
jaundice	желту́ха [zhylTUkha]
kidney stone	по́чечный ка́мень [POchichny KAmin']
lumbago	простре́л [praSTRYEL]
malaria	маляри́я [maliaRIya]
middle-ear infection	воспале́ние сре́днего у́ха [vaspaLYEniye SRYEDniva Ukha]
migraine	мигре́нь f [miGRYEN']
miscarriage	вы́кидыш [VYkidysh]
nausea	тошнота́ [tashnaTA]
nephritis	воспале́ние по́чек [vaspaLYEniye POchek]
nosebleed	кровотече́ние из но́са [kravatiCHEniye iz-NOsa]
pain	боль f [BOL']
pain in the side	боль f в боку́ [BOL' v-baKU]
paralysis	парали́ч [paraLICH]
pneumonia	воспале́ние лёгких [vaspaLYEniye LYOKHkikh]
poisoning	отравле́ние [atraVLYEniye]
polio	полиомиели́т [paliamiyiLIT]
pulled muscle	растяже́ние [rastiZHEniye]
rash	сыпь f [SYP']
rheumatism	ревмати́зм [rivmaTIZM]
rupture	гры́жа [GRYzha]
SARS	атипи́чная пневмони́я [atiPICHnaya pnivmoNIya]
sciatica	и́шиас [Ishyas]
shivering fit	озно́б [azNOP]
sinusitis	воспале́ние ло́бных па́зух [vaspaLYEniye LOBnykh PAzukh]
sore throat	боль f в го́рле [BOL' v-GORlye]
sprained	растя́нутый [raSTYAnuty]
stomach ache	желу́дочная боль [zhyLUdachnaya BOL']
stroke	(апоплекси́ческий) уда́р [(apaplikSIchiski) uDAR]
sunburn	со́лнечный ожо́г [SOLnichny aZHOK]
sunstroke	со́лнечный уда́р [SOLnichny uDAR]

swelling	опуха́ние [apuKHAniye], о́пухоль f [Opukhal']
swollen	опу́хший [aPUKHshy]
tachycardia	сердцебие́ние [sirtsybiYEniye]
tetanus	столбня́к [stalbNYAK]
tick	клещ [KLYESH]
to hurt	боле́ть ipf [baLYET']
to injure	ра́нить/пора́нить [RAnit'/paRAnit']
to itch	чеса́ться/почеса́ться [chiSAtsa/pachiSAtsa]
to sneeze	чиха́ть/чихну́ть [chiKHAT'/chikhNUT']
tonsillitis	воспале́ние минда́лин [vaspaLYEniye minDAlin]
torn ligament	разры́в свя́зок [razRYF SVYAzak]
tuberculosis	туберкулёз [tubirkuLYOS]
tumor	о́пухоль f [Opukhal']
typhus	тиф [TIF]
ulcer	я́зва [YAZva]
urge to vomit	позы́в к рво́те [paZYF k-RVOtye]
venereal disease	венери́ческая боле́знь [viniRIchiskaya baLYEZN']
wound	ра́на [RAna]
yellow fever	жёлтая лихора́дка [ZHOLtaya likhaRATka]

Body – Doctor – Hospital

abdomen	живо́т [zhyVOT]
anesthetic	нарко́з [narKOS]
ankle	лоды́жка [laDYSHka]
appendix	аппендикс [aPENdiks]
arm	рука́ sing [ruKA], ру́ки pl [RUki]
backbone	позвоно́чник [pazvaNOCHnik]
bandage	повя́зка [paVYASka]
bladder	мочево́й пузы́рь [machiVOY puZYR']
to bleed (wound)	кровоточи́ть ipf [kravataCHIT']
(person)	истека́ть/исте́чь кро́вью [istiKAT'/isTYECH KROv'yu]
blister	во́лдырь f [VOLdyr']
blood	кровь f [KROF']
blood group	гру́ппа кро́ви [GRUpa KROvi]
blood pressure	кровяно́е давле́ние [kraviNOye daVLYEniye]
bone	кость f [KOST']
bowel movement	стул [STUL]
brain	мозг [MOSK]
breast, chest	грудь f [GRUT']
to breathe	дыша́ть/вздохну́ть [dySHAT'/vzdakhNUT']

bronchial tubes	бро́нхи *m pl* [BRONkhi]
cardiologist	кардио́лог [kardiOlak]
certificate	свиде́тельство [sviDYEtil'stva]
collarbone	ключи́ца [klyuCHItsa]
cough	ка́шель *m* [KAshyl']
diagnosis	диа́гноз [diAGnas]
diet	дие́та [diYEta]
digestion	пищеваре́ние [pishivaRYEniye]
to disinfect	дезинфици́ровать *ipf a. pf* [dizinfiTSYravat']
doctor's medical certificate	больни́чный листо́к [bal'NICHny liSTOK]
drainage	дрена́ж [driNASH]
to dress	перевя́зывать/перевяза́ть [piriVYAzyvat'/piriviZAT']
ear	у́хо *sing* [Ukha], у́ши *pl* [Ushy]
eardrum	бараба́нная перепо́нка [baraBAnaya piriPONka]
esophagus	пищево́д [pishiVOT]
examination	осмо́тр [aSMOTR]
eye	глаз *sing* [GLAS], глаза́ *pl* [glaZA]
face	лицо́ [liTSO]
finger	па́лец [PAlits]
foot	ступня́ ноги́ [stupNYA NOgi]
gallbladder	жёлчный пузы́рь [ZHOLCHny puZYR']
hand	кисть *f* руки́ [KIST' ruKI]
head	голова́ [galaVA]
health insurance	медици́нская страхо́вка [midiTSYNskaya straKHOFka]
health insurance certificate	страхово́е свиде́тельство [strakhaVOye sviDYEtil'stva]
hearing	слух [SLUKH]
heart	се́рдце [SYERtse]
hip	бедро́ [biDRO]
hospital	больни́ца [bal'NItsa]
ill, sick	больно́й [bal'NOY]
infusion	влива́ние [vliVAniye], впры́скиван [FPRYskivaniye]
inguinal area	ни́жняя часть живота́ [NIZHniya CHAST' zhyvaTA]
injection, shot	уко́л [uKOL], инъе́кция [inYEKtsyya]
intestine	кишка́ [kishKA]
joint	суста́в [suSTAF]
kidney	по́чка [POCHka]
knee	коле́но [kaLYEna]
leg	нога́ *sing* [naGA], но́ги *pl* [NOgi]
lip	губа́ [guBA]

180

liver	печень f [PYEchin']
lung	лёгкое [LYOKHkaye]
male nurse	медбрат [midBRAT]
medical certificate	врачебное заключение [vraCHEBnaye zaklyuCHEniye]
menstruation	менструация [minstruAtsiya]
mouth	рот [ROT]
muscle	мускул [MUSkul], мышца [MYSHtsa]
nauseous (to feel)	тошнить/стошнить (+ dat) [tashNIT'/stashNIT']
nerve	нерв [NYERF]
nervous	нервный [NYERVny]
nose	нос [NOS]
nurse	медсестра [mitsiSTRA]
office hours	приёмные часы [priYOMnyye chiSY]
operation	операция [apiRAtsyya]
pacemaker	кардиостимулятор [kardiastimuLYAtar]
pregnancy	беременность f [birYEminast']
to prescribe	выписывать/выписать [vyPIsyvat'/VYpisat']
prosthesis	протез [praTYES]
pulse	пульс [PUL'S]
pus	гной [GNOY]
rib	ребро [riBRO]
scar	шрам [SHRAM], рубец [ruBYETS]
sexual organs	половые органы m pl [palaVYye ORgany]
shin	большая берцовая кость [bal'SHAya birTSOvaya KOST']
shoulder	плечо [pliCHO]
skin	кожа [KOzha]
specialist	врач-специалист [VRACH-spitsyaLIST]
spinal column	позвоночный столб [pazvaNOCHny STOLP]
spine	спина [spiNA]
splint	шина [SHYna]
sting	укол [uKOL]
to stitch up	зашивать/зашить [zashyVAT'/zaSHYT']
stomach	желудок [zhyLUdak]
surgeon	хирург [khiRURK]
to sweat	потеть/вспотеть [paTYET'/fspaTYET']
syringe	шприц [SHPRITS]
throat	горло [GORla]
toe	палец (на ноге) [PAlits (na-naGYE)]
tongue	язык [yiZYK]
tonsils	миндалины f pl [minDAliny]
ultrasound scan	осмотр ультразвуком [aSMOTR ul'traZVUkam]

unconscious	бессозна́тельный [bisaZNAtil'ny]
urine	моча́ [maCHA]
vaccination	приви́вка [priVIFka]
vaccination card	спра́вка о приви́вках [SPRAFka a-priVIFkakh]
virus	ви́рус [VIrus]
visiting hours	вре́мя посеще́ния [VRYEmya pasiSHEniya]
waiting room	приёмная [priYOMnaya]
ward	отделе́ние [addiLYEniye]
X-ray	рентге́новский сни́мок [rindGYEnafski SNImak]
to X-ray	просве́чивать/просвети́ть [praSVYEchivat'/prasviTIT']

At the Dentist's

I have a (terrible) toothache.
У меня́ (о́чень) боля́т зу́бы. [u-miNYA (Ochin') baLYAT ZUby]

This (upper/lower/front/back) tooth hurts.
Э́тот зуб (ве́рхний/ни́жний/пере́дний/за́дний) боли́т.
[Etat ZUP (VYERKHni/NIZHni/piRYEDni/ZADni) baLIT]

I've lost a filling.
У меня́ вы́пала пло́мба. [u-miNYA VYpala PLOMba]

I've broken a tooth.
У меня́ слома́лся зуб. [u-miNYA slaMALsa ZUP]

Please give/don't give me an injection.
Да́йте/Не дава́йте мне инъе́кцию, пожа́луйста.
[DAYtye/ni-daVAYtye MNYE inYEKtsyyu paZHAlusta]

bridge	мост [MOST]
cavity	дупло́ [duPLO]
crown	коро́нка [kaRONka]
dentures	проте́з [praTYES]
filling	пло́мба [PLOMba]
gums	десна́ [diSNA]
incisor	резе́ц [riZYETS]
jaw	че́люсть f [CHElyust']
molar	коренно́й зуб [kariNOY ZUP]
to take out/extract	удаля́ть/удали́ть [udaLYAT'/udaLIT']
temporary treatment	вре́менное лече́ние [VRYEminaye liCHEniye]
tooth	зуб [ZUP]
toothache	зубна́я боль [zubNAya BOL']
wisdom tooth	зуб му́дрости [ZUP MUdrasti]

ПОЧТА

ВЫЕМКА ПИСЕМ
ПРОИЗВОДИТСЯ
4 РАЗА В ДЕНЬ
с 8 до 19 час

A   18   A

Essentials from A to Z

Bank

When you change money in exchange offices, pay close attention to the terms, the commission, etc. Be careful: people who approach you in public and offer to exchange money at especially tempting rates are usually trying to defraud you. Larger cities often have ATMs (in hotels, for example), which accept at least the most common credit cards.

Could you please tell me where the nearest bank/exchange office/ATM is?
Вы не скажете мне, где здесь банк?/обменный пункт?/банкомат? [VY ni-SKAzhytye MNYE GDYE ZDYES' BANK/abMYEny PUNKT/bankaMAT]

I'd like to change ... euros/Swiss francs/dollars (into rubles).
Я бы хотел *m*/хотела *f* обменять ... евро/швейцарских франков/долларов (на рубли). [YA BY khaTYEL/khaTYEla abmiNYAT' ... YEVra/shviyTSARskikh FRANkaf/DOlaraf (na-ruBLI)]

Could you please tell me what the exchange rate is today?
Не могли бы Вы мне сказать, какой сегодня курс обмена? [ni-maGLI BY VY MNYE skaZAT' kaKOY siVOdnya KURS abMYEna]

I'd like to cash this traveler's check.
Я бы хотел *m*/хотела *f* обналичить этот трэвел-чек. [YA BY khaTYEL/khaTYEla abnaliCHIT' Etat TREvil-chek]

Please let me see ...
Покажите, пожалуйста, ... [pakaZHYtye paZHAlusta]

your identification.
Ваше удостоверение личности.
[VAshy udastvaRYEniye LICHnasti]

your passport.
Ваш паспорт. [VASH PASpart]

Sign here, please.
Подпишитесь здесь, пожалуйста. [patpiSHYtyis' ZDYES' paZHAlusta]

My card got stuck in the ATM.
Моя карточка застряла в банкомате.
[maYA KARtachka zaSTRYAla v-bankaMAtye]

account	....	счёт [SHOT]
amount	....	сумма [SUma]
ATM	....	банкомат [bankaMAT]
bank	....	банк [BANK]
bill	....	банкнота [bankNOta]
cash	....	наличные (деньги *f pl*)
		[naLICHnyye DYEN'gi]

cent	цент [TSENT]
to change	менять/обменять [miNYAT'/abmiNYAT']
check	чек [CHEK]
to write a check	выписывать/выписать чек [vyPIsyvat'/VYpisat' CHEK]
coin	монéта [maNYEta]
commission	комиссиóнная [kamisiOnaya]
credit card	кредитная кáрточка [kriDITnaya KARta]
currency	валюта [vaLYUta]
dollar	дóллар [DOlar]
exchange	обмéн дéнег [abMYEN DYEnik]
exchange rate	валютный курс [vaLYUTny KURS]
foreign currency	валюта [vaLYUta]
form	бланк [BLANK]
in cash	налиичный [naLICHny]
money	дéньги f pl [DYEN'gi]
money transfer	дéнежный перевóд [DYEnizhny piriVOT]
payment	платёж [plaTYOSH]
to pay out	выплáчивать/выплатить [vyPLAchivat'/VYplatit']
PIN number	шифр [SHYFR]
receipt	квитáнция [kviTANtsyya]
signature	пóдпись f [POTpis']
small change	мéлочь f [MYElach]
Swiss francs	швейцáрские фрáнки m pl [shviyTSARskiye FRANki]
transfer	перевóд [piriVOT]
wire transfer	телегрáфный перевóд [tiliGRAFny piriVOT]
traveler's check	туристический чек [turiSTIchiski CHEK] , трэвел-чек [TREvil-chek]

Photos

> also Photographic Materials

Would you mind taking a picture of us?
Не могли бы Вы нас сфотографировать?
[ni-maGLI BY VY NAS sfatagraFIravat']

That's really nice of you!
Это óчень любéзно! [Eta Ochin' lyuBYEZna]

Just press this button.
Нажмите на эту кнóпочку. [naZHMItye na-Etu KNOpachku]

You set the distance/aperture like this.

Расстоя́ние/Диафра́гма регули́руется вот так.

[rastaYAniye/diaFRAGma riguLIruyitsa VOT TAK]

May I take a picture of you?

Мо́жно Вас сфотографи́ровать? [MOZHna VAS sfatagraFIravat']

This will be a nice reminder of our vacation.

Так у нас бу́дет хоро́шая па́мять о на́шем о́тпуске.

[TAK u-NAS BUdit khaROshaya PAmit' a-NAshym OTpuskye]

camera	фотоаппара́т [fataapaRAT]
landscape format	горизонта́льный форма́т [garizanTAL'ny farMAT]
picture, photo(graph)	сни́мок [SNImak]
portrait format	вертика́льный форма́т [virtiKAL'ny farMAT]
snapshot	спонта́нный сни́мок [sponTAny SNImak]
to take a photo	фотографи́ровать/сфотографи́ровать [fatagraFIravat'/sfatagraFIravat']

Lost-and-Found Office

➢ also Police

Could you tell me where the lost-and-found is, please?

Вы не мо́жете мне сказа́ть, где здесь бюро́ нахо́док?

[VY ni-MOzhytye MNYE skaZAT' GDYE ZDYES' byuRO naKHOdak]

I've lost ...

Я потеря́л *m*/потеря́ла *f* ... *(+ acc)* [YA patiRYAL/patiRYAla ...]

I left my purse on the train.

Я забы́ла свою́ су́мочку в по́езде.

[YA zaBYla svaYU SUmachku f-POyizdye]

Would you please let me know if it turns up?

А Вы мо́жете мне сообщи́ть в слу́чае, е́сли су́мочка бу́дет на́йдена? [a VY MOzhytye MNYE saapSHIT' f-SLUchaye YEsli SUmachka BUdit NAYdina]

Here's my hotel address/my home address.

Вот мой а́дрес гости́ницы. [VOT MOY Adris gaSTInitsy]/
Вот мой дома́шний а́дрес. [VOT MOY daMASHny Adris]

Could you please tell me where the nearest police station is?
Вы не мо́жете мне сказа́ть, где здесь милице́йский уча́сток?
[VY ni-MOzhytye MNYE skaZAT' GDYE ZDYES' miliTSEYski uCHAstak]

I'd like to report ...
Я хочу́ заяви́ть ... [YA khaCHU zayiVIT' ...]

  a theft.
  о кра́же. [a-KRAzhy]

  an assault./a holdup.
  о нападе́нии. [a-napaDYEnii]

My ... has been stolen.
У меня́ укра́ли ... (+ acc). [u-miNYA uKRAli ...]

  purse
  су́мочку. [SUmachku]

  billfold
  бума́жник. [buMAZHnik]

  camera
  фотоаппара́т. [fataapaRAT]

  car/bike
  маши́ну. [maSHYnu]/велосипе́д. [vilasiPYET]

My car has been broken into.
Взлома́ли мою́ маши́ну. [vzlaMAli maYU maSHYnu]

... has been stolen from my car.
Из маши́ны укра́ли ... (+ acc). [iz-maSHYny uKRAli ...]

My son/My daughter is missing.
Мой сын потеря́лся. [MOY SYN patiRYALsa]/
Моя́ дочь потеря́лась. [maYA DOCH patiRYAlas']

This man is harassing me.
Э́тот мужчи́на пристаёт ко мне.
[Etat mushCHIna pristaYOT ka-MNYE]

Can you help me, please?
Не могли́ бы Вы мне помо́чь? [ni-maGLI BY VY MNYE paMOCH]

When exactly did it happen?
Когда́ и́менно э́то случи́лось? [kagDA Imina Eta sluCHIlas']

Your name and address, please.
Ва́ши фами́лия и а́дрес, пожа́луйста.
[VAshy faMIliya i Adris paZHAlusta]

You need to get in touch with your consulate.
Обрати́тесь в своё ко́нсульство. [abraTItyis' f-svaYO KONsul'stva]

to arrest . . . . арестова́ть *ipf a. pf* [aristaVAT']
assault, mugging . . . . нападе́ние [napaDYEniye]

187

to beat up	избива́ть/изби́ть [izbiVAT'/izBIT']
billfold, wallet	бума́жник [buMAZHnik]
to break into	взла́мывать/взлома́ть [VZLAmyvat'/vzlaMAT']
car radio	автомоби́льный радиоприёмник [aftamaBIL'ny radiapriYOMnik]
car registration (papers)	техпа́спорт [tikhPASpart]
check	чек [CHEK]
check card	че́ковая ка́рточка [CHEkavaya KARtachka]
coin purse	кошелёк [kashyLOK]
to confiscate	конфискова́ть ipf a. pf [kanfiskaVAT']
contraband	контраба́нда [kantraBANda]
court	суд [SUT]
credit card	креди́тная ка́рточка [kriDITnaya KARtachka]
crime	преступле́ние [pristuPLYEniye]
drugs	нарко́тик [narKOtik]
fault	вина́ [viNA]
to harass	пристава́ть/приста́ть к … (+ dat) [pristaVAT'/priSTAT' k-…]
ID/identification	(общеграждáнский) па́спорт [apshigrazhDANski PASpart]
judge	судья́ [suDYA]
key	ключ [KLYUCH]
lawyer, attorney	адвока́т [advaKAT]
to lose	теря́ть/потеря́ть [tiRYAT'/patiRYAT']
papers, documents m pl	докуме́нты m pl [dakuMYENty]
passport	заграни́чный па́спорт [zagraNICHny PASpart]
pickpocket	карма́нный вор [karMAny VOR]
police	мили́ция [miLItsya]
police car	милице́йский автомоби́ль [miliTSEYski aftamaBIL']
police custody	предвари́тельное заключе́ние [pridvaRItil'naye zaklyuCHEniye]
police officer	милиционе́р [militsyaNYER]
prison	тюрьма́ [tyur'MA]
rape	изнаси́лование [iznaSIlavaniye]
to report	заявля́ть/заяви́ть о … (+ prep) [zayiVLYAT'/zayiVIT' a-…]
sexual harassment	сексуа́льное домога́тельство [siksuAL'naye damaGAtil'stva]
theft	кра́жа [KRAzha]
thief	вор [VOR]
witness	свиде́тель/свиде́тельница [sviDYEtil'/sviDYEtil'nitsa]

Post Office

Could you tell me where ... is, please?
Вы не мо́жете мне сказа́ть, где здесь ...?
[VY ni-MOzhytye MNYE skaZAT' GDYE ZDYES' ...]

the nearest post office
ближа́йший почта́мт [bliZHAYshy pachTAMT]

the nearest mailbox
ближа́йший почто́вый я́щик
[bliZHAYshy pachTOvy YAshik]

How much is a letter/a postcard ...
Ско́лько сто́ит отпра́вить письмо́/откры́тку ...
[SKOL'ka STOit atPRAvit' piS'MO/atKRYTku ...]

to America?
в Аме́рику? [v-aMYEriku]

to the US?
в США? [f-SE-SHE-A]

to Canada?
в Кана́ду? [v-kaNAdu]

Three ... -ruble/... -kopeck stamps, please.
Мне, пожа́луйста, три почто́вые ма́рки на ... рубле́й, ... копе́ек.
[MNYE paZHAlusta TRI pachTOvyye MARki na- ... ruBLYEY, ... kaPYEyik]

I'd like to send this letter ...
Э́то письмо́ отпра́вьте ...[Eta piS'MO atPRAF'tye...]

by airmail.
а́виа. [Avia]

special delivery.
экспре́сс-по́чтой. [ekSPRYES-POCHtay]

certified.
заказно́й по́чтой. [zakazNOY POCHtay]

How long does a letter to the US take?
Как долго идёт письмо́ до США?
[KAK DOLga iDYOT piS'MO da-SE-SHE-A]

Do you have special issue stamps?
У вас есть коллекцио́нные ма́рки?
[u-VAS YEST kaliktsyOnyye MARki]

Can I send a fax from here?
Отсю́да мо́жно отпра́вить факс? [atSYUda MOZHna atPRAvit' FAKS]

address .... а́дрес [Adris]
addressee .... получа́тель *m* [paluCHAtil']

airmail	áвиа [Avia]
certified letter	заказно́е письмо́ [zakazNOye piS'MO]
charge, fee	пла́та [PLAta], сбор [ZBOR]
collection	вы́емка пи́сем [VYyimka PIsim]
customs declaration	таможенная деклара́ция [taMOzhynaya diklaRAtsyya]
declaration of value	объявле́ние це́нности [abyiVLYEniye TSEnasti]
fax, fax machine	факс [FAKS]
to fill out	заполня́ть/запо́лнить [zapalNYAT'/zaPOLnit']
form	бланк [BLANK]
to forward	пересыла́ть/пересла́ть [pirisyLAT'/piriSLAT']
letter	письмо́ [pis'MO]
mailbox	почто́вый я́щик [pachTOvy YAshik]
mailing form	бланк на посы́лку [BLANK na-paSYLku]
main post office	гла́вный почта́мт [GLAVny pachTAMT], главпочта́мт [glavpachTAMT]
parcel	посы́лка [paSYLka]
postage	почто́вый сбор [pachTOvy ZBOR]
post office	почта́мт [pachTAMT]
postcard	откры́тка [atKRYTka]
poste restante	до востре́бования [doh vasTREHbovaneeyah]
printed form	бланк [BLANK]
printed matter	бандеро́ль f [bandiROL']
sender	отправи́тель m [atpraVItil']
special delivery letter	сро́чное письмо́ [SROCHnaye piS'MO], экспре́сс-по́чта [ekSPRYES-POCHta]
special issue/ commemorative stamp	коллекцио́нная (почто́вая) ма́рка [kaliktsyOnaya (pachTOvaya) MARka]
stamp	почто́вая ма́рка [pachTOvaya MARka]
stamp machine	автома́т по прода́же ма́рок [aftaMAT pa-praDAzhy MArak]
telegram	телегра́мма [tiliGRAma]
telex	те́лекс [TYElyeks]
weight	вес [VYES]
zip code	почто́вый и́ндекс [pachTOvy INdiks]

Telephoning

Could you tell me where the nearest phone booth is?
Вы не мо́жете мне сказа́ть, где ближа́йшая телефо́нная бу́дка?
[VY ni-MOzhytye MNYE skaZAT' GDYE bliZHAYshyya tiliFOnaya BUTka]

I'd like a phone card, please.
Мне, пожа́луйста, телефо́нную ка́рточку.
[MNYE paZHAlusta tiliFOnuyu KARtachku]

What's the area code for ...?
Како́й код … *(+ gen)*? [kaKOY KOT …]

A domestic/an international long-distance call to ...
Междугоро́дный/Междунаро́дный разгово́р с … *(+ instr)*.
[mizhdugaRODny/mizhdunaRODny razgaVOR s-…]

I'd like to make a collect call.
Я хочу́ заказа́ть разгово́р за счёт вызыва́емого абоне́нта.
[YA khaCHU zakaZAT' razgaVOR za-SHOT vyzyVAyimava abaNYENta]

Please go to booth number ...
Иди́те в каби́ну № … [iDItye f-kaBInu NOmir …]

A Telephone Conversation

> The person answering the phone says "Алло́" [aLO] ("Hello")
> or "Слу́шаю" [SLUshayu] ("I'm listening"). Apart from private
> conversations between friends, telephone calls are usually kept
> very short and quite matter-of-fact.

This is ... (speaking).
Это говори́т … [Eta gavaRIT …]

Hello, who's speaking, please?
Алло́, с кем я говорю́? [aLO s-KYEM YA gavaRYU]

Hello, my name is ...
Здра́вствуйте, меня́ зову́т … [ZDRASTvuytye miNYA zaVUT …]

May I please speak to Mr./Mrs. ...?
Мо́жно поговори́ть с господи́ном …?/с госпожо́й …?
[MOZHna pagavaRIT' s-gaspaDInam …/s-gaspaZHOY …]

I'm sorry, he's/she's not here.
К сожале́нию, его́/её нет. [k-sazhaLYEniyu yiVO/yiYO NYET]

Could he/she return your call?
Мо́жет ли он/она́ перезвони́ть Вам?
[MOzhyt li ON/aNA pirizvaNIT' VAM]

Would you like to leave a message?
Хоти́те оста́вить сообще́ние? [khaTItye aSTAvit' saapSHEniye]

Please tell him/her that I called.
Скажи́те ему́/ей, пожа́луйста, что я позвони́л.
[skaZHYtye yiMU/YEY paZHAlusta SHTO YA pazvaNIL]

"The number you have reached is not in service."
«Вы́бранный Ва́ми но́мер неве́рный»
[VYbrany VAmi NOmir niVYERny]

Before departure, ask your cell phone carrier about roaming terms and conditions in Russia. It may be less expensive to purchase a prepaid SIM card once you arrive. The Russian SIM cards, however, always are valid only for a certain territory, and when you leave it, roaming charges are due. Generally, charges are assessed for incoming calls as well, unless the call involves the same service provider within a network.

I'd like a SIM card, please.
СИМ-ка́рту, пожа́луйста. [SIM-KARtu paZHAlusta]
　with roaming/without roaming.
　с ро́умингом [s-ROumingam]/**без ро́уминга** [biz-ROuminga]

What area is this SIM card valid for?
Како́й охва́т террито́рии э́той СИМ-ка́рты?
[kaKOY aKHVAT tiriTOrii Etay SIM-KARty]

Please give me a list of the rates.
Да́йте, пожа́луйста, распеча́тку тари́фов.
[DAYtye paZHAlusta raspiCHATku taRIfaf]

Do you have debit cards for the service provider ...?
Креди́тные ка́рточки прова́йдера … есть?
[kriDITnyye KARtachki praVAYdira … YEST]

How many minutes can I talk with a ... -ruble card?
Ско́лько мину́т я могу́ говори́ть по ка́рточке за … рубле́й?
[SKOL'ka miNUT YA maGU gavaRIT pa-KARtachkye za-… ruBLYEY]

to answer the phone	снима́ть/снять тру́бку [sniMAT'/SNYAT' TRUPku]
answering machine	автоотве́тчик [aftaatVYETshik]
area code	телефо́нный код [tiliFOny KOT]
busy	за́нятый [ZAnyity]
(phone) call	звоно́к [zvaNOK]
to call, to phone	звони́ть/позвони́ть (по телефо́ну) (+ dat) [zvaNIT'/pazvaNIT' (pa-tiliFOnu)]
call, conversation	разгово́р [razgaVOR]
cell phone	моби́льник [maBIL'nik]
cellular phone	моби́льный телефо́н [maBIL'ny tiliFON], со́товый телефо́н [SOtavy tiliFON]
charge, fee	пла́та [PLAta], сбор [ZBOR]
collect call	телефо́нный разгово́р, опла́чиваемый вызыва́емым абоне́нтом [tiliFOny razgaVOR aPLAchivayimy vyzyVAyimym abaNYENtam]

connection	связь *f* [SVYAS']
to dial	набира́ть/набра́ть [nabiRAT'/naBRAT']
directory assistance	спра́вочная слу́жба [SPRAvachnaya SLUZHba]
international call	междунаро́дный разгово́р [mizhdunaRODny razgaVOR]
local call	городско́й разгово́р [garatSKOY razgaVOR]
long-distance call *(domestic/international)*	междугоро́дный/междунаро́дный разгово́р [mizhdugaRODny/ mizhdunaRODny razgaVOR]
person-to-person call	предвари́тельная зая́вка [pridvaRItil'naya zaYAFka]
phone booth	телефо́нная бу́дка [tiliFOnaya BUTka]
phone number	но́мер (телефо́на) [NOmir (tiliFOna)]
receiver	тру́бка [TRUPka]
telephone	телефо́н [tiliFON]
telephone book	телефо́нный спра́вочник [tiliFOny SPRAvachnik]
telephone card	телефо́нная ка́рточка [tiliFOnaya KARta]
yellow pages	жёлтые страни́цы *f pl* [ZHOLtyye straNItsy]

Internet Café

There are Internet cafés in many places, frequently in larger post offices as well. The rates usually specify a minimum charge. The longer the session, the better the rate. By the way: on both the Russian and the English keyboards, you will find the @ symbol on the same key as the number 2.

Is there an Internet café near here?
Где здесь побли́зости Интерне́т-кафе́?
[GDYE ZDYES' paBLIzasti intirNYET-kaFYE]

How much does an hour/a quarter-hour cost?
Ско́лько сто́ит оди́н час?/пятна́дцать мину́т?
[SKOL'ka STOit aDIN CHAS/pitNAtsat' miNUT]

Can I print a page, please?
Я могу́ распеча́тать страни́цу? [YA maGU raspiCHAtat' straNItsu]

I can't get a connection.
У меня́ не устана́вливается связь.
[u-miNYA ni-ustaNAVlivayitsa SVYAS']

May I transfer the photos from my digital camera to a CD here?
Мо́жно у Вас переписа́ть фотогра́фии из цифрово́го
фотоаппара́та на компакт-ди́ск? [MOZHno u VAS perepiSAT'
fotoGRAfy is tsyfraVOva fotoapaRAta na KOMpakt-DISK]

Toilet and Bathroom

Public restrooms usually do not provide toilet paper in the
stalls. You can get toilet paper either from the restroom
attendant or take some off a roll at the entrance. There may
be none available at all, so it is wise to carry an emergency
supply in your purse or pants pocket.

Where is the restroom, please?
Где здесь туале́т? [GDYE ZDYES' tuaLYET]

Could I use your restroom/bathroom, please?
Могу́ ли я воспо́льзоваться Ва́шим туале́том?
[maGU liYA vaSPOL'zavatsa VAshym tuaLYEtam]

Could I have the key for the restroom, please?
Не дади́те мне ключ от туале́та?
[ni-daDItye MNYE KLYUCH at-tuaLYEta]

Please give me some toilet paper.
Да́йте, пожа́луйста, туале́тную бума́гу.
[DAYtye paZHAlusta tuaLYETnuyu buMAgu]

clean	чи́стый [CHIsty]
dirty	гря́зный [GRYAZny]
flush	спуск воды́ [SPUSK vaDY]
Men	мужско́й [mushSKOY], «М»
sanitary napkins	гигиени́ческие прокла́дки *f pl* [gigiyiNIchiskiye praKLATki]
sink	ра́ковина [RAkavina]
soap	мы́ло [MYla]
stand-up toilet	туале́т без унита́за [tuaLYET biz-uniTAza]
tampons	тампо́ны *m pl* [tamPOny]
toilet paper	туале́тная бума́га [tuaLYETnaya buMAga]
towel	полоте́нце [palaTYENtse]
Women	же́нский [ZHENski], «Ж»

A Short Guide to Russian Grammar

General Rules of Spelling

Certain sequences of letters are not permissible under the rules of Russian spelling:

- The letters ж, ч, ш, щ can never be followed by ы, ю, я, but only by и, у, а. The letters г, к, х are never followed by ы, but only by и.

- Russian does not allow an unstressed о to follow ж, ч, ш, щ, ц; instead, е is used.

One example is the word река́ *nom* (river) реки́ *gen* (of the river). According to the pattern for this declension, the genitive form should end in -ы, but the rule above does not allow that.

These rules must be followed with all inflected forms!

The following changes can occur in the inflection (declension or conjugation) of some Russian words:

Consonant Change

Consonant changes occur primarily in the conjugation of verbs. The most important consonant changes are:

г, д, з	→	ж
к, т	→	ч
т	→	щ
с, х	→	ш
ск, ст	→	щ
б; в; м; п	→	бл, вл; мл; пл

- иска́ть (to search) → я ищу́ (I search)
  люби́ть (to love) → я люблю́ (I love)

Change in Stress

- Word stress is free and variable: голова́ *nom sing* (head), го́ловы (heads).
- With verbs that undergo a change in the position of the stress when conjugated, the infinitive and the 1st person singular usually are stressed on the ending, while the other personal forms are stressed on the syllable preceding the ending:
  to look (at): смотре́ть, смотрю́, смо́тришь

Fleeting Vowels

- The vowels е and о may be dropped from the last syllable or inserted in it:

оте́ц *nom*	(father)	→	отца́ *gen* (of the father)
о́кна *nom pl*	(windows)	→	о́кон *gen pl* (of the windows)

Important verbs in which consonant changes, changes in stress, or fleeting vowels occur are listed on pages 210–212.

Articles

Russian has neither a definite article ("the") nor an indefinite article ("a, an"): у́лица means the street *or* a street.

Nouns

Gender

Russian has three grammatical genders. In the nominative case, the gender of a noun usually can be recognized by its final letter:

Final Letter	Gender	Example	
Consonant	masculine *m*	дом *m*	house
а *or* я	feminine *f*	у́лица *f*	street
е, ё, *or* о	neuter *n*	сло́во *n*	word
ь	either *m* or *f*	день *m* пло́щадь *f*	day square

- This book indicates the gender of nouns ending in -ь, as well as nouns that are exceptions to the patterns above.
- Capitalization is less common in Russian than in English. For example, months, days of the week, and nationalities are not capitalized.

Declension

Russian has six cases. The inflected forms indicate the function of a word within a sentence or phrase.

1.	Nominative	*nom*	Subject (who/what?)
2.	Genitive	*gen*	Possession, quantity, negation ("of")
3.	Dative	*dat*	Indirect object ("to/for")
4.	Accusative	*acc*	Direct object (whom/what?)
5.	Instrumental	*instr*	Shows means (by/with what?)
6.	Prepositional	*prep*	Shows location, etc.— (always with prepositions)

It is primarily the endings of words that change when they are declined. In addition to nouns, adjectives, pronouns, and numbers are also declined.

This book indicates the case that is required with certain prepositions and following certain verbs.

Animate/Inanimate Nouns

For all masculine nouns in the singular and plural and for plural nouns of all declensions, Russian has two sets of endings, depending on whether the word denotes an animate being or an inanimate object.

Animate being → accusative = genitive	Inanimate Being → accusative = nominative
муж *nom* (husband) му́жа *gen* му́жа *acc*	стол *nom* (table) стола́ *gen* стол *acc*

All the declension tables are based on inanimate nouns. For animate nouns, the accusative forms, which are identical to the genitive forms, are indicated with *.

Types of Declensions (based on inanimate nouns)

For information on the terms "hard" and "soft" as they apply to letters and/or sounds, see page 7.

1. Type One: *Masculine*

The stem ends in a hard sound, as in стака́н (glass).

	nom	*gen*	*dat*	*acc*	*instr*	*prep*
sing	стака́н-	-а	-у	-*	-ом	-е
pl	-ы	-ое	-ам	-у*	-ами	-ах

* For animate nouns: accusative = genitive

- Deviations from this pattern exist, in accordance with the rules of spelling (see page 95).
  Examples: га́лстук *nom sing* (necktie), га́лстуки *nom pl*

The stem ends in a soft sound, as in рубль (ruble)

	nom	*gen*	*dat*	*acc*	*instr*	*prep*
sing	рубл-ь	-я́	-ю́	-ь*	-ём	-é
pl	-й	-éй	-я́м	-й*	-я́ми	-я́х

- In the same way: nouns ending in -й:, such as музе́й *nom* (museum), музе́я *gen*, except: музе́ев *gen pl*

1. Type One: *Neuter*

Hard final sound, as in сло́во (word)

	nom	*gen*	*dat*	*ac*	*instr*	*prep*
sing	сло́в-о	-а	-у	-о	-ом	-е
pl	-á	-	-áм	-á	-áми	-áх

The stem ends in a soft sound, as in мо́ре (ocean)

	nom	gen	dat	acc	instr	prep
sing	мо́р-е	-я	-ю	-е	-ем	-е
pl	-я	-ей	-ям	-я	-ями	-ях

- In the same way: stressed ending in -ё, as in жильё (dwelling), жилья́, except: жильём *instr*, жи́лий *gen pl*
- In the same way: final sound of -ие, as in зда́ние (building) *nom*, зда́ния *gen*, except: зда́нии *prep* and зда́ний *gen pl*

2. Type Two: *Feminine*

The stem ends in a hard sound, as in ка́рта (map)

	nom	gen	dat	acc	instr	prep
sing	ка́рт-а	-ы	-е	-у	-ой	-е
pl	-ы	-	-ам	-ы*	-ами	-ах

- Deviations from this pattern exist, in accordance with the rules of orthography (page 195), as in река́ *nom* (river), реки́ *gen*

The stem ends in a soft sound, as in неде́ля (week)

	nom	gen	dat	acc	instr	prep
sing	неде́л-я	-и	-е	-ю	-ей	-е
pl	-и	-ь	-ям	-и*	-ями	-ях

- In the same way: final -ия, as in исто́рия *nom* (history), исто́рии *gen*, except: исто́рии *dat and prep* and исто́рий *gen pl*

3. Type Three: *Feminine*

The stem ends in a soft sound, as in пло́щадь (square)

	nom	gen	dat	acc	instr	prep
sing	пло́щад-ь	-и	-и	-ь	-ью	-и
pl	-и	-ей	-ям	-и*	-ями	-ях

Adjectives

Adjectives are always given in the masculine singular form in this book.

Types of Declensions (based on inanimate words)

The stem ends in a hard sound, as in но́вый (new)

	nom	gen	dat	acc	instr	prep
sing m	но́в-ый	-ого	-ому	-ый*	-ым	-ом
sing f	-ая	-ой	-ой	-ую	-ой	-ой
sing n	-ое	-ого	-ому	-ое	-ым	-ом
pl	-ые	-ых	-ым	-ые*	-ыми	-ых

* For animate words: accusative = genitive
- Deviations from this pattern exist, in accordance with the rules of orthography (page 195), as in высо́кий m nom (high), высо́кая f nom, высо́кое n nom, высо́кого m gen, etc.
- In the same way: adjectives ending in -о́й, -а́я, -о́е, -ы́е. Here the endings are always stressed, as in большо́й m nom (big), большо́го m gen

The stem ends in a soft sound, as in ли́шний (superfluous)

	nom	gen	dat	acc	instr	prep
sing m	ли́шн-ий	-его	-ему	-ий*	-им	-ем
sing f	-яя	-ей	-ей	-юю	-ей	-ей
sing n	-ее	-его	-ему	-ее	-им	-ем
pl	-ие	-их	-им	-ие*	-ими	-их

- Deviations from this pattern exist, in accordance with the rules of orthography (page 195), as in: горя́чий m nom (hot), горя́чая f nom, горя́чую f acc, горя́чее n nom
- Other words that have adjective endings are also declined like adjectives:
- ordinal numerals, such as пя́тый m nom (fifth), пя́того m gen
- substantivized adjectives, such as моро́женое nom ("something frozen," ice cream), моро́женого gen
- various participles and pronouns with adjective endings, such as the relative pronoun кото́рый m nom, кото́рого m gen
- Most adjectives also have an indeclinable short form, which can be used only predicatively. Its endings are -(zero ending) m, -a f, -о n, -ы pl. These words often undergo a change in the position of the stress, as in краси́вый (beautiful), short forms: краси́в m, краси́ва f, краси́во n, краси́вы pl

→ Э́то — краси́вая карти́на. This is a beautiful picture.
Э́та карти́на краси́ва. or
Э́та карти́на краси́вая. This picture is beautiful.

Comparison of Adjectives

The comparative can be formed in two ways. Like English, Russian has three degrees of comparison: positive, comparative, and superlative.

1. Compound comparison

To form the comparative degree, simply place the indeclinable word более (more) in front of the adjective. For the superlative degree ("most"), use самый, which must agree with the adjective in case, number, and gender.

These forms are mostly used attributively:

Positive	красивая картина	beautiful picture
Comparative	более красивая картина	more beautiful picture
Superlative	самая красивая картина	most beautiful picture

2. Simple comparison

To form the comparative degree, replace the ending with -ee. For the superlative degree, add the word всего (or, for things that can be counted, всех) after the comparative.

Positive	Картина красивая.	The picture is beautiful.
Comparative	Картина красивее.	The picture is more beautiful.
Superlative	Картина красивее всех.	The picture is most beautiful.

The superlative degree can also be formed by adding the suffix -ейший or айший to the adjective. These forms are inflected like adjectives and are mostly used attributively. Frequently they serve only to intensify the adjective's meaning:

Красивейшая картина   The most beautiful picture
                          The extremely beautiful picture

If the comparison is used to contrast different things, the object of comparison is either preceded by чем or is in the genitive case:
Картина красивее чем фотография. *Or*
Картина красивее фотографии. The picture is more beautiful than the photo.

Adverbs

Adverbs are usually derived from adjectives by replacing the endings -ый and -ой with -о and the ending -ий with -e or -о, as in быстрый *adj* → быстро *adv* (quickly).
The ending -ский is replaced by -ски, and this form is often preceded by по-, as in русский *adj* → по-русски *adv* (Russian).

Pronouns

Personal Pronouns

		nom	gen	dat	acc	instr	prep
1st pers. sing	(I)	я	меня́	мне	меня́	мной	мне
2nd pers. sing	(you)	ты	тебя́	тебе́	тебя́	тобо́й	тебе́
3rd pers. sing	(he)	он	его́	ему́	его́	им	нём
3rd pers. sing	(she)	она́	её	ей	её	ей	ней
3rd pers. sing	(it)	оно́	его́	ему́	его́	им	нём
1st pers. pl	(we)	мы	нас	нам	нас	иами	нас
2nd pers. pl	(you)	вы	вас	вам	вас	ва́ми	вас
3rd pers. pl	(they)	они́	их	им	их	ими	них

- All third-person forms are preceded by н- when they depend directly on a preposition: от него́ (from him)
- In addition to the personal pronouns, there exists a **reflexive pronoun**, which is used when the subject and object of a sentence are identical. It is the same for all persons, singular and plural, and has the same form as ты in the singular:
  - Он ви́дит его́. (He sees him.) Он ви́дит себя́. (He sees himself.)
  - Ты ви́дишь себя́. (You see yourself.)
  - Вы говори́те о себе́. (You're talking about yourself/yourselves.)
- Personal pronouns may be omitted in the nominative:
  - Я говорю́. or Говорю́. (I speak.)
- The forms of the second person plural (вы, etc.) also function as a polite form of "you".

Possessive Pronouns

	Obj.		nom	gen	dat	acc	instr	prep
1st pers. sing	m	(my)	мой	моего́	моему́	мой*	мои́м	моём
	f	(my)	моя́	мое́й	мое́й	мою́	мое́й	мое́й
	n	(my)	моё	моего́	моему́	моё	мои́м	моём
	pl	(my)	мои́	мои́х	мои́м	мои́*	мои́ми	мои́х
3rd pers. sing m		(his)	его́					
3rd pers. sing f		(her)	её					
3rd pers. sing n		(its)	его́					
1st pers. pl	m	(our)	наш	на́шего	на́шему	наш*	на́шим	на́шем
	f	(our)	на́ша	на́шей	на́шей	на́шу	на́шей	на́шей
	n	(our)	на́ше	на́шего	на́шему	на́ше	на́шим	на́шем
	pl	(our)	на́ши	на́ших	на́шим	на́ши*	на́шими	на́ших
3rd pers. pl		(their)	их					

*with an animate noun: accusative = genitive

- The possessive pronoun for the 2nd person singular, твой (your) has the same forms as мой, while the 2nd person plural, ваш (your) follows the pattern of наш:

> Я говорю́ о твоём до́ме. I'm talking about your house.
> Мы говори́м о ва́шем до́ме. We're talking about your house.

- The reflexive possessive pronoun свой is used when the subject and the owner of the object in a sentence are identical. It follows the same declensional pattern as мой:

> Ты говори́шь о своём до́ме. You're talking about your house.
> Она́ ви́дит её чемода́н. She sees her (another woman's) suitcase
>
> Она́ ви́дит свой чемода́н. She see her (own) suitcase.
> Вы ви́дите свой чемода́н. You (pl) see your suitcase.

Interrogative Pronouns

	nom	gen	dat	acc	instr	prep
who	кто	кого́	кому́	кого́	кем	ком
what	что	чего́	чему́	что	чем	чём

- The interrogative pronouns како́й and кото́рый (which) are declined like adjectives (see page 199).

Demonstrative Pronouns

	nom	gen	dat	acc	instr	prep
sing m (this)	э́тот	э́того	э́тому	э́тот*	э́тим	э́том
sing f (this)	э́та	э́той	э́той	э́ту	э́той	э́той
sing n (this)	э́то	э́того	э́тому	э́то	э́тим	э́том
pl (these)	э́ти	э́тих	э́тим	э́ти*	э́тими	э́тих
sing m (that)	тот	того́	тому́	тот*	тем	том
sing f (that)	та	той	той	ту	той	той
sing n (that)	то	того́	тому́	то	тем	том
pl (those)	те	тех	тем	те*	те́ми	тех

* for animate words: accusative = genitive

Relative Pronouns

The relative pronoun кото́рый is declined like an adjective: кни́га, кото́рую чита́ю (the book [which, that] I'm reading)

Numerals

- A list of the cardinal and ordinal numerals can be found on pages 24–25.
- The forms of nouns and adjectives following numerals depend on the numeral.

- after 2, 3, and 4, they are in the genitive singular;
- from 5 to 19, the genitive plural is required; above 19 it is the last digit that determines the case, and 0 acts like 10.

one ticket	–	оди́н биле́т
two tickets	–	два биле́та *gen sing*
five tickets	–	пять биле́тов *gen pl*

	nom	gen	dat	acc	instr	prep
sing m (one)	оди́н	одного́	одному́	оди́н*	одни́м	одно́м
sing f (one)	одна́	одно́й	одно́й	одну́	одно́й	одно́й
sing n (one)	одно́	одного́	одному́	одно́	одни́м	одно́м
two *m/n*	два	двух	двум	два*	двумя́	двух
two *f*	две	двух	двум	две*	двумя́	двух
three	три	трёх	трём	три*	тремя́	трёх
four	четы́ре	четырёх	четырём	четы́ре*	четырьмя́	четырёх
five	пять	пяти́	пяти́	пять	пятью́	пяти́

For example: с двумя́ чемода́нами (with two suitcases)
- The numerals шесть (six) to три́дцать (thirty) are declined like пять. The inflected forms of the numerals through де́сять (ten), as well as два́дцать (twenty) and три́дцать (thirty), are stressed on the ending, while the others are stressed on the stem.
  Both parts of the tens пятьдеся́т (fifty) to во́семьдесят (eighty) are declined like пять:

fifty:	пятьдеся́т *nom*, пяти́десяти *gen*
sixty:	шестьдеся́т *nom*, шести́десяти *gen*
seventy:	се́мьдесят *nom*, семи́десяти *gen*
eighty:	во́семьдесят *nom*, восьми́десяти *gen*

	nom	gen	dat	acc	instr	prep
forty	со́рок	сорока́	сорока́	со́рок	сорока́	сорока́
two hundred	две́сти	двухсо́т	двумста́м	две́сти	двумяста́ми	двухста́х

- These follow the pattern of со́рок:

ninety:	девяно́сто *nom*, девяно́ста *gen*
one hundred:	сто *nom*, ста *gen*

- Both parts of these are declined like две́сти:

three hundred:	три́ста *nom*, трёхсо́т *gen*
four hundred:	четы́рестра *nom*, четырёхсо́т *gen*
five hundred:	пятьсо́т *nom*, пятисо́т *gen*

  as well as the other hundreds through девятьсо́т (nine hundred)
- The numerals ты́сяча (one thousand), миллио́н (one million), and миллиа́рд (one billion) are declined like nouns.
- The ordinal numbers are declined like adjectives:

fifth:	пя́тый *m nom*, пя́того *m gen*

Verbs

Aspects

Most verbs occur in pairs that differ not in their meaning, but in their so-called aspect. The imperfective aspect *ipf* basically focuses on the process of the action being performed, while the perfective aspect *pf* calls attention to the completion of actions.

| to solve (a problem or s.th. similar) | решáть | *ipf* | ("to work on a solution") |
| | решúть | *pf* | ("to finish solving it") |

- Only imperfective verbs form a present tense.

The aspectual partners can differ from one another in various ways: The perfective aspect can be derived from the imperfective verb by attaching a prefix (for a list of possible prefixes, see page 210), as with звать *ipf* → позвáть *pf* (to call); the imperfective can be made into the perfective verb by attaching a syllable or a letter as a suffix (suffixes: -ыва, -ива, -а, -я, etc.), as with рассказáть *pf* → расскáзывать *ipf* (to tell); or both aspectual partners can have different stems, as with говорúть *ipf*/сказáть *pf* (to speak, to say).

In this book, both aspectual partners are always listed with a / separating them, with the imperfective aspect given first. If a verb has only one form, the aspect is indicated.

Conjugation

The conjugated forms of imperfective verbs express present action, while the conjugated forms of perfective verbs denote future action. This distinction is not taken into account in the tables below.

Conjugation I (so called e-conjugation)

Examples читáть (to read) and вернýть (to give back)

Infinitive		читá-ть	верн-ýть
Present	*1st pers. sing*	-ю	-ý
(Future)	*2nd pers. sing*	-ешь	-ёшь
	3rd pers. sing	-ет	-ёт
	1st pers. pl	-ем	-ём
	2nd pers. pl	-ете	-ёте
	3rd pers. pl	-ют	-ýт
Imperative	*sing*	-й	-й
	pl	-йте	-йте

- The endings of the second and third persons singular and the first and second persons plural contain -e- if they are unstressed, and -ё- if they are stressed.
- The endings of the first person singular and the third person plural contain -ю- if the ending is preceded by a vowel or a soft consonant; otherwise, they contain -у-.
- These have the same endings:
  Verbs ending in -ять such as to walk – гуля́ть, гуля́ю, гуля́ешь
  Verbs ending in -еть such as to be ill – боле́ть, боле́ю, боле́ешь
  Verbs ending in -овать and -евать (with a change in the stem), such as to organize – организова́ть, организу́ю, организу́ешь, as well as a few other verbs
- Verbs of this conjugational type, in which a consonant change occurs, usually retain this change throughout all persons, as in to write – писа́ть, пишу́, пи́шешь

Conjugation II (so-called и-conjugation)

Multi-syllable verbs ending in -ить, such as говори́ть (to speak)

Infinitive		говор-и́ть
Present	1ˢᵗ pers. sing	-ю́
(Future)	2ⁿᵈ pers. sing	-и́шь
	3ʳᵈ pers. sing	-и́т
	1ˢᵗ pers. pl	-и́м
	2ⁿᵈ pers. pl	-и́те
	3ʳᵈ pers. pl	-я́т
Imperative	sing	-и́
	pl	-и́те

- A consonant change in the first person singular regularly occurs in verbs of this conjugational type, as in to ask; to beg – проси́ть, прошу́, про́сишь
- A few other verbs with different endings are conjugated in exactly the same way.

Imperative

The imperative is formed like the conjugated forms starting with the second person singular, but with the stress of the first person singular. Add -й to the stem if a vowel precedes the ending; otherwise, add -и́, if the ending of the first person singular is stressed, or -ь, if it is unstressed. The plural is always formed by adding -те: to believe – ве́рить, ве́рю, ве́ришь; верь!, ве́рьте!

The affirmative imperative generally is formed from the perfective verb, while the negative imperative is based on the imperfective verb:

Расскажи́!	Tell!
Расскажи́те!	Tell!
Не расска́зывай!	Don't tell!
Не расска́зывайте!	Don't tell!

Past Tense

Forming the past tense of imperfective and perfective verbs entails taking into account the (grammatical) gender and number of the subject. The infinitive ending -ть is replaced by -л *m*, -ла *f*, -ло *n*, -ли *pl*.

to see	– ви́деть
(I *m*, you *m*, he) saw	– ви́дел *m*
(I *f*, you *f*, she) saw	– ви́дела *f*
(it) saw	– ви́дело *n*
(we, you, they) saw	– ви́дели *pl*

- Some verbs lack the -л of the masculine form.
- Frequently there is a change in stress among the various forms.
- In sentences where these past-tense forms occur, this book supplies all the relevant forms.

Future Tense

The future tense of imperfective and perfective verbs is formed in different ways.

1. Compound Future

Conjugated forms of быть (to be) (see page 210)
+ the infinitive of the imperfective verb:

чита́ть *ipf*	to read
→ Я бу́ду чита́ть.	I will read.

2. Simple Future

Conjugated forms of the perfective verb:

прочита́ть *pf*	to read (through)
→ Я прочита́ю.	I will read (through).

Reflexive Verbs

For the reflexive verb, the sylllable -ся is attached to the end of all forms; in forms that end in a vowel, this syllable is reduced to -сь:

мыть	to wash
мы́ться	to wash oneself
Я мо́юсь.	I wash myself.

Participles

There are four kinds of participles:

Present Active Participle	Present Passive Participle
(of imperfective verbs only) with the suffixes **-ющий, -ущий, -ящий, -ащий** as in чита́**ющий** (reading)	(of imperfective verbs only) with the suffixes **-емый, -имый** as in чита́**емый** (being read)
Past Active Participle	**Past Passive Particle**
(usually of perfective verbs) with the suffixes **-вший, -ший** as in прочита́**вший** (having read through)	(usually of perfective verbs) with the suffixes **-(е)нный, -тый** as in прочи́та**нный** (having been read through)

* They have the same endings as adjectives, and they also exist in long and short forms (see page 199).

"To Be"

The verb to be does not exist in the present:

Он студе́нт.	He is a student.	("He student.")
Э́то хорошо́.	That is fine.	("That fine.")

Negation is accomplished by using не:

Он не студе́нт.	He is not a student.	("He not student.")
Э́то не хорошо́.	That is not fine.	("That not fine.")

(For the past and future forms, see page 210: быть (to be))

"To Have"

To convey the meaning of to have, Russian uses a prepositional construction:
the preposition y + the logical object in the nominative case:

У меня́ су́мка. or У меня́ есть су́мка.	I have a bag. ("With me bag.")

Negation is accomplished by using нет, with the logical object in the genitive:

У меня́ нет су́мки.	I don't have a bag. ("With me not bag.")

To form the past and future tenses, the forms of быть (to be) are used (for forms, see page 210):

У меня́ была́ су́мка.	I had a bag.
У меня́ бу́дет су́мка.	I will have a bag.

Modals or Modal Auxiliaries

These words are used to express the speaker's attitude toward an action.

Necessity or Compulsion

The adjectival short form до́лжен *m*, должна́ *f*, должно́ *n*, должны́ *pl* is used to express "should, must, ought to, have to" when there is a sense of obligation or moral compulsion from within. They agree with the subject in gender and number but are not declined:

| Она́ должна́ чита́ть. | She ought to (has to, should, etc.) read. |

In the past and future, the forms of быть (to be) are used (for forms, see page 210):

| Она́ была́ должна́ чита́ть. | She was supposed to read. |
| Она́ бу́дет должна́ чита́ть. | She will have to read. |

Other Modals Expressing Necessity, Compulsion, Possibility, Desirability

These notions are expressed with impersonal adverbial constructions, with the logical subject in the dative or not translated at all.

1. мо́жно expresses possibility or permission

| Мне мо́жно кури́ть? | May I smoke? |
| Мо́жно кури́ть? | Is smoking allowed? |

The negative is нельзя́; "не мо́жно" does not exist (see below).

2. нельзя́ is the negative of мо́жно. If used with an imperfective verb, it means "not allowed to"; with a perfective verb, its meaning is "not able to."

Мне нельзя́ э́то открыва́ть. *ipf.*	I'm not allowed to open it.
Мне нельзя́ э́то откры́ть. *pf.*	I can't get it open.
Нельзя́ кури́ть!	No smoking (allowed)!

3. на́до and ну́жно express necessity and often suggest a certain compulsion from outside.

| Мне на́до звони́ть. | I have to make a phone call. |

The verb to need can also be translated with ну́жен *m*, нужна́ *f*, ну́жно *n*, нужны́ *pl*. This word agrees in number and gender with the logical object, which is in the nominative:

| Вам нужна́ су́мка. | You need a bag. |

In the past and future, the forms of быть (to be) (see forms on page 210) are used with all these expressions.

Мо́жно бы́ло кури́ть.	Smoking was allowed.
Вам была́ нужна́ су́мка.	You needed a bag.
Мне на́до бу́дет звони́ть.	I will have to make a phone call.

Verbs of Motion

Some verbs that express motion occur in pairs in the imperfective aspect, with one verb rendering *determined* motion in a single specific direction and the other indicating *nondetermined* motion.

nondetermined	determined	
ходи́ть	идти́	to walk, to go
е́здить	е́хать	to ride; to drive

Example: to go to the theater:
   ходи́ть в теа́тр (to attend the theater)
   идти́ в теа́тр (to be on the way to the theater)

- The perfective aspect of both verbs is usually formed by adding a prefix to the determined verb.
  Example: to go (by vehicle); to ride; to drive – е́здить, е́хать *ipf*/пое́хать *pf*

Questions

Intonation differs from English in that the voice is not raised, but lowered, at the end of a question. Use a rising intonation on the question word or on the word or sentence element being inquired about.

Intonation pattern:
   Do you like pancakes?   Вы лю́бите блины́?

Word order in "yes/no" questions is free; frequently, however, the word or sentence component in question is placed at the beginning. If the thing being asked about is the first element of the utterance, the interrogative particle ли may be used as the second element:

	Вы лю́бите блины́?	
or	Блины́ лю́бите?	Do you like pancakes?
or	Лю́бите вы блины́?	
or	Лю́бите ли вы блины́?	

Irregular Verbs

For each verb, the following forms are given here: the infinitive (English translation), the 1st person singular, the 2nd person singular. That allows the verb to be assigned to one of the conjugation patterns in the section beginning on page 204. You should continue conjugating the verb in accordance with the 2nd person singular form.

Additional forms are given only if they have special features (such as a change in stress). The past tense forms are given in this order: masculine - feminine - neuter - plural. If forms are omitted, they are identical to the preceding form. Verbs with a prefix (see page 204) usually are conjugated in the same way as verbs with no prefix (an exception: the prefix вы-, which is always stressed in perfective verbs). For verbs with identical prefixed and non-prefixed versions, only the non-prefixed forms are given here.

These are important prefixes: в-, во-, въ-, вз-, взо,- взъ-, вс-, воз-, вос-, вы-, до-, за-, из-, изо-, изъ-, ис-, на-, над-, надо-, о-, об-, обо-, объ-, от-, ото-, отъ-, пере-, по-, под-, подо-, подъ-, пред-, предо-, предъ-, при-, про-, раз-, разо-, разъ-, рас-, с-, со-, съ-, у-. For verbs that have both a reflexive and a non-reflexive form, only the non-reflexive form is given. To form the reflexive, see page 206.

бежа́ть (run), бегу́, бежи́шь, бегу́т 3rd p. pl; беги́(те)!
бить (hit), бью, бьёшь; бей(те)!
боя́ться (be afraid), бою́сь, бои́шься
брать (take), беру́, берёшь; брал, брала́, бра́ло
бро́сить (throw), бро́шу, бро́сишь
буди́ть (wake), бужу́, бу́дишь
быть (be – no present tense!), бу́ду, бу́дешь; был, была́, бы́ло; будь(те)!
вари́ть (cook, boil), варю́, ва́ришь
везти́ (drive, convey), везу́, везёшь; вёз, везла́
вести́ (lead, conduct), веду́, ведёшь; вёл, вела́
взгляну́ть (look, glance), взгляну́, взгля́нешь
взять (take), возьму́, возьмёшь; взял, взяла́, взя́ло, взя́ли
ви́деть (see), ви́жу, ви́дишь
води́ть (lead; drive), вожу́, во́дишь
возврати́ть (give back), возвращу́, возврати́шь

вози́ть (drive, convey), вожу́, во́зишь
врать (lie, tell lies), вру, врёшь; врал, врала́, вра́ло
встава́ть (get up), встаю́, встаёшь
встать (get up), вста́ну, вста́нешь; встань(те)!
встре́тить (meet, greet), встре́чу, встре́тишь
гляде́ть (look), гляжу́, гляди́шь
гото́вить (prepare), гото́влю, гото́вишь
дава́ть (give), даю́, даёшь
дари́ть (present with), дарю́, да́ришь
дать (give), дам, дашь, даст, дади́м, дади́те, даду́т; дал, дала́, да́ли; дай(те)!
дви́гать (move), дви́жу, дви́жешь
дели́ть (divide), делю́, де́лишь
держа́ть (hold), держу́, де́ржишь
е́здить (drive), е́зжу, е́здишь
есть (eat), ем, ешь, ест, еди́м, еди́те, едя́т; ел, е́ла, е́ли, ешь(те)!

éхать (drive), éду, éдешь; поезжáй(те)!

ждать (wait), жду, ждёшь; ждал, ждалá, ждáло

жечь (burn), жгу, жжёшь, жжёт, жжём, жжёте, жгут; жёг, жгла; жги(те)!

жить (live), живý, живёшь; жил, жи лá, жи́ло

забы́ть (forget), забýду, забýдешь; забы́л; забýдь(те)!

закры́ть (close), закрóю, закрóешь

замéтить (notice), замéчу, замéтишь

звать (call), зовý, зовёшь; звал, звалá, звáло

идти́ (go), идý, идёшь; шёл, шла, шло, шли; иди́(те)! (with prefix, e.g.:) пойти́, пойдý, пойдёшь; пошёл; пойди́(те)!

искáть (seek), ищý, и́щешь

исчéзнуть (disappear), исчéзну, исчéзнешь; исчéз, исчéзла

класть (put, lay, place), кладý, кладёшь

красть (steal), крадý, крадёшь

кричáть (cry, shout), кричý, кричи́шь

купи́ть (buy), куплю́, кýпишь

лежáть (lie), лежý, лежи́шь

летéть (fly), лечý, лети́шь

лечи́ть (cure), лечý, лéчишь

лечь (lie), лягу, ля́жешь; лёг, леглá; ляг(те)!

лови́ть (catch), ловлю́, лóвишь

ложи́ть (lay), ложý, лóжишь

ложи́ться (lie down), ложýсь, ложи́шься

люби́ть (love), люблю́, лю́бишь

молчáть (be silent), молчý, молчи́шь

мочь (be able, can), могý, мóжешь; мог, моглá

мыть (wash), мóю, мóешь; мóй(те)!

надéть (put on), надéну, надé нешь

начáть (begin), начнý, начнёшь; нáчал, началá, нáчало

нести́ (carry; wear), несý, несёшь; нёс, неслá

носи́ть (carry; wear), ношý, нóсишь

нрáвиться (please), нрáвлюсь, нрáвишься

обманýть (deceive), обманý, обмáнешь

отвéтить (answer), отвéчу, отвéтишь

откры́ть (open), открóю, открóешь

ошиби́ться (be mistaken), ошибýсь, ошибёшься

пасть (fall), падý, падёшь

петь (sing), пою́, поёшь

писáть (write), пишý, пи́шешь

пить (drink), пью, пьёшь; пил, пилá, пи́ло; пей(те)!

плáкать (cry), плáчу, плáчешь

плати́ть (pay), плачý, плáтишь

плыть (swim), плывý, плывёшь; плыл, плылá

показáть (show), покажý, покáжешь

получи́ть (receive, get), получý, полýчишь

помóчь (help), помогý, помóжешь; помóг, помоглá

поня́ть (understand), поймý, поймёшь; пóнял, понялá, пóняло

посети́ть (visit), посещý, посети́шь

предпочéсть (prefer), предпочтý, предпочтёшь; предпочёл, предпочлá

прибы́ть (arrive), прибýду, прибýдешь; при́был, прибылá, при́было

привы́кнуть (get used to), привы́кну, привы́кнешь; привы́к, привы́кла

пригласи́ть (invite), приглашý, пригласи́шь

прийти́ (come), придý, придёшь; пришёл, пришлá

приня́ть (receive), примý, при́мешь; при́нял, принялá, при́няло

продáть (sell), продáм, продáшь, продáст, продади́м,

продади́те, продаду́т;
про́дал, продала́, про́дало;
прода́й(те)!
проси́ть (ask for), прошу́, про́сишь
прости́ть (forgive), прощу́,
прости́шь
пря́тать (hide), пря́чу, пря́чешь
пусти́ть (let), пущу́, пу́стишь
расти́ (grow), расту́, растёшь;
рос, росла́
ре́зать (cut), ре́жу, ре́жешь
сади́ть (plant), сажу́, са́дишь
серди́ть (anger), сержу́, се́рдишь
сесть (sit down), ся́ду, ся́дешь;
сел; сядь(те)!
сиде́ть (sit), сижу́, сиди́шь
сказа́ть (say), скажу́, ска́жешь
слать (send), шлю, шлёшь
служи́ть (serve), служу́,
слу́жишь
слы́шать (hear), слы́шу,
слы́шишь
смотре́ть (look), смотрю́,
смо́тришь
снять (take off; photograph; rent),
сниму́, сни́мешь; снял, сняла́,
сня́ло
согласи́ться (agree), соглашу́сь,
согласи́шься

спасти́ (save), спасу́, спасёшь;
спас, спасла́
спать (sleep), сплю, спишь;
спал, спала́, спа́ло
спроси́ть (ask), спрошу́,
спро́сишь
ста́вить (put), ста́влю, ста́вишь
стать (begin; become), ста́ну,
ста́нешь; стань(те)!
стоя́ть (stand), стою́, стои́шь
терпе́ть (suffer), терплю́,
те́рпишь
торопи́ть (hurry), тороплю́,
торо́пишь
тра́тить (spend), тра́чу, тра́тишь
узнава́ть (hear, find out), узнаю́,
узнаёшь
умере́ть (die), умру́, умрёшь;
у́мер, умерла́
учи́ть (learn), учу́, у́чишь
хвати́ть (seize; suffice), хвачу́,
хва́тишь
ходи́ть (go), хожу́, хо́дишь
хоте́ть (want), хочу́, хо́чешь,
хо́чет, хоти́м, хоти́те, хотя́т
шуме́ть (make a noise), шумлю́,
шуми́шь
шути́ть (joke), шучу́, шу́тишь

A

a [a] and

абонемéнт [abaniMYENT] subscription

абсцéсс [apsTSES] abscess

авари́йная световáя сигнализáция [avaRInaya svitaVAya signaliZAtsyya] emergency flashers

авари́йная слýжба [avaRInaya SLUZHba] road patrol

авáрия [avaRIya] breakdown, accident

áвгуст [AVgust] August

áвиа [Avia] airmail

авиакомпáния [aviakamPAniya] airline

авиапочтóй [aviaPOCHtay] via airmail

автóбус [aFTObus] bus

автóбус-шаттл [aFTObus-SHATL] shuttle bus

автóбус-экспрéсс [aFTObus-ikSPRYES] airport bus

автовокзáл [aftavagZAL] bus station

автомагистрáль f [aftamagiSTRAL'] freeway, highway

автомáт [aftaMAT] automat; submachine gun

автомáт по продáже билéтов [aftaMAT pa-praDAzhy biLYEtaf] ticket machine

автоматическая передáча [aftamaTIchiskaya piriDAcha] automatic transmission

автоматический [aftamaTIchiski] automatic

автоотвéтчик [aftaatVYETshik] answering machine

автоспýск [aftaSPUSK] self-timer, automatic shutter release

автостóп [aftaSTOP] hitchhiking

автостоя́нка [aftastaYANka] stopping place, rest area

агéнтство [aGYENTstva] agency

адáптер [aDAPtir] adapter

адвокáт [advaKAT] lawyer

администрáция [adminiSTRAtsyya] administration; reception desk

áдрес [Adris] address

Áзия [Aziya] Asia

акварéль f [akvaRYEL'] watercolor

акклиматизи́роваться ipf a. pf [aklimatiZIravatsa] to get acclimated

аккумуля́тор [akumuLYAtar] accumulator, battery

аккумуля́тор хóлода [akumuLYAtar KHOlada] freezer pack

акт [AKT] act

актёр / актри́са [akTYOR/akTRIsa] actor/actress

аллерги́ческий рини́т [alirGIchiski riNIT] hay fever

аллерги́я [alirGIya] allergy

алтáрь m [alTAR'] altar

альпини́зм [al'piNIZM] mountain climbing, mountaineering

алюми́ниевая фольгá [alyuMInivaya fal'GA] aluminum foil

Амéрика [aMYErika] America

америкáнец / америкáнка [amiriKAnits/amiriKANka] American (man, woman)

ангинá [anGIna] chest pain

англи́йский [anGLIYski] English

Áнглия [ANgliya] England

анекдóт [anigDOT] joke

антибиóтик [antibiOtik] antibiotic

антиква́рный магази́н [antiKVARny magaZIN] antiques store

антифри́з [antiFRIS] antifreeze

антра́кт [anTRAKT] *(theater)* intermission

аплодисме́нты *m pl* [aplodisMYENty] applause

аппара́т [apaRAT] gadget

аппети́т [apiTIT] appetite

апре́ль *m* [aPRYEL'] April

апте́ка [apTYEka] pharmacy

арбу́з [arBUS] watermelon

аре́нда [aRYENda] rent

арестова́ть *ipf a. pf* [aristaVAT'] to arrest

а́рка [ARka] arch

археоло́гия [arkhiaLOgiya] archeology

архите́ктор [arkhiTYEKtar] architect

архитекту́ра [arkhitikTUra] architecture

аспири́н [aspiRIN] aspirin

а́стма [ASTma] asthma

ателье́ [atiL'YE] tailoring/dressmaking establishment

аэро́бика [aeRObika] aerobics

аэропо́рт [aeraPORT] airport

аэропорто́вые сбо́ры *m pl* [aeraparTOvyye ZBOry] airport tax

Б

ба́бочка [BAbachka] butterfly; bowtie

ба́бушка [BAbushka] grandmother

бага́ж [baGASH] baggage

бага́жная ка́сса [baGAZHnaya KAsa] baggage counter

бага́жник [baGAZHnik] trunk *(of car)*

бага́жное отделе́ние [baGAZHnaye addiLYEniye] baggage office

бадминто́н [badminTON] badminton

байда́рка [bayDARka] paddle boat

бак [BAK] tank

бакенба́рды *f pl* [bakinBARdy] sideburns

бал [BAL] *(dance)* ball

бале́т [baLYET] ballet

балко́н [balKON] balcony

ба́мпер [BAMpir] bumper

бандеро́ль *f* [bandiROL'] *(postal)* printed matter

банк [BANK] bank

ба́нка [BANka] can, jar

банкно́та [bankNOta] banknote, bill

банкома́т [bankaMAT] ATM

бар [BAR] bar

бараба́нная перепо́нка [baraBAnaya piriPONka] eardrum

бара́нина [baRAnina] mutton, lamb

барахо́лка [baraKHOLka] flea market

баро́кко [baROka] baroque

баскетбо́л [baskidBOL] basketball

бассе́йн [baSYEYN] swimming pool

батаре́йка [bataRYEYka] battery

ба́шня [BASHnya] tower

бебифо́н [bibiFON] baby monitor

бе́гать *ipf* [BYEgat'] to run, jog, race

бе́дный [BYEDny] poor

бедро́ [biDRO] hip

бежа́ть/побежа́ть [biZHAT'/pabiZHAT'] to run, race

бе́жевый [BYEzhyvy] beige

без + *gen* [BYES] without

безалкого́льный [bizalkaGOL'ny] nonalcoholic

безве́трие [bizVYEtriye] calm

безвку́сный [bizFKUSny] tasteless

безопа́сная була́вка [bizaPASnaya buLAFka] safety pin

безопáсный [bizaPASny] safe

безрабóтный [bizraBOTny] unemployed

белокýрый [bilaKUry] blond

бéлый [BYEly] white

бельё [biL'YO] laundry *(textiles)*

бельевáя верёвка [bilyiVAya viRYOFka] clothesline

бéрег [BYErik] shore, coast

берéменность *f* [biRYEminast'] pregnancy

бесплáтный [bisPLATny] free, gratis

беспокóиться/обеспокóиться (о + *prep)* [bispaKOitsa/abispaKOitsa] to worry (about)

беспóшлинный [bisPOshliny] duty-free

бессознáтельный [bisaZNAtil'ny] unconscious

бессóнница [biSOnitsa] insomnia

бессты́дный [biSTYDny] shameless, indecent

бéшеный [BYEshiny] enraged

бигудú *f pl* [biguDI] hair rollers

бижутéрия [bizhuTYEriya] costume jewelry

бикúни *n* [biKlini] bikini

билéт [biLYET] ticket (of admission)

билéт в óба концá [biLYET v-Oba kanTSA] round-trip ticket

билéт на... поéздок [biLYET na-... paYEZdak] pass for ... trips

билéтная кácca [biLYETnaya KAsa] ticket window/counter

бинт [BINT] bandage

бирюзá [biryuZA] turquoise

бирюзóвый [biryuZOvy] turquoise

благодарúть/поблагодарúть + *acc* [blagadaRIT'/pablagadaRIT'] to thank

бланк [BLANK] (printed) form

блéйзер [BLYEYzir] blazer

ближáйший [bliZHAYshy] nearest

блúжний свет [BLIZHni SVYET] dimmed lights

блúзкий (к + *dat)* [BLISki (k-...)] near, close

блúзко [BLISka] *adv* near, close

блокнóт [blakNOT] writing pad

блýзка [BLUSka] blouse

блюдо [BLYUda] dish (of food), course

блюдо дня [BLYUda DNYA] daily special

блюдце [BLYUtse] saucer

бог/богúня [BOK/baGInya] god/goddess

богáтый [baGAty] rich

богослужéние [bagasluZHEniye] religious service

бокáл [baKAL] wine glass

бóлее [BOliye ...] *adv used to form comparative*, more than

болéзнь *f* [baLYEZN'] illness, disease

болéть *ipf* + *acc* [baLYET'] to hurt, be painful

болеутоля́ющее [baliutaLYAyushiye] painkiller

болóто [baLOta] swamp, marsh

болт [BOLT] bolt

боль *f* [BOL'] pain

больнúца [balNItsa] hospital

больнóй [bal'NOY] ill, sick

бóльше + *gen or* чем + *nom* [BOL'she ..., CHEM ...] more than

большóй [bal'SHOY] large, big

бородá [baraDA] beard

ботанúческий сад [bataNIchiski SAT] botanical gardens

боя́ться *ipf* [baYAtsa] to be afraid

браслéт [braSLYET] bracelet

брат [BRAT] brother

брать/взять [BRAT'/VZYAT'] to take

брать/взять взаймы́ (у + *gen)* [BRAT'/VZYAT' vzayMY (u-...)] to borrow *(from s.o.)*

брать/взять напрокáт [BRAT'/ VZYAT' napraKAT] to rent

брúтвенный аппарáт [BRITviny apaRAT] shaver

брить(ся)/побри́ть(ся) [BRIT'(sa)/paBRIT'(sa)] to shave (o.s.)
бритьё [briT'YO] shave
бро́нза [BRONza] bronze
брони́рование [braNIravaniye] reservation
брони́ровать/заброни́ровать [braNIravat'/pabraNIravat'] to reserve
бро́нхи *m pl* [BRONkhi] bronchial tubes
бро́ня [BROnya] reservation
бро́шка [BROSHka] brooch, pin
брю́ки *f pl* [BRYUki] pants
буди́льник [buDIL'nik] alarm clock
буди́ть/разбуди́ть [buDIT'/razbuDIT'] to wake
бу́дущее [BUdushiye] future
бу́дущий [BUdushi] future
бу́ква [BUKva] letter *(alphabet)*
буке́т [buKYET] bouquet
букси́ровать/отбукси́ровать [bukSIravat'/adbukSIravat'] to tow (away)
буксиро́вочный автомоби́ль [buksiROvachny aftamaBIL'] tow truck
буксиро́вочный трос [buksiROvachny TROS] tow rope
була́вка [buLAFka] pin; safety pin
бу́лочка [BUlachka] roll, bun
бу́лочная [BUlachnaya] bakery
бума́га [buMAga] paper
бума́жник [buMAZHnik] billfold, wallet
бума́жный [buMAZHny] paper
бу́ря [BUrya] storm
бутербро́д [butirBROT] open-face sandwich
буты́лка [buTYLka] bottle
буты́лочка с со́ской [buTYLka s-SOskay] baby bottle
буфе́т [buFYET] breakfast buffet; snack bar
бу́хта [BUKHta] bay
бы́вший [BYFshy] former
бы́стрый [BYstry] fast, rapid

быть [BYT'] to be
бэбиси́ттер [bebiSItir] babysitter
бюро́ [byuRO] office
бюро́ обслу́живания тури́стов [byuRO apSLUzhyvaniya tuRIstaf] tourist information office
бюро́ по тури́зму [byuRO pa-tuRIZmu] tourism office
бюстга́льтер [byuzdGAL'tir] bra

В

в + *acc* [f-...] *(location)* to, into; at (...o'clock)
в + *prep* [f-...] in
в бу́дущем [v-BUdushim] in the future
в доро́ге [v-daROgye] on the road
в друго́м ме́сте [v-druGOM MYEStye] somewhere else
в сре́днем [f-SRYEDnim] *adv* on the average
ваго́н [vaGON] railroad car
ваго́н-рестора́н [vaGON-ristaRAN] dining car
ва́жный [VAZHny] important
ва́за [VAza] vase
валю́та [vaLYUta] currency
валю́тный курс [vaLYUTny KURS] exchange rate
ва́нна [VAna] bathtub
ва́нная [VAnaya] bathroom
варёный [vaRYOny] boiled
варе́нье [vaRYEn'ye] jam
вари́ть/свари́ть [VArit'/SVArit'] to boil; to cook
варьете́ [varieTE] variety show
вас *gen, acc* [VAS] you (familiar)
Вас *gen, acc* [VAS] you (polite)
ва́та [VAta] (absorbent) cotton
ва́тная па́лочка [VATnaya PAlachka] cotton swab

ваш *m*/ва́ша *f*/ва́ше *n*/ва́ши *pl*
[VASH/VAsha/VAshe/VAshy] your

вверх [VVYERKH] up, upward(s)

вдове́ц/вдова́ [vdaVYETS/vdaVA]
widower/widow

вдруг [VDRUK] *adv* suddenly

вегетариа́нский [vigitariANski]
vegetarian

ве́жливый [VYEZHlivy] polite

везде́ [viZDYE] everywhere

век [VYEK] century

вели́кий [viLIki] great

вели́чие [viLIchiye] greatness

величина́ [vilichiNA] size

велосипе́д [vilasiPYET] bicycle

велоспо́рт [vilaSPORT] biking

вентиля́тор [vintiLYAtar] fan

верёвка [viRYOFka] string; rope

ве́рить/пове́рить (в + *acc)*
[VYErit/paVYErit'(f-...)] to believe

верну́ться ➢ возвраща́ться

ве́рный [VYERny] true

вероя́тный [viraYATny] probable

вертика́льный форма́т
[virtiKAL'ny farMAT] portrait format

верх [VYERKH] top; acme

верхо́м [virKHOM] on horseback

верши́на [virSHYna] summit, peak

вес [VYES] weight

весёлый [viSYOly] cheerful

весло́ [viSLO] oar

весна́ [viSNA] spring

ве́тер [VYEtir] wind

ветрово́е стекло́ [vitraVOye
stiKLO] windshield

ве́тряная о́спа [VYEtrinaya Ospa]
chicken pox

ветчина́ [vichiNA] ham

ве́чер [VYEchir] evening

вечери́нка [vichiRINka] party

вече́рнее пла́тье [viCHERniye
PLAt'ye] formal dress

ве́чером [VYEchiram] in the
evening

вещь *f* [VYESH] thing

взгляд [VZGLYAT] glance, look

вздохну́ть ➢ дыша́ть

взла́мывать/взлома́ть
[VZLAmyvat/vzlaMAT'] to break
open

взлома́ть ➢ взла́мывать

взро́слый [VZROsly] adult

взять ➢ брать

вид [VIT] type; prospect; aspect
(verb)

ви́део [VIdia] video (film)

видеока́мера [vidiaKAmira] video
camera

видеокассе́та [vidiakaSYEta] video
cassette

видеомагнитофо́н
[vidiamagnitaFON] video recorder

ви́деть/уви́деть [VIdit'/uVIdit'] to
see

ви́за [VIza] visa

византи́йский [vizanTIYski]
Byzantine

ви́лка [VILka] fork; plug

ви́лла [VIla] villa

вина́ [viNA] fault

виндсёрфинг [vintSYERfink]
windsurfing

ви́нный [VIny] *adj* wine

вино́ [viNO] *n* wine

виново́дочный магази́н
[vinaVOdachny magaZIN] liquor
store

виногра́д [vinaGRAT] grapes

виногра́дный са́хар [vinaGRADny
SAkhar] dextrose

винт [VINT] screw

ви́рус [VIrus] virus

витри́на [viTRIna] store window

включа́ть/включи́ть [fklyuCHAT'/
fklyuCHIT'] to turn on; include

включённый [fklyuCHOny]
included; turned on

включи́ть ➢ включа́ть

вкус [FKUS] taste

вку́сный [FKUSny] tasty

владе́лец/владе́лица [vlaDYElits/
vlaDYElitsa] owner

влива́ние [vliVAniye] infusion

вме́сте [VMYEStye] *adv* together

вме́сто + *gen* [VMYESta] instead (of)

вне + *gen* [VNYE] outside

внеза́пный [vniZAPny] sudden

внизу́ [vniZU] below

внима́ние [vniMAniye] attention

внук/вну́чка [VNUK/VNUCHka] grandson/granddaughter

вну́тренний двор [VNUtriny DVOR] inner courtyard

вну́тренний полёт [VNUtriny paLYOT] domestic flight

внутри́ + *gen* [vnuTRI] inside; within

во вре́мя + *gen* [va-VRYEmya] during

во́время [VOvrimya] *adv* on time

вода́ [vaDA] water

води́тель/ница [vaDItil'/nitsa] driver

води́тельские права́ [vaDItil'skiye praVA] driver's license

во́дный [VODny] *adj* water

во́дный велосипе́д [VODny vilasiPYET] paddle boat

водола́з [vadaLAS] diver

водопа́д [vadaPAT] waterfall

возврати́ть ➢ возвраща́ть

возврати́ться ➢ возвраща́ться

возвраща́ть/возврати́ть [vazvraSHAT'/vazvraTIT'] to give back

возвраща́ться/верну́ться [vazvraSHAtsa/virNUtsa] to go back, return

возвраще́ние домо́й [vazvraSHEniye daMOY] return trip

во́здух [VOZdukh] air

возду́шный [vazDUSHny] *adj* air

возмо́жный [vazMOZHny] possible

во́зраст [VOZrast] age

войди́те! [vayDItye] Come in!

войти́ ➢ входи́ть

вокза́л [vagZAL] train station

вокру́г + *gen* [vaKRUK] around

волды́рь *f* [VOLdyr'] blister

волейбо́л [valiyBOL] volleyball

волне́ние [valNYEniye] rough seas; agitation

во́лосы *m pl* [VOlasy] hair

воня́ть *ipf (+ instr)* [vaNYAT'] to reek (of)

вопро́с [vaPROS] question

вор [VOR] thief

воро́та *n pl* [vaROta] gate

воскресе́нье [vaskriSYEn'ye] Sunday

воспале́ние [vaspaLYEniye] inflammation

воспале́ние ло́бных па́зух [vaspaLYEniye LOBnykh PAzukh] sinusitis

воспале́ние сре́днего у́ха [vaspaLYEniye SRYEDniva Ukha] inflammation of the middle ear

воспрепя́тствовать ➢ препя́тствовать

восто́к [vaSTOK] east

восто́чный [vaSTOCHny] eastern

восхити́тельный [vaskhiTItil'ny] delightful

восхищённый *(+ instr)* [vaskhiSHOny] delighted (with)

впаде́ние [fpaDYEniye] confluence

вперёд [fpiRYOT] forward

впереди́ [fpiriDI] in front

впечатля́ющий [fpichatLYAyushi] impressive

впры́скивание [FPRYskivaniye] injection

врата́рь *m* [vraTAR'] goalkeeper

врач [VRACH] doctor, physician

враче́бное заключе́ние [vraCHEBnaye zaklyuCHEniye] medical certificate

врач-специали́ст [VRACH-spitsyaLIST] medical specialist

вред [VRYED] harm, damage

вре́менный [VRYEminy] temporary

вре́мя *n* [VRYEmya] time

вре́мя *n* го́да [VRYEmya GOda] season

вре́мя от вре́мени [VRYEmya at-VRYEmini] now and then

все [FSYE] everybody, all

всё [FSYO] everything, all

всегда [fsigDA] always

всё-таки [FSYO-taki] nevertheless

вспомнить ➢ помнить

вспотеть ➢ потеть

вспышка [FSPYSHka] flash (attachment)

вставать/встать [fstaVAT'/FSTAT'] to get up, rise

встретить ➢ встречать

встреча [FSTRYEcha] meeting

встречать/встретить + acc [fstriCHAT'/FSTRYEtit'] to meet; greet

вторник [FTORnik] Tuesday

второе (блюдо) [ftaROye (BLYUda)] entrée, main course

второй [ftaROY] second

второстепенная дорога [ftarastiPYEnaya daROga] secondary road

вход [FKHOD] entry; entrance

входить/войти [fkhaDIT'/vayTI] to come in

входной [fkhadNOY] adj entrance

вчера [fchiRA] yesterday

въезд [VYEST] entrance; freeway ramp; entry

Вы [VY] (polite form) you

вы pers pron [VY] you

выбирать/выбрать [vybiRAT'/VYbrat'] to pick out, select

выбор [VYbar] selection

выбрать ➢ выбирать

вывеска [VYviska] notice, sign

выгладить ➢ гладить

выгода [VYgada] advantage

выдача багажа [VYdacha baGAzha] baggage claim

выезд [VYyist] departure; going out

выигрывать/выиграть [vylgryvat'/VYigrat'] to win

выйти ➢ выходить

выключатель m [vyklyuCHAtil'] switch

вылет [VYlit] take-off, (plane) departure

вылечить ➢ лечить

вымыть ➢ мыть

вымыться ➢ мыться

выписывать/выписать [vyPIsyvat'/VYpisat'] to prescribe

выпить ➢ пить

выплачивать/выплатить [vyPLAchivat'/VYplatit'] to pay (out)

выражение [vyraZHEniye] expression

высокий [vySOki] high, tall

высокое напряжение [vySOkaye napriZHEniye] high voltage

высота [vysaTA] height

высохнуть ➢ сохнуть

выставка [VYstafka] exhibition

выстирать ➢ стирать

высушить ➢ сушить

выхлоп [VYkhlap] (car) muffler

выход [VYkhat] exit

выходить/выйти [vykhaDIT'/VYti] to go out, get out

выходить/выйти замуж за... + acc [vykhaDIT'/VYti ZAmush za-...] to marry (a man)

вышивка [VYshyfka] embroidery

вязаная кофта [VYAzanaya KOFta] cardigan

Г

габаритные фары m pl [gabaRITnyye FАry] parking lights

газ [GAS] gas

газета [gaZYEta] newspaper

газетный киоск [gaZYETny kiOSK] newsstand

газовый [GAzavy] adj gas

газовый баллон [GAzavy baLON] gas cartridge

газо́н [gaZON] lawn

га́зы *m pl* [GAzy] flatulence

галантере́я [galantiRYEya] drugstore, dry goods store

галере́я [galiRYEya] gallery

га́лстук [GALstuk] necktie

гандбо́л [gandBOL] handball

гара́ж [gaRASH] garage

гара́нтия [gaRANtiya] guarantee

гардеро́б [gardiROP] coat check

гастроно́м [gastraNOM] delicatessen

гвозди́ка [gvazDIka] carnation

генера́тор [giniRAtar] generator

гигиени́ческая прокла́дка [gigiyiNIchiskaya praKLATka] sanitary napkin, panty liner

гид [GIT] guide

гимна́стика [gimNAstika] gymnastics

гла́вный [GLAVny] *adj* main, chief

гла́вным о́бразом [GLAVnym Obrazam] *adv* mainly

главпочта́мт [glafpachTAMT] main post office

гла́дить/вы́гладить [GLAdit'/ VYgladit'] to iron

глаз [GLAS], *pl* глаза́ [glaZA] eye

глазны́е ка́пли *f pl* [GLAZnyye KApli] eye drops

гли́на [GLIna] clay

гли́ссер [GLIsir] hydroplane

глубо́кий [gluBOki] *adj* deep

глубоко́ [glubaKO] *adv* deeply

глу́пый [GLUpy] dumb, stupid

глухо́й [gluKHOY] deaf

глухонемо́й [glukhaniMOY] deaf-mute

гляде́ть/погляде́ть [glyaDYET'/ paglyaDYET'] to look

гнило́й [gniLOY] rotten

гной [GNOY] pus

говори́ть/поговори́ть [gavaRIT'/ pagavaRIT'] to speak, talk

говори́ть/сказа́ть [gavaRIT'/ skaZAT'] to say

говя́дина [gaVYAdina] beef

год [GOT] year

гол [GOL] *(sports)* goal

голова́ [galaVA] head

головна́я боль [galaVNAya BOL'] headache

головокруже́ние [galavakruZHEniye] dizziness

голо́дный [gaLODny] hungry

гололе́дица [galaLYEditsa] ice-covered ground

го́лый [GOly] naked, bare

гольф [GOL'F] golf

го́ночные лы́жи *f pl* [GOnachnyye LYzhy] cross-country skis

го́ночный велосипе́д [GOnachny vilasiPYET] racing bike

гонча́рные изде́лия [ganCHARnyye izDYEliya] earthenware

гонча́рня [ganCHARnya] *(place)* pottery

гора́ [gaRA] mountain

горизонта́льный форма́т [garizanTAL'ny farMAT] landscape format

го́рло [GORla] neck, throat

го́рничная [GORnichnaya] chambermaid

го́рный велосипе́д [GORny vilasiPYET] mountain bike

го́рный перехо́д [GORny piriKHOT] mountain pass

го́род [GOrat] city, town

городска́я стена́ [garatSKAya stiNA] city wall

городско́й авто́бус [garatSKOY aFTObus] city bus

городско́й разгово́р [garatSKOY razgaVOR] *(telephone)* local call

горо́х [gaROKH] peas

горчи́ца [garCHItsa] mustard

го́ры *f pl* [GOry] mountains

го́рький [GOR'ki] bitter

горя́чая вода́ [gaRYAchaya vaDA] hot water

горя́чий [gaRYAchi] hot

господи́н [gaspaDIN] Mr.

госпожа [gaspaZHA] Mrs./Ms.

гостеприимство [gastipriIMstva] hospitality

гость m/гостья f [GOST'/GOst'ya] guest

государство [gasuDARstva] state

готовить/приготовить [gaTOvit'/ prigaTOvit'] to prepare

готовый [gaTOvy] prepared, ready

гравюра [graVYUra] engraving

градусник [GRADusnik] thermometer

гражданство [grazhDANstva] citizenship

грамм [GRAM] gram

граница [graNItsa] border

графика [GRAfika] drawing(s); graphic art

графин [graFIN] carafe

гребная лодка [gribNAya LOTka] rowboat

гренок [griNOK] toast

грести/погрести [griSTI/pagriSTI] to row

гриб [GRIP] mushroom

гриль m [GRIL'] grill

грипп [GRIP] flu

гроза [graZA] thunderstorm

громкий [GROMki] loud

громкоговоритель m [gramkagavaRItil'] (loud)speaker

грот [GROT] grotto

грудной ребёнок [grudNOY riBYOnak] infant

грудь f [GRUT'] breast, chest

грузовик [gruzaVIK] truck

группа [GRUpa] group

группа крови [GRUpa KROvi] blood group

груша [GRUsha] pear

грязный [GRYAZny] dirty

губа [guBA] lip

губная помада [gubNAya paMAda] lipstick

гулять/погулять [guLYAT'/ paguLYAT'] to go for a walk

да [DA] yes

давать/дать [daVAT'/DAT'] to give

давление [daVLYEniye] pressure

далёкий [daLYOki] adj distant

далеко [daliKO] adv far

дальний свет [DAL'ni SVYET] bright lights

дамба [DAMba] dam

дамская сумочка [DAMskaya SUmachka] purse, handbag

дарить/подарить [daRIT'/ padaRIT'] to present (with)

дата [DAta] date

дата рождения [DAta raZHDYEniya] date of birth

дать ➢ давать

дача [DAcha] country cottage

дверной код [dvirNOY KOT] door code

дверь f [DVYER'] door

двигатель m [DVIgatil'] motor

движение [dviZHEniye] movement; traffic

двойной [dvayNOY] double

двор [DVOR] courtyard

дворец [dvaRYETS] palace

двухъярусная кровать [dvukhYArusnaya kraVAT'] bunk bed

девичья фамилия [DYEvichya faMIliya] maiden name

девочка [DYEvachka] (little) girl

девушка [DYEvushka] (young) girl

дедушка m [DYEdushka] grandfather

дежурная [diZHURnaya] concierge, "floor lady"

дезинфицировать ipf a. pf [dizinfiTSYravat'] to disinfect

дезинфицирующее средство [dizinfiTSYruyushiye SRYETstva] disinfectant дезодора́нт [dizadaRANT] deodorant

действи́тельный [diystVItil'ny] real, actual; valid

дека́брь m [diKABR'] December

де́лать/сде́лать [DYElat'/ZDYElat'] to do

де́ло [DYEla] matter; business

денатури́рованный спирт [dinatuRIravany SPIRT] denatured alcohol

де́нежный [DYEnizhny] adj money

день m [DYEN'] day

день m рожде́ния [DYEN' raZHDYEniya] birthday

де́ньги f pl [DYEN'gi] money

дере́вня [diRYEVnya] village

де́рево [DYEriva] tree; wood

держа́ть ipf [dirZHAT'] to hold

десе́рт [diSYERT] dessert

десна́ [diSNA] gums

де́тская площа́дка [DYETskaya plaSHATka] playground

де́тский [DYETski] children's, child's

Де́тский мир [DYETski MIR] toy store

дешёвый [diSHOvy] cheap

джаз [DZHAS] jazz

джем [DZHEM] jam

джи́нсы m pl [DZHYNSy] jeans

диабе́т [diaBYET] diabetes

диабе́тик [diaBYEtik] diabetic

диа́гноз [diAGnos] diagnosis

дива́н(-крова́ть) [diVAN(-kraVAT')] sleeper sofa

дие́та [diYEta] diet

диети́ческое пита́ние [diyiTIchiskaye piTAniye] diet food; bland diet

ди́кий [DIki] wild

дире́кция [diRYEKtsyya] management (office)

дирижёр [diriZHOR] conductor

дискоте́ка [diskaTYEka] discotheque

дифтери́я [diftiRIya] diphtheria

дли́нный [DLIny] long

для + gen [dli-...] for

днём [DNYOM] in the daytime

до + gen [da-...] up to, until; before (point in time)

до востре́бования [da-vaSTRYEbavaniya] poste restante

до обе́да [da-aBYEda] before midday

добавля́ть/доба́вить [dabaVLYAT'/daBAvit'] to add

Добро́ пожа́ловать! [daBRO paZHAlavat'] Welcome!

дове́рие (к + dat) [daVYEriye (k-...)] confidence (in)

дово́льно [daVOL'na] adv rather

дово́льный [daVOL'ny] satisfied

догова́риваться/договори́ться [dagaVArivatsa/dagavaRItsa] to agree (on)

догово́р [dagaVOR] contract

договори́ться ➤ догова́риваться

дождли́вый [dazhDLIvy] rainy

дождь m [DOSHT'] rain

докуме́нты m pl [dakuMYENty] papers, documents

долг [DOLK] debt; duty

до́лгий [DOLgi] (time) long

до́лжен m/должна́ f/должно́ n/должны́ pl + inf [DOLzhyn/dalzhNA/dalzhNO/dalzhNY] must, should, have to

доли́на [daLIna] valley

дом [DOM] house

до́ма [DOma] at home

дома́шнее живо́тное [daMASHnyye zhyVOTnaye] pet

дома́шний [daMASHni] homemade

домкра́т (автомоби́льный) [damKRAT (aftamaBIL'ny)] (lifting) jack

допла́та [daPLAta] additional charge, surcharge

дополни́тельный [dapalNItil'ny] additional

допусти́мый [dapuSTImy] permissible

доро́га [daROga] road

до́рого [DOraga] adv dearly, expensively

дорого́й [daraGOY] adj expensive

доро́жная су́мка [daROZHnaya SUMka] travel bag

доро́жно-тра́нспортное происше́ствие [daROZHna-TRANSpartnaye praiSHESTviye] traffic accident

доро́жный указа́тель [daROZHny ukaZAtil'] road sign

достава́ть/доста́ть [dastaVAT'/daSTAT'] to reach; obtain

доста́точно [daSTAtachna] adv enough; rather

доста́ть ➤ достава́ть

достопримеча́тельность f [dastaprimiCHAtil'nast'] sight, place of interest

досту́пный [daSTUPny] accessible

до́ллар [DOlar] dollar

дочь [DOCH], pl до́чери [DOchiri] daughter

дре́вний [DRYEVni] ancient

дрова́ n pl [draVA] firewood

друг [DRUK] friend

друго́й [druGOY] other, another

дружи́ть ipf с + instr [druZHYT's-...] to be friends with

ДТП [de-te-PE] traffic accident

ду́мать/поду́мать (о + prep) [DUmat'/paDUmat' (a-...)] to think (about)

дупло́ [duPLO] cavity (in a tooth)

духи́ m pl [duKHI] perfume

душ [DUSH] shower

ду́шный [DUSHny] humid

ды́ня [DYnya] honeydew melon

дыра́ [dyRA] hole

дыша́ть/вздохну́ть [dySHAT'/vzdakhNUT'] to breathe

Е

е́вро [YEVra] euro

Евро́па [yiVROpa] Europe

европе́ец/европе́йка [yivraPYEits/yivraPYEYka] European

европе́йский [yivraPYEYski] European

еда́ [yiDA] food; meal

едва́ [yiDVA] hardly, scarcely

еди́нственный [yiDINstviny] only

её pers pron f gen; acc [yiYO] her

её poss pron f [yiYO] her

ежего́дный [yizhyGODny] annual

ежедне́вно [yizhyDNYEVna] daily

ежеме́сячный [yizhyMYEsichny] monthly

еженеде́льный [yizhyniDYEL'ny] weekly

ежеча́сно [yizhyCHASna] hourly

езда́ [yizDA] driving; journey

е́здить ipf [YEZdit'] to drive

е́здить ipf верхо́м [YEZdit' virKHOM] to ride a horse

ей pers pron f dat [YEY] to/for her

ЕС [YE-ES] EU

е́сли [YESli] if

есте́ственный [yiSTYEstviny] natural

есть (not conjugated) [YEST] there is, there are

есть/пое́сть [YEST'/paYEST'] to eat

е́хать/пое́хать [YEkhat'/poYEkhat'] to drive

ещё [yiSHO] still; (some) more

Ж

жа́лко! [ZHALka] Too bad!

жа́ловаться/пожа́ловаться (на + acc) [ZHAlavatsa/paZHAlavatsa (na-...)] to complain (about) жаль! [ZHAL'] Pity!

жара́ [zhaRA] heat

жа́реный [ZHAriny] roasted

жа́ркий [ZHARki] *(weather)* hot

жва́чка [ZHVACHka] chewing gum

ждать/подожда́ть [ZHDAT'/ padaZHDAT'] to wait

же [ZHE] but, and

жела́ть/пожела́ть [zhyLAT'/ pazhyLAT'] to wish, desire

жёлтый [ZHOLty] yellow

желу́док [zhyLUdak] stomach

жёмчуг [ZHEMchuk] pearl

жена́ [zhyNA] wife

жена́тый [zhyNAty] married *(to a woman)*

жени́ться *ipf a. pf* на... + *prep* [zhyNItsa na-...] to marry *(a woman)*

же́нский [ZHENski] woman's, female

же́нщина [ZHENshina] woman

жест [ZHEST] gesture

жёсткий [ZHOSTki] tough

жёстов язы́к [ZHEstaf yiZYK] sign language, language of gestures

живо́й [zhyVOY] live; lively

живописец [ZHYvapisits] painter

жи́вопись *f* [ZHYvapis'] painting

живо́т [zhyVOT] abdomen

живо́тное [zhyVOTnaye] animal

жи́дкий [ZHYTki] *adj* liquid

жи́дкость *f* [ZHYTkast'] liquid

жизнь *f* [ZHYZN'] life

жила́я ко́мната [zhyLAya KOMnata] living room

жиле́т [zhyLYET] vest, waistcoat

жи́рный [ZHYRny] fatty, greasy

жи́тель/ница [ZHYtil'/nitsa] inhabitant

жить *ipf* [ZHYT'] to live, reside

журна́л [zhurNAL] magazine

за + *acc* [za-...] for; in place of

за + *instr* [za-...] behind

забавля́ться *ipf* [zabaVLYAtsa] to have a good time

заба́вный [zaBAVny] amusing

заблужда́ться *ipf* [zabluZHDAtsa] to be mistaken

забо́титься/позабо́титься о + *prep* [zaBOtitsa/pazaBOtitsa a-...] to take care of

заброни́ровать ➤ брони́ровать

забыва́ть/забы́ть [zabyVAT'/ zaBYT'] to forget

заво́д [zaVOT] factory

за́втра [ZAFtra] tomorrow

за́втрак [ZAFtrak] breakfast

за́втракать/поза́втракать [ZAFtrakat'/paZAFtrakat'] to eat breakfast

заграни́ца [zagraNItsa] abroad

заграни́чный па́спорт [zagraNICHny PASpart] passport for travel abroad

за́дний [ZADni] rear, back

за́дний ход [ZADni KHOT] reverse gear

заже́чь ➤ зажига́ть

зажига́ние [zazhyGAniye] ignition

зажига́ть/заже́чь [zazhyGAT'/ zaZHECH] to ignite

заинтересова́ться ➤ интересова́ться

зака́з [zaKAS] order

заказно́е письмо́ [zakazNOye piS'MO] registered letter

заключе́ние [zaklyuCHEniye] conclusion; confinement

закрича́ть ➤ крича́ть

закры́тый [zaKRYty] closed

заку́ска [zaKUska] appetizer, hors d'oeuvre

зал [ZAL] hall

зал ожида́ния [ZAL azhyDAniya] waiting room

зали́в [zaLIF] bay

зало́г [zaLOK] deposit

заме́на [zaMYEna] replacement

заменя́ть/замени́ть [zamiNYAT'/zamiNIT'] to replace

замёрзнуть ➢ мёрзнуть

замеча́ть/заме́тить [zamiCHAT'/zaMYEtit'] to notice, note

замо́к [zaMOK] lock

за́мок [ZAmak] castle

за́мужем [ZAmuzhym] married *(to a man)*

заму́жняя [zaMUZHniya] married *(to a man)*

за́нятый [ZAnyity] busy, occupied

за́падный [ZApadny] western

запа́с [ZApas] reserve, supplies

запа́сный [zaPASny] spare; emergency

за́пах [ZApakh] smell

запере́ть ➢ запира́ть

запечённый [zapiCHOny] au gratin

запира́ть/запере́ть [zapiRAT'/zapiRYET'] to lock (up)

запи́сывать/записа́ть [zaPIsyvat/zapiSAT'] to write down

заплати́ть ➢ плати́ть

запове́дник [zapaVYEDnik] national park; nature reserve

заполня́ть/запо́лнить [zapalNYAT'/zaPOLnit'] to fill out

запо́р [zaPOR] constipation

запреща́ть/запрети́ть [zapriSHAT'/zapriTIT'] to forbid, ban

запрещено́! [zaprishiNO] Prohibited!

зараже́ние кро́ви [zaraZHEniye KROvi] blood poisoning

зара́зный [zaRAZny] contagious

зарегистри́роваться ➢ регистри́роваться

заря́дное устро́йство [zaRYADnaye uSTROYstva] charging device

заряжа́ть/заряди́ть [zariZHAT'/zariDIT'] to charge (battery)

засвиде́тельствовать ➢ свиде́тельствовать

засте́нчивый [zaSTYENchivy] shy

зато́р [zaTOR] constipation; (traffic) jam

захоте́ть ➢ хоте́ть

зашива́ть/заши́ть [zashyVAT'/zaSHYT'] to sew

защи́та [zaSHIta] protection

зая́вка [zaYAFka] application; order

заявля́ть/заяви́ть (о... + *prep*) [zayiVLYAT'/zayiVIT' (a-...)] to report, declare

звезда́ [zviZDA] star

звони́ть/позвони́ть (по телефо́ну) + *dat* [zvaNIT'/pazvaNIT' (pa-tiliFOnu)] to call (on the phone)

звоно́к [zvaNOK] call, ring; bell

звук [ZVUK] sound

зда́ние [ZDAniye] building

здесь [ZDYES'] here

здоро́вый [zdaROvy] healthy

зелёная страхова́я ка́рта [ziLYOnaya strakhaVAya KARta] green insurance card

зелёный [ziLYOny] green

земля́ [zimLYA] earth; land; ground

земля́к/земля́чка [zimLYAK/zimLYACHka] (fellow) countryman/woman

земляни́ка [zimliNIka] strawberry

зе́ркало [ZYERkala] mirror

зима́ [ziMA] winter

зи́мний [ZIMni] *adj* winter

злой [ZLOY] angry; wicked

змея́ [zmiYA] snake

знак [ZNAK] sign

знак авари́йной остано́вки [ZNAK avaRIYnay astaNOFki] warning triangle

знако́мство [znaKOMstva] acquaintance

знако́мый [znaKOmy] well-known

знамени́тый [znamiNIty] famous

знать *ipf* [ZNAT'] to know

значе́ние [znaCHEniye] meaning

зна́чить *ipf* [ZNAchit'] to mean

зову́т, *acc* + ~ [zaVUT] to be called

золоти́стый [zalaTIsty] golden

зо́лото [ZOlata] gold

зо́нт(ик) [ZONtik] umbrella

зоопа́рк [zaaPARK] zoo

зре́лый [ZRYEly] ripe

зри́тель/ница [ZRItil'/nitsa] spectator

зуб [ZUP] tooth

зубна́я боль [zubNAya BOL'] toothache

зубна́я па́ста [zubNAya PAsta] toothpaste

зубочи́стка [zubaCHISTka] toothpick

И

и [I] and

игла́ [iGLA] needle

игра́ [iGRA] game

игра́ть/сыгра́ть [iGRAT'/syGRAT'] to play

игру́шки *f pl* [iGRUSHki] toys

иде́я [iDYEya] idea

идти́/пойти́ [iTI/payTI] to go

из + *gen* [is-...] from; out of

избива́ть/изби́ть [izbiVAT'/izBIT'] to beat (up)

изве́стие [izVYEstiye] news

извине́ние [izviNYEniye] excuse; apology

извиня́ть(ся)/извини́ть(ся) [izviNYAT'(sa)/izviNIT'(sa)] to excuse (o.s.)

изде́ржки *f pl* [izDYERSHki] expenses

изжо́га [iZHOga] heartburn

из-за + *gen* [iz-za-...] because of

изнаси́лование [iznaSIlavaniye] rape

изуча́ть/изучи́ть [izuCHAT'/ izuCHIT'] to study

и́ли [Ili] or

и́ли ... и́ли ... [Ili .. Ili ...] either ... or ...

име́ть *ipf* [iMYET'] to have, to own

име́ть *ipf* вкус + *gen* [iMYET' FKUS] to taste (of)

и́мя *n* [Imya] first name

инвали́д [invaLIT] disabled person

инвали́дная коля́ска [invaLIDnaya kaLYAska] wheelchair

иногда́ [inagDA] sometimes

иностра́нец/иностра́нка [inaSTRAnits/inaSTRANka] foreigner

иностра́нный [inaSTRAny] foreign

инстру́кция [inSTRUKtsyya] instructions

инструме́нт [instruMYENT] instrument; tool

инсули́н [insuLIN] insulin

интере́сный [intiRYESny] interesting

интересова́ться/заинтересо-ва́ться *(+ instr)* [intirisaVAtsa/zaintirisaVAtsa] to be interested (in)

инфе́кция [inFYEKtsyya] infection

информи́ровать(ся) *ipf a. pf* [infarMIravat'(sa)] to inform (o.s.)

инциде́нт [intsyDYENT] incident

инъе́кция [inYEKtsyya] injection

иска́ть/поиска́ть [iSKAT'/ paiSKAT'] to seek, look for

иску́сство [isKUstva] art

испо́рченный [isPORchiny] spoiled

испуга́ться ➢ пуга́ться

истека́ть/исте́чь кро́вью [istiKAT'/iSTYECH KROvyu] *(person)* to bleed

исте́чь ➢ истека́ть

исто́рия [iSTOriya] history

226

исто́чник [iSTOCHnik] spring; source

исчисля́ть/исчи́слить [ishchiSLYAT'/ishCHIslit'] to estimate, calculate

ита́к [iTAK] thus

их *pers pron pl gen, acc* [IKH] them

их *poss pron pl* [IKH] their

ию́ль *m* [iYUL'] July

ию́нь *m* [iYUN'] June

Й

йо́га [YOga] yoga

йо́гурт [YOgurt] yogurt

йод [YOT] iodine

К

к + *dat* [k-...] to; for

к сожале́нию [k-sazhaLYEniyu] unfortunately

каблу́к [kaBLUK] heel

ка́ждый [KAZHdy] every, each

казино́ [kaziNO] casino

как [KAK] how; as

как раз [KAK RAS] just

калькуля́тор [kal'kuLYAtar] pocket calculator

ка́мбала [KAMbala] flounder

камени́стый [kamiNIsty] stony

ка́мень *m* [KAmin'] stone

ка́мера [KAmira] camera; inner tube

ка́мера хране́ния [KAmira khraNYEniya] checkroom, locker

Кана́да [kaNAda] Canada

кана́л [kaNAL] canal

кана́т [kaNAT] cable, rope

кана́тная доро́га [kaNATnaya daROga] cableway

кани́кулы *f pl* [kaNIkuly] holidays, vacation

кани́стра [kaNIstra] canister

кано́э [kaNOe] canoe

канцтова́ры *m pl* [kantstaVAry] stationery

капита́н [kapiTAN] captain

ка́пля [KAplya] drop

капо́т дви́гателя [kaPOT DVIgatilya] (engine) hood

капу́ста [kaPUsta] cabbage

карава́н [karaVAN] trailer

каранда́ш [karanDASH] pencil

кардиостимуля́тор [kardiastimuLYAtar] pacemaker

карма́н [karMAN] pocket

карма́нный вор [karMAny VOR] pickpocket

ка́рта [KARta] map

карти́на [karTIna] painting

карто́фель *m* [karTOfil'] potatoes

ка́ско [KASka] comprehensive insurance

ка́сса [KAsa] ticket office; cashier

кассе́та [kaSYEta] cassette

ката́ться *ipf* (на + *prep*) [kaTAtsa na-...] to roll; drive, ride (on, in)

като́к [kaTOK] ice skating rink

кафе́ [kaFYE] café

ка́чество [KAchistva] quality

ка́шель *m* [KAshyl'] cough

каю́та [kaYUta] cabin, stateroom

квадра́тный метр [kvaDRATny MYETR] square meter

кварти́ра [kvarTIra] apartment

квита́нция [kviTANtsiya] receipt

кекс [KYEKS] cake

ке́мпер [KYEMpir] RV, camper

ке́мпинг [KYEMpink] camping; campground

кера́мика [kiRAmika] ceramics

кероси́н [kiraSIN] kerosene

кéтчуп [KYEchup] ketchup

килогра́мм [kilaGRAM] kilogram

киломéтр [kilaMYETR] kilometer

кинó [kiNO] movies; movie theater

ки́слый [KISly] sour

кисть *f* руки́ [KIST' ruKI] hand

кита́йский [kiTAYski] Chinese

кишка́ [kishKA] intestine

кла́дбище [KLADbishe] cemetery, graveyard

кла́ксон [KLAKsan] (car) horn

класс [KLAS] class

классици́зм [klasiTSYZM] classicism

класси́ческий [klaSIchiski] classical

класть/положи́ть [KLAST'/ palaZHYT'] to put

кли́мат [KLImat] climate

ключ [KLYUCH] key

ключи́ца [klyuCHItsa] collarbone

кни́га [KNIga] book

кни́жка-раскра́ска [KNISHka-rasKRAska] coloring book

кни́жный магази́н [KNIZHny magaZIN] bookstore

когда́ [kagDA] when, whenever

код [KOT] code

кóжа [KOzha] skin

кóжаный [KOzhany] leather

кокóс [kaKOS] coconut

колбаса́ [kalbaSA] sausage

колгóтки *f pl* [kalGOTki] pantyhose

колéно [kaLYEna] knee

колесó [kaliSO] wheel

кóлики *f pl* [KOliki] colic

коллéга [kaLYEga] colleague

коллекциóнная (почтóвая) ма́рка [kaliktsyOnaya (pachTOvaya) MARka] special-issue stamp

колокóльня [kalaKOL'nya] steeple

колóнна [kaLOna] column

колóть/кольну́ть [kaLOT'/ kal'NUT'] to stab; prick

кóлышек [KOlyshyk] tent peg

кольну́ть ➢ колóть

кольцó [kal'TSO] ring

кома́нда [kaMANda] team

кома́р [kaMAR] mosquito

комéдия [kaMYEdiya] comedy

комиссиóнная [kamisiOnaya] commission

кóмната [KOMnata] room

компа́кт-ди́ск [kampagd-DISK] CD (compact disc)

кóмпас [KOMpas] compass

компетéнтный [kampiTYENTny] responsible

кóмплексное блю́до [KOMpliksnaye BLYUda] set menu

комплéкт [kamPLYEKT] set

компози́тор [kampaZItar] composer

компóстер [kamPOstir] ticket-punching machine

компости́ровать/прокомпости́ровать [kampaSTIravat'/ prakampaSTIravat'] to punch/date a ticket

конвéрт [kanVYERT] envelope

конди́терская [kanDItirskaya] pastry shop

кондиционéр [kanditsyaNYER] air conditioner

кондýктор [kanDUKtar] conductor

конéц [kaNYETS] end

конéчно [kaNYESHna] *adv* naturally, of course

конéчный [kaNYECHny] *adj* last; final

консервооткрыва́тель *m* [kansirvaatkryVAtil'] can opener

консéрвы *m pl* [kanSYERvy] canned goods

кóнсульство [KONsul'stva] consulate

конта́кт [kanTAKT] contact

контраба́нда [kantraBANda] contraband

контролёр [kantraLYOR] inspector, ticket collector

контрóль *m* [kanTROL'] checking, inspection

конфеты *m pl* [kanFYEty] candies, bonbons

конфисковать *ipf & pf* [kanfiskaVAT'] to confiscate

концерт [kanTSERT] concert

кончено [KONchina] *adv* all over

кончено [KONchinaye] finished, settled

коньки *m pl* [kan'KI] ice skates

копия [KOpiya] copy

корабль *m* [kaRABL'] ship

корзина [karZIna] basket

коричневый [kaRICHnivy] brown

коробка скоростей [kaROPka skaraSTYEY] transmission

король/королева [kaROL'/karaLYEva] king/queen

коронка [kaRONka] crown (dental)

короткий [kaROTki] short

короткое замыкание [kaROTkaye zaMYkaniye] short circuit

короткометражка [karatkamiTRASHka] short film

корь *f* [KOR'] measles

косметический [kasmiTIchiski] cosmetic

костыль *m* [kaSTYL'] crutch

кость *f* [KOST'] bone

костюм [kaSTYUM] costume

кофе *m* [KOfye] coffee

кофеварка [kafiVARka] coffee machine

кошелёк [kashyLYOK] coin purse

кошка [KOSHka] cat

КПП [KA-PE-PE] border crossing

краб [KRAP] crab

кража [KRAzha] theft

край [KRAY] area, region

крайний [KRAYni] extreme; emergency

кран [KRAN] water faucet

красивый [kraSIvy] beautiful; fine

красить/покрасить [KRAsit'/paKRAsit'] to dye

краснуха [krasNUkha] German measles

красный [KRASny] red

красный перец [KRASny PYErits] paprika

красть/украсть [KRAST'/uKRAST'] to steal

кратковременный [kratkaVRYEminy] brief, short-lived

краткосрочный [kratkaSROCHny] short-term

креветка [kriVYETka] shrimp

кредитная карточка [kriDITnaya KARtachka] credit card

крем [KRYEM] cream

крепость *f* [KRYEpast'] castle, fortress

кресельная канатная дорога [KRYEsil'naya kaNATnaya daROga] chair lift

кресло [KRYEsla] armchair

крест [KRYEST] cross

кричать/закричать [kriCHAT'/zakriCHAT'] to shout, cry

кровать *f* [kraVAT'] bed

кровообращение [kravaabraSHEniye] circulation

кровотечение [kravatiCHEniye] bleeding

кровоточить *ipf* [kravataCHIT'] *(wound)* to bleed

кровь *f* [KROF'] blood

кровяное давление [kraviNOye daVLYEniye] blood pressure

кролик [KROlik] rabbit

кроме + *gen* [KROmye] except(ing)

кроме того [KROmye taVO] moreover, besides

круг [KRUK] circle

круглый [KRUgly] round

круиз [kruIS] cruise

крутой [kruTOY] steep

крыло [kryLO] wing

крыша [KRYsha] roof

крюк [KRYUK] hook

ксилография [ksilaGRAfiya] wood engraving

кто-нибудь [KTO-nibut'] someone, anyone

кудри *f pl* [KUdri] curls

кузе́н / кузи́на [kuZYEN/kuZIna] cousin

кукуру́за [kukuRUza] corn

куло́н [kuLON] pendant

культу́ра [kul'TUra] culture

купа́льная ша́почка [kuPAL'naya SHApachka] bathing cap

купа́льник [kuPAL'nik] bathing suit

купа́льный хала́т [kuPAL'ny khaLAT] bathrobe

купе́ [kuPYE] *(train)* compartment

купи́ть ➤ покупа́ть

ку́пол [KUpal] dome, cupola

кури́ть / покури́ть [kuRIT'/pakuRIT'] to smoke *(tobacco)*

ку́рица [kuRItsa] chicken

куро́рт [kuRORT] health resort, spa

курс(ы) [KURsy] course

ку́ртка [KURTka] jacket

куря́щий [kuRYAshi] smoker

куса́ть / укуси́ть [kuSAT'/ukuSIT'] to bite, sting *(insect, etc.)*

куса́ться *ipf* [kuSAtsa] to bite

кусо́к [kuSOK] piece

ку́хня [KUKHnya] kitchen

Л

лавро́вый лист [laVROvy LIST] bay leaf

лак для ногте́й [LAK dlia-nakTYEY] nail polish

ла́мпа [LAMpa] lamp

ла́мпочка [LAMpachka] light bulb

лапша́ [lapSHA] noodles

ла́сковый [LAskavy] affectionate; tender

ла́сты *m pl* [LAsty] swim fins

ле́вый [LYEvy] left

лёгкая атле́тика [LYOKHkaya atLYEtika] track and field

лёгкий [LYOKHki] *adj* light

легко́ [likhKO] *adv* lightly; easily

лёгкое [LYOKHkaye] lung

лёд [LYOT] ice

лежа́ть *ipf* [liZHAT'] to lie

ле́звие [LYEZviye] razor blade

лека́рство [liKARSTva] medicine

лён [LYON] linen

лени́вый [liNIvy] lazy

лес [LYES] forest, woods

ле́стница [LYESnitsa] stairs

лета́ть *ipf* [liTAT'] to fly

лете́ть / полете́ть [liTYET'/ paliTYET'] to fly

ле́то [LYEta] summer

лечи́ть / вы́лечить [liCHIT'/ VYlichit'] to treat *(medically)*

лечь ➤ ложи́ться

ли *interrogative particle* [li] whether, if

лило́вый [liLOvy] lilac

лимо́н [liMON] lemon

лимона́д [limaNAT] soda pop, soft drink

ли́нза [LINza] lens

ли́ния [LIniya] line

лист [LIST] leaf; sheet *(paper)*

литр [LITR] liter

лифт [LIFT] elevator

лицо́ [liTSO] face; person

ли́чность *f* [LICHnast'] person, personality

ли́чные све́дения [LICHnyye SVYEdiniya] personal information

ли́чный [LICHny] personal

лови́ть / пойма́ть [laVIT'/payMAT'] to catch

ло́дка [LOTka] boat

лоды́жка [laDYSHka] ankle

ло́жа [LOzha] *(theater)* box

ложи́ться / лечь [laZHYtsa/LYECH] to lie down

ло́жка [LOSHka] spoon

ло́мтик [LOMtik] slice

ло́шадь *f* [LOshat'] horse

луг [LUG] meadow

лук [LUK] onion; bow

лук-поре́й [LUK-paRYEY] leek

луна́ [luNA] moon

лу́чший [LUchy] better, best

лы́жа [LYzha] ski

лы́жный [LYZHny] *adj* ski

лыжня́ [lyzhNYA] ski trail

льго́та [L'GOta] privilege, advantage; reduction (price)

любе́зный [lyuBYEZny] courteous, amiable, nice

люби́мец *m*/люби́мица *f* [lyuBImits/lyuBImitsa] favorite

люби́ть *ipf* [lyuBIT'] to love, like

любо́вь *f* [lyuBOF'] love

любопы́тный [lyubaPYTny] curious

лю́ди *m pl* [LYUdi] people

люк [LYUK] sunroof

M

магази́н [magaZIN] store, shop

магнитофо́н [magnitaFON] tape player

мазь *f* [MAS'] ointment

май [MAY] May

ма́ленький [MAlin'ki] small

ма́ло [MAla] little; not much

ма́льчик [MAL'chik] boy

маргари́н [margaRIN] margarine

ма́рлевый бинт [MARlivy BINT] gauze bandage

март [MART] March

маршру́т [marshRUT] route

масли́на [maSLIna] olive

ма́сло [MAsla] oil, butter

масса́ж [maSASH] massage

мастерска́я [mastirSKAya] workshop, repair shop

материа́л [matiriAL] material

матра́с [maTRAS] mattress

мать [MAT'] mother

маши́на [maSHYna] machine; car

мая́к [maYAK] lighthouse

ме́бель *f* [MYEbil'] furniture

мёд [MYOT] honey

медбра́т [midBRAT] male nurse

медици́нский [midiTSYNski] medical

ме́дленный [MYEdliny] slow

медсестра́ [mitsisTRA] female nurse

ме́жду + *instr* [MYEZHdu] between, among

междугоро́дный [mizhdugaRODny] intercity

междугоро́дный разгово́р [mizhdugaRODny razgaVOR] domestic long-distance call

междунаро́дный [mizhdunaRODny] international

междунаро́дный опознава́тельный знак [mizhdunaRODny apaznaVAtil'ny ZNAK] *(car)* nationality plate

междунаро́дный полёт [mizhdunaRODny paLYOT] international flight

междунаро́дный разгово́р [mizhdunaRODny razgaVOR] international call

мели́рование [miLIravaniye] highlights *(hair)*

ме́лочь *f* [MYElach] small change

мемориа́л [mimariAL] memorial

менструа́ция [minstruAtsyya] menstruation

меню́ *n* [miNYU] menu

меня́ *acc* [miNYA] me

меня́ть/поменя́ть [miNYAT'/pamiNYAT'] to change

мёрзнуть/замёрзнуть [MYORznut'/zaMYORznut'] to freeze

мероприя́тие [mirapriYАtiye] event

ме́стность *f* [MYESnast'] district; locality

ме́стный [MYESny] local

ме́сто [MYEsta] place

местожи́тельство [mistaZHYtil'stva] place of residence

ме́сяц [MYEsits] month

метр [MYETR] meter

метро́ [miTRO] subway

мех [MYEKH] fur

мечта́ [michTA] dream; ambition

меша́ть/помеша́ть + dat [miSHAT'/pamiSHAT'] to interfere

мешо́к [miSHOK] bag; sack

мигре́нь f [miGRYEN'] migraine

ми́дия [MIdiya] Venus mussel

микроволно́вая печь [mikravalnOVaya PYECH] microwave oven

микрокалькуля́тор [mikrakal'kuLYAtar] pocket calculator

миксту́ра от ка́шля [mikSTUra at-KAshlya] cough syrup

милиционе́р [militsyaNYER] police officer

мили́ция [miLItsyya] police

миллиме́тр [miliMYETR] millimeter

ми́лый [MIly] dear

ми́мо + gen [MIma] past, by

минда́ль m [minDAL'] almonds

минера́льная вода́ [miniRAL'naya vaDA] mineral water

ми́ни-гольф [MIni-gol'f] miniature golf

мину́та [miNUta] minute

мир [MIR] world; peace

ми́ска [MIska] bowl; basin

младе́нец [mlaDYEnits] baby

мне dat [MNYE] (to, for) me

мне́ние (о + prep) [MNYEniye (a-...)] opinion (on, about)

мно́го [MNOga] much; many

моби́льник [maBIL'nik] cell phone

моби́льный телефо́н [maBIL'ny tiliFON] mobile cellular phone

моги́ла [maGIla] grave, tomb

мо́да [MOda] fashion

моде́ль f [maDYEL'] model

мо́дный [MODny] fashionable

мо́жет быть [MOzhyt BYT'] maybe, perhaps

мо́жно adv (dat + ~) + inf [MOZHna] can; may; possible

моза́ика [maZAika] mosaic

мозг [MOSK] brain

мой m/моя́ f/моё n/мои́ pl [MOY/maYA/maYO/maI] my

мо́йка [MOYka] sink

мо́крый [MOkry] wet

мол [MOL] pier; jetty

моли́ться/помоли́ться [maLItsa/pamaLItsa] to pray

мо́лния [MOLniya] lightning

молодо́й [malaDOY] young

молоко́ [malaKO] milk

молото́к [malaTOK] hammer

моло́чная [maLOCHnaya] milk/dairy store

моме́нт [maMYENT] moment

монасты́рь m [manaSTYR'] cloister, monastery

моне́та [maNYEta] coin

мо́ре [MOrye] sea, ocean

морко́вь f [marKOF'] carrots

моро́женое [maROzhynaye] ice cream

моро́з [maROS] frost

морска́я боле́знь [marSKAya baLYEZN'] seasickness

морско́й язы́к [marSKOY yiZYK] sole

мост [MOST] bridge

мо́стик [MOstik] footbridge

моте́ль m [maTYEL'] motel

моча́ [maCHA] urine

мочево́й пузы́рь [machiVOY puZYR'] bladder

мочь/смочь [MOCH/SMOCH] to be able; can

муж [MUSH] husband

мужско́й [mushSKOY] men's

мужчи́на [mushCHIna] man

музе́й [muZEY] museum

му́зыка [MUzyka] music

музыка́льный [muzyKAL'ny] musical

232

мука́ [muKA] flour

мультфи́льм [mul'tFIL'M] cartoon film

му́скул [MUskul] muscle

му́сор [MUsar] garbage, trash

мусоросбо́рник [musaraZBORnik] trash can

му́ха [MUkha] fly

мы [MY] we

мы́ло [MYla] soap

мыть/вы́мыть [MYT'/VYmyt'] to wash; to rinse

мы́ться/вы́мыться [MYtsa/VYmytsa] to wash o.s.

мы́шца [MYSHtsa] muscle

мю́зикл [MYUzikl] musical *(theater)*

мя́гкий [MYAKHki] soft, mild

мясна́я ла́вка [miSNAya LAFka] butcher shop

мясно́й фарш [miSNOY FARSH] ground meat

мя́со [MYAsa] meat

мяч [MYACH] ball

Н

на + *acc* [na-...] on, onto; to

на + *prep* [na-...] at; on; by

на са́мом де́ле [na-SAmam DYElye] in (actual) fact

на у́лице [na-Ulitse] in the street; outdoors

на́бережная [NAbirizhnaya] quay

наве́рное [naVYERnaye] probably

наверху́ [navirKHU] upstairs

награ́да [naGRAda] reward

над + *instr* [nat-...] over; above

наде́яться/понаде́яться [naDYEyitsa/panaDYEyitsa] to hope

надое́дливый [nadaYEDlivy] boring; tiresome

на́дпись *f* [NATpis'] inscription

надувно́й [naduVNOY] inflatable

наза́д [naZAT] back; backwards

называ́ться/назва́ться [nazyVAtsa/naZVAtsa] to be called, be named

найти́ ➤ находи́ть

наказа́ние [nakaZAniye] punishment

накло́нный [naKLOny] sloping

наконе́ц [nakaNYETS] *adv* finally; at last

нале́во [naLYEva] on/to the left

наливно́е [naliVNOye] on tap

нали́чный [naLICHny] (in) cash

нам *dat* [NAM] (to, for) us

наоборо́т [naabaROT] *adv* on the contrary, vice versa

нападе́ние [napaDYEniye] assault

написа́ть ➤ писа́ть

напи́ток [naPItak] beverage

направле́ние [napraVLYEniye] direction

напра́во [naPRAva] on/to the right

напро́тив + *gen* [naPROtif] opposite, facing

напряже́ние [napriZHEniye] tension, voltage

нарисова́ть ➤ рисова́ть

нарко́з [narKOS] anesthesia

наро́д [naROT] people; nation

наро́дный [naRODny] popular; national

нару́чные часы́ *m pl* [naRUCHnyye chiSY] wristwatch

нас *acc* [NAS] us

насеко́мое [nasiKOmaye] insect

наслажда́ться/наслади́ться + *instr* [naslaZHDAtsa/naslaDItsa] to enjoy

на́сморк [NAsmark] head cold

насо́с [naSOS] pump

насто́йка [naSTOYka] liqueur

насто́льный те́ннис [naSTOL'ny TYEnis] table tennis, ping-pong

настоя́щий [nastaYAshi] genuine; present

натюрмо́рт [natyurMORT] still life

научи́ться ➤ учи́ться

нау́шники [naUSHniki] headphones

находи́ть/найти́ [nakhaDIT'/nayTI] to find

находи́ться *ipf* [nakhaDItsa] to be located

нахо́дки *f pl* [naKHOTki] finds

национа́льный костю́м [natsyaNAL'ny kaSTYUM] national costume

нача́ло [naCHAla] beginning

нача́льник [naCHAL'nik] boss

начина́ть/нача́ть [nachiNAT'/naCHAT'] to begin

наш *m*/на́ша *f*/на́ше *n*/на́ши *pl* [NASH/NAsha/NAshe/NAshy] our

не [ni-...] not

не за́мужем *f* [ni-ZAmuzhym] single, unmarried

не хвата́ть/не хвати́ть + *gen* [ni-khvaTAT'/ni-khvaTIT'] to be lacking, not enough

не́бо [NYEba] sky

нева́жный [niVAZHny] insignificant; poor

невероя́тный [niviraYATny] incredible

невозмо́жный [nivazMOZHny] impossible

негати́вный [nigaTIVny] negative

неда́вно [niDAVna] recently

неде́ля [niDYElya] week

недоразуме́ние [nidarazuMYEniye] misunderstanding

нежи́рный [niZHYRny] *(food)* lean

не́жный [NYEZHny] tender

незнако́мый [niznaKOmy] unknown

неиспра́вность *f* [niisPRAVnast'] defect, fault

некраси́вый [nikraSIvy] ugly

не́кто [NYEKta] somebody

некуря́щий [nikurYAshi] nonsmoker

нельзя́ *adv + inf ipf* [nil'ZYA] It's not allowed

нельзя́ *adv + inf pf* [nil'ZYA] It's not possible

немно́го [niMNOga] a little; somewhat

немо́й [niMOY] mute

необходи́мый [niapkhaDImy] necessary

необыкнове́нный [niabyknaVYEny] extraordinary, unusual

непо́лный пансио́н [niPOLny pansiON] half-board *(two meals)*

непра́вильный [niPRAvil'ny] wrong, incorrect

непреме́нно [nipriMYEna] *adv* certainly, surely

неприго́дный [nipriGODny] useless

неприя́тный [nipriYATny] unpleasant

непромока́емый [nipramaKAyimy] waterproof

нерв [NYERF] nerve

не́рвный [NYERVny] nervous

не́сколько + *gen pl* [NYEskal'ka] several; a few

несно́сный [niSNOsny] unbearable

несча́стный слу́чай [nishCHASny SLUchay] accident

нет [NYET] no; not

нет + *gen* [NYET] there is/are no...

нигде́ [niGDYE] nowhere

ни́же + *gen* [NIzhe] below

ни́жнее бельё [NIZHniye biL'YO] underwear

ни́жний [NIZHni] *adj* lower; bottom

ни́жняя соро́чка [NIZHniya saROCHka] undershirt

ни́зкий [NIski] low; inferior

никако́й [nikaKOY] no

никогда́ [nikagDA] never

никто́ [niKTO] no one, nobody

ничего́ [nichiVO] nothing

ничья́ [niCHYA] tie *(score)*

но [NO] but

Нового́дний ве́чер [navaGODny VYEchir] New Year's Eve

но́вый [NOvy] new

нога́ [naGA], pl но́ги [NOgi] leg

нож [NOSH] knife

но́жницы f pl [NOZHnitsy] scissors

но́жницы f pl для ногте́й
[NOZHnitsy dlia-nakTYEY] nail
scissors

но́мер [NOmir] number; hotel
room

номерно́й знак [namirNOY ZNAK]
license plate

норма́льный [narMAL'ny] normal;
all right

нос [NOS] nose

носи́ть ipf [naSIT'] to carry; wear

носки́ m pl [naSKI] socks

носово́й плато́к [nasaVOY plaTOK]
handkerchief

носо́чки m pl [naSOCHki] ankle
socks

но́тный магази́н [NOTny
magaZIN] (sheet) music store

ноутбу́к [noutBUK] notebook

ночева́ть/переночева́ть
[nachiVAT'/pirinachiVAT']
to spend
the night

ночле́г [nachLYEK] place to sleep;
accommodations

ночни́к [NOCHnik] bedside lamp;
nightlight

ночно́й клуб [nachNOY KLUP]
nightclub

ночно́й сто́лик [nachNOY STOlik]
bedside table

ночь f [NOCH] night

но́чью [NOchyu] at night

ноя́брь m [naYABR'] November

нра́виться/понра́виться
(dat + ~) [NRAvitsa/paNRAvitsa]
to please (s.o.); to like

нуди́зм [nuDIZM] nudism

нужда́ться (в + prep) [nuzhDAtsa
(f-...)] to need, require

ну́жный [NUZHny] necessary

нут [NUT] chickpeas

ныря́ть/нырну́ть [nyRYAT'/
nyrNUT'] to dive

ню́хать/поню́хать [NYUkhat'/
paNYUkhat'] to smell (something)

O

о + prep [a-...] about, of; on

о́ба m, n/о́бе f [Oba/Obye] both

обгоня́ть/обогна́ть [abgaNYAT'/
abaGNAT'] (traffic) to pass

обе́д [aBYET] lunch

обезжи́ренный [abiZHYriny] low-
fat

обеспоко́иться ≻ беспоко́иться

обеща́ть ipf a. pf [abiSHAT'] to
promise

оби́да [aBIda] insult

о́блако [Oblaka] cloud

о́блачный [Oblachny] cloudy

обма́н [abMAN] deception, fraud

обме́н [abMYEN] exchange (of
money)

обме́нивать/обменя́ть
[abMYEnivat'/abmiNYAT'] to
exchange

обме́нный пункт [abMYEny
PUNKT] (money) exchange office

обменя́ть ≻ обме́нивать

о́бморок [OBmarak] faint

обогна́ть ≻ обгоня́ть

обра́доваться ≻ ра́доваться

о́браз [Obras] image; mode, way

обрати́ть ≻ обраща́ть

обра́тный [aBRATny] reverse;
opposite

обраща́ть/обрати́ть [abraSHAT'/
abraTIT'] to turn

обручённый [abruCHOny] engaged

обслу́живание [apSLUzhyvaniye]
service

о́бувь f [Obuf'] footwear

обуче́ние [abuCHEniye] education,
training

обхо́д [apKHOT] detour

обходна́я доро́га [apkhaDNAya daROga] bypass

о́бщая цена́ [OPshaya tsyNA] flat rate

обще́ственный [apSHESTviny] public

объе́зд [abYEST] detour

объекти́в [abyikTIF] lens, objective

обы́чный [aBYCHny] usual, customary

о́вощи *m pl* [Ovashi] vegetables

огнеопа́сный [agniaPASny] inflammable

огнетуши́тель *m* [agnituSHYtil'] fire extinguisher

ого́нь *m* [aGON'] fire

огоро́д [agaROT] vegetable garden

огуре́ц [aguRYETS] cucumber

ода́лживать/одолжи́ть [aDALzhyvat'/adalZHYT'] to lend

одева́ть/оде́ть [adiVAT'/aDYET'] to put on

оде́жда [aDYEZHda] clothing

оде́ть ➢ одева́ть

одея́ло [adiYAla] blanket

оди́н *m*/ одна́ *f*/ одни́ *pl* [aDIN/adNA/adNI] one; alone

одина́ковый [adiNAkavy] equal

одино́кий [adiNOki] lonely

одна́жды [adNAZHdy] once; one day

одновреме́нный [adnaVRYEminy] simultaneous

однодне́вная экску́рсия [adnaDNYEvnaya ekSKURsiya] day trip

однодне́вный [adnaDNYEny] one-day

однонеде́льный [adnaniDYEL'ny] one-week

одноцве́тный [adnaTSVETny] one-color, plain

одолжи́ть ➢ ода́лживать

оживлённый [azhyvLYOny] lively

ожида́ть *ipf* [azhyDAT'] to expect

ожо́г [aZHOK] burn

о́зеро [Ozira] lake

озно́б [aZNOP] shivering fit

окно́ [akNO] window

о́коло + *gen* [Okala] next to, beside; about

оконча́тельный [akanCHAtil'ny] final; complete

о́корок [Okarak] ham

окруже́ние [akruZHEniye] surroundings

октя́брь *m* [akTYABR'] October

о́кунь *m* [Okun'] perch

оли́вковое ма́сло [aLIFkaye MAsla] olive oil

он [ON] he

она́ *pers pron f* [aNA] she

они́ *pers pron pl* [aNI] they

опа́здывать/опозда́ть (на + *acc*) [aPAZdyvat'/apaZDAT'] to be late (for)

опаса́ться *ipf* + *gen* [apaSAtsa] to fear

опа́сность *f* [aPASnast'] danger

опа́сный [aPASny] dangerous

о́пера [Opira] opera

опера́ция [apiRAtsyya] operation

опере́тта [apiRYEta] operetta

опи́сывать/описа́ть [aPIsyvat'/apiSAT'] to describe

опла́кивать/опла́кать (+ *acc*) [aPLAkivat'/aplaKAT'] to complain (about)

опозда́ние [apaZDAniye] delay

опозда́ть ➢ опа́здывать

определённый [apridiLYOny] definite; explicit

опры́сканный [aPRYskany] (*vegetables, etc.*) sprayed

о́птик [OPtik] optician

опуха́ние [apuKHAniye] swelling

о́пухоль *f* [Opukhal'] tumor

опу́хший [aPUKHshy] swollen

опя́ть [aPYAT'] again

ора́нжевый [aRANzhyvy] (*color*) orange

о́рден [ORdin] order, decoration

оре́х [aRYEKH] nut

оркéстр [arKYESTR] orchestra

оса́ [aSA] wasp

освежéние [asviZHEniye] refreshment

óсень *f* [Osin'] fall, autumn

осма́тривать/осмотрéть [aSMAtrivat'/asmaTRYET'] to see, visit

осмóтр [aSMOTR] examination; visit

осмотрéть ➤ осма́тривать

осóбенный [aSObiny] special, particular

остава́ться/оста́ться [astaVAtsa/aSTAtsa] to stay, remain

остана́вливаться/останови́ться [astaNAvlivatsa/astanaVItsa] to stop

останóвка [astaNOFka] stop; stay

оста́тки *f pl* [aSTATki] remains

оста́ться ➤ остава́ться

Осторóжно! [astaROZHna] Caution!, Look out!

осторóжный [astaROZHny] cautious

óстров [Ostraf] island

óстрый [Ostry] sharp; spicy

от + *gen* [at-...] from, away from

отбивна́я котлéта [adbivNAya katLYEta] cutlet

отбукси́ровать ➤ букси́ровать

отварнóй [atvarNOY] boiled

отвéтить ➤ отвеча́ть

отвéтственный [atVYETstviny] responsible

отвеча́ть/отвéтить [atviCHAT'/atVYEtit'] to answer; answer for

отдава́ть/отда́ть [addaVAT'/adDAT'] to give back; hand in

отделéние [addiLYEniye] department; ward

отдохну́ть ➤ отдыха́ть

óтдых [ODdykh] rest; recreation

отдыха́ть/отдохну́ть [addyKHAT'/addakhNUT'] to rest; take a vacation

отéц [aTYETS] father

отка́зываться/отказа́ться (от + *gen*) [atKAzyvatsa/atkaZAtsa] to refuse

откла́дывать/отложи́ть [atKLAdyvat'/ atlaZHYT'] to postpone

открыва́лка [atkryVALka] bottle opener

открыва́ть/откры́ть [atkryVAT'/atKRYT'] to open; discover

откры́тка [atKRYTka] postcard

откры́тый [atKRYty] open

откры́ть ➤ открыва́ть

отли́в [atLIF] low tide, ebb

отли́чный [atLICHny] excellent

отложи́ть ➤ откла́дывать

отменя́ть/отмени́ть [atmiNYAT'/ atmiNIT'] to cancel

отоплéние [ataPLYEniye] heating

отправи́тель *m* [atpraVItil'] sender

отправлéние [atpraVLYEniye] departure

óтпуск [OTpusk] vacation; leave

отравлéние [atraVLYEniye] poisoning

отремонти́ровать ➤ ремонти́ровать

óтчество [Ochistva] patronymic

отъезжа́ть/отъéхать [atyiZHAT'/ atYEkhat'] to depart

официа́льный [afitsyAL'ny] official

официа́нт/ка [afitsyANT/ka] waiter/waitress

оформлéние [afarmLYEniye] *(customs)* clearance

охлажда́ющая вода́ [akhlazhDAyushaya vaDA] coolant

охóтничий парк [aKHOTnichi PARK] game preserve

охóтно [aKHOTna] gladly

охра́на [aKHRAna] protection

очарова́тельный [acharaVAtil'ny] charming

óчень [Ochin'] very

óчередь *f* [Ochirit'] (waiting) line

оши́бка [aSHYPka] error

па́дать/упа́сть [PAdat'/uPAST'] to fall

паке́т [paKYET] plastic bag

паке́тик [paKYEtik] small bag; tea bag

пала́тка [paLATka] tent

пала́ты *f pl* [paLAty] palace

па́лец [PAlits] finger; toe

пало́мничество [paLOMnichistva] pilgrimage

па́луба [PAluba] deck

пальто́ [pal'TO] coat

па́мятник [PAmitnik] monument

пансио́н [pansiON] boarding house, pension

па́ра + *gen pl* [PAra] pair

парали́ч [paraLICH] paralysis

парашюти́зм [parashuTIZM] sky-diving

па́реный [PAriny] steamed

пари́к [paRIK] wig

парикма́хер [parikMAkhir] hairdresser; barber

парк [PARK] park

паро́ль *m* [paROL'] password

паро́м [paROM] ferry

парохо́д [paraKHOT] steamer

парте́р [parTYER] *(theater)* orchestra (seats)

па́русная ло́дка [PArusnaya LOTka] sailboat

парфюме́рия [parfyuMYEriya] perfume and cosmetics store

па́спорт [PASpart] passport

па́спортный контро́ль [PASpartny kanTROL'] passport inspection

пассажи́р/ка [pasaZHYR/ka] passenger

Па́сха (Христо́ва) [PASkha (khriSTOva)] Easter

па́хнуть *ipf* [PAKHnut'] to smell (of)

паховая гры́жа [pakhaVAya GRYzha] hernia

па́хта [PAKHta] buttermilk

певе́ц/певи́ца [piVYETS/piVItsa] singer

педа́ль *f* акселера́тора [piDAL' aksiliRAtara] gas pedal, accelerator

педиа́тр [pidiATR] pediatrician

пейза́ж [piyZASH] landscape

пелёнки *f pl* [piLYONki] diapers

пе́на [PYEna] foam

пе́пельница [PYEpilnitsa] ashtray

пе́рвое (блю́до) [PYERvaye (BLYUda)] soup, first course

пе́рвый [PYERvy] first

пе́рвый эта́ж [PYERvy eTASH] first floor

перебива́ть/переби́ть [piribiVAT'/piriBIT'] to interrupt

перевести́ ≻ переводи́ть

перево́д [piriVOT] translation; *(money)* transfer

переводи́ть/перевести́ (с + *gen* на + *acc*) [pirivaDIT'/piriviSTI] to translate

перево́дчик/перево́дчица [piriVOTshik/piriVOTshitsa] translator

перевя́зывать/перевяза́ть [piriVYAzyvat'/pirivyaZAT'] *(wound)* to bandage; dress

перед + *instr* [pirit-...] before; in front of

перед тем [pirit-TYEM] before

переда́ча [piriDAcha] transmission; transfer

передвижно́й буфе́т [piridvizhNOY buFYET] *(train)* snack cart

перекрёсток [piriKRYOstak] intersection

перело́м ко́сти [piriLOM KOsti] *(bone)* fracture

переме́на [piriMYEna] change

переме́нчивый [piriMYENchivy] changeable

переночева́ть ≻ ночева́ть

переодева́ться/переоде́ться [piriadiVAtsa/piriaDYEtsa] to change one's clothes

переправля́ть(ся)/перепра́вить ть(ся) (че́рез + acc) [piripraVLYAtsa/piriPRAvitsa (chiris-...)] to cross (a river)

перепу́тать ➤ пу́тать

переры́в [piriRYF] break; intermission

переса́дка [piriSATka] change, transfer

пересла́ть ➤ пересыла́ть

переставать/переста́ть [piristaVAT'/piriSTAT'] to stop

пересыла́ть/пересла́ть [pirisyLAT'/piriSLAT'] to forward

переу́лок [piriUlak] alley, lane

перехо́д [piriKHOT] crossing

переходни́к [pirikhoDNIK] adapter

пе́рец [PYErits] pepper

пе́речница [PYErichnitsa] peppermill

пери́ла n pl [piRIla] railings

перочи́нный но́жик [piraCHIny noZHYK] pocket knife

перро́н [piRON] (train station) platform

пе́рсик [PYERsik] peach

перча́тки f pl [pirCHATki] gloves

пе́сня [PYEsnya] song

песо́к [piSOK] sand

песо́чница [piSOCHnitsa] sandbox

пёстрый [PYOstry] colorful, multi-colored

петру́шка [piTRUshka] parsley

петь/спеть [PYET'/SPYET'] to sing

печа́льный [piCHAL'ny] sad

печа́ть f [piCHAT'] stamp; seal

печёнка [piCHONka] (food) liver

печёночный паште́т [piCHOnachny paSHTYET] liver paté

печёный [piCHOny] baked

пе́чень f [PYEchin'] liver

пече́нье [piCHEn'ye] cookies

пешехо́д [pishyKHOT] pedestrian

пешехо́дная зо́на [pishyKHODnaya ZOna] pedestrian zone

пеще́ра [piSHEra] cave

пивна́я [piVNAya] tavern, beer joint

пи́во [PIva] beer

пило́т [piLOT] pilot

пинце́т [pinTSET] tweezers

пиро́г [piROK] pie, pastry

писа́ть/написа́ть [piSAT'/napiSAT'] to write

пи́сьменный [PIs'miny] written

письмо́ [piS'MO] letter

пита́ние [piTAniye] food

пить/вы́пить [PIT'/VYpit'] to drink

питьева́я вода́ [pitiVAya vaDA] drinking water

пищеваре́ние [pishivaRYEniye] digestion

пищево́д [pishiVOT] esophagus

пищево́е отравле́ние [pishiVOye atraVLYEniye] food poisoning

пла́вание [PLAvaniye] swimming; voyage

пла́вательный круг [PLAvatil'ny KRUK] life buoy

пла́вать ipf [PLAvat'] to swim

пла́вать ipf под па́русом [PLAvat' pat-PArusam] to sail

пла́вки f pl [PLAFki] bathing trunks

плака́т [plaKAT] poster

пла́кать ipf [PLAkat'] to cry

план го́рода [PLAN GOrada] city map

планери́зм [planiRIZM] gliding

пла́стика [PLAstika] plastic art

пла́стырь m [PLAstyr'] band-aid

пла́та [PLAta] charge; fare

пла́та за прое́зд [PLAta za-praYEST] highway toll

платёж [plaTYOSH] payment

плати́ть/заплати́ть [plaTIT'/zaplaTIT'] to pay

плато́к [plaTOK] shawl; handkerchief

пла́тье [PLAt'ye] dress

плацка́рта [platsKARta] reserved-seat ticket

плацка́ртный ваго́н [platsKARTny vaGON] *(train)* car with reserved seats

плащ [PLASH] raincoat

плёнка [PLYONka] film

пле́чики *m pl* [PLYEchiki] coat hanger

плечо́ [pliCHO] shoulder

плита́ [pliTA] stove

пли́тка [PLITka] hot-plate

пловец́/пловчи́ха [plaVYETS/plafCHIkha] swimmer

пло́мба [PLOMba] *(tooth)* filling

пло́ский [PLOski] flat; shallow

плохо́й [plaKHOY] bad, poor

пло́щадь *f* [PLOshat'] square

плыть/поплы́ть [PLYT'/paPLYT'] to swim

пляж [PLYASH] beach

по + *dat* [pa-...] through; by; along

по бу́дням [pa-BUdnim] on weekdays

по кра́йней ме́ре [pa-KRAYniy MYErye] at least

по ме́ньшей ме́ре [pa-MEN'SHEY MYErye] at least

побежа́ть ➤ бежа́ть

поблагодари́ть ➤ благодари́ть

побри́ть(ся) ➤ брить(ся)

по́вар/повари́ха [POvar/pavaRIkha] cook

пова́ренная кни́га [pavaRYOnaya KNIga] cookbook

пове́рить ➤ ве́рить

повора́чивать/поверну́ть [pavaRAchivat'/pavirNUT'] to turn; turn around

поворо́т [pavaROT] curve

поврежда́ть/повреди́ть [pavriZHDAT'/pavriDIT'] to injure, damage

поврежде́ние [pavriZHDYEniye] injury, damage

повторя́ть/повтори́ть [paftaRYAT'/paftaRIT'] to repeat

пове́зка [paVYASka] bandage

погляде́ть ➤ гляде́ть

поговори́ть ➤ говори́ть

пограни́чный контро́льно-пропускно́й пункт [pagraNICHny kanTROL'na-prapuSKNOY PUNKT] border crossing

погрести́ ➤ грести́

погуля́ть ➤ гуля́ть

под + *instr* [pat-...] under, underneath

подари́ть ➤ дари́ть

пода́рок [paDArak] gift

подво́д [padVOT] supply, feed; lead

подво́дный [padVOdny] underwater, submarine

подгу́зники *f pl* [padGUzniki] diapers

подкра́шивать/подкра́сить [patKRAshyvat'/patKRAsit'] to touch up, color

по́длинник [POdlinik] original

по́длинный [POdliny] authentic, original

подмётка [padMYOTka] *(shoe)* sole

подожда́ть ➤ ждать

подойти́ ➤ подходи́ть

подпи́сывать/подписа́ть [patPIsyvat'/patpiSAT'] to sign

по́дпись *f* [POTpis'] signature

подро́бный [paDROBny] detailed

подру́га [paDRUga] girlfriend

по-друго́му [pa-druGOmu] differently

подтвержда́ть/подтверди́ть [patvirZHDAT'/patvirDIT'] to confirm

поду́мать ➤ ду́мать

поду́шка [paDUshka] pillow

подходи́ть/подойти́ [patkhaDIT'/padayTI] to approach, draw near

подъём [paD'YOM] incline, slope

подъёмник [paD'YOMnik] elevator; ski lift

по́езд [POyist] train

поездка [paYESTka] trip; tour

поехать ≻ ехать

пожаловаться ≻ жаловаться

пожарная команда [paZHARnaya kaMANda] fire department

пожарный извещатель [paZHARny izviSHAtil'] fire alarm

пожелать ≻ желать

позаботиться ≻ заботиться

позавтракать ≻ завтракать

позавчера [pazafchiRA] the day before yesterday

позади [pazaDI] behind, at the back

позади + gen [pazaDI] behind

позвонить ≻ звонить

позвоночный столб [pazvaNOCHny STOLP] spinal column

поздний [POZny] late

поздравить ≻ поздравлять

поздравление [pazdraVLYEniye] congratulation

поздравлять/поздравить + acc (c + instr) [pazdraVLYAT'/ paZDRAvit' ... s-...] to congratulate s.o. (on ...)

позже [POzhy] later

позыв [paZYF] desire, inclination

поискать ≻ искать

поймать ≻ ловить

пойти ≻ идти

показывать/показать [paKAzyvat'/pakaZAT'] to show, display

покидать/покинуть [pakiDAT/ paKInut'] to leave

покрасить ≻ красить

покрышка [paKRYshka] lid; tire cover

покупатель/ница [pakuPAtil'/ nitsa] customer

покупать/купить [pakuPAT'/ kuPIT'] to buy

покурить ≻ курить

пол [POL] floor

полагать ipf [palaGAT'] to suppose, believe

полагаться/положиться на + acc [palaGAtsa/palaZHYtsa na-...] to rely, depend (on)

полароид [palaROit] instant camera

полдень m [POLdin'] midday, noon

поле [POlye] field

полёт [paLYOT] flight

полететь ≻ летать, лететь

полиомиелит [paliamiLIT] polio

полкило [palkiLO] half a kilo

полный [POLny] full

полный пансион [POLny pansiON] full board (meals)

половина [palaVIna] half

половинный [palaVIny] half

положение [palaZHEniye] situation

положить ≻ класть

положиться ≻ полагаться

полотенце [palaTYENtse] towel

получатель m [paluCHAtil'] addressee, recipient

получать/получить [paluCHAT'/ paluCHIT'] to receive, get

помазок [pamaZOK] shaving brush

поменять ≻ менять

поместиться ≻ помещаться

поместье [paMYEst'ye] estate

помешать ≻ мешать

помещаться/поместиться [pamiSHAtsa/pamiSTItsa] to go in, fit in

помещение [pamiSHEniye] building; premises

помидор [pamiDOR] tomato

помнить/вспомнить + acc [POMnit'/FSPOMnit'] to remember

помогать/помочь [pamaGAT'/ paMOCH] to help, assist

помогите! [pamaGItye] Help!

помолиться ≻ молиться

помочь ≻ помогать

помощь f [POmash] help

помыть ≻ мыть

понадеяться ➤ надеяться

понедельник [paniDYEL'nik]
Monday

понимать/понять [paniMAT'/
paNYAT'] to understand

понос [paNOS] diarrhea

понравиться ➤ нравиться

понюхать ➤ нюхать

понять ➤ понимать

попадать/попасть (в + acc)
[papaDAT'/paPAST' (f-...)] to
reach; get (to, into)

попасть ➤ попадать

поперечный миелит
[papiRYECHny miyiLIT]
quadriplegia

поплыть ➤ плавать, плыть

попробовать ➤ пробовать

попросить ➤ просить

попутешествовать ➤
путешествовать

попытаться ➤ пытаться

поразговаривать ➤
разговаривать

поранить ➤ ранить

порог [paROK] threshold

порт [PORT] port, harbor

портал [parTAL] portal

портной/портниха [partNOY/
partNIkha] tailor/seamstress

портрет [parTRYET] portrait

портье [parT'YE] porter

поручни m pl [POruchni] handrails

порция [PORtsyya] portion, serving

порыв ветра [paRYF VYEtra] gust
of wind

посадка [paSATka] boarding;
emplaning

посадочный талон [paSAdachny
taLON] boarding card

посёлок [paSYOlak] settlement

посещать/посетить [pasiSHAT'/
pasiTIT'] to visit

посещение [pasiSHEniye] visit

послать ➤ посылать

после + gen [POslye ...] after

после обеда [POslye aBYEda] in
the afternoon

последний [paSLYEDni] last

послезавтра [pasliZAftra] day after
tomorrow

послесезонный период
[paslisiZOny piRIat] off-season

послушать ➤ слушать

посмеяться ➤ смеяться

посмотреть ➤ смотреть

посоветовать ➤ советовать

посольство [paSOL'stva] embassy

поспешить ➤ спешить

пост [POST] fast(ing); Lent

поставить ➤ ставить

постараться ➤ стараться

постельное бельё [paSTYEL'naye
biL'YO] bed linens

посуда [paSUda] dishes

посудомоечная машина
[pasudaMOyichnaya maSHYna]
dishwasher

посылать/послать [pasyLAT'/
paSLAT'] to send

посылка [paSYLka] parcel

потанцевать ➤ танцевать

потерять ➤ терять

потеть/вспотеть [paTYET'/
fspaTYET'] to sweat

потеха [paTYEkha] fun,
amusement

потолок [pataLOK] ceiling

потом [paTOM] then; afterwards

потому что [pataMU SHTO]
because

поторопиться ➤ торопиться

потратить ➤ тратить

потребление [patriBLYEniye] use

потянуть ➤ тянуть

поудить ➤ удить

похожий (на + acc) [paKHOzhy
(na-...)] similar, like

поцеловать ➤ целовать

поцелуй [patsyLUY] kiss

почерк [POchirk] handwriting

почесаться ➤ чесаться

почечный камень [POchichny KAmin'] kidney stone

починить ➢ чинить

почистить ➢ чистить

почка [POCHka] kidney

почтамт [pachTAMT] post office

почти [pachTI] almost

почтовая марка [pachTOvaya MARka] stamp

почтово-сберегательная книжка [pachTOva-zbiriGAtil'naya KNISHka] postal savings book

почтовый индекс [pachTOvy INdiks] zip code

почтовый ящик [pachTOvy YAshik] mailbox

почувствовать ➢ чувствовать

пошлина [POshlina] customs duty

поэтому [paEtamu] therefore

пояс [POyis] belt

правильный [PRAvil'ny] correct

правительство [praVItil'stva] government

правый [PRAvy] right

праздник [PRAZnik] holiday, festival

практический [prakTIchiski] practical

прачечная [PRAchichnaya] laundry

пребывать/пребыть (в + prep) [pribyVAT'/priBYT' (f-...)] to stay (in)

предварительно [pridvaRItil'na] beforehand, in advance

предлагать/предложить [pridlaGAT'/pridlaZHYT'] to offer, suggest

предложение [pridlaZHEniye] suggestion; sentence

предложить ➢ предлагать

предмет [pridMYET] object, thing

предохранитель [pridakhraNItil'] safety fuse

предписание [pritpiSAniye] instructions

предпоследний [pritpaSLYEdni] next-to-last

представление [pritstaVLYEniye] presentation; performance

предупредительный треугольник [pridupriDItil'ny triuGOL'nik] warning triangle (road safety device)

прежде всего [PRYEzhdye vsiVO] above all

прежде чем [PRYEzhdye CHEM] before

презерватив [prizirvaTIF] condom

премьера [priM'YEra] premiere

преподавать/преподать (+ dat + acc) [pripadaVAT'/pripaDAT'] to teach

препятствовать/воспрепятствовать [priPYATstvavat'/vaspriPYATstvavat'] to prevent

преступление [pristuPLYEniye] crime

приблизительно [pribliZItil'na] approximately

прибор [priBOR] silverware, cutlery

прибывать/прибыть [pribyVAT'/priBYT'] to arrive

прибыль f [PRIbyl'] profit

прибытие [priBYtiye] arrival

прибыть ➢ прибывать

приветствовать ipf a. pf [priVYETstvavat'] to greet (s.o.)

прививка [priVIFka] vaccination

привык m/привыкла f/привыкли pl [priVYK/priVYKla/priVYkli] accustomed, used

приглашать/пригласить [priglaSHAT'/priglaSIT'] to invite

пригород [PRIgarat] suburb

пригородный поезд [PRIgaradny POyist] commuter train

приготовить ➢ готовить, приготовлять

приготовлять/приготовить [prigataVLYAT'/prigaTOvit'] to prepare приезжа́ть / прие́хать [priyiZHAT'/ priYEkhat'] to come *(by vehicle)*

прие́зжий [priYEzhy] newcomer, visitor

прие́мные часы́ [priYOMnyye chiSY] office hours

прие́хать ➤ приезжа́ть

приземле́ние [prizimLYEniye] landing

прийти́ ➤ приходи́ть

прикладно́е иску́сство [priklaDNOye isKUstva] applied arts

прилета́ть / прилете́ть [priliTAT'/ priliTYET'] to come *(by plane)*

прили́в [priLIF] flood

приме́р [priMYER] example

приме́рный [priMYERny] approximate

принадлежа́ть *ipf + dat* [prinadliZHAT'] to belong

принести́ ➤ приноси́ть

принима́ть / приня́ть [priniMAT'/ priNYAT'] to receive

приноси́ть / принести́ [prinaSIT'/ priniSTI] to bring (along)

при́нятый [PRInyity] accepted, usual

приня́ть ➤ принима́ть

приправля́ть / припра́вить [pripraVLYAT'/priPRAvit'] to season, flavor

приро́да [priROda] nature; scenery

присма́тривать / присмотре́ть (за + *instr*) [priSMAtrivat'/ prismaTRYET' (za-...)] to keep an eye on

приспосо́бленный для инва ли́дных коля́сок [prispaSObliny dlia-invaLIDnykh kaLYAsak] wheelchair-accessible

приспосо́бленный для инва ли́дов [prispaSObliny dlia-invaLIdaf] suitable for the disabled

пристава́ть / приста́ть (к + *dat*) [pristaVAT'/priSTAT' (k-...)] to bother

при́ступ [PRIstup] fit, attack

приходи́ть / прийти́ [prikhaDIT'/ priyTI] to come *(on foot)*

прича́ливать / прича́лить (в + *prep*) [priCHAlivat'/priCHAlit' (f-...)] to dock (at)

причеса́ть ➤ причёсывать

причёска [priCHOska] hairdo, hairstyle

причёсывать / причеса́ть [priCHOsyvat'/prichiSAT'] to comb

причи́на [priCHIna] reason

причиня́ть / причини́ть [prichiNYAT'/prichiNIT'] to cause

прище́пка [priSHEPka] clothespin

прию́т [priYUT] shelter; refuge

прия́тный [priYATny] pleasant

пробле́ма [praBLYEma] problem

про́бовать / попро́бовать [PRObavat'/paPRObavat'] to try, taste

пробо́р [praBOR] *(hair)* part

прове́рить ➤ проверя́ть

прове́рка [praVYERka] inspection, check

проверя́ть / прове́рить [praviRYAT'/praVYErit'] to inspect, check

провожа́ть / проводи́ть [pravaZHAT'/pravaDIT'] to accompany; to see off

про́волока [PROvalaka] wire

прогно́з пого́ды [pragNOS paGOdy] weather forecast

програ́мма [praGRAma] program

програ́ммка [praGRAMka] program booklet

прогу́лка [praGULka] walk

продава́ть / прода́ть [pradaVAT'/ praDAT'] to sell

прода́жа [praDAzha] sale

продово́льственный магази́н [pradaVOL'stviny magaZIN] grocery store

продово́льствие [pradaVOL'stviye] foodstuffs

продолжа́ть/продо́лжить [pradalZHAT'/praDOLzhyt'] to continue; extend

продолжа́ться/продо́лжиться [pradalZHAtsa/pradalZHYtsa] to last

продо́лжить ➤ продолжа́ть

продо́лжиться ➤ продолжа́ться

проду́кт [praDUKT] product

проду́кты m pl [praDUKty] food products

прое́зд [praYEST] passing through; journey

проездно́й биле́т [prayizNOY biLYET] ticket

прозра́чный [prazRACHny] transparent

произведе́ние [praizviDYEniye] work; product

произнести́ ➤ произноси́ть

произноси́ть/произнести́ [praiznaSIT'/praizniSTI] to pronounce

прокомпости́ровать ➤ компости́ровать

промежу́точная поса́дка [pramiZHUtachnaya paSATka] stopover

пропуска́ть/пропусти́ть [prapuSKAT'/prapuSTIT'] to miss

просве́чивать/просвети́ть [praSVYEchivat'/prasviTIT'] to (take an) X-ray

проси́ть/попроси́ть (у + gen + gen) [praSIT'/papraSIT' (u-...)] to ask (s.o. for s.th.)

просну́ться ➤ просыпа́ться

проспе́кт [praSPYEKT] boulevard

прости́ться ➤ проща́ться

просто́й [praSTOY] simple

простре́л [praSTRYEL] lumbago

просту́да [prasTUda] (bad) cold

просыпа́ться/просну́ться [prasyPAtsa/prasNUtsa] to wake up

про́сьба [PROz'ba] request

проте́з [praTYES] prosthesis

про́тив + gen [PROtif...] against

противозача́точное [prativazaCHAtachnaye] contraceptive

противополо́жность f [prativapaLOZHnast'] opposite

противополо́жный [prativapaLOZHny] opposite, opposing

противоуго́нная сигнализа́ция [prativauGOnaya signaliZAtsyya] car alarm

профе́ссия [praFYEsiya] profession

прохла́дный [praKHLAdny] cool

прохо́д [praKHOT] passage

проце́нт [praTSENT] percent

проце́ссия [praTSEsiya] procession

прочита́ть ➤ чита́ть

про́чный [PROCHny] durable

прочь [PROCH] away, off

про́шлое (вре́мя) [PROshlaye (VRYEmya)] (the) past

про́шлый [PROshly] last

проща́ть/прости́ть [praSHAT'/praSTIT'] to forgive

проща́ться/прости́ться (с + instr) [praSHAtsa/praSTItsa (s-...)] to say goodbye (to)

пря́мо [PRYAma] straight ahead

прямо́й [priMOY] direct; straight

пря́ность f [PRYAnast'] spice

пти́ца [PTItsa] bird

пуга́ться/испуга́ться [puGAtsa/ispuGAtsa] to be frightened

пу́дра [PUdra] powder

пуло́вер [puLOvir] pullover, sweater

пульс [PUL'S] pulse

пунктуа́льный [punktuAL'ny] punctual

пусковы́е про́воды m pl [puskaVYye praVOdy] jumper cables

пусто́й [puSTOY] empty

пу́стошь f [PUstash] waste ground

пусты́шка [puSTYshka] pacifier

пýтать/перепýтать [PUtat'/ piriPUtat'] to mix up

путеводи́тель *m* [putivaDItil'] travel guide

путешéствовать/попутешéствовать [putiSHEstvavat'/paputiSHEstvavat'] to travel

путь *m* [PUT'] track; way

пчелá [pchiLA] bee

пыль *f* [PYL'] dust

пытáться/попытáться [pyTAtsa/ papyTAtsa] to try

пьéса [P'YEsa] *(theater)* play

пья́ный [P'YAny] drunk

пя́тница [PYATnitsa] Friday

пятнó [pitNO] spot, stain

P

рабóта [raBOta] work

рабóтать *ipf* [raBOtat'] to work; function

рабóчий день [raBOchi DYEN'] workday

равни́на [ravNIna] plain

рáвный [RAVny] equal

рад *m*/рáда *f*/рáды *pl (+ dat)* [RAT/RAda/RAdy] happy (about)

рада́рный контрóль скóрости [raDARny kanTROL' SKOrasti] radar-controlled speed

радиáтор [radiAtor] *(car)* radiator

рáдио [RAdia] radio

радионя́ня [radiaNYAnya] baby monitor

радиоприёмник [radiapriYOMnik] receiver (radio)

рáдоваться/обрáдоваться *(+ dat)* [RAdavatsa/aBRAdavatsa] to be happy (about)

раз [RAS] once, one time

разбуди́ть ≻ буди́ть

развáлины *f pl* [raZVAliny] ruins

развивáть/разви́ть [razviVAT'/ raZVIT'] to develop

развлекáться/развлéчься [razvliKAtsa/razVLYECHsa] to enjoy o.s.

развлечéние [razvliCHEniye] entertainment

развлéчься ≻ развлекáться

разгáр сезóна [razGAR siZOna] high season

разговáривать/поразговáривать [razgaVArivat'/parazgaVArivat'] to speak, talk

разговóр [razgaVOR] conversation

размéр [razMYER] size

разочарóванный [razachiROvany] disappointed

разры́в свя́зок [razRYF SVYAzak] torn ligament

райóн [rayON] district, part of town

рак [RAK] cancer

ракéтка [raKYETka] racquet

рáковина [RAkavina] sink

раку́шка [raKUshka] mussel

рáна [RAna] wound

ранéние [raNYEniye] injury

рáненый [RAniny] injured

рáнить/порáнить [RAnit'/paRAnit'] to injure

рáно [RAna] early

рáньше [RAN'she] previously; earlier

раскóпки *f pl* [rasKOPki] excavations

расписáние [raspiSAniye] timetable

распродáжа [raspraDAzha] sale

рассерди́ться ≻ серди́ться

расскáзывать/рассказáть [rasKAzyvat'/raskaZAT'] to tell

расстоя́ние [rastaYAniye] distance

расстрóйство пищеварéния [rasTROYstva pishivaRYEniya] indigestion

растéние [rasTYEniye] plant

растяжёние [rastyiZHEniye] sprain, strain

растя́нутый [rasTYAnuty] sprained

расхо́д [rasKHOT] expense; consumption

расчёска [rasCHOska] comb

рво́та [RVOta] vomit

ребёнок [riBYOnak] child

ревмати́зм [rivmaTIZM] rheumatism

ревю́ n [riVYU] revue, show

регио́н [rigiON] region

регистра́ция [rigiSTRAtsyya] registration

регистри́ровать(ся)/зарегис-три́ровать(ся) [rigiSTRIravat'(sa)/zarigiSTRIravat'(sa)] to register, check in

регуля́рный [riguLYARny] regular

ре́дкий [RYETki] rare

режиссу́ра [rizhySUra] directed by

ре́заная ра́на [RYEzanaya RAna] cut

рези́на [riZIna] eraser; rubber

рези́новый [riZInavy] (adj) rubber

резьба́ [riz'BA] woodcarving

река́ [riKA] river

реклами́ровать ipf a. pf [riklaMIravat'] to publicize

рели́гия [riLIgiya] religion

реме́нь m безопа́сности [riMYEN' bizaPAsnasti] safety belt

ремо́нт [riMONT] repairs

ремонти́ровать/отремонти́ровать [rimanTIravat'/atrimanTIravat'] to repair

рентге́новский сни́мок [rindGYEnafski SNImak] X-ray (photograph)

репертуа́р [ripirtuAR] repertoire

рестора́н [ristaRAN] restaurant

реце́пт [riTSEPT] prescription; recipe

реша́ть/реши́ть [riSHAT'/riSHIT'] to decide; solve

реше́ние [riSHEniye] decision; solution

рини́т [riNIT] head cold

рис [RIS] rice

рисова́ть/нарисова́ть [risaVAT'/narisaVAT'] to draw; paint

рису́нок [riSUnak] drawing

ро́вный [ROvny] even, smooth

ро́дина [ROdina] homeland

роди́тели m pl [raDItili] parents

ро́дственный [ROTstviny] related

рожде́ние [razhDYEniye] birth

Рождество́ Христо́во [razhdisTVO khrisTOva] Christmas (Jan. 7th)

розе́тка [raZYETka] wall plug

ро́зовый [ROzavy] pink

рок [ROK] rock (music)

ро́лик [ROlik] roller skate

рома́шка [raMASHhka] chamomile

роско́шный [raSKOSHny] luxurious

рот [ROT] mouth

руба́шка [ruBASHka] shirt

рубе́ц [ruBYETS] scar

ру́йны f pl [rulny] ruins

рука́ [ruKA], pl ру́ки [RUki] arm

рука́в [ruKAF] sleeve

руководи́тель/ница [rukavaDItil'] manager, leader, head

ру́чка [RUCHka] ballpoint pen, fountain pen

ручно́й [ruchNOY] handmade

ры́ба [RYba] fish

ры́бья кость [RYbya KOST'] fishbone

ры́нок [RYnak] market

ры́хлый снег [RYKHly SNYEK] powder snow

рюкза́к [ryukZAK] backpack

ря́дом с + instr [RYAdam s-...] next to

С

с + gen [s-...] from, off

с + instr [s-...] with

с каки́х пор [s-kaKIKH POR] since then

сад [SAT] garden

сади́ться/сесть [saDItsa/SYEST'] to board, get on

сала́т [saLAT] salad

салфе́тка [salFYETka] napkin

саля́ми f pl [saLYAmi] salami

сам m/сама́ f/само́ n/са́ми pl [SAM/saMA/saMO/SAmi] ~self (myself, etc.)

самока́т [samaKAT] scooter

самообслу́живание [samaapSLUzhyvaniye] self-service

санда́лии f pl [sanDAlii] sandals

са́ни f pl [SAni] sled

санита́рный [saniTARny] sanitary

сантиме́тр [santiMYETR] centimeter

сапоги́ m pl [sapaGI] boots

сапо́жная щётка [saPOZHnaya SHOTka] shoe brush

сапо́жник [saPOZHnik] shoemaker

са́уна [SAuna] sauna

са́хар [SAkhar] sugar

сахари́н [sakhaRIN] artificial sweetener

сбива́ться/сби́ться с доро́ги [zbiVAtsa/ZBItsa s-daROgi] to lose one's way

сбор(ы) [ZBOR (ZBOry)] charge, fee

сва́дьба [SVAD'ba] wedding

свари́ть ➤ вари́ть

све́жий [SVYEzhy] fresh

сверх + gen [SVYERKH] over; in addition to

свет [SVYET] light; world

све́тлый [SVYETly] bright, light

светофо́р [svitaFOR] traffic light

свеча́ [sviCHA] candle

свеча́ зажига́ния [sviCHA zazhyGAniya] sparkplug

све́чка [SVYECHka] suppository

свиде́тель/свиде́тельница [sviDYEtil'/sviDYEtil'nitsa] witness

свиде́тельство [sviDYEtil'stva] certificate

свиде́тельствовать/засвиде́-тельствовать
(о + prep) [sviDYEtil'stvavat'/zasviDYEtil'stvavat' (a-...)] to certify, affirm

свини́на [sviNIna] pork

сви́нка [SVINka] mumps

сви́тер [SVItir] pullover, sweater

свобо́дный [svaBOdny] free; clear

свобо́дный от загражде́ний [svaBOdny at-zagraZHDYEniy] barrier-free

свод [SVOT] vault; arch

сво́дка пого́ды [SVOTka paGOdy] weather report

своевре́менный [svayiVRYEminy] adj timely, opportune

СВЧ-печь [es-ve-CHE-pyech] microwave oven

свя́зывать/связа́ть [SVYAzyvat'/sviZAT'] to connect, link

связь f [SVYAS'] contact, connection

свято́й [sviTOY] holy

свяще́нник [sviSHEnik] priest

сдава́ть/сдать [zdaVAT'/ZDAT'] to hand over; deliver

сдава́ть/сдать напрока́т [zdaVAT'/ZDAT' napraKAT] to rent, lease

сда́ча [ZDAcha] handing over; delivery; (money) change

сде́лать ➤ де́лать

сеа́нс [siANS] (movie) show(ing)

се́вер [SYEvir] north

се́верный [SYEvirny] northern

сего́дня (у́тром/ве́чером) [siVOdnya (Utram/VYEchiram)] today (this morning/this evening)

сезо́н [siZON] season

сейф [SYEYF] safe

сейча́с [siyCHAS] now; at once

сексуа́льное домога́тельство [siksuAL'naye damaGAtil'stva] sexual harassment

секу́нда [siKUNda] second

селёдка [siLYOTka] herring

село [siLO] village

сельдерей [sil'diRYEY] celery

сельдь f [SYEL'T'] herring

семья [siM'YA] family

сентябрь m [sinTYABR'] September

сервировать ipf a. pf [sirviraVAT']
to serve

сердечный [sirDYECHny] cordial;
sincere

сердиться/рассердиться
(на + acc) [sirDItsa/rasirDItsa
(na-...)] to be angry (about)

сердце [SYERtse] heart

серебристый [siriBRIsty] silvery

серебро [siriBRO] silver

середина [siriDIna] middle

сёрфинг [SYERfink] surfboard

серый [SYEry] gray

серьги f pl [SYER'gi] earrings

серьёзный [siRYOZny] serious

сестра [siSTRA] sister

сесть ≻ садиться

сетка [SYETka] net

сигара [siGAra] cigar

сигарета [sigaRYEta] cigarette

сигарка [siGARka] cigarillo

сидения [siDYEniya] chairlift

сиденье [siDYEn'ye] seat

сидеть [siDYET'] to sit

сила ветра [SIla VYEtra] wind
force

сильный [SIL'ni] strong

символ [SIMval] symbol

симпатичный [simpaTICHny] nice,
likable

синий [SIni] blue

сказать ≻ говорить

скала [skaLA] rock

скамейка [skaMYEYka] bench

скатерть f [SKAtirt'] tablecloth

скейтборд [skiydBORD] skateboard

скидка [SKITka] discount

складной [skladNOY] folding,
collapsible

скорая помощь [SKOraya POmash]
first aid; ambulance

скоро [SKOra] soon

скоростная дорога [skarasNAya
daROga] expressway

скорость f [SKOrast'] speed;
(transmission) gear

скульптор [SKUL'Ptar] sculptor

скульптура [skul'pTUra]
sculpture

скумбрия [SKUMbriya] mackerel

скучный [SKUchny] boring

слабительное [slaBItil'naye]
laxative

слабовидящий [slabaVIdyashi]
visually impaired

слабослышащий [slabaSLYshishi]
hearing impaired

слабый [SLAby] weak, poor

славяне [slaVYAnye] Slavs

славянский [slaVYANski] Slavic

сладкий [SLATki] sweet

сладости f pl [SLAdasti] candy

следующий [SLYEduyushi] the
next, the following

слепой/слепая [sliPOY/sliPAya]
blind man/woman

слива [SLIva] plum

сливки f pl [SLIFki] cream

слово [SLOva] word

сломанный [SLOmany] broken

служба [SLUZHba] service

слух [SLUKH] hearing

случай [SLUchay] case; event

случайный [sluCHAYny] chance,
accidental

слушать/послушать (+ acc)
[SLUshat'/paSLUshat'] to listen to
(s.o.), hear

слышать/услышать [SLYshat'/
uSLYshat'] to hear

смена [SMYEna] change; shift

сметана [smiTAna] sour cream

смешанный [SMYEshany] mixed

смешной [smishNOY] funny

смеяться/посмеяться (над
+ instr) [smiYAtsa/pasmiYAtsa
(nat-...)] to laugh (at)

смотреть/посмотреть
[smaTRYET'/pasmaTRYET'] to look
(at)

смотри́тель *m* [smaTRItil'] superintendent

смотрова́я площа́дка [smatraVAya plaSHATka] lookout point

смочь ➢ мочь

снару́жи [snaRUzhy] (on the) outside, outwardly

снача́ла [snaCHAla] first; at first

снег [SNYEK] snow

снима́ть/снять [sniMAT'/SNYAT'] to take off; to take, rent *(apartment)*

сни́мок [SNImak] photo(graph)

снотво́рное [snatVORnoye] sleeping pill

снять ➢ снима́ть

соба́ка [saBAka] dog

собира́ть/собра́ть [sabiRAT'/saBRAT'] to collect, gather

собо́р [saBOR] cathedral

собра́ть ➢ собира́ть

со́бственник/со́бственница [SOPstvinik/SOPstvinitsa] owner

со́бственный [SOPstviny] own, one's own

сове́т [saVYET] advice, tip

сове́товать/посове́товать [saVYEtavat'/pasaVYEtavat'] to recommend

совме́стный [saVMYESny] joint, combined

совсе́м [saFSYEM] *adv* quite; totally

содержа́ние [sadirZHAniye] content

сожале́ть *ipf* [sazhaLYET'] to regret

сок [SOK] juice

сокраще́ние [sakraSHEniye] abbreviation

со́лнечный [SOLnichny] sunny, sun

со́лнечный уда́р [SOLnichny uDAR] sunstroke

со́лнце [SONtse] sun

солнцезащи́тный фа́ктор [sontsyzaSHITny FAKtar] sun protection factor

соло́минка [saLOMinka] straw

соло́нка [saLONka] salt shaker

соль *f* [SOL'] salt

соля́рий [saLYAriy] solarium

сон [SON] dream

сообще́ние [saabSHEniye] report, announcement

сооруже́ние [saaruZHEniye] edifice, structure

соотве́тствующий [saatVYETstvuyushi] corresponding; appropriate

сопровожда́ть/сопроводи́ть [sapravaZHDAT'/sapravaDIT'] to accompany

соревнова́ние [sarivnaVAniye] contest, competition

сорт [SORT] sort, kind

сосе́д/ка [saSYET/ka] neighbor

соси́ска [saSIska] small sausage

со́ска [SOska] *(baby bottle)* nipple

состоя́ть *ipf* (из + *gen*) [sastaYAT' (is-...)] to consist (of)

состоя́ться *pf* [sastaYAtsa] to take place

сосу́д [saSUT] container, vessel

сосчита́ть ➢ счита́ть

со́товый телефо́н [SOtavy tiliFON] cellular phone

сотрясе́ние [satriSYEniye] concussion

со́ус [SOus] sauce, dressing

со́хнуть/вы́сохнуть [SOKHnut'/VYsokhnut'] to dry, get dry

сохраня́ть/сохрани́ть [sakhraNYAT'/sakhraNIT'] to keep, look after

со́чный [SOCHny] juicy

спа́льный ваго́н [SPAL'ny vaGON] sleeping car

спа́льня [SPAL'nya] bedroom

спа́ржа [SPARzha] asparagus

спаса́тельная ло́дка [spaSAtil'naya LOTka] lifeboat

спаса́тельный жиле́т [spaSAtil'ny zhyLYET] life jacket

спасáтельный круг [spaSAtil'ny KRUK] life buoy

спать *ipf* [SPAT'] to sleep

спектáкль *m* [spikTAKL'] *(theater)* performance

сперва́ [spirVA] at first

спеть ➤ петь

специа́льность *f* [spitsyAL'nast'] specialty

специа́льный [spitsyAL'ny] special; specialized

спе́ция [SPYEtsyya] spice

спеши́ть/поспеши́ть [spiSHYT'/ paspiSHYT'] to hurry; be in a hurry

спе́шный [SPYESHny] urgent, pressing

спидо́метр [spiDOmitr] speedometer

спина́ [spiNA] back, spine

спи́чка [SPICHka] match

споко́йно [spaKOYna] quietly

споко́йствие [spaKOYstviye] quiet, calm

спорт [SPORT] sport; sports

спорти́вная площа́дка [sparTIVnaya plaSHATka] sports field

спорти́вный [sparTIVny] *adj* sports

спортсме́н/ка [spartsMYEN/ka] sportsman/woman, athlete

спортто́вары *m pl* [sparttaVAry] sporting goods

спо́соб [SPOsap] method, way

спра́вка [SPRAFka] information; reference

спра́вка о приви́вках [SPRAFka a-priVIFkakh] vaccination card

спра́шивать/спроси́ть [SPRAshyvat'/spraSIT'] to ask

спуск [SPUSK] release; flush

спуск воды́ [SPUSK vaDY] water flushing

среда́ [sriDA] environment; Wednesday

средневеко́вье [sridniviKOv'ye] Middle Ages

сре́дний [SRYEDni] *adj* middle; average

сре́дство (от + *gen*) [SRYETstva (at-...)] remedy (for)

сро́чное письмо́ [SROCHnaya piS'MO] special delivery letter

ста́вить/поста́вить маши́ну [STAvit'/paSTAvit' maSHYnu] to park a car

стадио́н [stadiON] stadium

стака́н [staKAN] glass, tumbler

станови́ться/стать [stanaVItsa/ STAT'] to become

стара́ться/постара́ться [staRAtsa/ pastaRAtsa] to try hard

стари́нный [staRIny] ancient

ста́ртер [STARtir] starter

ста́рый [STAry] old

ста́туя [STAtuya] statue

стать ➤ станови́ться

стекло́ [stiKLO] glass; windshield

стеклоочисти́тель *m* [stiklaachisTItil'] windshield wiper

стена́ [stiNA] wall

стиль *m* [STIL'] style

стиль *m* моде́рн [STIL' maDYERN] Art Nouveau

стира́льная маши́на [stiRAL'naya maSHYna] washing machine

стира́льный порошо́к [stiRAL'ny paraSHOK] detergent (powder)

стира́ть/вы́стирать [stiRAT'/ VYstirat'] *(laundry)* to wash

сти́рка [STIRka] washing

сто́имость *f* [STOimast'] price, cost

сто́ить *ipf* [STOit'] to cost

стой! [STOY] Stop!

стол [STOL] table

стол нахо́док [STOL naKHOdak] lost-and-found (office)

столб [STOLP] column

столбня́к [stalbNYAK] tetanus

столе́тие [staLYEtiye] century

сто́лик для пелена́ния [STOlik dlia-piliNAniya] changing table

столи́ца [staLItsa] capital

столкнове́ние [stalknaVYEniye] collision

столо́вая [staLOvaya] dining room

стоп-кран [STOP-KRAN] emergency brake

сторона́ [staraNA] side

стоя́нка [staYANka] parking lot; rest stop

стоя́нка такси́ [staYANka taKSI] taxi stand

стоя́ть *ipf* [staYAT'] to stand

страна́ [straNA] country, land

страни́ца [straNItsa] *(book)* page

страхова́ние [strakhaVAniye] insurance

страхо́вка [straKHOFka] insurance

стра́шный [STRASHny] terrible

строи́тельный [straItil'ny] building, construction

стро́йка [STROYka] construction site

стро́йный [STROYny] slender

стул [STUL] chair; stool, bowel movement

ступе́нчатая причёска [stuPYENchataya priCHOska] layered cut

ступе́нь *f* [stuPYEN'] step

ступня́ ноги́ [stupNYA naGI] foot

стю́ард/стюарде́сса [STYUart/ styuarDYEsa] flight attendant

суббо́та [suBOta] Saturday

субти́тры *m pl* [supTItry] subtitle

суд [SUT] court

су́дно [SUdna] ship; vessel

су́дорога [SUdaraga] cramp

судья́ [suD'YA] judge

сукно́ [suKNO] cloth

сумасше́дший [sumaSHETshy] crazy

суме́ть ➤ уме́ть

су́мка [SUMka] bag

су́мка-холоди́льник [SUMka-khalaDIL'nik] cooler bag

су́мма [SUma] sum, amount

су́мочка [SUmachka] handbag

суп [SUP] soup

суперма́ркет [supirMARkit] supermarket

суста́в [suSTAF] joint

сухо́й [suKHOY] dry

су́ша [SUsha] dry land

суши́лка [suSHYLka] dryer

суши́ть/вы́сушить [suSHYT'/ VYsushyt'] to dry (s.th.)

сфотографи́ровать ➤ фотографи́ровать

схе́ма [SKHYEma] diagram; layout

схе́ма го́рода [SKHYEma GOrada] city map

сцепле́ние [stsyPLYEniye] clutch

счастли́вый [shiSLIvy] happy

сча́стье [SHASt'ye] luck, happiness

счёт [SHOT] account; bill

счита́ть/сосчита́ть [shiTAT'/ sashiTAT'] to pay

США [se-she-a] USA

съедо́бный [syiDOBny] edible

съезд [SYEZD] exit ramp

сыгра́ть ➤ игра́ть

сын [SYN], *pl* сыновья́ [synaVYA] son

сыр [SYR] cheese

сыро́й [syROY] raw, uncooked; damp

сы́тый [SYty] satisfied, full

T

таба́к [taBAK] tobacco

таба́чный [taBACHny] tobacco

табле́тка (от + *gen*) [taBLYETka (at-...)] tablet, pill (for)

так же ..., как [TAK ZHE ... KAK] just as ... as

так как [TAK KAK] since, as, because

тало́н [taLON] coupon, voucher

там [TAM] there

тамо́женная деклара́ция [taMOzhynaya dilkaRAtsyya] customs declaration

тамо́женные по́шлины *f pl* [taMOzhynyye POshliny] customs duties

тамо́жня [taMOzhnya] customs

тампо́н [tamPON] tampon

танцева́льный орке́стр [tantsyVAL'ny arKYESTR] dance band

танцева́льный теа́тр [tantsyVAL'ny tiATR] dance theater

танцева́ть/потанцева́ть [tantsyVAT'/patantsyVAT'] to dance

танцо́вщик/танцо́вщица [tanTSOFshik/tanTSOFshitsa] dancer

та́почки *f pl* [TApachki] sneakers, gym shoes

таре́лка [taRYELka] plate

тари́ф [tarRIF] tariff; rate

тари́ф выходно́го дня [tarRIF vykhaDNOva DNYA] weekend rate

твёрдый [TVYORdy] hard

твой *m*/твоя́ *f*/твоё *n*/твои́ *pl* [TVOY/tvaYA/tvaYO/tvaI] your

творо́г [tvaROK] cottage cheese

тво́рческий [TVORchiski] creative

теа́тр [tiATR] theater

теа́тр ма́лых форм [tiATR MAlykh FORM] operatta theater

теа́тр миниатю́р [tiATR miniaTYUR] cabaret

театра́льный [tiaTRAL'ny] theater; theatrical

тебе́ *pers pron dat* [tiBYE] (to, for) you

тебя́ *pers pron gen, acc* [tiBYA] you

телевизио́нный [tiliviziOny] *adj* television

телеви́зор [tiliVIzar] television set

телегра́мма [tiliGRAma] telegram

телегра́фный перево́д [tiliGRAFny piriVOT] wire transfer

теле́жка [tiLYESHka] baggage car

те́лекс [TYEliks] telex

телеобъекти́в [tiliabyikTIF] telephoto lens

телефо́н [tiliFON] telephone

телефони́ровать *ipf a. pf* [tilifaNIravat'] to (make a) telephone (call)

телефо́нная бу́дка [tiliFOnaya BUTka] phone booth

телефо́нная ка́рточка [tiliFOnaya KARtachka] phone card

телефо́нный [tiliFOny] *adj* telephone

телефо́нный код [tiliFOny KOT] area code

телефо́нный спра́вочник [tiliFOny SPRAvachnik] phone book

те́ло [tieLO] body

теля́тина [tiLYAtina] veal

тёмный [TYOMny] dark

температу́ра [timpiraTUra] temperature; fever

те́ннис [TYEnis] tennis

те́ннисная раке́тка [TYEnisnaya raKYETka] tennis racquet

тень *f* [TYEN'] shadow, shade

тёплый [TYOply] warm

те́рмос [TYERmas] thermos bottle

терпе́ние [tirPYEniye] patience

терра́са [tiRAsa] terrace, patio

теря́ть/потеря́ть [tiRYAT'/patiRYAT'] to lose

техни́ческий [tikhNIchiski] technical

техпа́спорт [tikhPASpart] car papers, car registration

тимья́н [tiM'YAN] thyme

типи́чный [tiPICHny] typical

тиф [TIF] typhus

ти́хий [TIkhi] quiet, still

тишина́ [tishyNA] stillness, silence

ткань *f* [TKAN'] fabric

тмин [TMIN] caraway

то же са́мое [TO ZHE SAmaye] the same thing

това́р [taVAR] article, merchandise

тогда́ [tagDA] then

тóже [TOzhe] also, too

ток [TOK] *(electrical)* current

тóлстый [TOLsty] fat; thick

тóлько [TOL'ka] only

тому́ наза́д, ... ~ [... taMU naZAT] *(with time expressions)* ago

тóнкий [TONki] thin

тонне́ль *m* [taNYEL'] tunnel

тóпливо [TOpliva] fuel

тóрмоз [TORmas] brakes

торопи́ться / поторопи́ться [taraPItsa/pataraPItsa] to hurry, hasten

тост [TOST] toast

тóстер [TOstir] toaster

тот *m* / та *f* / то *n* / те *pl* [TOT/TA/TO/TYE] that, those

тóчный [TOCHny] precise; accurate

тошнота́ [tashnaTA] nausea

траге́дия [traGYEdiya] tragedy

трамва́й [tramVAY] streetcar

тра́нспорт [TRANspart] transport(ation)

тра́пеза [TRApiza] meal

тра́тить / потра́тить [TRAtit'/paTRAtit'] to spend *(money)*

тре́звый [TRYEZvy] sober

тре́ккинг [TRYEkink] trekking

три́ллер [TRIlir] thriller

трóгать / трóнуть [TROgat'/TROnut'] to touch

тропа́ [traPA] path

трость *f* [TROST'] walking stick

тру́бка [TRUPka] phone receiver

тру́дный [TRUDny] difficult, hard

тру́сики *m pl* [TRUsiki] underpants, briefs

трусы́ *m pl* [truSY] shorts

тра́вел-чек [TREvil-chek] traveler's check

тря́пка [TRYAPka] washcloth

туале́т [tuaLYET] toilet; restroom

туале́тная бума́га [tuaLYETnaya buMAga] toilet paper

тума́н [tuMAN] fog

туне́ц [tuNYETS] tuna fish

тупо́й [tuPOY] stupid; obtuse

тураге́нтство [turaGYENTstva] travel agency

тури́ст / ка [tuRIST/ka] tourist

туристи́ческая ба́за (турба́за) [turiSTIchiskaya BAza (turBAza)] tourist camp

туристи́ческий [turiSTIchiski] tourist; travel

тури́стский [tuRISTski] hiking, walking

ту́фли *f pl* [TUfli] shoes

тушёный [tuSHOny] stewed, braised

тушь *f* для ресни́ц [TUSH dlia-riSNITS] mascara

ты [TY] you

ты́ква [TYKva] pumpkin, squash

тюрьма́ [tyur'MA] prison

тяжело́ [tyizhyLO] *adv* seriously, severely

тяжёлый [tyiZHOly] *adj* serious; heavy

тя́нуть / потя́нуть [TYAnut'/paTYAnut'] to pull

у + *gen* (есть) + *nom* [u-... (YEST)] have

у + *gen* [u-...] at; by

убира́ть / убра́ть [ubiRAT'/uBRAT'] to clear away; clean, make tidy

уведомля́ть / уве́домить [uvidaMLYAT']/uVYEdamit'] to inform

уве́ренный [uVYEriny] confident, sure

уви́деть ➤ ви́деть

у́гол [Ugal] corner

ýголь *m* [Ugal'] (char)coal

ýгорь *m* [Ugar'] eel

удáр [uDAR] stroke, blow

удéрживать/удержáть
[uDYERzhyvat'/udirZHAT'] to hold,
keep

удивля́ться/удиви́ться *(+ dat)*
[udiVLYAtsa/udiVItsa] to be
surprised (at)

уди́ть/поуди́ть [uDIT'/pauDIT'] to
fish, go fishing

удлини́тель *m* [udliNItil']
extension cord

удлиня́ть/удлини́ть [udliNYAT'/
udliNIT'] to extend

удóбный [uDOBny] comfortable

удовлетворённый
[udavlitvaRYOny] satisfied;
contented

удовóльствие [udaVOL'stviye]
pleasure

удостоверéние инвали́дности
[udastvaRYEniye invaLIDnasti]
disabled identification card

удостоверéние ли́чности
[udastvaRYEniye LICHnasti]
identification card

ýдочка [Udachka] fishing rod

удýшье [uDUshye] difficulty
breathing

уезжа́ть/уéхать *(в + acc)*
[uyiZHAT/uYEkhat' (f-...)] to leave
(for)

ужáсный [uZHAsny] awful

ужé [uZHE] already

ужé ... как ... [uZHE ... KAK ...]
since *(in time expressions)*

ýжин [Uzhyn] dinner

ýзкий [USki] narrow

узнава́ть/узна́ть [uznaVAT'/
uZNAT'] to learn, find out

уйти́ ➢ уходи́ть

указа́тель *m* [ukaZAtil'] notice;
road sign

указа́тель *m* поворóта [ukaZAtil'
pavaROta] blinker, turn indicator

укáзывать/указáть [uKAzyvat'/
ukaZAT'] to show, indicate

укóл [uKOL] injection

укрáсть ➢ крáсть

украшéние [ukraSHEniye]
decoration; jewelry

ýксус [UKsus] vinegar

укуси́ть ➢ куса́ть

ýлица [Ulitsa] street

умéть/сумéть [uMYET'/suMYET']
to be able; can

ýмный [UMny] intelligent

умывáльная [umyVAL'naya]
washroom

универмáг [univirMAK] department
store

университéт [univirsiTYET]
university

упаковáть ➢ упакóвывать

упакóвка [upaKOFka] packaging

упакóвывать/упаковáть
[upaKOvyvat'/upakaVAT'] to pack,
wrap

упáсть ➢ пáдать

употреби́тельный [upatriBItil'ny]
frequently used

употребля́ть/употреби́ть
[upatriBLYAT'/upatriBIT'] to use

упражня́ть *ipf* [upraZHNYAT'] to
practice

усáдьба [uSAD'ba] farm

услýга [usLUga] service

услы́шать ➢ слы́шать

успокáиваться/успокóиться
[uspaKAivatsa/uspaKOitsa] to calm
down

успокáивающее
[uspaKAivayushiye] tranquilizer,
sedative

успокóиться ➢ успокáиваться

устáлый [uSTAly] tired, weary

ýстрица [Ustritsa] oyster

ýстье [Ust'ye] mouth, opening

усы́ *m pl* [uSY] mustache

утверждáть/утверди́ть
[utvirZHDAT'/ utvirDIT'] to assert,
allege

утильсырьё [util'syr'YO] second-hand dealer

утоми́тельный [utaMItil'ny] strenuous

у́тро [Utra] morning

у́тром [Utram] in the morning

у́хо [Ukha], *pl* у́ши [Ushy] ear

ухо́д [uKHOT] care; maintenance

уходи́ть／уйти́ [ukhaDIT'/uyTI] to leave, go away

уча́ствовать *ipf* (в + *prep*) [uCHAstvavat' (f-…)] to take part (in)

учи́ться／научи́ться + *dat o. inf* [uCHItsa/nauCHItsa] to learn, study

учрежде́ние [uchriZHDYEniye] office; department

уши́б [uSHYP] bruise, contusion

уще́лье [uSHEL'ye] canyon, gorge

уще́рб [uSHERP] damage, harm

ую́тный [uYUTny] cozy; comfortable

Ф

фа́брика [FAbrika] factory

факс [FAKS] fax, fax machine

фальши́вый [fal'SHYvy] false, imitation

фами́лия [faMIliya] family name

фа́ра [FAra] headlight

фарфо́р [farFOR] porcelain

фарш [FARSH] ground meat

фарширо́ванный [farshyROvany] filled, stuffed

фаса́д [faSAT] façade

фасо́ль *m* [faSOL'] beans

февра́ль *m* [fiVRAL'] February

фейерве́рк [fiyirVYERK] fireworks

фен [FYEN] hair-dryer

фестива́ль *m* [fistiVAL'] festival

физи́ческий недоста́ток [fiZIchiski nidasTAtak] physical disability

фильм [FIL'M] film

фи́нская ба́ня [FINskaya BAnya] sauna

фиоле́товый [fiaLYEtavy] violet

фи́рма [FIRma] firm, company

фитнес-це́нтр [fitnis-TSENTR] fitness center

фойе́ [faYE] reception area

фольга́ [fal'GA] foil

фолькло́р [fal'kLOR] folklore

фона́рь *m* [faNAR'] headlight

фонта́н [fanTAN] fountain

фо́рма [FORma] form; shape

формуля́р [farmuLYAR] *(printed)* form

фотоаппара́т [fataapaRAT] camera

фотографи́ровать／сфотографи́ровать [fatagraFIravat/sfatagraFIravat'] (take a) photograph (of)

фотогра́фия [fataGRAfiya] photography

фронто́н [franTON] pediment

фрукт [FRUKT] fruit

фру́кты *m pl* [FRUKty] fruits

фуже́р [fuZHER] wine glass

фуникулёр [funikuLYOR] cable railway

футбо́л [fudBOL] soccer

футбо́лка [fudBOLka] t-shirt

X

химзави́вка [khimzaVIFka] perm(anent wave)

химчи́стка [khimCHISTka] dry cleaning

хиру́рг [khiRURK] surgeon

хлеб [KHLYEP] bread

хло́пок [KHLOpak] cotton

ходи́ть *ipf* [khaDIT'] to go, walk

хозтова́ры *m pl* [khastaVAry] household goods

хозя́ин/хозя́йка [khaZYAin/ khaZYAYka] owner; host/hostess

хокке́й на льду [khaKEY na-L'DU] ice hockey

холм [KHOLM] hill

холоди́льник [khalaDIL'nik] refrigerator

хо́лодно *adv, dat + ~* [KHOladna] (to be) cold

холо́дный [khaLODny] cold

холосто́й *m* [khalaSTOY] unmarried

холосто́й ход [khalaSTOY KHOT] neutral; idle

холостя́к [khalaSTYAK] bachelor

хор [KHOR] choir

хоро́ший [khaROshi] *adj* good

хорошо́ [kharaSHO] *adv* well

хоте́ть/захоте́ть [khaTYET'/ zakhaTYET'] to want

хотя́ [khaTYA] although

храм [KHRAM] temple

хране́ние [khraNYEniye] storage; keeping, custody

храпе́ть *ipf* [khraPYET'] to snore

хри́плый [KHRIply] hoarse

христиа́нство [khristANstva] Christianity

хруста́ль *m* [khruSTAL'] crystal

худо́й [khuDOY] thin, lean

ху́тор [KHUtar] farm

Ц

цветна́я капу́ста [tsvitNAya kaPUsta] cauliflower

цветно́й [tsvitNOY] colored

цвето́к [tsviTOK], *pl* цветы́ [tsviTY] flower

целова́ть/поцелова́ть [tsylaVAT'/ patsylaVAT'] to kiss

це́лый [TSEly] *adj* whole, entire

цель *f* [TSEL'] goal

цена́ [tsyNA] price

це́нность *f* [TSEnast'] value

це́нный [TSEny] valuable

цент [TSENT] cent

центр [TSENTR] center

центра́льный [tsynTRAL'ny] central

цепо́чка [tsyPOCHka] necklace

цепь *f* [TSEP'] chain

це́рковь *f* [TSERkaf'] church

цирк [TSYRK] circus

цифрово́й [tsyfraVOY] digital

Ч

чаевы́е [chiyiVVye] tip

чай [CHAY] tea

ча́йка [CHAYka] seagull

ча́йная ло́жка [CHAYnaya LOSHka] teaspoon

час [CHAS] hour

часова́я мастерска́я [chasaVAya mastirsKAya] watch repair shop

часо́вня [chiSOFnya] chapel

части́чный [chisTICHny] partial

ча́стный [CHASTny] private

ча́стый [CHASty] frequent

часть *f* [CHAST'] part

часы́ *m pl* [chiSY] clock, watch

часы́ *m pl* рабо́ты [chiSY raBOty] opening hours

ча́шка [CHASHka] cup

челове́к [chilaVYEK] person

че́люсть *f* [CHELyust'] jaw

чемода́н [chimaDAN] suitcase
червь *m* [CHERF'] worm
черда́к [chirDAK] attic
че́рез + *acc* [chiris-...] through; across, over
чере́шня [chiRYESHnya] cherry
чёрно-бе́лый фильм [CHORna-BYEly FIL'M] black-and-white film
чёрный [CHORny] black
чеса́ться/почеса́ться [chiSAtsa/pachiSAtsa] to itch
чесно́к [chiSNOK] garlic
четве́рг [chitVYERK] Thursday
чечеви́ца [chichiVItsa] lentil(s)
чини́ть/почини́ть [chiNIT'/pachiNIT'] to repair
чип-ка́рта [chip-KARta] chip card
число́ [chiSLO] number; date
чи́стить/почи́стить [CHIstit'/paCHIstit'] to clean
чи́стка [CHISTka] cleaning
чи́стый [CHIsty] clean
чита́ть/прочита́ть [chiTAT'/prachiTAT'] to read
чита́ть/прочита́ть по бу́квам [chiTAT'/prachiTAT' pa-BUKvam] to spell
чиха́ть/чихну́ть [chiKHAT'/chikhNUT'] to sneeze
что [SHTO] that; what
что за + *acc* [SHTO za-...] what kind of
что́бы + *inf* [SHTOby] in order to; so that
что́-нибудь [SHTO-nibut'] something
чу́вство [CHUstva] feeling
чу́вствовать/почу́вствовать (себя́) [CHUstvavat'/paCHUstvavat' (siBYA)] to feel
чуде́сный [chuDYESny] wonderful, marvelous
чулки́ *m pl* [chulKI] stockings

Ш

шампа́нское [shamPANskaye] champagne
шампу́нь *m* [shamPUN'] shampoo
ша́пка [SHAPka] cap
ша́риковая ру́чка [SHArikavaya RUCHka] ballpoint pen
шарф [SHARF] scarf
шве́дский стол [SHVYETski STOL] buffet
швейца́р [shviyTSAR] porter
швейца́рский фра́нк [shviyTSARski FRANK] Swiss franc
шёлк [SHOLK] silk
шерсть *f* [SHERST'] wool
шерстяно́й [shirstiNOY] wool(en)
ше́ствие [SHEstviye] procession
ши́на [SHYna] tire
ширина́ [shyriNA] width
широ́кий [shyROki] wide
шифр [SHYFR] code
шкаф [SHKAF] cupboard, closet
шко́ла [SHKOla] school
шко́льник/ница [SHKOL'nik/nitsa] pupil
шланг [SHLANK] hose
шлем [SHLYEM] helmet
шля́па [SHLYApa] hat
шля́па от со́лнца [SHLYApa at-SONtse] sunhat
шно́ркель *m* [SHNORkil'] snorkel
шнурки́ *m pl* (для о́буви) [SHNURki (dlia-Obuvi)] shoelaces
шокола́д [shakaLAT] chocolate
шо́рты *m pl* [SHORty] shorts
шоссе́ [shaSYE] highway
шо́у *n* [SHOu] show
шофёр [shaFYOR] driver
шпина́т [shpiNAT] spinach
шприц [SHPRITS] syringe
шрам [SHRAM] scar

шрифт [SHRIFT] type, print
штатив [shtaTIF] tripod
штепсель *m* [SHTYEPsil'] *(electric)* plug
штопор [SHTOpar] corkscrew
штормовка [shtarMOFka] parka
штраф [SHTRAF] *(monetary)* fine
шум [SHUM] noise
шутка [SHUTka] joke

Щ

щётка [SHOTka] brush

Э

экскурсия [eksKURsiya] tour, excursion
экскурсовод [ekskursaVOT] guide
экспонат [ekspaNAT] exhibit
экспресс-почта [ekSPRYES-POCHta] express mail
эластичный бинт [elasTICHny BINT] elastic bandage
элегантный [eliGANTny] elegant
электрический [elikTRIchiski] electrical
электричка [elikTRICHka] suburban train
электротовары *m pl* [eliktrataVAry] electrical goods
эпилепсия [epiLYEPsiya] epilepsy

эпоха [Epokha] epoch, era
этаж [eTASH] floor, story
этнографический музей [etnagraFIchiski muZYEY] museum of ethnography
этот *m*/эта *f*/это *n*/эти *pl* [Etat/Eta/Eto/Eti] this

ю

юбка [YUPka] skirt
ювелир [yuviLIR] jeweler
юг [YUK] south
южный [YUZHny] southern

я

я [YA] I
яблоко [YABlaka] apple
яд [YAT] poison
ядовитый [yadaVIty] poisonous
язва [YAZva] ulcer
язык [yiZYK] tongue; language
языковые курсы [yizykaVYye KURsy] language courses
яйцо [yiyTSO], *pl* яйца [YAYtsa] egg
январь *m* [yinVAR'] January
Япония [yiPOniya] Japan
ярмарка [YARmarka] fair
ясный [YAsny] clear
ящик [YAshik] box

English–Russian Dictionary

A

a little немного [niMNOga]
abbreviation сокращение [sakraSHEniye]
abdomen (lower) нижняя часть живота [NIZHniya CHAST' zhyvaTA]
about о + *prep* [a-...]
about this time в это время [v-Eta VRYEmya]
above над + *instr* [nat-...]
above all прежде всего [PRYEZHdye fsiVO]
abroad заграница [zagraNItsa]
abscess абсцесс [apsTSES]
accept *(invitation)* обещать *ipf a. pf* [abiSHAT']
accessible доступный [daSTUPny]
accident *(misfortune)* несчастный случай [niSHASny SLUchay]; *(minor)* авария [aVAriya]; *(traffic)* дорожно-транспортное происшествие [daROZHna-TRANSpartnaye praiSHESTviye], ДТП [de-te-PE]
accidental случайный [sluCHAYny]
accommodations ночлег [nachLYEK]
accompany, to провожать/проводить [pravaZHAT'/pravaDIT']
accompanying person сопровождающее лицо [sapravaZHDAyushiye liTSO]
account счёт [SHOT]
acquaintance знакомство [znaKOMstva]

across по + *dat* [pa-...]
across from напротив + *gen* [naPROtif]
act акт [AKT]
action movie боевик [bayiVIK]
actor/actress актёр/актриса [akTYOR/akTRIsa]
actually *(adv)* на самом деле [na-SAmam DYElye]
adapter адаптер [aDAPtir]; переходник [pirikhadNIK]
add, to добавлять/добавить [dabaVLYAT'/daBAvit']
additional дополнительный [dapalNItil'ny]
additional charge доплата [daPLAta]
additional costs дополнительные расходы *m pl* [dapalNItil'nyye rasKHOdy]
address адрес [Adris]
addressee получатель *m* [paluCHAtil']
admission charge входная плата [fkhadNAya PLAta]
(admission) ticket (входной) билет [(fkhadNOY) biLYET]
adult взрослый [VZROsly]
advance notice предварительная заявка [pridvaRItil'naya zaYAFka]
advance ticket sales предварительная продажа [pridvaRItil'naya praDAzha]
advantage выгода [VYgada]
advertise, to рекламировать *ipf a. pf* [riklaMIravat']
advice совет [saVYET]
aerobics аэробика [aeRObika]
after *(temporal)* после + *gen* [POslye ...]

afterwards пото́м [paTOM]

again опя́ть [aPYAT']

against про́тив + *gen* [PROtif ...]

age во́зраст [VOZrast]

agency аге́нтство [aGYENTstva]

ago тому́ наза́д [taMU naZAT]

agree on, to догова́риваться/
догово́ри́ться [dagaVArivatsa/
dagavaRItsa]

air во́здух [VOZdukh]

air conditioning кондиционе́р
[kanditsyaNYER]

air mattress надувно́й матра́с
[naduVNOY maTRAS]

air pump возду́шный насо́с
[vazDUSHny naSOS]

airline авиакомпа́ния
[aviakamPAniya]

airmail а́виа [Avia]

airport аэропо́рт [aeraPORT]

airport shuttle авто́бус-
экспре́сс [aFTObus-ekSPRYES]

airport tax аэропорто́вые
сбо́ры *m pl* [aeraparTOvyye ZBOry]

alarm clock буди́льник
[buDIL'nik]

alarm sign противоуго́нная
сигнализа́ция [prativauGOnaya
signaliZAtsyya]

allergy аллерги́я [alirGIya]

allowed допусти́мый
[dapuSTImy]

almonds минда́ль *m* [minDAL']

almost почти́ [pachTI]

alone оди́н *m*/ одна́ *fl* одни́ *pl*
[aDIN/adNA/adNI]

already уже́ [uZHE]

also то́же [TOzhe]

altar алта́рь *m* [alTAR']

although хотя́ [khaTYA]

aluminum foil (алюми́ниевая)
фольга́ [(alyuMInivaya) fal'GA]

always всегда́ [fsigDA]

ambulance ско́рая по́мощь
[SKOraya POmash]

America Аме́рика [aMYErika]

American америка́нец/
америка́нка
[amiriKAnits/amiriKANka]

amount су́мма [SUma]

amphitheater амфитеа́тр
[amfitiATR]

amusement park парк с
аттракцио́нами [PARK
s-atraktsyOnami]

ancient дре́вний [DRYEVny]

and и [i], a [a]

anesthesia нарко́з [narKOS]

angry злой [ZLOY]

animal живо́тное [zhyVOTnaye]

animated film мультфи́льм
[mul'tFIL'M]

ankle лоды́жка [laDYSHka]

anklets носо́чки *m pl* [naSOCHki]

announcement сообще́ние
[saapSHEniye]

annoying надое́дливый
[nadaYEDlivy]

annual ежего́дный [yizhyGODny]

answer the phone, to снима́ть/
снять тру́бку [sniMAT'/SNYAT'
TRUPku]

answer, to отвеча́ть/отве́тить
[atviCHAT'/atVYEtit']

answering machine
автоотве́тчик [aftaatVYETchik]

antibiotic антибио́тик
[antibiOtik]

antifreeze антифри́з [antiFRIS]

antiques store антиква́рный
магази́н [antiKVARny magaZIN]

anybody кто́-нибудь [KTO-nibut']

apartment кварти́ра [kvarTIra]

appetite аппети́т [apiTIT]

appetizer заку́ска [zaKUska]

applause аплодисме́нты *m pl*
[apladiSMYENty]

apple я́блоко [YAblaka]

appointment *(medical)* да́та
[DAta]; *(engagement)* встре́ча
[FSTRYEcha]

appropriate соотве́тствующий
[saatVYETstvuyushi]

approximate приме́рный [priMYERny]

approximately приблизи́тельно [pribliZItil'na]; о́коло + gen [Okala]

April апре́ль m [aPRYEL']

arch а́рка [ARka], свод [SVOT]

archeology археоло́гия [arkhiaLOgiya]

architect архите́ктор [arkhiTYEKtar]

architecture архитекту́ра [arkhitikTUra]

area край [KRAY]

area code телефо́нный код [tiliFOny KOT]

arm рука́ sing [ruKA], ру́ки pl [ruKI]

armchair кре́сло [kriyeSLO]

(a)round вокру́г + gen [vaKRUK]

arrest, to арестова́ть ipf a. pf [aristaVAT']

arrival прибы́тие [priBYtiye]; въезд [VYEST]

arrival time вре́мя прибы́тия [VRYEmya priBYtiya]

arrive, to прибыва́ть/прибы́ть [pribyVAT'/priBYT']

art иску́сство [isKUstva]

art nouveau стиль m моде́рн [STIL' maDYERN]

artificial sweetener сахари́н [sakhaRIN]

arts and crafts прикладно́е иску́сство [prikladNOye isKUstva]

ashtray пе́пельница [PYEpil'nitsa]

Asia А́зия [Aziya]

ask, to спра́шивать/спроси́ть [SPRAshyvat'/spraSIT']

ask, to (s.o. for s.th.) проси́ть/попроси́ть (у + gen + gen) [praSIT'/papraSIT' (u-...)]

asparagus спа́ржа [SPARzha]

aspect вид [VIT]

aspirin аспири́н [aspiRIN]

assert, to утвержда́ть/утверди́ть [utvirZHDAT'/utvirDIT']

asthma а́стма [ASTma]

at у + gen [u-...]; (time) в + acc [f-...]

at first сперва́ [spirVA]; снача́ла [snaCHAla]

at ground level на у́ровне земли́ [na-Uravnye zimLI]

at home до́ма [DOma]

at least по ме́ньшей ме́ре [pa-MYEN'shey MYErye]; по кра́йней ме́ре [pa-KRAYniy MYErye]

at lunchtime в по́лдень [f-POLdin']

at night но́чью [NOchyu]

at once сейча́с [siyCHAS]

at the back позади́ [pazaDI]

at the same time одновре́менно [adnaVRYEmina]

athlete спортсме́н/ка [spartsMYEN/ka]

athletic field спорти́вная площа́дка [sparTIVnaya plaSHATka]

ATM/automatic teller machine банкома́т [bankaMAT]

attack нападе́ние [napaDYEniye]

attention внима́ние [vniMAniye]

au gratin запечённый [zapiCHOny]

August а́вгуст [AVgust]

automatic автомати́ческий [aftamaTIchiski]

automatic transmission автомати́ческая переда́ча [aftamaTIchiskaya piriDAcha]

average сре́дний adj [SRYEDni]; on the average в сре́днем adv [f-SRYEDnim]

award о́рден [ORdin]

baby младе́нец [mlaDYEnits]
baby bottle буты́лочка с со́ской [buTYlachka s-SOskay]
baby food де́тское пита́ние [DYETskaye piTAniye]
baby monitor бебифо́н [bebiFON]; радионя́ня [radiaNYAnya]
babysitter бэбиси́ттер [bebiSItir]
bachelor холостя́к [khalaSTYAK]
back спина́ [spiNA]; наза́д [naZAT]
backache боль f в спине́ [BOL' f-spiNYE]
backpack рюкза́к [ryukZAK]
backwards обра́тно [aBRATna]
bad плохо́й [plaKHOY]
badminton бадминто́н [badminTON]
bag мешо́к [miSHOK]; паке́т [paKYET]
baggage бага́ж [baGASH]
baggage cart теле́жка [tiLYESHka]
baggage claim вы́дача багажа́ [VYdacha baGAzha]
baggage clearing (customs) оформле́ние и сда́ча багажа́ [afarMLYEniye izDAcha baGAzha]
baggage counter бага́жное отделе́ние [baGAZHnaye addiLYEniye]; бага́жная ка́сса [baGAZHnaya KAsa]
baggage room ка́мера хране́ния [KAmira khraNYEniya]
baked печёный [piCHOny]
bakery бу́лочная [BUlachnaya]
balcony балко́н [balKON]
ball (toy) мяч [MYACH]; (dance) бал [BAL]
ballet бале́т [baLYET]
ballpoint pen (ша́риковая) ру́чка [(SHArikavaya) RUCHka]

band гру́ппа [GRUpa]
band-aid пла́стырь m [PLAstyr']
bandage повя́зка [paVYASka]
bandage, to перевя́зывать/ перевяза́ть [piriVYAzyvat'/piriviZAT']
bank банк [BANK]
bar кафе́ [kaFYE]; пивна́я [pivNAya]; бар [BAR]
barber парикма́хер [parikMAkhir]
barely едва́ [yidVA]
Baroque баро́кко [baROka]
barrier-free свобо́дный от загражде́ний [svaBODny at-zagraZHDYEniy]
basket корзи́на [karZIna]
basketball баскетбо́л [baskidBOL]
bathing cap купа́льная ша́почка [kuPAL'naya SHApachka]
bathing suit купа́льник [kuPAL'nik]
bathing trunks пла́вки f pl [PLAFki]
bathrobe купа́льный хала́т [kuPAL'ny khaLAT]
bathroom ва́нная [VAnaya]
bathtub ва́нна [VAna]
battery батаре́йка [bataRYEYka]
battery charger заря́дное устро́йство [zaRYADnaye uSTROYstva]
bay бу́хта [BUKHta]; зали́в [zaLIF]
bay leaf лавро́вый лист [laVROvy LIST]
be able, to мочь/смочь [MOCH/SMOCH]; уме́ть/суме́ть [uMYET'/suMYET']
be afraid of, to опаса́ться ipf + gen [apaSAtsa]
be afraid, to боя́ться ipf [baYAtsa]
be against, to (быть) про́тив + gen [(BYT') PROtiv ...]
be allowed, to (dat +) мо́жно adv + inf [MOZHna]

be angry, to (about)
серди́ться/рассерди́ться (на
+ *acc*) [sirDItsa/rasirDItsa (na-...)]
be called, to *acc* = зову́т [...
zaVUT]; *(things)* называ́ться/
назва́ться [nazyVAtsa/nazVAtsa]
be for, to (быть) за + *acc* [(BYT')
za-...]
be friends with, to дружи́ть
ipf с + *instr* [druZHYT' s-...]
be glad (about), to ра́до-
ваться/обра́доваться (+ *dat*)
[RAdavatsa/aBRAdavatsa]
be in a hurry, to спеши́ть/
поспеши́ть [spiSHYT'/paspiSHYT']
be interested (in), to
интересова́ться/
заинтересова́ться (+ *instr*)
[intirisaVAtsa/zaintirisaVAtsa]
be lacking, to не хвата́ть/
не хвати́ть + *gen* [ni-khvaTAT'/
ni-khvaTIT']
be late (for), to опа́здывать/
опозда́ть (на + *acc*) [aPAZdyvat'/
apaZDAT' (na-...)]
be left (over), to остава́ться/
оста́ться [astaVAtsa/aSTAtsa]
be located, to находи́ться *ipf*
[nakhaDItsa]
be mistaken, to заблужда́ться
ipf [zabluZHDAtsa]
be surprised (at), to
удивля́ться/удиви́ться (+ *dat*)
[udiVLYAtsa/udiVItsa]
be thirsty, to хоте́ть/
захоте́ть пить [khaTYET'/
zakhaTYET' PIT']
be, to быть [BYT']
be used, to *(to s.th.)* (быть)
привы́к *m*/привы́кла
f/привы́кли *pl* [(BYT')
priVYK/priVYkla/priVYkli]
be worried (about), to
беспоко́иться/обеспоко́иться
(о + *prep*) [bispaKOitsa/
abispaKOitsa (a-...)]
beach пляж [PLYASH]

beach resort куро́рт [kuRORT]
beans фасо́ль *m* [faSOL']
beard борода́ [baraDA]
beat up, to избива́ть/изби́ть
[izbiVAT'/izBIT']
beautiful краси́вый [kraSIvy]
because потому́ что [pataMU
SHTO]; так как [TAK KAK]
because of из-за + *gen* [iz-za-...]
become, to станови́ться/
стать [stanaVItsa/STAT']
bed крова́ть *f* [kraVAT']
bed linen бельё [biL'YO]
bed linens посте́льное бельё
[pasTYEL'naye biL'YO]
bedroom спа́льня [SPAL'n'ya]
bedside table ночно́й сто́лик
[nachNOY STOlik]
bee пчела́ [pchiLA]
beef говя́дина [gaVYAdina]
beer пи́во [PIva]
before до + *gen* [da-...]; перед
тем [pirit-TYEM]; пре́жде чем
[PRYEzhdye CHEM]
begin, to начина́ть/нача́ть
[nachiNAT'/naCHAT']
beginning нача́ло [naCHAla]
behind за + *instr* [za-...]; позади́
+ *gen* [pazaDI]
beige бе́жевый [BYEzhyvy]
believe, to ве́рить/пове́рить
(в + *acc*) [VYErit/paVYErit' (f-...)]
belong, to принадлежа́ть *ipf*
+ *dat* [prinadliZHAT']
below внизу́ [vniZU]; ни́же + *gen*
[NIzhe]; под + *instr* [pat-...]
belt по́яс [POyis]
bench скаме́йка [skaMYEYka]
besides кро́ме того́ [KROmye
taVO]
best лу́чший [LUchy]
better лу́чший [LUchy]
between ме́жду + *instr*
[MYEZHdy]
beverage напи́ток [naPItak]
bicycle велосипе́д [vilasiPYET]
big большо́й [bal'SHOY]

bike helmet велосипéдный шлем [vilasiPYEDny SHLYEM]

bike path велосипéдная дорóжка [vilasiPYEDnaya daROga]

bike trip поéздка на велосипéде [paYESTka na-vilasiPYEDye]

bikini бикини *n* [biKIni]

bill банкнóта [bankNOta]; счёт [SHOT]

billfold бумáжник [buMAZHnik]

bird птица [PTItsa]

birthday день *m* рождéния [DYEN' raZHDYEniya]

bite, to кусáть/укусить [kuSAT'/ukuSIT']

bitter гóрький [GOR'ki]

black чёрный [CHORny]

black-and-white film чёрно-бéлый фильм [CHORna-BYEly FIL'M]

bladder мочевóй пузы́рь [machiVOY puZYR']

blanket одеяло [adiYAla]

blazer блéйзер [BLYEYzir]

bleed, to *(wound)* кровоточить *ipf* [kravaTOchit']; *(human)* истекáть/истéчь крóвью [istiKAT'/iSTYECH KROV'yu]

bleeding кровотечéние [kravatiCHEniye]

blind слепóй [sliPOY]

blind man/woman слепóй/слепáя [sliPOY/sliPAya]

blinker указáтель *m* поворóта [ukaZAtil' pavaROta]

blister вóлдырь *f* [VOLdyr']

blond белокýрый [bilaKUry]

blood кровь *f* [KROF']

blood group грýппа крóви [GRUpa KROvi]

blood poisoning заражéние крóви [zaraZHEniye KROvi]

blood pressure кровянóе давлéние [kraviNOye daVLYEniye]

blouse блýзка [BLUSka]

blue синий [SIny]

boarding card посáдочный талóн [paSAdachny taLON]

boarding house пансиóн [pansiON]

body тéло [TYEla]

boil варить/сварить [VArit'/SVArit']

boiled варёный [vaRYOny], отварнóй [atvarNOY]

bone кость *f* [KOST']

book книга [KNIga]

bookstore книжный магазин [KNIZHny magaZIN]

boots сапоги́ *m pl* [sapaGI]

border граница [graNItsa]

border crossing пограничный контрóльно-пропускнóй пункт [pagraNICHny kanTROL'na-prapuskNOY PUNKT]; КПП [ka-pe-PE]

boring скýчный [SKUCHny]

borrow, to *(from s.o.)* брать/взять взаймы́ (у + *gen*) [BRAT'/VZYAT' vzayMY (u-...)]

boss начáльник [naCHAL'nik]

botanical gardens ботанический сад [bataNIchiski SAT]

both óба *m, n*/óбе *f* [Oba/Obye]

bother, to приставáть/пристáть (к + *dat*) [pristaVAT'/priSTAT' (k-...)]

bottle бутылка [buTYLka]

bottle opener открывáлка [atkryVALka]

bouquet букéт [buKYET]

boutique салóн мóдных товáров [salon MODnykh taVAraf]

bowel movement стул [STUL]

bowl миска [MISka]

bowtie бáбочка [BAbachka]

box ящик [YAshik]; *(theater)* лóжа [LOzha]

boy мáльчик [MAL'chik]

bra бюстгáльтер [byusdGAL'tir]

bracelet браслéт [braSLYET]

brain мозг [MOSK]

braised тушёный [tuSHOny]
brake тóрмоз [TORmas]
bread хлеб [KHLYEB]
break перерыв [piriRYF]
break into, to взлáмывать/
взломáть [VZLAmyvat/vzlaMAT']
breakdown *(auto)* авáрия
[aVAriya]
breakfast зáвтрак [ZAFtrak]
breakfast buffet швéдский
стол [SHVYETski STOL]
breakfast room буфéт
[buFYET]; ресторáн [ristaRAN]
breathe, to дышáть/
вздохнýть [dySHAT'/vzdakhNUT']
bridge мост [MOST]
briefs трусы́ *m pl* [truSY]
bright lights *(car)* дáльний
свет [DAL'ni SVYET]
bring back, to приноси́ть/
принести́ обрáтно [prinaSIT'/
priniSTI aBRATna]
bring, to приноси́ть/принести́
[prinaSIT'/priniSTI]
brochure проспéкт [praSPYEKT]
broken слóманный [SLOmany]
bronchial tubes брóнхи *m pl*
[BRONkhi]
bronze брóнза [BRONza]
brooch брóшка [BROSHka]
brother брат [BRAT]
brown кори́чневый [kaRICHnivy]
bruise уши́б [uSHYP]
brush щётка [SHOTka]
building здáние [ZDAniye]
bumper бáмпер [BAMpir]
bunk bed двухъя́русная
кровáть [dvukhYArusnaya kraVAT']
bunny lift дéтский подъёмник
[DYETski padYOMnik]
burn ожóг [aZHOK]
burn ointment мазь *f* от
ожóгов [MAS' at-aZHOgaf]
bus автóбус [aFTObus]
bus station автовокзáл
[aftavagZAL]
but но [NO]

butcher shop мяснáя лáвка
[misNAya LAFka]
butter мáсло [MAsla]
buttermilk пáхта [PAKHta]
buy, to покупáть/купи́ть
[pakuPAT'/kuPIT']
bypass (road) обходнáя
дорóга [apkhadNAya daROga]
Byzantine византи́йский
[vizanTIYski]

C

cabaret теáтр миниатю́р [tiATR
miniaTYUR]
cabbage капýста [kaPUsta]
cabin (ship) каю́та [kaYUta]
cable railway фуникулёр
[funikuLYOR], подъёмник
[padYOMnik], канáтная дорóга
[kaNATnaya daROga]
café кафé [kaFYE]
cake пирóг [piROK]; кекс [KYEKS]
calculate, to исчисля́ть/
исчи́слить [ishchiSLYAT'/
ishCHIslit']
call звонóк [zvaNOK]
calm спокóйствие
[spaKOYstviye]; тишинá [tishyNA];
(weather) безвéтрие [bizVYEtriye]
calm down, to успокáиваться/
успокóиться [uspaKAivatsa/
uspaKOitsa]
camcorder видеокáмера
[vidiaKAmira]
camera фотоаппарáт
[fataapaRAT]
camp stove пли́тка [PLITka]
camp, to жить *ipf* в палáтке
[ZHYT' f-paLATkye]
camper (vehicle) кéмпер
[KYEMpir]

campground ке́мпинг [KYEMpink]

camping ке́мпинг [KYEMpink]

camping guide путеводи́тель *m* по ке́мпингам [putivaDItil' pa-KYEMpingam]

camping stove *(gas)* га́зовая пли́тка [GAzavaya PLITka]

can opener консервооткрыва́тель *m* [kansirvaatkryVAtil']

can: you can мо́жно *adv + inf* [MOZHna]; you can't нельзя́ *adv + inf pf* [nil'ZYA]

Canada Кана́да [kaNAda]

canal кана́л [kaNAL]

cancel, to отменя́ть/отмени́ть [atmiNYAT'/atmiNIT']

cancer рак [RAK]

candies конфе́ты *m pl* [kanFYEty]

candle свеча́ [sviCHA]

candy сла́дости *f pl* [SLAdasti]

candy store конди́терская [kanDItirskaya]

canned goods консе́рвы *m pl* [kanSYERvy]

canoe кано́э [kaNOe]

canyon уще́лье [uSHEL'ye]

cap (headgear) ша́пка [SHAPka]

capital столи́ца [staLItsa]

captain капита́н [kapiTAN]

car маши́на [maSHYna]

car radio автомоби́льный радиоприёмник [aftamaBIL'ny radiapriYOMnik]

car registration техпа́спорт (автомоби́ля) [tikhPASpart (aftamaBIl'ya)]

car with reserved seats *(train)* плацка́ртный ваго́н [platsKARTny vaGON]

carafe графи́н [graFIN]

caraway тмин [TMIN]

cardiac stimulant серде́чно-сосу́дистое сре́дство [sirDYECHna-saSUdistaye SRYETstva]

cardigan вя́заная ко́фта [VYAzanaya KOFta]

care (in need of) нужда́ющийся в ухо́де [nuZHDAyushi v-uKHOdye]

carnation гвозди́ка [gvazDIka]

carrots морко́вь *f* [marKOF']

cash нали́чный [naLICHny]

cashier's desk ка́сса [KAsa]

casino казино́ [kaziNO]

cassette кассе́та [kaSYEta]

cassette recorder кассе́тный магнитофо́н [kaSYETny magnitaFON]

castle за́мок [ZAmak]

cat ко́шка [KOSHka]

catch, to лови́ть/пойма́ть [laVIT'/payMAT']

cathedral собо́р [saBOR]

cauliflower цветна́я капу́ста [tsvitNAya kaPUsta]

cause, to причиня́ть/причини́ть [prichiNYAT'/prichiNIT']

Caution! Осторо́жно! [astaROZHna]

cautious осторо́жный [astaROZHny]

cave пеще́ра [piSHEra]

cavity *(in a tooth)* дупло́ [duPLO]

CD (compact disc) компа́кт-ди́ск [kampagd-DISK]

CD player CD-пле́йер [si-di-PLYEyir]

ceiling потоло́к [pataLOK]

celery сельдере́й [sil'diRYEY]

cell phone моби́льник [maBIL'nik]

cellular phone моби́льный телефо́н [maBIL'ny tiliFON]; со́товый телефо́н [SOtavy tiliFON]

cemetery кла́дбище [KLADbishe]

cent цент [TSENT]

center центр [TSENTR]

centimeter сантиме́тр [santiMYETR]

central центра́льный [tsynTRAL'ny]

central heating центра́льное
отопле́ние [tsynTRAL'naye
ataPLYEniye]
century столе́тие [staLYEtiye];
век [VYEK]
ceramics кера́мика [kiRAmika]
certain уве́ренный [uVYEriny];
определённый [apridiLYOny]
certificate свиде́тельство
[sviDYEtil'stva]
certified letter заказно́е
письмо́ [zakazNOye piS'MO]
certify, to свиде́тельствовать/
засвиде́тельствовать
(о + prep) [sviDYEtil'stvavat'/
zasviDYEtil'stvavat']
chain цепь f [TSEP']
chair стул [STUL]
chairlift кре́сельная кана́тная
доро́га [KRYEsil'naya kaNATnaya
daROga]; сиде́ния [siDYEniya]
chambermaid го́рничная
[GORnichnaya]
chamomile рома́шка [raMASHka]
champagne шампа́нское
[shamPANskaye]
change (a reservation), to
меня́ть/поменя́ть [miNYAT'/
pamiNYAT']
change clothes, to
переодева́ться/переоде́ться
[piriadiVAtsa/piriaDYEtsa]
change (money in return) сда́ча
[ZDAcha]
changing table сто́лик для
пелена́ния [STOlik dlia-piliNAniya]
chapel часо́вня [chiSOVnya]
charming очарова́тельный
[acharaVAtil'ny]
cheap дешёвый [diSHOvy]
check in, to регистри́роваться/
зарегистри́роваться
[rigiSTRIravatsa/zarigiSTRIravatsa]
checkroom гардеро́б [gardiROP]
cheerful весёлый [viSYOly]
cheese сыр [SYR]

cheese (hard) твёрдый сыр
[TVYORdy SYR]
cherry tree чере́шня
[chiRYESHnya]
chest грудь f [GRUT']
chest pain ангина [anGIna]
chewing gum жва́чка
[ZHVACHka]
chicken ку́рица [KUritsa]
chickenpox ве́тряная о́спа
[VYEtrinaya Ospa]
chickpeas нут [NUT]
child ребёнок [riBYOnak]
child-care service ухо́д за
детьми́ [uKHOT za-dit'MI]
children's де́тский [DYETski]
child's car seat де́тское
сиде́нье [DYETskaye siDYEnye]
Chinese кита́йский [kiTAYski]
chip card чип-ка́рта [chip-KARta]
chocolate шокола́д [shakaLAT]
choice вы́бор [VYbar]
choir хор [KHOR]
choose, to выбира́ть/вы́брать
[vybiRAT'/VYbrat']
chop отбивна́я котле́та
[adbivNAya katLYEta]
Christianity христиа́нство
[khristiANstva]
Christmas (Jan. 7th)
Рождество́ Христо́во
[razhdiSTVO khriSTOva]
church це́рковь f [TSERkaf']
cigar сига́ра [siGAra]
cigarette сигаре́та [sigaRYEta]
cigarillo сига́рка [siGARka]
circulation кровообраще́ние
[kravaabraSHEniye]
circus цирк [TSYRK]
city го́род [GOrat]
city bus городско́й авто́бус
[garatsKOY aFTObus]
city map план го́рода [PLAN
GOrada]; схе́ма го́рода
[SKHYEma GOrada]

city sightseeing tour
экску́рсия по го́роду
[ekSKURsiya pa-GOradu]

city wall городска́я стена́
[garatsKAya stiNA]

class класс [KLAS]

classical класси́ческий
[klaSIchiski]

classicism классици́зм
[klasiTSYZM]

clay гли́на [gliNA]

clean чи́стый [CHIsty]

clean, to убира́ть/убра́ть
[ubiRAT'/'uBRAT']; чи́стить/
почи́стить [CHIstit'/paCHIstit']

cleaning чи́стка [CHISTka]

clear я́сный [YAsny]

clearance sale распрода́жа
[raspraDAzha]

climate кли́мат [KLImat]

close (to) бли́зкий (к + *dat*)
[BLISki (k-...)]

closed закры́тый [zaKRYty]

closet шкаф [SHKAF]

cloth сукно́ [sukNO]

clothes dryer суши́лка для б
елья́ [suSHYLka dlia-biL'YA]

clothesline бельева́я верёвка
[biliVAya viRYOFka]

clothespin прище́пка
[priSHEPka]

clothing оде́жда [aDYEzhda]

cloud о́блако [Oblaka]

cloudy о́блачный [Oblachny]

clutch сцепле́ние [stsyPLYEniye]

coal у́голь *m* [Ugal']

coat пальто́ [pal'TO]

coat hangers пле́чики *m pl*
[PLYEchiki]

coconut коко́с [kaKOS]

coffee ко́фе *m* [KOfye]

coffeemaker кофева́рка
[kafiVARka]

cog railway зубча́тая желе́зная
доро́га [zupCHAtaya zhyLYEZnaya
daROga]

coin моне́та [maNYEta]

coin purse кошелёк [kashyLYOK]

cold просту́да [praSTUda];
холо́дный [khaLODny]

cold (sickness) на́сморк
[NAsmark]

cold, to be *dat* + хо́лодно *adv*
[KHOladna]

colic ко́лики *f pl* [KOliki]

collarbone ключи́ца [klyuCHItsa]

colleague колле́га [kaLYEga]

collect, to собира́ть/собра́ть
[sabiRAT'/saBRAT']

collision столкнове́ние
[stalknaVYEniye]

**collision and liability
insurance** части́чное
(страхова́ние) ка́ско
[chisTICHnaye (strakhaVAniye) KAska]

colored цветно́й [tsvitNOY]

colorful пёстрый [PYOstry]

coloring book
кни́жка-раскра́ска [KNISHka-
rasKRAska]

column коло́нна [kaLOna];
столб [STOLP]

comb расчёска [rashCHOska]

comb, to причёсывать/
причеса́ть [priCHOsyvat'/
prichiSAT']

come back, to возвраща́ться/
возврати́ться [vazvraSHAtsa/
vazvraTItsa]

Come in! войди́те! [vayDItye]

come in, to входи́ть/войти́
[fkhaDIT'/vayTI]

come, to *(on foot)* приходи́ть/
прийти́ [prikhaDIT'/priyTI]; *(by
vehicle)* приезжа́ть/прие́хать
[priyiZHAT'/priYEkhat']; *(by plane)*
прилета́ть/прилете́ть [priliTAT'/
priliTYET']

comedy коме́дия [kaMYEdiya]

comfortable ую́тный [uYUTny];
удо́бный [uDOBny]

commission комиссио́нная
[kamisiOnaya]

common употреби́тельный [upatriBItil'ny]; при́нятый [PRInity]; совме́стный [saVMYESny]

commuter train при́городный по́езд [PRIgaradny POyist]; электри́чка [elikTRICHka]

company фи́рма [FIRma]

compartment купе́ [kuPYE]

compass ко́мпас [KOMpas]

complain (about), to опла́кивать/опла́кать (+ acc) [aPLAkivat'/aPLAkat']; жа́ловаться/пожа́ловаться (на + acc) [ZHAlavatsa/paZHAlavatsa (na-...)]

composer композитор [kampaZItar]

comprehensive and liability insurance по́лное (страхова́ние) ка́ско [POLnaye (strakhaVAniye) KAska]

concert конце́рт [kanTSERT]

concierge, "floor lady" дежу́рная [diZHURnaya]

concussion сотрясе́ние мо́зга [satriSYEniye MOZga]

condom презервати́в [prizirvaTIF]

conductor дирижёр [diriZHOR]; конду́ктор [kanDUKtar]

confidence дове́рие (к + dat) [daVYEriye (k-...)]

confirm, to подтвержда́ть/подтверди́ть [patvirZHDAT'/patvirDIT']

confiscate, to конфискова́ть ipf a. pf [kanfiskaVAT']

congratulate s.o. on ..., to поздравля́ть/поздра́вить + acc с + instr [pazdraVLYAT'/paZDRAvit' ... s-...]

congratulations поздравле́ние [pazdraVLYEniye]

connect, to свя́зывать/связа́ть [SVYAzyvat'/sviZAT']

connection связь f [SVYAS']; (transportation) переса́дка [piriSATka]

consist (of), to состоя́ть ipf (из + gen) [sastaYAT' (is-...)]

constipation запо́р [zaPOR]

construction site стро́йка [STROYka]

consulate ко́нсульство [KONsul'stva]

contact конта́кт [kanTAKT]

contagious зара́зный [zaRAZny]

container су́дно [SUDna]; сосу́д [saSUT]

contents содержа́ние [sadirZHAniye]

contraband контраба́нда [kantraBANda]

contraceptive противозача́точное [prativazaCHAtachnaye]

contraceptive pill противозача́точная табле́тка [prativazaCHAtachnaya taBLYETka]

contract догово́р [dagaVOR]

convent монасты́рь m [manaSTYR']

conversation разгово́р [razgaVOR]

cook по́вар/повари́ха [POvar/pavaRIkha]

cook, to (prepare) гото́вить/пригото́вить [gaTOvit'/prigaTOvit']

cookbook пова́ренная кни́га [paVArinaya KNIga]

cookies (бискви́тное) пече́нье [(biSKVITnaye) piCHEnye]

cool прохла́дный [praKHLADny]

coolant охлажда́ющая вода́ [akhlaZHDAyushaya vaDA]

cooler bag су́мка-холоди́льник [SUMka-khalaDIL'nik]

copy ко́пия [KOpiya]

corkscrew што́пор [SHTOpar]

corn кукуру́за [kukuRUza]

corner у́гол [Ugal]

correct пра́вильный [PRAvil'ny]

corridor прохо́д [praKHOT]

cost, to сто́ить *ipf* [STOit']

costume jewelry бижуте́рия [bizhuTYEriya]

cottage cheese творо́г [tvaROK]

cotton хло́пок [KHLOpak]

cotton swab ва́тная па́лочка [VATnaya PAlachka]

cotton wool ва́та [VAta]

cough ка́шель *m* [KAshyl']

cough syrup миксту́ра от ка́шля [mikSTUra at-KAshlya]

count, to счита́ть/сосчита́ть [shiTAT]

country страна́ [straNA]

countryman/woman (fellow) земля́к/земля́чка [zimLYAK/zimLYACHka]

course курс [KURS], *(usually pl)*: ку́рсы [KURsy]; *(meal)* блю́до [BLYUda]

court (law) суд [SUT]

cousin кузе́н/кузи́на [kuZYEN/kuZIna]

crab краб [KRAP]

cramp су́дорога [SUdaraga]

crash helmet защи́тный шлем [zaSHITny SHLYEM]

crazy сумасше́дший [sumaSHETshy]

cream *(cosmetic)* (космети́ческий) крем [(kasmiTIchiski) KRYEM]

creative тво́рческий [TVORchiski]

credit card креди́тная ка́рточка [kriDITnaya KARta]

crime преступле́ние [pristuPLYEniye]

cross крест [KRYEST]

cross-country skis го́ночные лы́жи *f pl* [GOnachnyye LYzhy]

cross, to *(river)* перепра вля́ть(ся)/перепра́вить(ся) (че́рез + *acc*) [piripraVLYAtsa/ piriPRAvitsa [chiris-...]

crossing перехо́д [piriKHOT]

crown (dental) коро́нка [kaRONka]

cruise круи́з [kruIS]

crutch костыль *m* [kaSTYL']

cry, to пла́кать *ipf* [PLAkat']

crystal хруста́ль *m* [khruSTAL']

cucumber огуре́ц [aguRYETS]

culture культу́ра [kul'TUra]

cup ча́шка [CHASHka]

curious любопы́тный [lyubaPYTny]

curlers бигуди́ *f pl* [biguDI]

curls ку́дри *f pl* [KUdri]

currency валю́та [vaLYUta]

current *(elec.)* ток [TOK]

curve поворо́т [pavaROT]

customer покупа́тель/ница [pakuPAtil'/nitsa]

customs *(duty)* по́шлина [POshlina]; *(office)* тамо́жня [taMOZHnya]

customs declaration тамо́женная деклара́ция [taMOzhynaya diklaRAtsyya]

customs duty тамо́женные по́шлины *f pl* [taMOzhynyye POshliny]

cut (wound) ре́заная ра́на [RYEzanaya RAna]

cycling велоспо́рт [vilaSPORT]

D

daily ежедне́вно [yizhyDNYEVna]

dam да́мба [DAMba]

damage вред [VRYET], уще́рб [uSHERP]; поврежде́ние [pavriZHDYEniye]

damage, to поврежда́ть/ повреди́ть [pavriZHDAT'/ pavriDIT']

damp сыро́й [syROY]

dance band танцева́льный орке́стр [tantsyVAL'ny arKYESTR]

dance theater танцева́льный теа́тр [tantsyVAL'ny tiATR]

dance, to танцева́ть/пота нцева́ть [tantsyVAT'/patantsyVAT']

dancer танцо́вщик/танцо́вщица [tanTSOFshik/tanTSOFshitsa]

danger опа́сность f [aPASnast']

dangerous опа́сный [aPASny]

dark тёмный [TYOMny]

dark blue тёмно-си́ний [TYOMna-SIni]

dark green тёмно-зелёный [TYOMna-ziLYOny]

date число́ [chiSLO]

date of birth да́та рожде́ния [DAta raZHDYEniya]

daughter дочь sing [DOCH], до́чери pl [DOchiri]

day день m [DYEN']

day after tomorrow послеза́втра [pasliZAFtra]

day before yesterday позавчера́ [pazafchiRA]

day of arrival день m прибы́тия [DYEN' priBYtiya]

day pass однодне́вный биле́т [adnaDNYEVny biLYET]

day trip однодне́вная экску́рсия [adnaDNYEVnaya eksKURsiya]

deaf глухо́й [gluKHOY]

deaf-mute глухонемо́й [glukhaniMOY]

debt долг [DOLK]

December дека́брь m [diKABR']

decide, to реша́ть/реши́ть [riSHAT'/riSHYT']

deck па́луба [PAluba]

decoration украше́ние [ukraSHEniye]

deep, deeply глубо́кий adj [gluBOki], глубоко́ adv [glubaKO]

delay опозда́ние [apaZDAniye]

delicatessen гастроно́м [gastraNOM]

delicious вку́сный [FKUSny]

delightful восхити́тельный [vaskhiTItil'ny]

denatured alcohol денатури́рованный спирт [dinatuRIravany SPIRT]

deodorant дезодора́нт [dizadaRANT]

depart (from), to отъезжа́ть/ отъе́хать [atyiZHAT'/atYEkhat']

department store универма́г [univirMAK]

departure отправле́ние [atpraVLYEniye]; вы́езд [VYyist]

departure time вре́мя отпра вле́ния [VRYEmya atpraVLYEniya]

deposit, to (for safekeeping) сдава́ть/сдать на хране́ние [zdaVAT'/ZDAT' na-khraNYEniye]; (as security) отдава́ть/отда́ть в зало́г [addaVAT'/adDAT' v-zaLOK]

describe, to опи́сывать/ описа́ть [aPIsyvat'/apiSAT']

dessert десе́рт [diSYERT]

detailed подро́бный [paDROBny]

detergent стира́льный порошо́к [stiRAL'ny paraSHOK]

detour объе́зд [abYEST]; обхо́д [apKHOT]

develop, to развива́ть/ разви́ть [razviVAT'/razVIT']

dextrose (glucose) виногра́дный са́хар [vinaGRADny SAkhar]; глюко́за [glyuKOzah]

diabetes диабе́т [diaBYET]

diabetic диабе́тик [diaBYEtik]

diagnosis диа́гноз [diAGnos]

diapers пелёнки f pl [piLYONki]; подгу́зники f pl [padGUZniki]

diarrhea поно́с [paNOS]

diet дие́та [diYEta]

diet food диети́ческое пита́ние [diyiTIchiskaye piTAniye]

different друго́й [druGOY]

differently по-друго́му [padruGOmu]

difficult тру́дный [TRUDny]

difficulty breathing удушье [uDUshye]

digestion пищеварение [pishivaRYEniye]

digital цифровой [tsyfraVOY]

dimmed lights ближний свет [BLIZHni SVYET]

dining car вагон-ресторан [vaGON-ristaRAN]

dining room столовая [staLOvaya]

dinner ужин [Uzhyn]

diphtheria дифтерия [diftiRIya]

direct прямой [priaMOY]

directed by режиссура [rizhySUra]

direction направление [napraVLYEniye]

dirty грязный [GRYAZny]

disabled identification card удостоверение инвалидности [udastaviRYEniye invaLIDnasti]

disabled person инвалид [invaLIT]

disappointed разочарованный [razachaROvany]

disco(theque) дискотека [diskaTYEka]

discount скидка [SKITka]

discover, to открывать/ открыть [atkryVAT'/atKRYT']

dish (food) блюдо [BLYUda]

dish towel кухонное полотенце [KUkhanaye palaTYENtse]

dishes посуда [paSUda]

dishwasher посудомоечная машина [pasudaMOyichnaya maSHYna]

disinfect, to дезинфицировать ipf a. pf [dizinfiTSYravat']

disinfectant дезинфицирующее средство [dizinfiTSYruyushiye SRYETstva]

distance расстояние [rastaYAniye]

district район [rayON]

disturb, to мешать/помешать + dat [miSHAT'/pamiSHAT']

dive, to нырять/нырнуть [nyRYAT'/nyrNUT']

diver водолаз [vadaLAS]

diver's mask водолазная маска [vadaLAZnaya MAska]

dizziness головокружение [galavakruZHEniye]

do someone's hair, to делать/сделать причёску [DYElat'/ZDYElat' priCHOsku]

do, to делать/сделать [DYElat'/ ZDYElat']

dock мостик [MOstik]

dock (at), to причаливать/ причалить (в + prep) [priCHAlivat'/priCHAlit' (f-...)]

doctor врач [VRACH]

documents документы m pl [dakuMYENty]

dog собака [saBAka]

dome купол [KUpal]

domestic flight внутренний полёт [VNUtriny paLYOT]

done готовый [gaTOvy]

door дверь f [DVYER']

door code дверной код [dvirNOY KOT]

double двойной [dvayNOY]

downtown центр города [TSENTR GOrada]

draw, to рисовать/нарисовать [risaVAT'/narisaVAT']

drawing рисунок [riSUnak]

dream сон [SON]; (ambition) мечта [michTA]

dress платье [PLAt'ye]

dressing соус [SOus]

drink, to пить/выпить [PIT'/ VYpit']

drinking water питьевая вода [pityiVAya vaDA]

drive back, to ехать/поехать назад [YEkhat'/paYEkhat' naZAT] drive, to е́здить *ipf*, е́хать/поéхать [YEZdit', YEkhat'/paYEkhat']

driver шофёр [shaFYOR]

driver's license води́тельские-права́ [vaDItil'skiye praVA]

drop ка́пля [KAPlya]

drugstore галантере́я [galantiRYEya]; парфюме́рия [parfyuMYEriya]

drunk пья́ный [P'YAny]

dry сухо́й [suKHOY]

dry clean, to отдава́ть/отда́ть в химчи́стку [addaVAT'/adDAT' f-khimCHISTku]

dry land су́ша [SUsha]

dry, to *(get dry)* со́хнуть/вы́сохнуть [SOKHnut'/VYsakhnut']; *(make dry)* суши́ть/вы́сушить [suSHYT'/VYsushyt']

dumb глу́пый [GLUpy]

durable про́чный [PROCHny]

during во вре́мя + *gen* [va-VRYEmya]

during the day днём [DNYOM]

dust пыль *f* [PYL']

duty-free беспо́шлинный [bisPOshliny]

duty-free store магази́н беспо́шлинной торго́вли [magaZIN bisPOshlinay tarGOvli]

dye, to кра́сить/покра́сить [KRAsit'/paKRAsit']

E

ear у́хо *sing* [Ukha], у́ши *pl* [Ushy]

eardrops ка́пли *f pl* в у́ши [KApli v-Ushy]

eardrum бараба́нная перепо́нка [baraBAnaya piriLONka]

earlier ра́ньше *adv* [RAN'she]

early ра́но [RAna]

earrings се́рьги *f pl* [SYER'gi]

earth земля́ [ziMLYA]

eas(il)y легко́ *adv* [likhKO]

east восто́к [vaSTOK]

Easter Па́сха (Христо́ва) [PASkha (khriSTOva)]

eastern восто́чный [vaSTOCHny]

eat breakfast, to за́втракать/поза́втракать [ZAFtrakat'/paZAFtrakat']

eat, to есть *ipf* [YEST']

edible съедо́бный [syiDOBny]

edifice сооруже́ние [saaruZHEniye]

education обуче́ние [abuCHEniye]

eel у́горь *m* [Ugar']

egg яйцо́ *sing* [yiyTSO]; я́йца *pl* [YAYtsa]

either ... or ... и́ли ... и́ли ... [Ili ... Ili ...]

elastic bandage эласти́чный бинт [elaSTICHny BINT]

electric-powered wheelchair электри́ческая инвали́дная коля́ска [elikTRIchiskaya invaLIDnaya kaLYAska]

electric stove электри́ческая плита́ [elikTRIchiskaya pliTA]

electrical электри́ческий [elikTRIchiski]

electrical goods электротова́ры *m pl* [eliktrataVAry]

electrical outlet подво́д электри́чества [padVOT elikTRIchistva]

elegant элега́нтный [eliGANTny]

elevator подъёмник [padYOMnik]; лифт [LIFT]

elsewhere в друго́м ме́сте [v-druGOM MYEstye]

embassy посо́льство [paSOL'stva]

embroidery вы́шивка [VYshyfka]

emergency кра́йний слу́чай [KRAYni SLUchay]

emergency blinkers авари́йная светова́я сигнализа́ция [avaRIYnaya svitaVAya signaliZAtsyya]

emergency brake стоп-кран [STOP-KRAN]

emergency exit запа́сный вы́ход [zaPASny VYkhat]

emergency road service авари́йная слу́жба [avaRIYnaya SLUZHba]

empty пусто́й [puSTOY]

end коне́ц [kaNYETS]

end of the line коне́чная ста́нция [kaNYECHnaya STANtsyya]

engaged обручённый [abruCHOny]

English англи́йский [anGLIYski]; in English по-англи́йски [pa-anGLIYski]

enjoy oneself, to развлека́ться/развле́чься [razvliKAtsa/razVLYECHsa]

enjoy, to наслажда́ться/на слади́ться + instr [naslaZHDAtsa/naslaDItsa]

enough доста́точно adv [daSTAtachna]

entertaining заба́вный [zaBAVny]

entertainment развлече́ние [razvliCHEniye]

enthusiastic (about) восхищённый (+ instr) [vaskhiSHOny]

entrance въезд [VYEST]; вход [FKHOT]

entrée второе (блюдо) [ftaROye (BLYUda)]

envelope конве́рт [kanVYERT]

environment (окружа́ющая) среда́ [(akruZHAyushaya) sriDA]

epilepsy эпиле́псия [epiLYEPsiya]

error оши́бка [aSHYPka]

esophagus пищево́д [pishiVOT]

especially осо́бенный [aSObiny]

estate поме́стье [paMYEst'ye]

etching гравю́ра [graVYUra]

EU (European Union) Европе́йский сою́з [yivraPEISki saYUIS, ESE], ЕС

euro е́вро [YEvra]

Europe Евро́па [yivROpa]

evening ве́чер [VYEchir]

event мероприя́тие [mirapriYAtiye]

every ка́ждый [KAZHdy]

everyone все [FSYE]

everything всё [FSYO]

everywhere везде́ [viZDYE]

exact то́чный [TOCHny]

examination осмо́тр [aSMOTR]

example приме́р [priMYER]

excavations раско́пки f pl [raSKOPki]

excellent отли́чный [atLICHny]

except кро́ме + gen [KROmye]

exchange обме́н де́нег [apMYEN DYEnik]; переме́на [piriMYEna]; сме́на [SMYEna]

exchange office обме́нный пункт [abMYEny PUNKT]

exchange rate валю́тный курс [vaLYUTny KURS]

exchange, to обме́нивать/ обменя́ть [abMYEnivat'/abmiNYAT']

excursion экску́рсия [ekSKURsiya]

excuse извине́ние [izviNYEniye]

excuse (to apologize), to извиня́ть(ся)/извини́ть(ся) [izviNYAT'(sa)/izviNIT'(sa)]

exhausted уста́лый [uSTAly]

exhibit экспона́т [ekspaNAT]

exhibition вы́ставка [VYstafka]

exit вы́езд [VYyist]; вы́ход [VYkhat]

expect, to ожида́ть ipf [azhyDAT']

expenses изде́ржки f pl [izDYERSHki]

expensive, expensively дорого́й adj [daraGOY], до́рого adv [DOraga] explicit определённый [apridiLYOny]

expression выражéние [vyraZHEniye]

expressway скоростнáя дорóга [skarasNAya daROga]

extend, to продолжáть/ продóлжить [pradalZHAT'/ pradalZHYT']

extension cord удлинúтель *m* [udliNItil']

extraordinary необыкновéнный [niabyknaVYEny]

eye глаз *sing* [GLAS], глазá *pl* [glaZA]

eyedrops глазны́е кáпли *f pl* [glazNYye KApli]

fabric ткань *f* [TKAN']
façade фасáд [faSAT]
face лицó [liTSO]
factory фáбрика [FAbrika]; завóд [zaVOT]
faint óбморок [OBmarak]
fair я́рмарка [YARmarka]
fall *(season)* óсень [Osin']
fall, to пáдать/упáсть [PAdat'/ uPAST']
false *(incorrect)* непрáвильный [niPRAvil'ny]; *(not genuine)* фальшúвый [fal'SHYvy]
family семья́ [siM'YA]
family name фамúлия [faMIliya]
famous знаменúтый [znamiNIty]
fan вентиля́тор [vintiLYAtar]
far далёкий *adj* [daLYOki], далекó *adv* [daliKO]
fare стóимость *f* проéзда [STOimast' praYEZda]

farm хýтор [KHUtar]; усáдьба [uSAD'ba]
fashion мóда [MOda]
fashionable мóдный [MODny]
fast бы́стрый [BYstry]
fast(ing) пост [POST]
fat тóлстый [TOLsty]
father отéц [aTYETS]
fat(ty) жúрный [ZHYRny]
faucet крáн [KRAN]
favorite любúмец *m* /любúмица *f* [lyuBImits/lyuBImitsa]
fax, fax machine факс [FAKS]
February феврáль *m* [fiVRAL']
feel, to чýвствовать/ почýвствовать (себя́) [CHUstvavat'/paCHUstvavat' (siBYA)]
feeling чýвство [CHUstva]
fees плáта [PLAta]
ferry парóм [paROM]
festival фестивáль *m* [fistiVAL']; нарóдные гуля́ния [naRODnyye guLYAniya]
fever температýра [timpiraTUra]
few нéсколько + *gen pl* [NYEskal'ka]
field пóле [POlye]
fill out, to заполня́ть/ запóлнить [zapalNYAT'/zaPOLnit']
fill up, to *(with gas)* заправля́ться/запрáвиться (тóпливом) [zapraVLYAtsa/ zaPRAvitsa (TOplivam)]
filling *(tooth)* плóмба [PLOMba]
film *(movie)* фильм [FIL'M]; *(photo)* плёнка [PLYONka]
final окончáтельный [akanCHAtil'ny]
final конéчный *adj* [kaNYESHny]
finally наконéц *adv* [nakaNYETS]
find, to находúть/найтú [nakhaDIT'/nayTI]
finds нахóдки *f pl* [naKHOTki]
fine штраф [SHTRAF]
fine *(thin)* тóнкий [TONki]
finger пáлец [PAlits]
fire огóнь *m* [aGON']

fire alarm пожа́рный извеща́тель [paZHARny izviSHAtil']

fire department пожа́рная кома́нда [paZHARnaya kaMANda]

fire extinguisher огнетуши́тель *m* [agnituSHYtil']

fireworks фейерве́рк [fiyirVYERK]

first пе́рвый [PYERvy]

first aid ско́рая по́мощь [SKOraya POmash]

first course пе́рвое (блю́до) [PYERvaye (BLYUda)]

first floor пе́рвый эта́ж [PYERvy eTASH]

first gear пе́рвая ско́рость [PYERvaya SKOrast']

first name и́мя *n* [Imya]

fish ры́ба [RYba]

fishbone ры́бья кость [RYb'ya KOST']

fishing license лице́нзия на ло́влю рыб [liTSENziya na-LOvlyu RYP]

fishing rod у́дочка [Udachka]

fit *(in shape)* в фо́рме [f-FORmye]

fit, to подходи́ть/подойти́ [patkhaDIT'/padayTI]; *(into)* помеща́ться/помести́ться [pamiSHAtsa/pamiSTItsa]

fitness center фитнес-це́нтр [fitnis-TSENTR]

flash *(camera)* вспы́шка [FSPYSHka]

flask буты́лочка [buTYlachka]

flat пло́ский [PLOski]

flat rate о́бщая цена́ [OPshaya tsyNA]

flatulence га́зы *m pl* [GAzy]

flaw неиспра́вность *f* [niiSPRAVnast']

flea market барахо́лка [baraKHOLka]

flight полёт [paLYOT]

flip-flops рези́новые та́почки *f pl* [riZInavyye TApachki]

floor пол [POL]

floor *(story)* эта́ж [eTASH]

florist's shop цвето́чный магази́н [tsviTOCHny magaZIN]

flour мука́ [MUka]

flower цвето́к *sing* [tsviTOK], цветы́ *pl* [tsviTY]

flu грипп [GRIP]

flush(ing) (of water) спуск воды́ [SPUSK vaDY]

fly му́ха [MUkha]

fly, to лета́ть *ipf* [liTAT'], лете́ть/полете́ть [liTYET'/ paliTYET']

foam пе́на [PYEna]

fog тума́н [tuMAN]

folding wheelchair складна́я инвали́дная коля́ска [skladNAya invaLIDnaya kalYAska]

folk music наро́дная му́зыка [naRODnaya MUzyka]

folk play наро́дная пье́са [naRODnaya P'YEsa]

folklore фолькло́р [fal'kLOR]

folklore evening фолькло́рный ве́чер [fal'kLORny VYEchir]

food еда́ [yiDA]; продово́льствие [pradaVOL'stviye]

food poisoning пищево́е отравле́ние [pishiVOye atraVLYEniye]

foot ступня́ ноги́ [stupNYA naGI]

footwear о́бувь *f* [Obuf']

for *(destined ~)* для + *gen* [dlia-...]; *(in favor of)* за + *acc* [za-...]

foreign иностра́нный [inaSTRAny]

foreign currency валю́та [vaLYUta]

foreigner иностра́нец/ иностра́нка [inaSTRAnits/ inaSTRANka]

forget, to забыва́ть/забы́ть [zabyVAT'/zaBYT']

fork ви́лка [VILka]

form (blank) бланк [BLANK]

form (document) формуля́р [farmuLYAR]

formal attire вече́рнее пла́тье [viCHERniye PLAt'ye]

former бы́вший [BYFshi]

fortress кре́пость f [KRYEpast']

forward, to пересыла́ть/ пересла́ть [pirisyLAT'/piriSLAT']

forward(s) вперёд [fpiRYOT]

fountain фонта́н [fanTAN]

fracture перело́м ко́сти [piriLOM KOsti]

frankfurter соси́ска [saSIska]

fraud обма́н [abMAN]

free свобо́дный [svaBODny]

free (of charge) беспла́тный [bisPLATny]

freeway автомагистра́ль f [aftamagisTRAL']

freeway exit вы́езд (с автомагистра́ли) [VYyist (s-aftamagisTRAli)]

freeway on/off ramp въезд/ съезд [VYEST/SYEST]

freeze, to мёрзнуть/ замёрзнуть [MYORznut'/ zaMYORznut']

freezer pack аккумуля́тор хо́лода [akumuLYAtar KHOlada]

frequent ча́стый [CHAsty]

fresh све́жий [SVYEzhy]

Friday пя́тница [PYATnitsa]

friend (boy/girl) друг/подру́га [DRUK/paDRUga]

friendly любе́зный [lyuBYEZny]

frightened, to be пуга́ться/ испуга́ться [puGAtsa/ispuGAtsa]

from с + gen [s-...], от + gen [at-...]

from (origin) из + gen [is-...]

frost моро́з [maROS]

fruit фрукт [FRUKT]

fruit(s) фру́кты m pl [FRUKty]

full сы́тый [SYty]; по́лный [POLny]

full room and board по́лный пансио́н [POLny pansiON]

fun поте́ха [paTYEkha]

fur мех [MYEKH]

furious бе́шеный [BYEshyny]

furniture ме́бель f [MYEbil']

fuse предохрани́тель [pridakhraNItil']

future бу́дущий adv [BUdushi]; in (the) future в бу́дущем adv [v-BUdushim]

G

gadget аппара́т [apaRAT]

gallery галере́я [galiRYEya]

game игра́ [iGRA]

garage гара́ж [gaRASH]

garbage му́сор [MUsar]

garbage bag му́сорный мешо́к [MUsarny miSHOK]

garbage can мусоросбо́рник [musaraZBORnik]

garden сад [SAT]; (vegetable) огоро́д [agaROT]

garlic чесно́к [chiSNOK]

gas canister га́зовый балло́н [GAzavy baLON]

gas pedal педа́ль f акселера́тора [piDAL' aksiliRAtara]

gas stove га́зовая плита́ [GAzavaya pliTA]

gasoline canister кани́стра для бензи́на [kaNIstra dlia-binZIna]

gate воро́та n pl [vaROta]; (airport) вы́ход на поса́дку [VYkhat na-paSATku]

gauze bandage (ма́рлевый) бинт [(MARlivy) BINT]

gear ско́рость f [SKOrast']

generator генера́тор [giniRAtar]

gentle ла́сковый [LAskavy]

genuine настоя́щий [nastaYAshi]; *(original)* по́длинный [POdliny]

German measles красну́ха [kraSNUkha]

get acclimated, to акклиматизи́роваться *ipf a. pf* [aklimatiZIravatsa]

get out, to выходи́ть/вы́йти [vykhaDIT'/VYti]

get, to получа́ть/получи́ть [paluCHAT'/paluCHIT']

get up, to встава́ть/встать [fstaVAT'/FSTAT']

gift пода́рок [paDArak]

girl *(little)* де́вочка [DYEvachka]; *(young)* де́вушка [DYEvushka]

give as a present, to дари́ть/ подари́ть [daRIT'/padaRIT']

give back, to возвраща́ть/ возврати́ть [vazvraSHAT'/ vazvraTIT']

give,to дава́ть/дать [daVAT'/ DAT']

glad (about) рад *m*/ра́да *f*/ ра́ды *pl* (+ dat) [RAT/RAda/RAdy]

gladly охо́тно [aKHOTna]

glare ice гололе́дица [galaLYEditsa]

glass стака́н [staKAN]

gliding планери́зм [planiRIZM]

gloves перча́тки *f pl* [pirCHATki]

go away, to уходи́ть/уйти́ [ukhaDIT'/uyTI]

go fishing, to уди́ть/поуди́ть [uDIT'/pauDIT']

go for a walk, to гуля́ть/ погуля́ть [guLYAT'/paguLYAT']

go out, to выходи́ть/вы́йти [vykhaDIT'/VYti]

go, to ходи́ть *ipf*, идти́/пойти́ [khaDIT', iTI/payTI]

goal *(aim)* цель *f* [TSEL']; *(sports)* гол [GOL]

goalkeeper вратáрь *m* [vraTAR']

god/goddess бог/боги́ня [BOK/baGInya]

gold зо́лото [ZOlata]

golden золоти́стый [zalaTIsty]

golf гольф [GOL'F]

gone прочь [PROCH]

good хоро́ший *adj* [khaROshy]

government прави́тельство [praVItil'stva]

gram грамм [GRAM]

grandfather де́душка *m* [DYEdushka]

grandmother ба́бушка [BAbushka]

grandson/granddaughter внук/вну́чка [VNUK/VNUCHka]

grapes виногра́д [vinaGRAT]

graphic arts гра́фика [GRAfika]

gratis беспла́тно [bisPLATna]

grave моги́ла [maGIla]

gray се́рый [SYEry]

great вели́кий [viLIki]

greatness вели́чие [viLIchiye]

green зелёный [ziLYOny]

green insurance card зелёная страхова́я ка́рта [ziLYOnaya strakhaVAya KARta]

greet, to приве́тствовать *ipf a. pf* [priVYETstvavat']

grill гриль *m* [GRIL']

grilled на гри́ле [na-GRIlye]

groceries проду́кты *m pl* [praDUKty]

grocery store продово́льственный магази́н [pradaVOL'stviny magaZIN]

grotto грот [GROT]

ground meat (мясно́й) фарш [(miSNOY) FARSH]

group гру́ппа [GRUpa]

guarantee гара́нтия [gaRANtiya]

guest гость *m*/го́стья *f* [GOST'/GOST'ya]

guide гид [GIT]; экскурсово́д [ekskursaVOT]

guided tour экску́рсия (с экскурсово́дом) [ekSKURsiya (s-ekskursaVOdam)]

guilt вина́ [viNA]

gums десна́ [diSNA]

gust of wind порыв ветра
[paRYF VYEtra]
gymnastics гимнастика
[gimNAstika]

H

hair волосы *m pl* [VOlasy]
hair-dryer фен [FYEN]
hairdo причёска [priCHOska]
hairdresser парикмахер
[parikMAkhir]
half половина [palaVIna];
половинный *adj* [palaVIny]
half-board неполный пансион
[niPOLny pansiON]; завтрак и
ужин [ZAFtrak i Uzhyn]
hall зал [ZAL]
ham ветчина [vichiNA]; окорок
[Okarak]
hammer молоток [malaTOK]
hand кисть *f* руки [KIST' ruKI]
hand cream крем для рук
[KRYEM dlia-RUK]
hand in, to отдавать/отдать
[addaVAT'/adDAT']
handball гандбол [gandBOL]
handing over передача
[piriDAcha]
handkerchief носовой платок
[nasaVOY plaTOK]
handmade ручной [ruchNOY]
handrails поручни *m pl*
[POruchni]
happiness счастье [SHCHAst'ye]
happy счастливый [shchiSLIvy]
happy (about) рад *m*/рада *f*/
рады *pl* (+ dat) [RAT/RAda/RAdy]
hard *(arduous)* трудный
[TRUDny]; *(solid)* твёрдый
[TVYORdy]

hardware строительные
товары *m pl* [straltil'nyye taVAry]
hat шляпа [SHLYApa]
have a good time, to
забавляться *ipf* [zabaVLYAtsa]
have, to у + *gen* (есть) + *nom*
[u-… (YEST)], иметь *ipf* [iMYET']
have to (should), to (быть)
должен *m*/должна *f*/должно
n/должны *pl* + *inf* [(BYT')
DOLzhyn/dalZHNA/dalZHNO/
dalZHNY]
hay fever аллергический
ринит [alirGIchiski riNIT]
he он [ON]
head голова [galaVA]
headache головная боль
[galaVNAya BOL']
headlight фонарь *m* [faNAR']
headphones наушники
[naUSHniki]
health food store магазин
диетических продуктов
[magaZIN diyiTIchiskikh praDUKtaf]
health insurance медицинская
страховка [midiTSYNskaya
straKHOFka]
healthy здоровый [zdaROvy]
hear, to слышать/услышать
[SLYshat'/uSLYshat']
hearing слух [SLUKH]
hearing-impaired
слабослышащий [slabaSLYshashi]
heart сердце [SYERtse]
heart attack сердечный
приступ [sirDYECHny PRIstup]
heartburn изжога [iZHOga]
heat жара [zhaRA]
heating отопление [ataPLYEniye]
heavy тяжёлый *adj* [tiZHOly]
heel каблук [kaBLUK]
height высота [vysaTA]
help помощь *f* [POmash]; Help!
Помогите! [pamaGItye]
help, to помогать/помочь
[pamaGAT'/paMOCH]

her её *pers pron f acc* [yiYO]
her её *poss pron f* [yiYO]; ей *pers pron f dat* [YEY]
here здесь *f* [ZDYES']
hernia паховая грыжа [pakhaVAya GRYzha]
herring сельдь [SYEL'T'], селёдка [siLYOTka]
high высокий [vySOki]
high tide прилив [priLIF]
high voltage высокое напряжение [vySOkaye napriZHEniye]
highlights *(hair)* мелирование [miLIravaniye]
highway шоссе [shaSYE]
hiking map туристская карта [tuRISTskaya KARta]
hiking path туристская тропа [tuRISTskaya traPA]
hill холм [KHOLM]
hip бедро [biDRO]
historical district старая часть города [STAraya CHAST' GOrada]
historical preservation охрана памятников [aKHRAna PAmitnikaf]
history история [iSTOriya]
hit, to *(the target)* попадать/ попасть (в + *acc*) [papaDAT'/ paPAST' (f-...)]
hitchhiking автостоп [aftaSTOP]
hoarse хриплый [KHRIply]
hold держать *ipf* [dirZHAT']
hole дыра [DYra]
holiday праздник [PRAZnik]
holy святой [sviaTOY]
homemade домашний [daMASHny]
homeowner хозяин/ хозяйка (дома) [khaZYAin/khaZYAYka (DOma)]
honey мёд [MYOT]

hood *(car)* капот двигателя [kaPOT DVIgatilya]
hook крюк [KRYUK]
hope, to надеяться/ понадеяться [naDYEyitsa/ panaDYEyitsa]
horn *(auto)* клаксон [klakSON]
horse лошадь *f* [LOshat']
horseback ride выезд верхом [VYyist virKHOM]
hose шланг [SHLANK]
hospital больница [bal'NItsa]
hospitality гостеприимство [gastiprilMstva]
host/hostess хозяин/хозяйка (дома) [khaZYAin/khaZYAYka (DOma)]
hot горячий [gaRYAchi]; *(weather)* жаркий [ZHARki]
hot air balloon воздушный баллон [vazDUSHny baLON]
hot water горячая вода [gaRYAchaya vaDA]
hour час [CHAS]
hourly ежечасно [yizhyCHASna]
house дом [DOM]
house number номер дома [NOmir DOma]
household goods хозтовары *m pl* [khastaVAry]
hovercraft глиссер [GLIsir], судно на воздушной подушке [SUDna na-vazDUSHnay paDUSHkye]
how как [KAK]
humid душный [DUSHny]
hungry, (to be) (быть) голоден *m*/голодна *f*/голодны *pl* [(BYT') GOladin/galaDNA/GOladny]
hurry, to торопиться/ поторопиться [taraPItsa/ pataraPItsa]
hurt, to болеть + *acc* [baLYET']
husband муж [MUSH]

I

I я [YA]

ice лёд [LYOT]

ice cream мороженое [maROzhynaye]

ice hockey хоккей на льду [khaKYEY na-L'DU]

ice skates коньки *m pl* [kan'KI]

ice skating бег на коньках [BYEK na-kan'KAKH]

ice-skating rink каток [kaTOK]

idea идея [iDYEya]

identification удостоверение личности [udastaviRYEniye LICHnasti]

if если [YEsli]

ignition зажигание [zazhyGAniye]

ignition key ключ зажигания [KLYUCH zazhyGAniya]

illness болезнь *f* [baLYEZN']

immediately сейчас [siyCHAS]

important важный [VAZHny]

impossible невозможный [nivazMOzhny]

impressive впечатляющий [fpichatLYAyushi]

in в + *prep* [v-...]; into в + *acc* [v-...]

in advance предварительно [pridvaRItil'na]

in charge компетентный [kampiTYENTny]

in front впереди [fpiriDI]

in front of перед + *instr* [PYErit-...]

in order to чтобы + *inf* [SHTOby]

in the afternoon после обеда [POslye aBYEda]

in the evening вечером [VYEchiram]

in the first place во-первых [va-PYERvykh]

in the morning утром [Utram]; до обеда [da-aBYEda]

in the third place в-третьих [f-TRYEtikh]

incident инцидент [intsyDYENT]

incline подъём [padYOM]

included включённый [fklyuCHOny]

incredible невероятный [niviraYATny]

indigestion расстройство пищеварения [raSTROYstva pishivaRYEniya]

infection инфекция [inFYEKtsyya]

inflammable огнеопасный [agniaPASny]

inflammation воспаление [vaspaLYEniye]

inform (s.o.), to информировать(ся) *ipf a. pf* [infarMIravat'(sa)]

inform, to уведомлять/ уведомить [uvidaMLYAT'/ uVYEdamit']

information справка [SPRAFka]

infusion вливание [vliVAniye], впрыскивание [FPRYskivaniye]

inhabitant житель/ница [ZHYtil'/nitsa]

injure, to ранить/поранить [RAnit/paRAnit']

injured раненый [RAniny]

injury ранение [raNYEniye]

inner courtyard внутренний двор [VNUtriny DVOR]

inner tube камера (шины) [KAmira (SHYny)]

inscription надпись *f* [NATpis']

insect насекомое [nasiKOmaye]

inside внутри [vnuTRI]

insomnia бессонница [biSOnitsa]

instant camera полароид [palaROit]

instead of вместо + *gen* [VMYEsta]

institution учреждение [uchriZHDYEniye]

insulin инсулин [insuLIN]

insult обида [aBIda]

insurance страхова́ние [strakhaVAniye]

intelligent у́мный [UMny]

intercity bus междугоро́дный авто́бус [mizhdugaRODny afTObus]

interesting интере́сный [intiRYESny]

intermission антра́кт [anTRAKT]

international междунаро́дный [mizhdunaRODny]

international call междунаро́дный разгово́р [mizhdunaRODny razgaVOR]

international flight междунаро́дный полёт [mizhdunaRODny paLYOT]

interrupt, to перебива́ть/перебы́ть [piribiVAT'/piriBIT']

intersection перекрёсток [piriKRYOstak]

intestine кишка́ [kishKA]

intolerable несно́сный [niSNOsny]

invite, to приглаша́ть/пригласи́ть [priglaSHAT'/priglaSIT']

iodine (tincture of) насто́йка йо́да [naSTOYka YOda]

iron, to гла́дить/вы́гладить [GLAdit'/VYgladit']

island о́стров [Ostraf]

itch, to чеса́ться/почеса́ться [chiSAtsa/pachiSAtsa]

J

jack *(auto)* автомоби́льный домкра́т [aftamaBIL'ny damKRAT]

jacket ку́ртка [KURTka]

jam варе́нье [vaRYEn'ye]; джем [DZHEM]

January янва́рь *m* [yinVAR']

Japan Япо́ния [yiPOniya]

jar ба́нка [BANka]

jaw че́люсть *f* [CHElyust']

jazz джаз [DZHAS]

jeans джи́нсы *m pl* [DZHYNsy]

jewelry store ювели́рный магази́н [yuviLIRny magaZIN]

jog, to бе́гать *ipf* [BYEgat']

joint суста́в [suSTAF]

joke шу́тка [SHUTka]; анекдо́т [anigDOT]

judge судья́ [suD'YA]

juice сок [SOK]

juicy со́чный [SOCHny]

July ию́ль *m* [iYUL']

jumper cables пусковы́е про́воды *m pl* [puskaVYye PROvady]

June ию́нь *m* [iYUN']

just как раз [KAK RAS]

just as ... as так же ..., как [TAK ZHE ..., KAK]

K

keep an eye (on), to присма́тривать/присмотре́ть (за + *instr*) [prisMAtrivat'/prismaTRYET' (za-...)]

keep, to уде́рживать/удержа́ть [uDYERzhyvat'/udirZHAT']

keep, to сохраня́ть/сохрани́ть [sakhraNYAT'/sakhraNIT']

kerosene кероси́н [kiraSIN]

ketchup ке́тчуп [KETchup]

key ключ [KLYUCH]

kidney по́чка [POCHka]

kidney stone по́чечный ка́мень [POchichny KAmin']

kilogram килогра́мм [kilaGRAM]

kilometer киломе́тр [kilaMYETR]

kind любе́зный [lyuBYEZny]

king коро́ль [kaROL']

kiss поцелу́й [patsyLUY]

kiss, to целова́ть/поцелова́ть [tsylaVAT'/patsylaVAT']

kitchen ку́хня [KUKHnya]

knee коле́но [kaLYEna]

knife нож [NOSH]

know, to знать *ipf* [ZNAT']

L

lake о́зеро [Ozira]

lamb бара́нина [baRAnina]

lamp ла́мпа [LAMpa]

land земля́ [zimLYA]

landing приземле́ние [prizimLYEniye]

landscape пейза́ж [piyZASH]

landscape format горизонта́льный форма́т [garizanTAL'ny farMAT]

lane *(alley)* переу́лок [piriUlak]

language язы́к [yiZYK]

language course языковы́е ку́рсы [yizykaVYye KURsy]

last после́дний [paSLYEDni]; *(previous)* про́шлый [PROshly]

last, to продолжа́ться/ продо́лжиться [pradalZHAtsa/ praDOLzhytsa]

late по́здний [POZny]

later по́зже [POzhe]

laugh, to смея́ться/ посмея́ться (над + *instr*) [smiYAtsa/pasmiYAtsa]

laundromat пра́чечная на самообслу́живание [PRAchichnaya na-samaapSLUzhyvaniya]

laundry сти́рка [STIRka]; *(place)* пра́чечная [PRAchichnaya]

lavatory умыва́льная [umyVAL'naya]

lawn газо́н [gaZON]

lawyer адвока́т [advaKAT]

laxative слаби́тельное сре́дство [slaBItil'naye SRYETstva]

layered cut ступе́нчатая причёска [stuPYENchataya priCHOSka]

lazy лени́вый [liNIvy]

leaf лист [LIST]

lean *(person)* худо́й [khuDOY]; *(meat)* нежи́рный [niZHYRny]

learn, to учи́ться/научи́ться + *dat o. inf* [uCHItsa/nauCHItsa]

learn, to узнава́ть/узна́ть [uznaVAT'/uZNAT']

leather goods кожгалантере́йные изде́лия [kazhgalantiRYEYnyye izDYEliya]

leather jacket ко́жаная ку́ртка [KOzhanaya KURTka]

leave (for), to уезжа́ть/ уе́хать (в + *acc*) [uyiZHAT'/uYEkhat' (f-...)]

leave, to покида́ть/поки́нуть [pakiDAT'/paKInut']

leek лук-поре́й [luk-paRYEY]

left ле́вый [LYEvy]

left (on/to the) нале́во [naLYEva]

leg нога́ *sing* [naGA], но́ги *pl* [NOgi]

legal alcohol limit допусти́мое содержа́ние алкого́ля в крови́ [dapuSTImaye zadirZHAniye alkaGOlya f-kraVI]

lemon лимо́н [liMON]

lend, to *(to s.o.)* ода́лживать/ одолжи́ть [aDALzhyvat'/ adalZHYT']

lengthen, to удлиня́ть/ удлини́ть [udliNYAT'/udliNIT']

lens ли́нза [LINza]; *(camera)* объекти́в [abyikTIF]

lentil чечеви́ца [chichiVItsa]

letter письмо́ [piS'MO]

lettuce салáт [saLAT]

license plate номернóй знак [namirNOY ZNAK]

lie down, to ложи́ться/лечь [laZHYtsa/LYECH]

lie, to лежáть *ipf* [liZHAT']

life жизнь *f* [ZHYZN']

life buoy плáвательный круг [PLAvatil'ny KRUK]

life jacket спасáтельный жилéт [spaSAtil'ny zhyLYET]

life preserver спасáтельный круг [spaSAtil'ny KRUK]

lifeboat спасáтельная лóдка [spaSAtil'naya LOTka]

light лёгкий *adj* [LYOKHki]; свет [SVYET]

light blue свéтло-си́ний [SVYETla-SIni]

light bulb (электри́ческая) лáмпочка [(elikTRIchiskaya) LAMpachka]

light green свéтло-зелёный [SVYETla-ziLYOny]

light, to зажигáть/зажéчь [zazhyGAT'/zaZHECH]

lighthouse маяк [maYAK]

lightning мóлния [MOLniya]

like, to люби́ть *ipf* [lyuBIT']

lilac лилóвый [liLOvy]

line ли́ния [LIniya]

line (waiting) óчередь *f* [Ochirit']

linen лён [LYON]

lip губá [guBA]

lipstick губнáя помáда [gubNAya paMAda]

liquid *(adj)* жи́дкий [ZHYTki]

liquor store виновóдочный магази́н [vinaVOdachny magaZIN]

listen to s.o., to слýшать/ послýшать + *acc* [SLUshat'/paSLUshat']

listen to, to слýшать/ послýшать [SLUshat'/paSLUshat']

liter литр [LITR]

little (a) немнóго [niMNOga]

little (few) мáло [MAla]

live music живáя мýзыка [zhyVAya MUzyka]

live, to жить *ipf* [ZHYT']

lively оживлённый [azhyVLYOny]

liver пéчень *f* [PYEchin']; *(food)* печёнка [piCHONka]

liver paté печёночный паштéт [piCHONachny pashTYET]

living room жилáя кóмната [zhyLAya KOMnata]

local мéстный [MYESny]

local call городскóй разговóр [garadSKOY razgaVOR]

locality мéстность *f* [MYESnast']

lock замóк [zaMOK]

lock, to запирáть/заперéть [zapiRAT'/zapiRYET']

locker кáмера хранéния [KAmira khraNYEniya]

lonely одинóкий [adiNOki]

long *(in linear extent)* дли́нный [DLIny]; *(distant)* далёкий [daLYOki]; *(time)* дóлгий [DOLgi]

long-distance phone call *(domestic/international)* междугорóдный/между-нарóдный разговóр [mizhdugaRODny/mizhdunaRODny razgaVOR]

look взгляд [VZGLYAT]

look at, to смотрéть/ посмотрéть [smaTRYET'/ pasmaTRYET']

look for, to искáть/поискáть [iSKAT'/paiSKAT']

look, to глядéть/поглядéть [gliDYET'/pagliDYET']

lookout point смотровáя площáдка [smatraVAya plaSHATka]

lose one's way, to сбивáться/ сби́ться с дорóги [zbiVAtsa/ ZBItsa z-daROgi]

lose, to теря́ть/потеря́ть [tiRYAT'/patiRYAT']

lost-and-found office стол находок [STOL naKHOdak]

loud гро́мкий [GROMki]

loudspeaker громкоговори́тель *m* [gramkagavaRItil']

love любо́вь *f* [lyuBOF']

love, to люби́ть *ipf* [lyuBIT']

low ни́зкий [NISki]

low-fat обезжи́ренный [abiZHYriny]

low tide отли́в [atLIF]

lower ни́жний *adj* [NIZHni]

lumbago простре́л [praSTRYEL]

lunch обе́д [aBYET]

lung лёгкое [LYOKHkaye]

luxurious роско́шный [raSKOSHny]

M

machine маши́на [maSHYna]

mackerel ску́мбрия [SKUMbriya]

magazine журна́л [zhurNAL]; (illustrated) (иллюстри́рован-ный) журна́л [(ilyuSTRIravany) zhurNAL]

maiden name де́вичья фами́лия [DYEvichya faMIliya]

mailbox почто́вый я́щик [pachTOvy YAshik]

main гла́вный *adj* [GLAVny]

main highway гла́вная доро́га [GLAVnaya daROga]

main post office гла́вный почта́мт [GLAVny pachTAMT], главпочта́мт [glafpachTAMT]

main train station гла́вный вокза́л [GLAVny vagZAL]

mainly гла́вным о́бразом *adv* [GLAVnym Obrazam]

make a phone call, to телефони́ровать *ipf a. pf* [tilifaNIravat']

make, to де́лать/сде́лать [DYElat'/ZDYElat']

man мужчи́на [mushCHIna]

management дире́кция [diRYEKtsyya]; администра́ция [adminiSTRAtsyya]

manager руководи́тель/ница [rukavaDItil'/nitsa]

map (географи́ческая) ка́рта [(giagraFIchiskaya) KARta]

March март [MART]

margarine маргари́н [margaRIN]

market ры́нок [RYnak]

married (to a woman) жена́тый [zhyNAty]; (to a man) заму́жняя [zaMUZHniya], за́мужем [ZAmuzhym]

marry, to (a woman) жени́ться *ipf a. pf* на ... + *prep* [zhyNItsa na-...]; (a man) выходи́ть/вы́йти за́муж за ... + *acc* [vykhaDIT'/VYti ZAmush za-...]

mascara тушь *f* для ресни́ц [TUSH dlia-risNITS]

mass (rel.) богослуже́ние [bagasluZHEniye]

massage масса́ж [maSASH]

match спи́чка [SPICHka]; (contest) соревнова́ние [sarivnaVAniye]

material материа́л [matiriAL]

mattress матра́с [maTRAS]

May май [MAY]

maybe мо́жет быть [MOzhyt BYT']

me *acc* меня́ [miNYA]

me (to, for) *dat* мне [MNYE]

meadow луг [LUK]

meal еда́ [yiDA]; тра́пеза [TRApiza]

mean, to зна́чить *ipf* [ZNAchit']

meaning значе́ние [znaCHEniye]

measles корь *f* [KOR']

meat мя́со [MYAsa]

medical certificate враче́бное заключе́ние [vraCHEBnaye zaklyuCHEniye]

medical insurance card страхово́е свиде́тельство [strakhaVOye sviDYEtil'stva]

medical specialist врач-специали́ст [VRACH-spitsyaLIST]

medicine лека́рство [liKARstva]

meet (s.o.), to встреча́ть/встре́тить + *acc* [fstriCHAT'/FSTRYEtit']

melon *(honeydew)* ды́ня [DYnya]; *(water~)* арбу́з [arBUS]

memorial мемориа́л [mimariAL]

men's мужско́й [mushSKOY]

menstruation менструа́ция [minstruAtsyya]

menu меню́ *n* [miNYU]

meter метр [MYETR]

method спо́соб [SPOsap]

microwave oven микроволно́вая печь [mikravalNOvaya PYECH]; СВЧ-печь [es-ve-CHE-PYECH]

middle середи́на [siriDIna]

Middle Ages средневеко́вье [sridniviKOv'ye]

middle ear infection воспале́ние сре́днего у́ха [vaspaLYEniye SRYEDniva Ukha]

migraine мигре́нь *f* [miGRYEN']

mild мя́гкий [MYAKHki]

milk молоко́ [malaKO]

milk store моло́чная [maLOCHnaya]

millimeter миллиме́тр [miliMYETR]

mineral water минера́льная вода́ [miniRAL'naya vaDA]

mini-bar (in hotel room) бар в но́мере [BAR v-NOmirye]

miniature golf ми́ни-гольф [MIni-gol'f]

minute мину́та [miNUta]

mirror зе́ркало [ZYERkala]

miscalculate, to обсчи́тываться/обсчита́ться [apSHItyvatsa/apshiTAtsa]

misfortune несча́стный слу́чай [niSHASny SLUchay]

miss, to *(let pass)* пропуска́ть/пропусти́ть [prapuSKAT'/prapuSTIT']

mistake оши́бка [aSHYPka]

mistake for, to пу́тать/перепу́тать [PUtat'/piriPUtat']

misunderstanding недоразуме́ние [nidarazuMYEniye]

mixed сме́шанный [SMYEshany]

model моде́ль *f* [maDYEL']

moment моме́нт [maMYENT]

monastery монасты́рь *m* [manaSTYR']

Monday понеде́льник [paniDYEL'nik]

money де́ньги *f pl* [DYEN'gi]

money transfer де́нежный перево́д [DYEnizhny piriVOT]

month ме́сяц [MYEsits]

monthly ежеме́сячный [yizhyMYEsichny]

monument па́мятник [PAmitnik]

moon луна́ [luNA]

more than бо́льше + *gen o.* чем + *nom* [BOL'she … CHEM …]; бо́лее + *gen* [BOliye …]

morning у́тро [Utra]

mosaic моза́ика [maZAika]

mosquito кома́р [kaMAR]

motel моте́ль *m* [maTYEL']

mother мать [MAT']

motor дви́гатель *m* [DVIgatil']

mountain гора́ [gaRA]

mountain bike го́рный велосипе́д [GORny vilasiPYET]

mountain climbing альпини́зм [al'piNIZM]

mountains го́ры *f pl* [GOry]

mouth рот [ROT]; *(of river)* у́стье [Ust'ye], впаде́ние [fpaDYEniye]

movie theater кино́ [kiNO]

Mr. господи́н [gaspaDIN]

Mrs., Ms. госпожа́ [gaspaZHA]

much мно́го [MNOga]

muffler *(car)* выхлоп [VYkhlap]

mumps свинка [SVINka]

muscle мускул [MUSkul]; мышца [MYSHtsa]

museum музей [muZYEY]

museum of ethnography этнографический музей [etnagraFIchiski muZYEY]

mushroom гриб [GRIP]

music музыка [MUzyka]

music hall варьете [var'yiTE]

music store нотный магазин [NOTny magaZIN]; магазин музыкальных инструментов [magaZIN muzyKAL'nykh instruMYENtaf]

musical мюзикл [MYUzikl]

mussel ракушка [raKUSHka]

mustache усы *m pl* [uSY]

mustard горчица [garCHItsa]

mute немой [niMOY]

mutton баранина [baRAnina]

my мой *m*/моя *f*/моё *n*/мои *pl* [MOY/maYA/maYO/mal]

N

nail polish лак для ногтей [LAK dlia-nakTYEY]

nail scissors ножницы *f pl* для ногтей [NOZHnitsy dlia-nakTYEY]

name *(first)* имя [Imya]; *(patronymic)* отчество [Ochistva]; *(last)* фамилия [faMIliya]

napkin салфетка [salFYETka]

narrow узкий [USki]

national costume (национальный) костюм [(natsyaNAL'ny) kaSTYUM]

national park заповедник [zapaVYEDnik]

nationality гражданство [grazhDANstva]

nationality plate *(auto)* международный опознавательный знак [mizhdunaRODny apaznaVAtil'ny ZNAK]

native country родина [ROdina]

natural естественный [yiSTYEstviny]

naturally конечно *adv* [kaNYESHna]

nature природа [priROda]

nausea позыв к рвоте [paZYF k-RVOtye]; тошнота [tashnaTA]

near близко *adv* [BLISka]; у + *gen* [u-...]

necessary необходимый [niapkhaDImy]; нужный [NUZHny]

necklace цепочка [tsyPOCHka]

necktie галстук [GALstuk]

need, to нуждаться (в + *prep*) [nuZHDAtsa (f-...)]; (быть) нужный [(BYT') NUZHny]

needle игла [iGLA]

negative негативный [nigaTIVny]

neighbor сосед/ка [saSYET/ka]

nerve нерв [NYERF]

nervous нервный [NYERvny]

net сетка [SYETka]

neutral (gear) холостой ход [khalaSTOY KHOT]

never никогда [nikagDA]

nevertheless всё-таки [FSYO-taki]

new новый [NOvy]

New Year's Day Новый год [NOvy GOT]

New Year's Eve Новогодний вечер [navaGODny VYEchir]

newborn грудной ребёнок [grudNOY riBYOnak]

news известие [izVYEstiye]

newspaper газета [gaZYEta]

newsstand киоск [kiOSK]

next *(in order)* следующий [SLYEduyushi]; *(nearest)* ближайший [bliZHAYshy]

next, to рядом с + *instr* [RYAdam s-...]

next to the last предпоследний [pritpaSLYEDni]

next year в следующем году [f-SLYEduyushim gaDU]

nice милый [MIly]; любезный [lyuBYEZny]; симпатичный [simpaTICHny]

night ночь *f* [NOCH]

nightclub ночной клуб [nachNOY KLUP]

nipple *(of bottle)* соска [SOska]

nobody никто [niKTO]

noise шум [SHUM]

non-alcoholic безалкогольный [bizalkaGOL'ny]

non-smoker некурящий [nikuRYAshi]

none никакой *pron* [nikaKOY]

noodles лапша [lapSHA]

noon полдень *m* [POLdin']

normal нормальный [narMAL'ny]

normally обычно *adv* [aBYCHna]

north север [SYEvir]

northern северный [SYEvirny]

nose нос [NOS]

not не [ni-...], нет [NYET]

Not allowed! Запрещено! [zaprishiNO]

notebook блокнот [blakNOT]; ноутбук [noutBUK]

nothing ничего [nichiVO]

notice, to замечать/заметить [zamiCHAT'/zaMYEtit']

November ноябрь *m* [naYABR']

now сейчас [siyCHAS]

now and then время от времени [VRYEmya at-VRYEmini]

nowhere нигде [niGDYE]

nude голый [GOly]; обнажённая натура [abnaZHOnaya naTUra]

nudist beach пляж нудистов [PLYASH nuDIstaf]

number номер [NOmir]; *(date)* число [chiSLO]

number (train) номер вагона [NOmir vaGOna]

nurse (female) медсестра [mitsiSTRA]

nurse (male) медбрат [midBRAT]

nut орех [aRYEKH]

O

oar весло [viSLO]

object предмет [pridMYET]

obtain, to доставать/достать [dastaVAT'/daSTAT']

occupied занятый [ZAnity]

October октябрь *m* [akTYABR']

off-season послесезонный период [paslisiZOny piRlat]

offer предложение [pridlaZHEniye]

offer, to предлагать/преложить [pridlaGAT'/pridlaZHYT']

office учреждение [uchriZHDYEniye]; бюро [byuRO]

office hours приёмные часы [priYOMnyye chiSY]

official официальный [afitsyAL'ny]

often часто [CHASta]

oil масло [MAsla]

oil change смена масла [SMYEna MAsla]

oil painting живопись *f* маслом [ZHYvapis' MAslam]

ointment мазь *f* [MAS']

old старый [STAry]

olive маслина [masLIna]

olive oil оливковое масло [aLIFkavaye MAsla]

on на + *prep* [na-...]
on-board wheelchair
бортова́я инвали́дная коля́ска
[bartaVAya invaLIDnaya kaLYAska]
on tap наливно́е [nalivNOye]
on the contrary наоборо́т *adv*
[naabaROT]
on the way в доро́ге [v-daROgye]
on time во́время *adv* [VOvrimya]
on weekdays по бу́дням [pa-
BUdnyam]
once раз [RAS]; *(once upon a time)*
одна́жды [adNAzhdy]
one-colored одноцве́тный
[adnaTSVYETny]
one-day excursion
однодне́вная экску́рсия
[adnaDNYEVnaya eksKURsiya];
(hiking) однодне́вный похо́д
[adnaDNYEVny paKHOT]
onion лук (ре́пчатый) [LUK
(ripCHAty)]
only то́лько [TOL'ka];
еди́нственный [yiDINstviny]
onto на + *acc* [na-...]
open откры́тый [atKRYty]
open-face sandwich
бутербро́д [butirBROT]
open, to открыва́ть/откры́ть
[atkryVAT'/atKRYT']
opening hours часы́ *m pl*
рабо́ты [chiSY raBOty]
opera о́пера [Opira]
operation опера́ция [apiRAtsyya]
operetta опере́тта [apiRYEta]
operetta theater теа́тр ма́лых
форм [tiATR MAlykh FORM]
opinion мне́ние (о + *prep*)
[MNYEniye (a-...)]
opposite противополо́жный
[prativapaLOZHny];
противополо́жность *f*
[prativapaLOZHnast']
optician о́птик [OPtik]
or и́ли [Ili]
orange *(color)* ора́нжевый
[aRANzhyvy]

orchestra орке́стр [arKYESTR]
orchestra circle *(theater)*
партёр [parTYER]
order зака́з [zaKAS]
origin исто́чник [isTOCHnik]
original по́длинник [POdlinik]
our(s) наш *m*/на́ша *f*/на́ше *n*/
на́ши *pl* [NASH/NAsha/NAshe/
NAshy]
out of order сло́манный
[SLOmany]
outlet *(electrical)* розе́тка
[raZYETka]
outside вне [VNYE]
outside (on the) снару́жи
[snaRUzhy]; *(outdoors)* на у́лице
[na-Ulitse]
over сверх [SVYERKH]; *(at an end)*
ко́нчено *adv* [KONchino]
own со́бственный [SOPstviny]
owner владе́лец/ владе́лица
[vlaDYElits/vlaDYELitsa];
со́бственник/
со́бственница [SOPstvinik/
SOPstvinitsa]
oyster у́стрица [Ustritsa]

P

pacemaker кардиостимуля́тор
[kardiastimuLYAtar]
pacifier пусты́шка [puSTYSHka]
pack, to упако́вывать/
упакова́ть [upaKOvyvat'/
upakaVAT']
packaging упако́вка [upaKOFka]
paddle boat байда́рка
[bayDARka]; во́дный велосипе́д
[VODny vilasiPYET]
page страни́ца [straNItsa]
painkiller болеутоля́ющее
[baliutaLYAyushiye]

paint (art), to рисова́ть/
нарисова́ть кра́сками
[risaVAT'/narisaVAT' KRASkami]
painter (art) жи́вописец
[ZHYvapisits]
painting карти́на [karTIna];
жи́вопись f [ZHYvapis']
pair па́ра + gen pl [PAra]
palace дворе́ц [dvaRYETS];
пала́ты f pl [paLAty]
pants брю́ки f pl [BRYUki]
panty liner гигиени́ческая
прокла́дка [gigiyiNIchiskaya
praKLATka]
pantyhose колго́тки f pl
[kalGOTki]
paper бума́га [buMAga]; adj
бума́жный [buMAZHny]
paprika кра́сный пе́рец
[KRASny PYErits]
parachuting парашюти́зм
[parashuTIZM]
parade ше́ствие [SHESTviye]
paralysis парали́ч [paraLICH]
paraplegia попере́чный
миели́т [papiRYECHny miyiLIT]
parcel посы́лка [paSYLka]
parents роди́тели m pl [raDItili]
park парк [PARK]
park a car, to ста́вить/
поста́вить маши́ну [STAvit'/
paSTAvit' maSHYnu]
parka штормо́вка [shtarMOFka]
parking lights габари́тные
фа́ры m pl [gabaRITnyye FAry]
parking lot стоя́нка [staYANka],
автостоя́нка [aftastaYANka]
parsley петру́шка [piTRUSHka]
part часть f [CHAST']; (in hair)
пробо́р [praBOR]
party вечери́нка [vichiRINka]
pass for ... trips биле́т на ...
пое́здок [biLYET na-... paYEZdak]
pass (mountain) го́рный
перехо́д [GORny piriKHOT]
pass, to (traffic) обгоня́ть/
обогна́ть [abgaNYAT'/abaGNAT']

passage прое́зд [praYEST]
passenger пассажи́р/ка
[pasaZHYR/ka]
passport (заграни́чный)
па́спорт [(zagraNIChny) PASpart]
passport control па́спортный
контро́ль [PASpartny kanTROL']
password паро́ль m [paROL']
past про́шлое (вре́мя)
[PROSHlaye (VRYEmya)]; ми́мо
+ gen [MIma]
pastry shop конди́терская
[kanDItirskaya]
patience терпе́ние [tirPYEniye]
patronymic о́тчество [Ochistva]
pay attention, to обраща́ть/
обрати́ть внима́ние [abraSHAT'/
abraTIT' vniMAniye]
pay, to плати́ть/заплати́ть
[plaTIT'/zaplaTIT']; выпла́чивать/
вы́платить [vyPLAchivat'/VYplatit']
payment платёж [plaTYOSH]
peach пе́рсик [PYERsik]
peak верх [VYERKH]
peak season разга́р сезо́на
[razGAR siZOna]
pear гру́ша [GRUsha]
pearl же́мчуг [ZHEMchuk]
peas горо́х [gaROKH]
pedestrian пешехо́д
[pishyKHOT]
pedestrian zone пешехо́дная
зо́на [pishyKHODnaya ZOna]
pediatrician педиа́тр [pidiATR];
де́тский врач [DYETski VRACH]
pediment фронто́н [franTON]
penalty (fine) штраф [SHTRAF]
pencil каранда́ш [karanDASH]
pendant куло́н [kuLON]
people лю́ди m pl [LYUdi];
(nation) наро́д [naROT]
pepper пе́рец [PYErits]
pepper mill пе́речница
[PYErichnitsa]
percent проце́нт [praTSENT]
perch о́кунь m [Okun']

performance представле́ние [pritstaVLYEniye]; *(theater)* спекта́кль *m* [spikTAKL']; *(movie)* сеа́нс [siANS]

perfume духи́ *m pl* [duKHI]

perfume store парфюме́рия [parfyuMYEriya]

period эпо́ха [ePOkha]

perm(anent wave) химзави́вка [khimzaVIFka]

person ли́чность *f* [LICHnast']

person, people челове́к *sing* [chilaVYEK]; лю́ди *pl* [LYUdi]

personal ли́чный [LICHny]

personal data ли́чные све́дения [LICHnyye SVYEdiniya]

pet дома́шнее живо́тное [daMASHniye zhyVOTnaye]

pharmacy апте́ка [apTYEka]

phone booth телефо́нная бу́дка [tiliFOnaya BUTka]

phone card телефо́нная ка́рточка [tiliFOnaya KARtachka]

phone in the room (hotel) телефо́н в но́мере [tiliFON v-NOmirye]

phone number но́мер (телефо́на) [NOmir (tiliFOna)]

phone, to звони́ть/позвони́ть (по телефо́ну) + *dat* [zvaNIT'/ pazvaNIT' (pa-tiliFOnu)]

photo сни́мок [SNImak]

photograph, to фотографи́ровать/ сфотографи́ровать [fatagraFIravat'/sfatagraFIravat']

photographic supplies фототова́ры *m pl* [fatataVAry]

photography фотогра́фия [fataGRAfiya]

physical disability физи́ческий недоста́ток [fiZIchiski nidaSTAtak]

pick out, to выбира́ть/ вы́брать [vybiRAT'/VYbrat']

pick up, to встреча́ть/ встре́тить + *acc* [fstriCHAT'/ FSTRYEtit']

pickpocket карма́нный вор [karMAny DVOR]

pickup service обра́тный подъём [aBRATny paDYOM]

picture карти́на [karTIna]

piece кусо́к [kuSOK]

pier мол [MOL]

pilgrimage site ме́сто пало́мничества [MYESta paLOMnichistva]

pill (for) табле́тка (от + *gen*) [taBLYETka (at-…)]

pillow поду́шка [paDUSHka]

pilot пило́т [piLOT]

pin number шифр [SHYFR]; код [KOT]; паро́ль *m* [paROL']

pink ро́зовый [ROzavy]

place ме́сто [MYESta]

place of birth ме́сто рожде́ния [MYESta raZHDYEniya]

place of residence местожи́тельство [mistaZHYtil'stva]

place setting прибо́р [priBOR]

place to sleep ночле́г [nachLYEK]

plaice ка́мбала [KAMbala]

plain равни́на [ravNIna]

plant расте́ние [raSTYEniye]

plastic wrap прозра́чная фольга́ [praZRACHnaya fal'GA]

plate таре́лка [taRYELka]

platform перро́н [piRON]

play *(theater)* пье́са [P'YEsa]

play, to игра́ть/сыгра́ть [iGRAT'/syGRAT']

playground де́тская площа́дка [DYETskaya plaSHATka]

pleasant прия́тный [priYATny]

please, to нра́виться/ понра́виться [NRAvitsa/ paNRAvitsa]

pleasure удово́льствие [udaVOL'stviye]

plug штéпсель *m* [SHTYEPsil'], вѝлка [VILka]

plum слѝва [SLIva]

pocket calculator (микро)калькулятор [(mikra)kalkuLYAtar]

pocket knife перочѝнный нóжик [piraCHIny NOzhyk]

poison яд [YAT]

poisoning отравлéние [atraVLYEniye]

poisonous ядовѝтый [yadaVIty]

police милѝция [miLItsyya]

police car милицéйский автомобѝль [miliTSEYski aftmaBIL']

police custody предварѝтельное заключéние [pridvaRItil'naye zaklyuCHEniye]

police officer милиционéр [militsyaNYER]

polio полиомиелѝт [paliamiyiLIT]

polite вéжливый [VYEZHlivy]

poor бéдный [BYEDny]

porcelain фарфóр [farFOR]

pork свинѝна [sviNIna]

port порт [PORT]

portal портáл [parTAL]

porter швейцáр [shviyTSAR]; портьé [parT'YE]

portion пóрция [PORtsyya]

portrait портрéт [parTRYET]

portrait format вертикáльный формáт [virtiKAL'ny farMAT]

possible возмóжный [vazMOZHny]

post office почтáмт [pachTAMT]

postage почтóвый сбор [pachTOvy ZBOR]

postal savings book почтóво-сберегáтельная книжка [pachTOva-zbiriGAtil'naya KNISHka]

postcard открытка [atKRYTka]

poste restante до востребóвания [da-vaSTRYEbavaniya]

poster плакáт [plaKAT]

postpone, to отклáдывать/отложѝть [atKLAdyvat'/atlaZHYT']

potatoes картóфель *m* [karTOfil']

pottery *(place)* гончáрня [ganCHARnya]; *(wares)* гончáрные издéлия [ganCHARnyye izDYEliya]

pound *(half kilo)* полкилó [palkiLO]

powder пýдра [PUdra]

powder snow рыхлый снег [RYKHly SNYEK]

power boat мотóрная лóдка [maTORnaya LOTka]

practical практѝческий [prakTIchiski]

practice, to упражнять *ipf* [upraZHNYAT']

pray, to молѝться/помолѝться [maLItsa/pamaLItsa]

pre-season врéмя до начáла сезóна [VRYEmya da-naCHAla siZOna]

pregnancy берéменность *f* [biRYEminast']

premiere премьéра [priM'YEra]

premises *(building)* помещéние [pamiSHEniye]

prepare, to готóвить/приготóвить [gaTOvit'/prigaTOvit']

prescribe, to выпѝсывать/выписать [vyPIsyvat'/VYpisat']

prescription рецéпт [riTSEPT]

pretty красѝвый *adj* [kraSIvy]

prevent, to препятствовать/воспрепятствовать [priPYATstvavat'/vaspriPYATstvavat']

previously рáньше [RAN'she]

price цена́ [tsyNA]

priest свящéнник [sviSHEnik]

printed matter бандерóль *f* [bandiROL']

prison тюрьмá [tyur'MA]

private чáстный [CHASTny]

293

privilege, advantage; reduction (price) льгота [L'GOta]
probable вероятный [viraYATny]
probably наверное [naVYERnaye]
problem проблема [praBLYEma]
procession процессия [praTSEsiya]
product произведение [praizviDYEniye]; продукт [praDUKT]
profession профессия [praFYEsiya]
profit прибыль f [PRIbyl']
program программа [praGRAma]
program booklet программка [praGRAMka]
pronounce, to произносить/произнести [praiznaSIT'/praizniSTI]
prosthesis протез [praTYES]
public общественный [apSHESTviny]
pull, to тянуть/потянуть [TYAnut'/paTYAnut']
pullover свитер [SVItir]; пуловер [puLOvir]
pulse пульс [PULS']
pumpkin тыква [TYKva]
punctual точный [TOCHny]; пунктуальный [punktuAL'nyy]
punishment наказание [nakaZAniye]
pupil школьник/ница [SHKOL'nik/nitsa]
purple фиолетовый [fiaLYEtavy]
purse сумка [SUMka]; (дамская) сумочка [(DAMskaya) SUmachka]
pus гной [GNOY]
put in a rinse, to подкрашивать/подкрасить [patKRAshyvat'/patKRAsit']
put on, to одевать/одеть [adiVAT'/aDYET']
put, to класть/положить [KLAST'/palaZHYT']

quality качество [KAchistva]
queen королева [karaLYEva]
question вопрос [vaPROS]
quiet тихий [TIkhi]
quietly спокойно [spaKOYna]
quite совсем adv [saFSYEM]

rabbit кролик [KROlik]
racing bike гоночный велосипед [GOnachny vilasiPYET]
racquet ракетка [raKYETka]
radar-controlled speed радарный контроль скорости [raDARny kanTROL' SKOrasti]
radiator радиатор [radiAtar]
radio радио [RAdio]
rail(ings) перила n pl [piRIla]
rain дождь m [DOSHT']
rain shower кратковременный дождь [kratkaVRYEminy DOSHT']
raincoat непромокаемый плащ [nipramaKAyimy PLASH]
rainy дождливый [dazhDLIvy]
ramp наклонный въезд [naKLOny VYEST]
ramp (for wheelchairs) наклонный въезд (для инвалидных колясок) [naKLOny VYEST (dlia-invaLIDnykh kaLYAsak)]
rape изнасилование [iznaSIlavaniye]
rare редкий [RYETki]
rate per kilometer тариф за километр [tarif za-kilaMYETR]
rather (quite) довольно adv [daVOL'na]
raw сырой [syROY]

razor blade ле́звие [LYEZviye]

read, to чита́ть/прочита́ть [chiTAT'/prachiTAT']

reading lamp ночни́к [nachNIK]

ready гото́вый [gaTOvy]

real действи́тельный [diySTVItil'ny]; *(genuine)* настоя́щий [nastaYAshi]

rearview mirror зе́ркало за́днего ви́да [ZYERkala ZADniva VIda]

reason причи́на [priCHIna]

receipt квита́нция [kviTANtsyya]

receive, to принима́ть/приня́ть [priniMAT'/priNYAT']; получа́ть/получи́ть [paluCHAT'/paluCHIT']

receiver *(phone)* тру́бка [TRUPka]

recently неда́вно [niDAVna]

reception area фойе́ [faYE]

reception (desk) администра́ция [adminiSTRAtsyya]

recommend, to сове́товать/посове́товать [saVYEtavat'/pasaVYEtavat']

red кра́сный [KRASny]

red wine кра́сное вино́ [KRASnaye viNO]

refreshment освеже́ние [asviZHEniye]

refrigerator холоди́льник [khalaDIL'nik]

refuse, to отка́зываться/отказа́ться (от + *gen*) [atKAzyvatsa/atkaZAtsa (ay-...)]

region регио́н [rigiON]

register, to регистри́ровать *ipf a. pf* [rigiSTRIravat']

registration регистра́ция [rigiSTRAtsyya]

regret, to сожале́ть *ipf* [sazhaLYET']

regular регуля́рный [riguLYARny]

regulation предписа́ние [pritpiSAniye]; инстру́кция [inSTRUKtsyya]

related ро́дственный [ROTstviny]

religion рели́гия [riLIgiya]

rely on, to полага́ться/положи́ться на + *acc* [palaGAtsa/palaZHYtsa na-...]

remains оста́тки *f pl* [aSTATki]

remedy (for) сре́дство (от + *gen*) [SRYETstva (at-...)]

remember, to по́мнить/вспо́мнить + *acc* [POMnit'/FSPOMnit']

rent аре́нда [aRYENda]

rent, to брать/взять напрока́т [BRAT'/VZYAT' napraKAT]; сдава́ть/сдать напрока́т [zdaVAT'/ZDAT' napraKAT]; *(apartment)* снима́ть/снять [sniMAT'/SNYAT']

repair ремо́нт [riMONT]

repair shop мастерска́я [mastirsKAya]

repair, to чини́ть/почини́ть [chiNIT'/pachiNIT']; ремонти́ровать/отремонти́ровать [rimanTIravat'/atrimanTIravat']

repeat, to повторя́ть/повтори́ть [paftaRYAT'/paftaRIT']

repertoire репертуа́р [ripirtuAR]

replace, to заменя́ть/замени́ть [zamiNYAT'/zamiNIT']

replacement заме́на [zaMYEna]

report, to заявля́ть/заяви́ть (о ... + *prep*) [zayiVLYAT'/zayiVIT' (a-...)]

request про́сьба [PROz'ba]

reservation бро́ня [BROnya]; брони́рование [braNIravaniye]

reserve, to брони́ровать/заброни́ровать [braNIravat'/zabraNIravat']

responsible отве́тственный [atVYETstviny]

rest о́тдых [ODdykh]

rest area (авто)стоя́нка [(afta)staYANka]

rest, to (have a) отдыха́ть/отдохну́ть [addyKHAT'/addakhNUT']

return, to возвраща́ться/
верну́ться [vazvraSHAtsa/
vazvraTItsa]

return trip обра́тный путь
[aBRATny PUT']

reverse обра́тный [aBRATny]

reverse gear за́дний ход [ZADni
KHOT]

reward награ́да [naGRAda]

rheumatism ревмати́зм
[rivmaTIZM]

rice рис [RIS]

rich бога́тый [baGAty]

ride a bike, to ката́ться на
велосипе́де [kaTAtsa na-
vilasiPYEdye]

ride a horse, to е́здить *ipf*
верхо́м [YEZdit' virKHOM]

ridiculous смешно́й [smishNOY]

right пра́вый [PRAvy]

right (on/to the) напра́во
[naPRAva]

ring кольцо́ [kal'TSO]; *(sound)*
звоно́к [zvaNOK]

ripe зре́лый [ZRYEly]

river река́ [riKA]

road доро́га [daROga]

road map ка́рта
автомоби́льных доро́г [KARta
aftamaBIL'nykh daROK]

roasted жа́реный [ZHAriny]

rock скала́ [skaLA]

rock (music) рок [ROK]

roll бу́лочка [BUlachka]

roller skate ро́лик [ROlik]

roof кры́ша [KRYsha]

room ко́мната [KOMnata]

rope кана́т [kaNAT]

rosé (wine) ро́зовое вино́
[ROzavaye viNO]

rotten *(food etc.)* гнило́й [gniLOY]

rough seas волне́ние (мо́ря)
[valNYEniye (MOrya)]

round кру́глый [KRUgly]

roundtrip ticket биле́т в о́ба
конца́ [biLYET v-Oba kanTSA]

route маршру́т [marshRUT]

row, to грести́/погрести́
[griSTI/pagriSTI]

rowboat гребна́я ло́дка
[griBNAya LOTka]

rubber boat надувна́я ло́дка
[naduVNAya LOTka]

rubber boots рези́новые
сапоги́ *m pl* [riZInavyye sapaGI]

ruins разва́лины *f pl* [razVAliny];
руи́ны *f pl* [ruIny]

run, to бе́гать *ipf*, бежа́ть/
побежа́ть [BYEgat', biZHAT'/
pabiZHAT']

sack мешо́к [miSHOK]

sad печа́льный [piCHAL'ny]

safe сейф [SYEYF]; безопа́сный
[bizaPASny]

safety belt реме́нь *m*
безопа́сности [riMYEN'
bizaPASnasti]

safety pin (безопа́сная)
була́вка [(bizaPASnaya) buLAFka]

sail, to пла́вать *ipf* под
па́русом [PLAvat' pat-PArusam]

sailboat па́русная ло́дка
[PArusnaya LOTka]

salad сала́т [saLAT]

salami саля́ми *f pl* [saLYAmi]

salt соль *f* [SOL']

salt shaker соло́нка [saLONka]

same ра́вный [RAVny];
одина́ковый [adiNAkavy]

sand песо́к [piSOK]

sandals санда́лии *f pl* [sanDAlii]

sandbox песо́чница
[piSOCHnitsa]

sanitary facilities санита́рно-гигиени́ческие устро́йства [saniTARna-gigiyiNIchiskiye usTROYstva]

sanitary napkin гигиени́ческая прокла́дка [gigiyiNIchiskaya praKLATka]

satisfied дово́льный [daVOL'ny]; удовлетворённый [udavlitvaRYOny]

Saturday суббо́та [suBOta]

sauce со́ус [SOus]

saucer блю́дце [BLYUtse]

sauna са́уна [SAuna]; фи́нская ба́ня [FINskaya BAnya]

sausage колбаса́ [kalbaSA]

say goodbye, to проща́ться/прости́ться (с + *instr*) [praSHAtsa/praSTItsa (s-…)]

say, to говори́ть/сказа́ть [gavaRIT'/skaZAT']

scar шрам [SHRAM]; рубе́ц [ruBYETS]

scarf шарф [SHARF]

school шко́ла [SHKOla]

scissors но́жницы *f pl* [NOZHnitsy]

scooter самока́т [samaKAT]

screw винт [VINT]; болт [BOLT]

sculptor ску́льптор [SKUL'ptar]

sculpture пла́стика [PLAstika]; скульпту́ра [skul'pTUra]

sea мо́ре [MOrye]

seagull ча́йка [CHAYka]

seasickness морска́я боле́знь [marsKAya baLYEZN']

season вре́мя *n* го́да [VRYEmya GOda]; сезо́н [siZON]

season, to приправля́ть/приправить [pripraVLYAT'/priPRAvit']

seasoning пря́ность *f* [PRYAnast']; спе́ция [SPYEtsyya]

seat сиде́нье [siDYEn'ye]

seat reservation *(train)* плацка́рта [platsKARta]

second секу́нда [siKUNda]; второ́й [ftaROY]

second-hand store утильсырьё [util'syR'YO]

secondary road второстепе́нная доро́га [ftoraSTYEpenaya daROga]

second(ly) во-вторы́х [va-ftaRYKH]

security check контро́ль *m* безопа́сности [kanTROL' bizaPASnasti]

security deposit зало́г [zaLOK]

see, to ви́деть/уви́деть [VIdit'/uVIdit']

self-service самообслу́живание [samaapSLUzhyvaniye]

self-timer автоспу́ск [aftaSPUSK]

self: myself, etc. сам *m/* сама́ *f/*само́ *n/*са́ми *pl* [SAM/saMA/saMO/SAmi]

sell, to продава́ть/прода́ть [pradaVAT'/praDAT']

send, to посыла́ть/посла́ть [pasyLAT'/paSLAT']

sender отправи́тель *m* [atpraVItil']

sentence предложе́ние [pridlaZHEniye]

September сентя́брь *m* [sinTYABR']

serious серьёзный [siRYOZny]

serve, to сервирова́ть *ipf a. pf* [sirVIravat']

service обслу́живание [apSLUzhyvaniye]

services for the disabled слу́жба социа́льной по́мощи [SLUZHba satsyAL'nay POmashi]

set meal ко́мплексное блю́до [KOMpliksnaye BLYUda]

settlement посёлок [paSYOlak]

severely тяжело́ *adv* [tizhyLO]

sew, to зашива́ть/заши́ть [zashyVAT'/zaSHYT']

sexual harassment
сексуа́льное домога́тельство
[siksuAL'naye damaGAtil'stva]

shadow тень *f* [TYEN']

shaking chills озно́б [aZNOP]

shameless бессты́дный
[biSTYDny]

shampoo шампу́нь *m*
[shamPUN']

shape фо́рма [FORma]

shave бритьё [briT'YO]

shave (o.s.), to брить(ся)/
побри́ть(ся) [BRIT'(sa)/
paBRIT'(sa)]

shaver бри́твенный аппара́т
[BRITviny apaRAT]

shaving brush помазо́к
[paMAzak]

she она́ *pers pron f* [aNA]

shelter (for tourists)
тури́стский прию́т [tuRISTski
priYUT]

shin больша́я берцо́вая кость
[bal'SHAya birTSOvaya KOST']

ship кора́бль *m* [kaRABL'], су́дно
[SUDna]

shirt руба́шка [ruBASHka]

shoe brush сапо́жная щётка
[saPOZHnaya SHOTka]

shoe polish крем для о́буви
[KRYEM dlia-Obuvi]

shoelaces шнурки́ *m pl* (для
о́буви) [SHNURki (dlia-Obuvi)]

shoemaker сапо́жник
[saPOZHnik]

shore (морско́й) бе́рег
[(marSKOY) BYErik]

short коро́ткий [kaROTki]

short circuit коро́ткое
замыка́ние [kaROTkaye
zamyKAniye]

short film короткометра́жка
[karatkamiTRASHka]

short-term краткосро́чный
[kratkaSROCHny]

shorts шо́рты *m pl* [SHORty]

shot *(injection)* уко́л [uKOL];
инъе́кция [inYEKtsyya]

shoulder плечо́ [pliCHO]

shout, to крича́ть/закрича́ть
[kriCHAT'/zakriCHAT']

show ревю́ *n* [riVYU]; шо́у *n*
[SHOu]

show, to пока́зывать/пока-
за́ть [paKAzyvat'/pakaZAT'];
ука́зывать/указа́ть

shower душ [DUSH]

shrimp креве́тка [kriVYETka]

shutter *(camera)* спуск [SPUSK]

shuttle bus авто́бус-шаттл
[aFTObus-shatl]

shy засте́нчивый [zaSTYENchivy]

sick больно́й [bal'NOY]

side сторона́ [staraNA]

sideburns бакенба́рды *f pl*
[bakinBARdy]

sight *(place of interest)*
достопримеча́тельность *f*
[dastaprimiCHAtil'nast']

sign *(road)* указа́тель *m*
[ukaZAtil']; *(signboard)* вы́веска
[VYviska]; знак [ZNAK]

sign language же́стов язы́к
[ZHEstaf yiZYK]

sign (road) (доро́жный)
указа́тель [(daROZHny) ukaZAtil']

sign, to подпи́сывать/
подписа́ть [patPIsyvat'/patpiSAT']

signature по́дпись *f* [POTpis']

silk шёлк [SHOLK]

silk painting жи́вопись *f* на
шёлке [ZHYvapis' na-SHOLkye]

silver серебро́ [siriBRO]

silverware прибо́р [priBOR]

silver(y) серебри́стый
[siriBRIstry]

similar похо́жий (на + *acc*)
[paKHOzhy (na-...)]

simple просто́й [praSTOY]

simultaneous одновреме́нный
[adnaVRYEminy]

since *prep* с + *gen* [s-...]

since when *conj* с каки́х пор [s-kaKIKH POR]

sincere серде́чный [sirDYECHny]

sing, to петь/спеть [PYET'/ SPYET']

singer певе́ц/певи́ца [piVYETS/ piVItsa]

sink мо́йка для посу́ды [MOYka dlia-paSUdy]; ра́ковина [RAkavina]

sinusitis воспале́ние ло́бных па́зух [vaspaLYEniye LOBnykh PAzukh]

sister сестра́ [sisTRA]

sit, to сади́ться/сесть [saDItsa/SYEST']

situation положе́ние [palaZHEniye]

size величина́ [vilichiNA]; *(clothing)* разме́р [razMYER]

skateboard скейтбо́рд [skiydBORT]

ski лы́жа [LYzha]; *adj* лы́жный [LYZHny]

ski, to ката́ться на лы́жах [kaTAtsa na-LYzhakh]

ski track лыжня́ [lyzhNYA]

skin ко́жа [KOzha]

skirt ю́бка [YUPka]

sky не́бо [NYEba]

Slavic славя́нский [slaVYANski]

Slavs славя́не [slaVYAnye]

sled са́ни *f pl* [SAni]

sleep, to спать *ipf* [SPAT']

sleeper sofa дива́н(крова́ть) [diVAN(kraVAT')]

sleeping car спа́льный ваго́н [SPAL'ny vaGON]

sleeping pill снотво́рное [snaTVORnaye]

sleeve рука́в [ruKAF]

slender стро́йный [STROYny]

slice ло́мтик [LOMtik]

slow ме́дленный [MYEDliny]

small ма́ленький [MAlin'ki]

small change ме́лочь *f* [MYElach]

smell за́пах [ZApakh]

smell (of), to *(stink)* воня́ть *ipf* *(+ instr)* [vaNYAT']

smell, to па́хнуть *ipf* [PAKHnut']; *(s. th.)* ню́хать/поню́хать [NYUkhat'/paNYUkhat']

smoke, to *(tobacco)* кури́ть/ покури́ть [kuRIT'/pakuRIT']

smoker куря́щий [kuRYAshi]

smoking compartment купе́ для куря́щих [kuPYE dlia-kuRYAshikh]

smooth ро́вный [ROVny]

snack заку́ска [zaKUska]

snack bar буфе́т [buFYET]

snake змея́ [zmiYA]

sneakers гимнасти́ческие ту́фли *f pl* [gimnaSTIchiskiye TUfli]

sneeze, to чиха́ть/чихну́ть [chiKHAT'/chikhNUT']

snore, to храпе́ть *ipf* [khraPYET']

snorkel шно́ркель *m* [SHNORkil']

snow снег [SNYEK]

snow tire зи́мняя ши́на [ZIMniya SHYna]

so that что́бы [SHTOby]

soap мы́ло [MYla]

sober тре́звый [TRYEzvy]

soccer футбо́л [fudBOL]

socks носки́ *m pl* [naSKI]

soft мя́гкий [MYAKHki]

soft cheese мя́гкий сыр [MYAKHki SYR]

soft drink лимона́д [limaNAT]

solarium соля́рий [saLYAri]

sole *(fish)* морско́й язы́к [marsKOY yiZYK]; *(shoe)* подмётка [padMYOTka]

some не́сколько *+ gen pl* [NYEskal'ka]

somebody не́кто [NYEKta]

something что́-нибудь [SHTO-nibut']

sometimes иногда́ [inagDA]

son сын *sing* [SYN], сыновья́ *pl* [synaV'YA]

song пе́сня [PYESnya]

soon ско́ро [SKOra]

sore throat боль *f* в го́рле [BOL' v-GORlye]

sort *(kind, brand)* сорт [SORT]

sound звук [ZVUK]

soup суп [SUp]; пе́рвое (блю́до) [PYERvaye BLYUda]

soup bowl глубо́кая таре́лка [gluBOkaya taRYELka]

sour ки́слый [KIsly]

sour cream смета́на [smiTAna]

south юг [YUK]

southern Ю́жный [YUZHny]

souvenir shop сувени́рный магази́н [suviNIRny magaZIN]

spare wheel запасно́е колесо́ [zapasNOye kaliSO]

spark plug свеча́ зажига́ния [sviCHA zazhyGAniya]

speak, to говори́ть/поговори́ть [gavaRIT'/pagavaRIT']

special специа́льный [spitsyAL'ny]

special delivery letter сро́чное письмо́ [SROCHnaye piS'MO]; экспре́сс-по́чта [ekSPRYES-POCHta]

special-issue stamp коллекцио́нная (почто́вая) ма́рка [kaliktsyOnaya (pachTOvaya) MARka]

specialty специа́льность *f* [spitsyAL'nast']

spectator зри́тель/ница [ZRItil'/nitsa]

speed ско́рость *f* [SKOrast']

speedometer спидо́метр [spiDOmitr]

spell, to чита́ть/прочита́ть по бу́квам [chiTAT'/prachiTAT' pa-BUKvam]

spend the night, to ночева́ть/переночева́ть [nachiVAT'/pirinachiVAT']

spend, to *(money)* тра́тить/потра́тить [TRAtit'/paTRAtit']

spicy о́стрый [Ostry]

spinach шпина́т [shpiNAT]

spinal column позвоно́чный столб [pazvaNOCHny STOLP]

spoiled испо́рченный [isPORchiny]

spoon ло́жка [LOSHka]

sporting goods спортто́вары *m pl* [sparttaVAry]

sport(s) спорт [SPORT]

sprain растяже́ние [rastiZHEniye]

sprained растя́нутый [rasTYAnuty]

sprayed *(vegetables, etc.)* опры́сканный [aPRYskany]

spring весна́ [viSNA]

square пло́щадь *f* [PLOshat']

square meter квадра́тный метр [kvaDRATny MYETR]

stab, to коло́ть/кольну́ть [kaLOT'/kal'NUT']

stadium стадио́н [stadiON]

stain пятно́ [pitNO]

stairs ле́стница [LYESnitsa]

stamp почто́вая ма́рка [pachTOvaya MARka]; *(seal)* печа́ть *f* [piCHAT']

stamp one's ticket, to компости́ровать/прокомпости́ровать [kampaSTIravat'/prakampaSTIravat']

stamp-vending machine автома́т по прода́же ма́рок [aftaMAT pa-praDAzhy MArak]

stand, to стоя́ть *ipf* [staYAT']

star звезда́ [zvizDA]

starter ста́ртер [STARtir]

state госуда́рство [gasuDARstva]

stationery почто́вая бума́га [pachTOvaya buMAga]; канцтова́ры *m pl* [kantstaVAry]

statue ста́туя [STAtuya]

stay (in), to пребыва́ть/пребы́ть (в + *prep*) [pribyVAT'/priBYT' (f-...)]

stay, to остава́ться/оста́ться [astaVAtsa/aSTAtsa]

steal, to красть/укра́сть [KRAST'/uKRAST']

steamed па́реный [PAriny]
steamship парохо́д [paraKHOT]
steep круто́й [kruTOY]
steeple колоко́льня [kalaKOL'nya]
step ступе́нь f [stuPYEN']
steward/stewardess стю́ард/
стюарде́сса [STYUart/
styuarDYEsa]
still ещё [yiSHO]
still life натюрмо́рт [natyurMORT]
sting, to (insect) куса́ть/
укуси́ть [kuSAT'/ukuSIT']
stock запа́с [zaPAS]
stockings чулки́ m pl [chulKI]
stomach желу́док [zhyLUdak];
живо́т [zhyVOT]
stomachache желу́дочная
боль [zhyLUdachnaya BOL']
stone ка́мень m [KAmin']
stony камени́стый [kamiNIsty]
Stop! Стой! [STOY]
stop (bus, etc.) остано́вка
[astaNOFka]
stop, to остана́вливаться/
останови́ться [astaNAvlivatsa/
astanaVItsa]; переставать/
переста́ть [piristaVAT'/pirisTAT']
stopover промежу́точная
поса́дка [pramiZHUtachnaya
paSATka]
store window витри́на [viTRIna]
storm бу́ря [BUrya]
story расска́з [raSKAS]
stove f плита́ [pliTA]
straight прямо́й [priMOY]
straight ahead пря́мо [PRYAma]
strange незнако́мый
[niznaKOmi]
straw соло́минка [saLOMnika]
strawberries земляни́ка
[zemliNIka]
street у́лица [Ulitsa]
streetcar трамва́й [tramVAY]
strenuous утоми́тельный
[utaMItil'ny]
string верёвка [viRYOFka]
stroke уда́р [uDAR]

strong си́льный [SIL'ny]
study, to учи́ться ipf [uCHItsa];
изуча́ть/изучи́ть + acc
[izuCHAT'/izuCHIT']
stuffed фарширо́ванный
[farshyROvany]
stupid тупо́й [tuPOY]
style стиль m [STIL']
subject to duty облага́емый
по́шлиной [ablaGAyimy POshlinay]
subtitles субти́тры m pl [supTItry]
suburb при́город [PRIgarat]
subway метро́ [miTRO]
sudden внеза́пный adj
[vniZAPny]
suddenly вдруг adv [VDRUK]
sugar са́хар [SAkhar]
suggestion предложе́ние
[pridlaZHEniye]
suit костю́м [kaSTYUM]
suitable for the disabled
приспосо́бленный для
инвали́дов [prispaSObliny
dlia-invaLIdaf]
suitcase чемода́н [chimaDAN]
sum су́мма [SUma]
summer ле́то [LYEta]
summer cottage да́ча [DAcha]
summit верши́на [virSHYna]
sun со́лнце [SONtse]
sun cream крем от со́лнца
[KRYEM at-SONtse]
sun protection factor
солнцезащи́тный фа́ктор
[santsyzaSHITny FAKtar]
sunburn со́лнечный ожо́г
[SOLnichny aZHOK]
Sunday воскресе́нье
[vaskriSYEn'ye]
sunhat шля́па от со́лнца
[SHLYApa at-SONtsa]
sunny со́лнечный [SOLnichny]
sunroof люк [LYUK]
sunscreen защи́та от со́лнца
[zaSHIta at-SONtsa]
sunstroke со́лнечный уда́р
[SOLnichny uDAR]

suntan oil ма́сло от со́лнца [MAsla at-SONtsa]

supermarket суперма́ркет [supirMARkit]

supervisor смотри́тель *m* [smaTRItil']

suppose, to полага́ть *ipf* [palaGAT']

suppository све́чка [SVYECHka]

surely *(without fail)* непреме́нно *adv* [nipriMYEna]

surf, to ката́ться *ipf* на доске́ [kaTAtsa na-daSKYE]

surfboard се́рфинг [SYERfink]

surgeon хиру́рг [khiRURK]

surroundings окруже́ние [akruZHEniye]

swamp боло́то [baLOta]

sweat pants спорти́вные брю́ки [sparTIVnyye BRYUki]

sweat to поте́ть/вспоте́ть [paTYET'/fspaTYET']

sweet сла́дкий [SLATki]

sweet wine сла́дкое [SLATkaye]

swelling опуха́ние [apuKHAniye]; о́пухоль *f* [Opukhal']

swim fins ла́сты *m pl* [LAsty]

swim, to пла́вать *ipf,* плыть/ поплы́ть [PLAvat', PLYT'/paPLYT']

swimmer плове́ц/ пловчи́ха [plaVYETS/plafCHIkha]

swimming lessons курс по пла́ванию [KURS pa-PLAvaniyu]

swimming pool бассе́йн [baSYEYN]

Swiss franc швейца́рский фра́нк [shviyTSARski FRANK]

switch выключа́тель *m* [vyklyuCHAtil']

switch on, to включа́ть/ включи́ть [fklyuCHAT'/fklyuCHIT']

swollen опу́хший [aPUKHshy]

symbol си́мвол [SIMval]

symphony concert симфони́ческий конце́рт [simfaNIchiski kanTSERT]

syringe шприц [SHPRITS]

t-shirt футбо́лка [fudBOLka]

table стол [STOL]

table tennis насто́льный те́ннис [naSTOL'ny TYEnis]

tablecloth ска́терть *f* [SKAtirt']

taillight за́дняя фа́ра [ZADniya FAra]; за́дний фона́рь [ZADni faNAR']

tailor/dressmaker портно́й/ портни́ха [partNOY/partNIkha]

tailor's shop ателье́ [atiL'YE]

take along, to брать/взять с собо́й [BRAT'/VZYAT' s-saBOY]

take care of (s.th.), to забо́титься/позабо́титься о + *prep* [zaBOtitsa/pazaBOtitsa]

take part (in), to уча́ствова ть *ipf* (в + *prep*) [uCHAstvavat (f-…)]

take place, to состоя́ться *pf* [sastaYAtsa]

take, to брать/взять [BRAT'/ VZYAT']

takeoff вы́лет [VYlit]

talk, to разгова́ривать/ поразгова́ривать [razgaVArivat'/ parazgaVArivat']

tampon тампо́н [tamPON]

tank бак [BAK]

taste вкус [FKUS]

taste good, to *(to s.o.) (dat +)* нра́виться/понра́виться [NRAvitsa/paNRAvitsa]

taste like, to *(s.th.)* име́ть *ipf* вкус + *gen* [iMYET' FKUS]

taste, to про́бовать/ попро́бовать [PRObavat'/ paPRObavat']

tasteless безвку́сный [bisFKUSny]

taxi driver води́тель/ница такси́ [vaDItil'/nitsa takSI]

taxi stand стоя́нка такси́ [staYANka takSI]

tea чай [CHAY]

tea bags чай в паке́тиках [CHAY f-paKYEtikakh]

teach, to преподава́ть/ преподать + dat + acc [pripadaVAT'/pripadaDAT']

team кома́нда [kaMANda]

teaspoon ча́йная ло́жка [CHAYnaya LOSHka]

telegram телегра́мма [tiliGRAma]

telephone телефо́н [tiliFON]

telephone book телефо́нный спра́вочник [tiliFOny SPRAvachnik]

telephoto lens телеобъекти́в [tiliabyikTIF]

television lounge телевиз- ио́нная ко́мната [tiliviziOnaya KOMnata]

television set телеви́зор [tiliVIzar]

telex те́лекс [TYEliks]

tell, to расска́зывать/ рассказа́ть [raSKAzyvat'/ raskaZAT']

temperature температу́ра [timpiraTUra]

temple храм [KHRAM]

temporary вре́менный [VRYEminy]

tender не́жный [NYEZHny]

tennis те́ннис [TYEnis]

tennis racquet те́ннисная раке́тка [TYEnisnaya raKYETka]

tent пала́тка [paLATka]

tent peg ко́лышек f [KOlyshyk]

terrace терра́са [tiRAsa]

terrible стра́шный [STRASHny]; ужа́сный [uZHASny]

terrific чуде́сный [chuDYESny]

tetanus столбня́к [stalbNYAK]

thank, to благодари́ть/ поблагодари́ть + acc [blagadaRIT'/pablagadaRIT']

that что [SHTO]

that (those) тот m/та f/то n/ те pl [TOT/TA/TO/TYE]

the same thing то же са́мое [TO ZHE SAmaye]

theater теа́тр [tiATR]

theater ensemble театра́льна я тру́ппа [tiaTRAL'naya TRUpa]

theft кра́жа [KRAzha]

their их poss pron pl [IKH]

them их pers pron pl acc [IKH]

then тогда́ [tagDA]

there там [TAM]

there is/are есть [YEST']; нет + gen [NYET]

therefore поэ́тому [paEtamu]

thermometer гра́дусник [GRAdusnik]

thermos bottle те́рмос [TYERmas]

they они́ pers pron pl [aNI]

thief вор [VOR]

thin то́нкий [TONki]; (slim) худо́й [khuDOY]

thing (object) вещь f [VYESH]; (matter, affair) де́ло [DYEla]

think (about), to ду́мать/ подумать (о + prep) [DUmat'/ paDUmat' (a-...)]

this evening сего́дня ве́чером [siVOdnya VYEchiram]

this morning сего́дня у́тром [siVOdnya Utram]

this, these э́тот m/э́та f/э́то n/ э́ти pl [Etat/Eta/Eto/Eti]

threshold поро́г [paROK]

thriller три́ллер [TRIlir]

throat го́рло [GORla]

through че́рез + acc [CHEris-...]

thunderstorm гроза́ [graZA]

Thursday четве́рг [chitVYERK]

thus ита́к [iTAK]

thyme тимья́н [tiM'YAN]

ticket (проездно́й) биле́т [(prayizNOY) biLYET]

ticket counter биле́тная ка́сса [biLYETnaya KAsa]

ticket machine автома́т по
прода́же биле́тов [aftaMAT
pa-praDAzhy biLYEtaf]

ticket office ка́сса [KAsa]

ticket-punching machine
компо́стер [kamPOstir]

ticket-taker контролёр
[kantraLYOR]

tie *(score)* ничья́ [niCHYA]

time вре́мя *n* [VRYEmya]

timely своевре́менный *adj*
[svayiVRYEminy]

timetable расписа́ние
[raspiSAniye]

tip *(advice)* сове́т [saVYET];
(gratuity) чаевы́е [chayiVYye]

tire ши́на [SHYna]

tired уста́лый [usTAly]

to *(place)* в + *acc* [f-...], к + *dat*
[k-...]

to к + *dat* [k-...]; *(in order ~)*
что́бы [SHTOby]

toast *(bread)* грено́к [griNOK];
(drinking) тост [TOST]

toaster то́стер [TOstir]

tobacco таба́к [taBAK]

tobacco store таба́чный
магази́н [taBACHny magaZIN]

today сего́дня [siVOdnya]

today's special блю́до дня
[BLYUda DNYA]

toe па́лец (на ноге́) [PAlits (na-
naGYE)]

together вме́сте [VMYEStye]

toilet туале́т [tuaLYET]

toilet paper туале́тная бума́га
[tuaLYETnaya buMAga]

toll пла́та за прое́зд [PLAta
za-praYEST]

tomato помидо́р [pamiDOR]

**tomorrow (morning/
evening)** за́втра (у́тром/
ве́чером) [ZAFtra (Utram/
VYEchiram)]

tongue язы́к [yiZYK]

tool инструме́нт [instruMYENT]

tooth зуб [ZUP]

toothache зубна́я боль
[zubNAya BOL']

toothbrush зубна́я щётка
[zubNAya SHOTka]

toothpaste зубна́я па́ста
[zubNAya PASta]

toothpick зубочи́стка
[zubaCHISTka]

torn ligament разры́в свя́зок
[razRYF SVYAzak]

touch, to тро́гать/тро́нуть
[TROgat'/TROnut']

tough жёсткий [ZHOSTki]

tour group гру́ппа тури́стов
[GRUpa tuRIstaf]

tour guide гид [GIT];
экскурсово́д [ekskursaVOT];
путеводи́тель *m* [putivaDItil']

tourist тури́ст/ка [tuRIST/ka]

tourist camp туристи́ческая
ба́за (турба́за) [turisTIchiskaya
BAza (turBAza)]

tourist information office
бюро́ по тури́зму [byuRO
pa-tuRIZmu]; бюро́ обслу́жива-
ния тури́стов [byuRO
apSLUzhyvaniya tuRIstaf]

tow (away), to букси́ровать/
отбукси́ровать [bukSIravat'/
adbukSIravat']

tow rope буксиро́вочный трос
[buksiROvachny TROS]

tow truck буксиро́вочный
автомоби́ль [buksiROvachny
aftamaBIL']

to(ward) к + *dat* [k-...]

towel полоте́нце [palaTYENtse]

tower ба́шня [BASHnya]

towing service слу́жба
техни́ческой по́мощи [SLUZHba
tikhNIchiskay POmashi]

toy store магази́н игру́шек
[magaZIN iGRUshyk]; Де́тский
мир [DYETSky MIR]

toys игру́шки *f pl* [iGRUSHki]

track *(train)* путь *m* [PUT']

track and field лёгкая атлётика [LYOKHkaya atLYEtika]

trade fair ярмарка [YARmarka]

traffic движение [dviZHEniye]

traffic accident дорожно-транспортное происшествие [daROZHna-TRANSpartnaye praiSHESTviye]; ДТП [de-te-PE]

traffic jam затор [zaTOR]

traffic light светофор [svitaFOR]

tragedy трагедия [traGYEdiya]

trailer караван [karaVAN]

train поезд [POyist]

train station вокзал [vagZAL]

tranquilizer успокаивающее средство [uspaKAivayushiye SRYETstva]

transfer (money) (денежный) перевод [(DYEnizhny) piriVOT]

translate (from … to), to переводить/перевести (с + gen на + acc) [pirivaDIT'/piriviSTI (s-…)]

translation перевод [piriVOT]

translator переводчик/переводчица [piriVOTshik/ piriVOTshitsa]

transmission передача [piriDAcha]; коробка скоростей [kaROPka skaraSTYEY]

transportation service транспортные услуги [TRANSpartnyye uSLUgi]

travel agency турагентство [turaGYENTstva]

travel bag дорожная сумка [daROZHnaya SUMka]

travel, to путешествовать/попутешествовать [putiSHESTvavat'/paputiSHESTvavat']

traveler's check туристический чек [turiSTIchiski CHEK]; трэвел-чек [TREvil-chek]

treat, to *(medically)* лечить/вылечить [liCHIT'/VYlichit']

tree дерево [DYERiva]

trekking треккинг [TRYEkink]

triangular safety reflector предупредительный треугольник [pridupriDItil'ny triUgal'nik]; знак аварийной остановки [ZNAK avaRIYnay astaNOFki]

trip поездка [paYESTka]

trip, drive езда [yizDA]

trip home возвращение домой [vazvraSHEniye daMOY]

tripod штатив [shtaTIF]

truck грузовик [gruzaVIK]

true верный [VYERny]

trunk (car) багажник [baGAZHnik]

try hard, to стараться/постараться [staRAtsa/pastaRAtsa]

try, to *(taste)* пробовать/попробовать [PRObavat'/paPRObavat']; *(make an effort)* пытаться/попытаться [pyTAtsa/papyTAtsa]

Tuesday вторник [fTORnik]

tumbler стакан [staKAN]

tumor опухоль *f* [Opukhal']

tuna тунец [tuNYETS]

tunnel тоннель *m* [taNYEL']

turn back, to поворачивать/повернуть обратно [pavaRAchivat'/pavirNUT' aBRATna]

turquoise бирюза [birYUza]; бирюзовый *adj* [biryuZOvy]

tweezers пинцет [pinTSET]

typhus тиф [TIF]

typical типичный [tiPICHny]

U

ugly некрасивый [nikraSIvy]

ulcer язва [YAZva]

umbrella зо́нт(ик) [ZONT(ik)]

unconscious бессозна́тельный [bisaZNAtil'ny]

under под + *instr* [pat-...]

underpants тру́сики *m pl* [TRUsiki]

underpass тонне́ль *m* [taNYEL']

undershirt ни́жняя соро́чка [NIZHniya saROCHka]

understand, to понима́ть/поня́ть [paniMAT'/paNYAT']

underwater подво́дный [padVODny]

underwear ни́жнее бельё [NIZHniye biL'YO]

unemployed безрабо́тный [bizraBOTny]

unfortunately к сожале́нию [k-sazhaLYEniyu]

unimportant нева́жный [niVAZHny]

university университе́т [univirsiTYET]

unmarried (man) холосто́й *m*/ не за́мужем *f* [khalaSTOY/ ni-ZAmuzhym]

unpleasant неприя́тный [nipriYATny]

unsuited неприго́дный [nipriGODny]

until до + *gen* [da-...]

unusual необыкнове́нный [niabyknaVYEny]

up вверх [VVYERKH]

upstairs наверху́ [navirKHU]

urgent спе́шный [SPYESHny]

urine моча́ [maCHA]

us нам *dat* [NAM], нас *acc* [NAS]

USA США [se-she-a]

use, to употребля́ть/ употреби́ть [upatriBLYAT'/ upatriBIT']

usual обы́чный [aBYCHny]

V

vacation кани́кулы *f pl* [kaNIkuly]; о́тпуск [OTpusk]

vacation cottage да́ча [DAcha]

vaccination приви́вка [priVIFka]

vaccination card спра́вка о приви́вках [SPRAFka a-priVIFkakh]

valid действи́тельный [diySTVItil'ny]

valley доли́на [daLIna]

valuables це́нные ве́щи [TSEnyye VYEshi]

value це́нность *f* [TSEnast']

variable переме́нчивый [piriMYENchivy]

vase ва́за [VAza]

vault свод [SVOT]

veal теля́тина [tiLYAtina]

vegetables о́вощи *m pl* [Ovashi]

vegetarian вегетариа́нский [vigitariANski]

vending machine автома́т [aftaMAT]

Venus mussel ми́дия [MIdiya]

verify, to проверя́ть/прове́рить [praviRYAT'/praVYErit']

very о́чень [Ochin']

vest жиле́т [zhyLYET]

video camera видеока́мера [vidiaKAmira]

video film ви́део [VIdia]; видеофи́льм [vidiaFIL'M]

video recorder видео- магнитофо́н [vidiamagnitaFON]

videocassette видеокассе́та [vidiakaSYEta]

view вид [VIT]

view, to осма́тривать/ осмотре́ть [aSMAtrivat'/ asmaTRYET']

view(ing) осмо́тр [aSMOTR]

villa ви́лла [VIla]

village дере́вня [diRYEVnya]; село́ [siLO]

vinegar у́ксус [UKsus]

virus ви́рус [VIrus]

visa ви́за [VIza]

visit посеще́ние [pasiSHEniye]

visit, to посеща́ть/посети́ть [pasiSHAT/pasiTIT']

visiting hours вре́мя посеще́ния [VRYEmya pasiSHEniya]

visually impaired слабови́дящий [slabaVIdyishi]

volleyball волейбо́л [valiyBOL]

voltage (электри́ческое) напряже́ние [(elikTRIchiskaye) napriZHEniye]

vomit рво́та [RVOta]

voucher тало́н [taLON]

wading pool де́тский бассе́йн [DYETski baSYEYN]

wait, to ждать/подожда́ть [ZHDAT'/padaZHDAT']

waiter/waitress официа́нт/ка [afitsyANT/ka]

waiting room зал ожида́ния [ZAL azhyDAniya]

wake, to буди́ть/разбуди́ть [buDIT'/razbuDIT']

wake up, to просыпа́ться/ проснуться [prasyPAtsa/prasNUtsa]

walk прогу́лка [praGULka]

walking stick трость f [TROST']

wall стена́ [stiNA]

want, to хоте́ть/захоте́ть [khaTYET'/zakhaTYET']; жела́ть/пожела́ть [zhyLAT'/pazhyLAT']

ward (hospital) отделе́ние [addiLYEniye]

warm тёплый [TYOply]

wash dishes, to мыть/помы́ть (посу́ду) [MYT'/paMYT' (paSUdu)]

wash, to мыть/вы́мыть [MYT'/VYmyt']; (laundry) стира́ть/ вы́стирать [stiRAT'/VYstirat']; (o.s.) мы́ться/вы́мыться [MYTsa/VYmatsa]

washcloth тря́пка [TRYAPka]

washing machine стира́льная маши́на [stiRAL'naya maSHYna]

wasp оса́ [aSA]

waste ground пу́стошь f [PUstash']

watch, to смотре́ть/ посмотре́ть [smaTRYET'/ pasmaTRYET']

watchmaker's shop часова́я мастерска́я [chasaVAya mastirSKAya]

water вода́ [vaDA]; во́дный adj [VODny]

water canister кани́стра для воды́ [kaNIstra dlia-vaDY]

water consumption потреб ле́ние воды́ [patriBLYEniye vaDY]

water wings надувны́е кры́лышки для пла́вания [naduvNYye KRYlyshki dlia-PLAvaniya]

watercolor акваре́ль f [akvaRYEL']

watercolor painting акваре́льная жи́вопись [akvaRYEL'naya ZHYvapis']

waterfall водопа́д [vadaPAT]

way (road) доро́га [daROga], путь m [PUT']

we мы [MY]

weak сла́бый [SLAby]

wear, to носи́ть ipf [naSIT']

weather forecast прогно́з пого́ды [praGNOS paGOdy]

weather report сво́дка пого́ды [SVOTka paGOdy]

wedding сва́дьба [SVAD'ba]

Wednesday среда́ [sriDA]

week неде́ля [niDYElya]

weekend special rate тариф выходно́го дня [taRIF vykhadNOva DNYA]

weekly еженеде́льный [yizhiniDYEL'ny]

weekly pass однонеде́льный биле́т [adnaniDYEL'ny biLYET]; абонеме́нт [abaniMYENT]

weight вес [VYES]

Welcome! Добро́ пожа́ловать! [daBRO paZHAlavat']

well хорошо́ adv [kharaSHO]

well-known знако́мый [znaKOmy]

western за́падный [ZApadny]

Western (movie) ве́стерн [VYEstirn]

wet мо́крый [MOkry]

wet suit водола́зный костю́м [vadaLAZny kaSTYUM]

wharf на́бережная [NAbirizhnaya]

what что [SHTO]; ~ kind of что за + acc [SHTO za....]

What a shame! жа́лко! [ZHALka]; жаль! [ZHAL']

wheel колесо́ [kaliSO]

wheelchair инвали́дная коля́ска [invaLIDnaya kaLYAska]

wheelchair-accessible приспосо́бленный для инвали́дных коля́сок [prispaSObliny dliainvaLIDnykh kaLYAsak]

wheelchair-accessible parking автостоя́нка для инвали́дов [aftastaYANka dlia-invaLIdaf]

wheelchair-accessible restroom туале́т [tuaLYET]; приспосо́бленный для инвали́дов [prispaSObliny dlia-invaLIdaf]

when когда́ [kagDA]

whether ли (interrogative particle) [li]

whipping cream сли́вки f pl [SLIFki]

white бе́лый [BYEly]

white wine бе́лое вино́ [BYElaye viNO]

whole це́лый adj [TSEly]

wide широ́кий [shyROki]

widower/widow вдове́ц/ вдова́ [vdaVYETS/vdaVA]

width ширина́ [shyriNA]

wife жена́ [zhyNA]

wig пари́к [paRIK]

wild ди́кий [DIki]

wildlife park охо́тничий парк [aKHOTny PARK]

win, to выи́грывать/вы́играть [vylgryvat'/VYigrat']

wind ве́тер [VYEtir]

wind direction направле́ние ве́тра [napraVLYEniye VYEtra]

wind velocity си́ла ве́тра [SIla VYEtra]

window окно́ [akNO]

window seat ме́сто у окна́ [MYEsta u-akNA]

windshield ветрово́е стекло́ [vitraVOye stiKLO]

windshield wiper стеклоочисти́тель m [stiklaachiSTItil']

windsurfing виндсе́рфинг [vintSYERfink]

wine вино́ [viNO]; ви́нный adj [VIny]

wine glass бока́л [baKAL]; фуже́р [fuZHER]

wing крыло́ [kryLO]

winter зима́ [ziMA]

wire про́волока [PROvalaka]

wire transfer телегра́фный перево́д [tiliGRAFny piriVOT]

wisdom tooth зуб му́дрости [ZUP MUdrasti]

with с + instr [s-...]

without без + gen [byes-...]

witness свиде́тель/ свиде́тельница [sviDYEtil'/ sviDYEtil'nitsa]

woman же́нщина [ZHENshina]

women's же́нский [ZHENski]

wonderful чуде́сный [chuDYESny]

wood де́рево [DYEriva]; *(for fire)* дрова́ *n pl* [draVA]

woodcarving резьба́ [riz'BA]

woodcut(ting) ксилогра́фия [ksilaGRAfiya]

woods лес [LYES]

wool шерсть *f* [SHERST']

woolen шерстяно́й [shyrstiNOY]

word сло́во [SLOva]

work рабо́та [raBOta]

work, to рабо́тать *ipf* [raBOtat']

workday рабо́чий день [raBOchi DYEN']

world мир [MIR]; свет [SVYET]

worm червь *m* [CHERF']

worry (about), to беспоко́иться/обеспоко́иться (о + *prep*) [bispaKOitsa/ abispaKOitsa (o-...)]

wound ра́на [RAna]

wristwatch нару́чные часы́ *m pl* [naRUCHnyye chiSY]

write down, to запи́сывать/ записа́ть [zaPIsyvat'/zapiSAT']

write, to писа́ть/написа́ть [piSAT'/napiSAT']

writing шрифт [SHRIFT]; *(hand~)* по́черк [POchirk]

written пи́сьменный [PIS'miny]

yard двор [DVOR]

year год [GOT]

yellow жёлтый [ZHOLty]

yellow pages жёлтые страни́цы *f pl* [ZHOLtyye straNItsy]

yesterday (morning/evening) вчера́ (у́тром/ве́чером) [fchiRA (Utram/VYEchiram)]

yoga йо́га [YOga]

yogurt йо́гурт [YOgurt]

you *(familiar form)* ты [TY]; *(polite form) pers pron* вы [VY]; вас *acc* [VAS]

you (to, for) *(familiar)* тебе́ [tiBYE]

young молодо́й [malaDOY]

young lady де́вушка [DYEvushka]

young people молоды́е лю́ди [malaDYye LYUdi]

your ваш *m*/ва́ша *f*/ва́ше *n*/ ва́ши *pl* [VASH/VAsha/VAshe/ VAshy]

your *(familiar)* твой *m*/твоя́ *f*/ твоё *n*/твои́ *pl* [TVOY/tvaYA/ tvaYO/tvaI]

X-ray рентге́новский сни́мок [rindGYEnafski SNImak]

X-ray, to просве́чивать/ просвети́ть [praSVYEchivat'/ prasviTIT']

zip code почто́вый и́ндекс [pachTOvy INdiks]

zoo зоопа́рк [zaaPARK]

ENGLISH–RUSSIAN DICTIONARY